PRAISE FOR *NEVER SILENT*

"Bishop Thad Barnum is a courageous and faithful man who cares not so much about his own personal well-being as he does about the well-being of the church of Jesus Christ. He tells the truth even when the truth is hard truth to tell. In this faithful narrative he shows clearly how the North American church is fast losing its distinctive message and then how the gospel is being sent back to North America through the gracious providence of God. Having witnessed what is happening to the churches of North America firsthand, I can assure you that this is not just a message for Anglicans, or for mainline churches, but a general, faithful wake-up call for all Christians and churches."

—DR. JOHN H. ARMSTRONG,
President, ACT 3

"We desperately need to recover the passion for truth and orthodoxy of which this book speaks. I'm grateful for the message of this book—rousing us from our apathy, forcing us to face the responsibility we each possess to love, defend, and preach the gospel at all costs."

—CHUCK COLSON,
Founder, Prison Fellowship

"'Then you will know the truth, and the truth will set you free' (John 8:32).

"With two specific qualities—a gift for expository preaching and a passion for evangelizing lost souls for Christ—Bishop Thaddeus Rockwell Barnum has been appointed by God to tell the unique story of the Third World missionaries' battle for the soul of the American church.

"As a gifted expository preacher, Bishop Barnum took great care to measure every story of the movement against the truth as revealed in the Bible. Thus he weaved through the webs of documents and events to give us the true picture behind the war of propaganda and publicity.

"With the passion of an evangelist, Bishop Barnum fixes his eyes on Jesus as he tells the real story of the power of the gospel to convict hearts and convert souls. In the midst of the crisis of faith and the collapse of spiritual leadership in the church today, Bishop Barnum sees that this is the only way to save the church in America.

"Through personal experiences of two servants of God from Rwanda, Bishop John Rucyahana and Archbishop Emmanuel Kolini, the horror of the genocide in Rwanda is linked clearly to the spiritual genocide in America. How could anyone keep silent when the souls of our people are being ushered into hell for eternal death?

"My prayer for everyone who reads this book is that you too 'will know the truth, and the truth will set you free.'"

—YONG PING CHUNG
Retired Primate, Southeast Asia

"As I read this book I realized that Thad Barnum and John Rucyahana are modern prophets. This volume contains both a warning and a challenge from God. The church is under massive assault, there is a raging war for souls, and many Christians in the Western world—especially those in mainline denominations—are snoozing while the fire is spreading. Barnum's book should be read by all evangelical clergy and the men and women in our seminaries. Personally, I intend to get this book into the hands of my students and as many pastors as possible."

—LYLE W. DORSETT,
Billy Graham Professor of Evangelism, Beeson Divinity School

"Thaddeus Rockwell Barnum has written a personal and engaging account of the dawn of renewal in one of Christendom's great Communions. His book unveils one dimension of that increasingly important story: how Third-world missionaries are now bringing the gospel to the US. I am grateful for his book."

—MARK GALLI,
Senior Managing Editor, *Christianity Today*

"These amazing and absorbing pages are a ringing testimony to three things together: heroic faith and faithfulness following the Rwanda genocide; dogged faith and obedience in the birth of AMIA; and increasing faith and vision in the author, who came to see that passivity in face of heresy and sin can never please God. Objectively unfolded, coolly expressed, and meticulously documented, this triple tale with its inner links needed to be told in this way, and to all who seek the good of souls and the glory of God amid the current Anglican agony I commend it now as a 'must read.'"

—J. I. PACKER,
Professor of Theology

"Bishop Thad has responded in obedience to the prompting of the Holy Spirit to write about God's move in the United States church. I am also grateful that the Lord chose to use me in the reformation process of His church in America."

—THE RT. REV. JOHN K. RUCYAHANA,
Bishop, Shyira Diocese, Rwanda

NEVER
SILENT

OTHER BOOKS BY THADDEUS ROCKWELL BARNUM

Remember Eve

Where Is God in Suffering and Tragedy?

NEVER SILENT

SILENT

How Third World Missionaries Are Now
Bringing the Gospel to the US

THADDEUS BARNUM

eleison
PUBLISHING

Eleison Publishing, Colorado Springs, CO 80909
publisher@eleisonpub.com

NEVER SILENT

The Web addresses (URLs) mentioned throughout this book are solely offered as
a resource to the reader. The citation of these Web sites does not in any way imply
an endorsement on the part of the authors or the publisher, nor do the authors or
publisher vouch for their content for the life of this book.

Cover Design: *dlp*Studios
Editor: Craig A. Bubeck
Third Printing, 2011
Printed in the United States of America
3 4 5 6 7 8 9 Printing/Year 15 14 13 12 11

For information and to order this book, visit neversilentbook.com

ISBN: 978-0-615-20694-3
LCCN: 2008928932

To the first Anglican invaders from the Global South who believed—
as Richard Baxter once said—that "it's better that men should be
disorderly saved, than orderly damned, and that the Church
be disorderly preserved than orderly destroyed."[1]

ALEXANDER AND HERMA MUGE
JOHN AND HARRIET RUCYAHANA
EMMANUEL AND FREDA KOLINI
MOSES AND CYNTHIA TAY
YONG PING CHUNG AND JULIA

For Zion's sake I will not keep silent,

for Jerusalem's sake I will not remain quiet,

till her righteousness shines out like the dawn,

her salvation like a blazing torch.

ISAIAH 62:1

CONTENTS

FOREWORD

by Rick Warren

A second reformation has begun in the church — one that will alter history just as much as the first Reformation did.

This time, however, the epicenter for defending the truth is in Africa, not Europe. Men with great names such as Kolini, Orumbi, Rucyahana, Akinola, and others, along with Asian names such as Yong and Tay, are courageously leading the way. Each of these men is a personal friend of mine, and I have observed their integrity, compassion, commitment to Christ, and wisdom at close range.

What is the battle? First and foremost, it is a courageous stand for truth — for the unchangeable authority of God's Word, the Holy Scriptures, and for the uniqueness of Jesus Christ, the Son of God, and our Savior and Lord.

In a world that is increasingly turning from orthodoxy to rapid relativism, some church leaders are walking away from "the faith once delivered to the saints." Their immorality has poisoned their theology.

God warns us to separate ourselves from those who claim the name of Christ but refuse to obey him. "They will betray their friends, be reckless, be puffed up with pride, and love pleasure rather than God. They will act religious, but they will reject the power that could make them godly. Stay away from people like that!" (2 Tim. 3:4–5 NLT).

This powerful book is a behind-the-scenes account of the tragic decline and slide into heresy of much of the American Episcopal Church, along with the ascendency of the Anglican Church in Africa.

Read it, learn from it, and take a stand where you need to stand for truth in your life.

DR. RICK WARREN
Sr. Pastor, Saddleback Church
Author, *The Purpose Driven Life*
Global PEACE Plan

ACKNOWLEDGMENTS

Erilynne and I had front-row seats when these missionaries began to invade the US. It changed our lives. I had to write their story.

We have been in ministry with John and Harriet Rucyahana for twenty years. Together, with many others, we formed the Mustard Seed Project to accomplish ministries such as a Babies Home in Hoima, Uganda; and the Sonrise School in Ruhengeri, Rwanda. These ministries are helping to sponsor and bless African children in the name of Jesus (www.mustardseedproject.org).

I am thankful for our US staff, Bob Dwyer and Joyce Wingett—our dear friends.

Erilynne and I are also blessed by our staff at ARIEL, a ministry promoting the mighty work of biblical discipleship. They have prayed for me on this writing project, and I am thankful for each one (www.arielpawleys.org). I am especially indebted to those who committed to pray regularly: Barbara Counts, Dick and Joan Fossum, David and Nancy Bryan, Sallie Ross, Paul Wolff, my incredible sister Kate Oches, and our dad, Malcolm Barnum, who has been a deep well of love and encouragement.

Craig Bubeck, publisher for Eleison, saw the vision of this book reaching beyond Anglicans, while keeping the details of the story alive. Craig gathered a gifted team to make this project come to life, among whom were our editor, Mary McNeil; our indexer, Nancy Kopper; and our designers, Robert de la Peña and Pat Reinheimer. I am amazed by his gifting, and we are both indebted to Jeff Dunn for his vision and bringing us together. I also want to thank Joe Murphy, Chip Edgar, Dan Claire, and his sister Catherine for extending unimaginable kindness to me in helping garner such strong support for this book.

I have to add that the writing took far longer than Erilynne and I had hoped. And no one has had so much influence in seeing this project through as Ken Ross (Senior Pastor of International Anglican Church, Colorado Springs, CO). He called, he emailed, he demanded chapters out of me, and then refused to hear me complain that I was too busy. He brought to this work his unique gift of insight, direction, critique, and vision. He believed in this work and in me. He has been my brother in Christ from our earliest days at our beloved Prince of Peace Church in Hopewell Township, Pennsylvania, and I am beyond thankful for him.

Finally, Erilynne and I both remember fondly our family at All Saints, Pawleys Island, South Carolina. Thank you for your welcome of us. We extend our love to our church family at Apostles in Fairfield, Connecticut (www.apostlesct.org) and to our four beautiful daughters and their families who, to our greatest joy, hold to the testimony of Jesus.

—Thaddeus Rockwell Barnum
Trumbull, Connecticut
April 10, 2008

BURNING APATHY

Y̶ou don't care?" John reacted immediately, his voice unconsciously rising.[1]

The clergyman responded apologetically: "It's not my denomination. It's not my problem."

The pain struck deep. John Rucyahana is an African missionary to the States.[2] In 1994 his country of Rwanda suffered unimaginable genocide. His people cried for help. As a matter of documented history, the world heard that cry, saw their suffering, and did nothing. Nearly one million perished. Rwandans know these words too well: *Not my problem.*

"You think there's a firewall between you and the Episcopalians?" John asked.

The clergyman had no response.

John wouldn't relent. "What do you think happened in November 2003 when they consecrated an openly gay bishop in New Hampshire? They invoked the name of the Lord Jesus Christ over that man—the same One who died for you, who saved you. They did it publicly, for all the world to see. That didn't move you? Who can sit back and do nothing when the One you love is being mocked and spit on?"

Still no reaction.

John pressed harder: "They laid hands on that man. They called on the Holy Spirit to bless and consecrate him. You know the Holy Spirit doesn't do that. He will not bless sin." John lifted his hands, palms up, pleadingly. "So what spirit came upon him? What spirit was released into your country on that day? Do you know?" His eyes were wide and fixed on the minister. "Aren't you troubled by that? Isn't there something inside you rising up to

15

protect the Christians in your country?"

Finally, the clergyman's eyes fell away, and he shook his head slightly.

John's voice took on an urgency. "How can you say, "Not my problem"? Fire is raging in the house of God. Can't you feel the heat? Doesn't the smoke fill your nostrils with burning pain? How can you pretend that your people are safe? Who told you there were firewalls between denominations?"

The clergyman looked back up and did his best to show concern. But he remained distant, unaffected.

John knew it and reacted sharply. "You Americans sleep while the devil goes after your children."

●　●　●

The clergyman's response is not new—like so many others, he becomes defensive. He tells John his church is thriving. People are coming to saving faith. Their church is profoundly impacting their world for Christ—locally, nationally, internationally. So he has no time to waste on irrelevant, radical liberals. He has one focus: his church, his mission.

John shakes his head. He can never accept this argument, just as he couldn't in 1994 when the nations of the world turned their collective back on his native land, also too busy to help. As he always had said, "Everyone had their self-interests, and Rwanda wasn't one of them."

He fires back: "These radical liberals you shrug off are persecuting evangelical Christians all across your country. Congregations are being evicted from their buildings, their assets frozen by church lawyers. Clergy are put on trial and deposed for contesting the heresy of their bishops. They are thrown out of their church homes, cut off from health plans, and many are suffering poverty. You have no time for them? Can you walk away when your brothers and sisters are crying out in pain? You have a duty before the Lord. Go to them, no matter what. Stand with them against these forces of evil!"

The clergyman seems genuinely taken aback at this. "I didn't know." He confesses he saw the Episcopal Church as harmless. "They are leaders of the gay movement."

John smiles. "They have done their job well."

"What do you mean?"

"It's not about the gay issue," John says. "It's true, they are the first. They have done what no one in church history has ever done before.[3] But they are deceiving the world. They have one purpose in mind: to attack the Bible, to deny the gospel, and to condemn all Christians who believe that Jesus Christ is the only way to eternal life.[4] You see, they claim the Holy Spirit has spoken to them. He has given them a new gospel that blatantly contradicts His own Bible."

"You're kidding me." The clergyman's voice is more incredulous than he intends.

"I am not kidding you," John insists. "I will tell you a story about a man named Bishop Peter Lee of Virginia." John fixes his eyes intently on the clergyman's. "Do you want to hear it?"

He reluctantly nods.

"In 2003, he voted for the gay bishop in New Hampshire. Concerning that vote, he told the *New York Times*, 'I'll be remembered as a bishop who did the right thing.'[5]

"Then he participated in the consecration of a new bishop in Washington, DC, named John Chane. Of course, John Chane is an activist for the gay movement. But Chane's sin goes much deeper. That man is a heretic. He publicly denies the Christian faith, saying the Lord Jesus Christ never rose from the dead.[6] Knowing this, Peter Lee helped make Chane a bishop and leader in the church.

"Then days later, Lee made this statement for the entire world to hear: 'If you must make a choice between heresy and schism, always choose heresy. For as a heretic, you are only guilty of a wrong opinion. As a schismatic, you have torn and divided the body of Christ. Choose heresy every time.'"[7]

John pauses and takes an article from his briefcase. He waves it lightly in the air. "Chuck Colson, founder of Prison Fellowship — maybe you've heard of him at least?"

The pastor rolls his eyes and, smiling, nods.

"Colson heard that statement and immediately rose up. He refused to remain silent. It didn't matter that it came from Episcopalians. No! The gospel must be defended. Christians must be protected. Christian leaders have a duty before God to 'banish and drive away all wrong and strange doctrines that are contrary to God's Word.'[8] That's what we do. Listen to what Colson said:

> I can think of nothing more dangerous. What Lee is basically saying
> is that we can tolerate anything within the Church just to keep the

Church together. . . . American Christians of all stripes — evangelical, as well as liberal — no longer take truth seriously. . . . like Bishop Lee, we've fallen into a mushy ecumenism, believing that doctrines and distinctions make little or no difference. But our forebears, particularly in the Reformation tradition, didn't shed their blood for retirement plans, for buildings, or for a cozy sense that everybody is okay. They shed their blood for the truth.[9]

Finally, the clergyman is visibly impacted. "Colson is right," he admits. "Truth comes first. It's truth that brings unity in Christ, not vice versa. That's what I teach; but putting it into practice, now, that's hard."

"It's not hard," the African says. "It's a choice."

The clergyman backs up, as if John has pushed him. He hesitates, not wanting to confess, but out it pours: "I wrestle with that choice all the time. Do I speak the truth, or do I keep the peace? It happened again a month ago. I got news about an elder in our church. The Bible is clear: I must go, confront, and bring him under discipline. But I didn't do it. I know how it works. The moment that story gets out, and it would, I'd have a mess on my hands — scandal, division, media coverage. I said to myself, *No, I can't go through that right now.* Remorse etches into his face and his glance falls away. "I made the choice to turn my head."

John lets the other man's words hang in the air for a moment. But finally, again he reacts — he can't help it. No one can turn his or her head without John feeling the burning pain of Rwanda 1994 and the unforgettable sin: *No one came to help. Not my problem.*

He speaks as he had said it a thousand times before:

Never turn your head. Never walk away.
Never cover your ears to the cry of those in need.
Never close your heart to those suffering in sin.
Never refuse the cost. Did the Lord Jesus Christ do that at Calvary?
Neither should you.

The clergyman stares into the black face of the African missionary. As hard as it is to hear, it is true, and he knows it. In his mind flash a half dozen times he'd made the same decision, and always for the same reasons: to keep peace, to prize image, to make life easier. He knew it was wrong, but somehow he has learned to shrug it off. So even now he tries to argue with himself: *It's not that big a sin. It's not like Rwanda. It's not like the Episcopalians.*

He wants to believe it.

John hands him the copy of Chuck Colson's article. "The truth must be lived. Compromise for the sake of unity and peace, and you are no different than Peter Lee."

His mind protests still. *That's not true.* He wants to say it out loud, but can't. The weight of his sin is coming down on him. No, he isn't like Peter Lee. Because he doesn't believe unity trumps truth . . . ever. But then why wasn't he living that way?

The question thunders inside him: *But you knew it was wrong?* For the first time the words sink deep, and it scares him. The knot in his stomach swells. The palms of his hands bead with sweat.

"I turn my head to protect myself. It's that simple."

"But you are a Christian," John quietly counters, without missing a beat.

He is nodding now. "I want to give up everything for Jesus. But I don't do it."

"That's when we build firewalls," John says, a slight smile on his lips. "We put them up and pretend the fire won't touch us. Then we close our ears so we can't hear people screaming on the other side."

Now his eyes are closed. "I know that."

"But you are in the same house." John's voice rises slightly with an urgency.

The clergyman's eyes flash open and dart straight at John. No one will push him like this. No one holds him accountable. Why not? And why this African? "I've heard about you," he acknowledges. "Missionaries coming from the South to re-evangelize the North. You've come to help us."

"We were asked to come," John states matter-of-factly. "The fire raging in the Episcopal Church is everywhere, spreading through denominations, from church to church. The Episcopalians may be the first. But they are only doing in public what others do in secret. The devil is at work in your culture, and your Christian leaders are not strong enough to stop him."

His eyes fall away again. "Some of us aren't paying attention."

"You need to hear this story. You may not be Episcopalian, but what happened to them is already happening to you. The firewalls between Christian churches in the First World must come down. No one should feel safe. No Christian leader who belongs to Jesus, and I mean truly converted by the saving power of the Lord Jesus Christ, has the right to turn his or her head and look away."

"But we do, constantly."

John is still smiling slightly, his voice soft but urgent. "It's time to stop."

"You have to understand. We're too proud to even think we need help."

"But now you know. You can smell the smoke. You can see the fire raging. No more pretending. It's time to do something about it. Lift up your voice. Turn your head back to the fire. Knock down the firewalls and come join us in the work. If you remain silent, the fire will soon consume you."

And at that moment, the clergyman can feel himself making the choice to turn toward the heat. It surprises him, but suddenly he remembers his first days as a Christian in his late teens. Back then, he wanted nothing more than to give his life for Jesus. That zeal! That faith to risk! What happened to it? What had he become? "I want to hear the story," he tells John.

John's smile grows. "But you said, 'not my problem'?"

"I know."

John nods, and then pauses. He points his finger at the clergyman. "I have to tell you a secret." He chuckles. "In Africa, we call *you* the dark continent."

"Ha! That's what we called you."

"Not anymore. You brought the gospel to us years ago. And now here we are, bringing it right back."

PART 1

DARK
CONTINENTS

CHAPTER 1

THE AFRICAN PRIEST

*I**Love Idi Amin.*

I had just picked up this small book by the late Ugandan bishop Festo Kivengere in early December 1988. I had never heard a Christian man speak like this before. How could anybody love Idi Amin? He was a Muslim terrorist, president of Uganda from 1971 to 1979, a wild beast of a man whose armies slaughtered hundreds of thousands of Ugandans, who ripped the infrastructure of the country to shreds, polluted their waters, destroyed their cattle, and brought a paralyzing fear into the hearts of the young. Yet this bishop did not write about Amin and all the evils he committed against the nation and before God. No, he wrote about his own personal sin. The Spirit of God had brought him under conviction for his own wrongdoing.

Festo confessed that his hatred for the acts of Amin, and the grief he bore for the countless deaths and the constant humiliation of his people, had slowly hardened into bitterness. He hated Amin himself, not just his acts, and that hatred was consuming him. It was making it difficult to pray, and even more difficult to share the love of Jesus Christ with others. He was being called by God to repent of this sin.

I could not believe what I was reading.

I had to face my own attitude towards President Amin and his agents. The Holy Spirit showed me that I was getting hard in my spirit, and that my hardness and bitterness toward those who were persecuting us could only bring spiritual loss. This would take away my ability to communicate the love of God. . . . So I had to ask for forgiveness from the Lord, and for grace to love President Amin more . . . for he is one of those for whom Christ shed His precious blood. As long as he is still alive . . . Pray for him.[1]

I read the book a second time. Festo began his writing with the story of an Anglican missionary bishop from England, James Hannington, who, in 1885, first brought the good news of Jesus Christ into Uganda. The bishop did not make it across the Nile River. King Kabaka Mwanga ordered him killed, fearing this stranger was "planning to take over the country." As he lay dying from a spear wound in the hut of a native chief, the bishop spoke his most remembered words: "I am now going to die at your hands, Mr. Chief, but I want you to tell your king that my blood has bought this way into Uganda."[2]

Festo wrote about Ugandan children who were martyred for their Christian faith in the late 1800s and who left their legacy by saying, "Tell his Majesty that he has put our bodies in the fire, but we won't be long in the fire. Soon we shall be with Jesus, which is much better. But ask him to repent and change his mind, or he will land in a place of eternal fire and desolation." And then they sang a song that today, in Uganda, is called the "Martyr's Song": "O that I had wings like the angels, I would fly away and be with Jesus!"[3]

The high cost of being a Christian in Uganda continued in the 1900s. Festo wrote of the life and death of his colleague, the Most Reverend Janani Luwum, archbishop of Uganda, who was murdered on February 16, 1977, at the hands of President Amin. "We were also told," wrote Bishop Festo, "that he was praying aloud for his captors when he died."[4]

This little book seemed bigger than life to me. Did I have this kind of faith? Does it only come in a time of intense affliction and persecution, or is it intended for every Christian? The Bible teaches that "everyone who wants to live a godly life in Christ Jesus will be persecuted" (2 Tim. 3:12). In my context, I thought this meant losing a friend, a colleague, a family member, someone deeply connected to me, maybe even my job, all because of my commitment to "the word of God and the testimony of Jesus" (Rev. 1:9).

But in the African context, persecution is taken to a different level. Was I willing to suffer in this way, let alone die for my confession of Christ? What would I do in the time of testing? Would I deny Him, as Peter did the night the Lord Jesus was captured? Would I hesitate, rationalize, work a deal, compromise, "Go along to get along," and pretend the rooster wasn't crowing for me? Or would I have the faith to stand as these Ugandan Christians had?

Just asking the questions made me realize how untested I was. I was a sheltered, spoiled, overeducated, and underworked American Christian who had never truly experienced authentic opposition. What did I know about the cost of being a disciple of the Lord Jesus Christ? How could I relate to these two Anglican bishops, in two different centuries, let alone the young children who willingly died for the sake of the gospel? How could I understand Bishop Festo, a Christian leader modeling the New Testament command to love our enemies? There was something about Festo — the conviction of his faith, the depth of his Christian character — that pricked my heart deeply and left me wanting more.

Why, I wondered, hadn't I read this story in seminary?

●　●　●

It was the second Sunday of Advent 1988, a few weeks before Christmas. I was the rector of an Episcopal church just outside Pittsburgh, Pennsylvania. It was a new church situated only miles from the airport in one direction and an evangelical Episcopal seminary in another. We had just completed our first building project in late October, which gave us a seating capacity four times greater than the average Sunday attendance. We were building for the future, believing God had called us to be local missionaries impacting our small piece of the world for Christ.

That morning, fifteen minutes before the second service, I was putting on my robe and staring out the office window as a light shower of snowflakes filled the sky. I was thinking about the morning's sermon and my desire to share part of Bishop Festo's testimony, when I heard a knock on the door and saw Joyce Wingett, our church administrator, come in. Behind her was an African priest carrying his robe and Bible. I turned to greet them.

"Good morning, Joyce. John, I'm glad you're here. Thank you for being part of the service today," I said, reaching out my hand to shake his.

"Oh, my brother, it is my pleasure," he said clearly but with a noticeable African accent. They both shed their winter jackets, looking relieved to get out of the cold.

John . . . I could not pronounce his last name. He had come to the

United States in late August to study at the seminary nearby. Sometime in late September, he came to our Sunday service. At that time, we were renting space in a local fire hall down the road. I can still picture him sitting in the back row on the right side. He was there when the bishop of Pittsburgh, Alden Hathaway, dedicated our new building a few weeks later. I had not spent any time with John, which I deeply regretted, simply because I had been too busy with church matters and the building project. By November, he had been coming regularly. It did not seem right to me that an Anglican priest was sitting in the church and not participating in the service. And so, one day, late that month, I called him up and asked if he would like to help out on a Sunday in December and then have lunch afterward. He gladly accepted, and this morning, of all mornings, was our first time serving together.

"John, I know you're from Africa, but I'm not sure where. Have you ever been to East Africa?"

"My brother, I am an East African," he said, slipping on his robe and fastening the top button.

"What about Uganda? Have you ever been there?"

"That is my country. I was exiled from my homeland of Rwanda during the civil war of 1959. I have lived in Uganda ever since."

"Then you have heard of Idi Amin?" I asked, redundantly.

"Yes, I have. I have seen that evil man face to face as he danced in our streets as a madman, his machine guns on either hip. I was no more than two feet from him." He paused, looking straight at me. "I also know his soldiers. They have had their guns at my head, jammed against my temple."

"What?"

"They came looking for my bishop. I was the vicar of St. Peter's Cathedral in Hoima town. I was sitting in my office when the soldiers banged on the door and told me at gunpoint that I was going to die because my bishop had escaped the country. I told them straightaway that my bishop was sitting in his office that very moment. When they heard this, they told me that if he was there, I would live. If not, I would die. They dragged me to his office with their guns pressing into my head."

"And?"

"By God's grace, he was sitting at his desk, just as I told them."

"John, unbelievable. I can't imagine it."

"Actually, there were many times like that. In the middle of the day, soldiers would shoot at us simply because we tried to take dead bodies off the road and give them proper burial. It was a very scary time. We never knew what they would do next. Nobody was safe. Everybody lost somebody they loved. The number of widows and orphans was just too much," he said, wincing at the thought. "The country still hasn't recovered."

It was almost time for the service.

"What about Bishop Festo Kivengere? Did you know him?"

"I knew the late Festo and his wife, Mera, and their children. He was my brother in Christ. I have eaten at his home and shared fellowship with him many times. I knew him well." He also knew Festo's writings and the book *I Love Idi Amin*.

As we prayed for the service and made our way to the sanctuary, I turned to John and told him briefly that I had planned on sharing Festo's testimony in the sermon. He nodded approvingly, but I couldn't help think that this moment was providential. Who was I to share this story when John was there, in Uganda, during the days of Festo and Amin?

"John, would you help me with the sermon today?"

He looked puzzled but said yes without hesitation. "What do you want me to do?"

"Tell us your story. Tell us what it was like to be a Christian under Idi Amin's rule."

He simply nodded.

That Sunday I did what I had never done before. I came to that time in the sermon when I would normally give an illustration to the main point, and instead, I introduced John.

This diminutive African priest with a light brown face, a gentle yet passionate voice, stood in front of the congregation that morning and thanked the Lord for the opportunity to speak. He was forty-three years old. He had come to the United States to study, privileged to receive an American scholarship, leaving his wife and five children behind.

He had experienced the saving power of Jesus Christ during the East African revival and, leaving his job as a schoolteacher, become a lay evangelist in his early twenties. He traveled through the country, starting several new churches as a layperson. Eventually, he went to seminary at Bishop Tucker Theological College in Uganda and became an ordained Anglican clergyman. He served as a parish priest, an acting vicar of a cathedral, and an archdeacon over many churches. Regardless of his various offices, a single passion guided his life. He told us he knew the Lord had called him to a specific work.

"I thank God that a group of believers came to the school where I was teaching as a young man. They were talking about Jesus Christ who saved them. The Holy Spirit convicted me that I was a sinner. He told me I needed Jesus in my life. It was then that I became a Christian. A few days later, the Lord gave me a vision while I was sleeping. I saw Him handing me a Bible and telling me to preach. I took it, and I saw two more books. One was the book of condemnation and the other was the book of life. As I began to preach the Bible, I saw the Lord Jesus Christ take names out of the book where people were destined for eternal judgment and transfer them into His book of life. When I woke up, I knew the Lord had spoken to me and called me into His service. People need to hear about Jesus. They need to have their names in the book of life."

He paused a minute, and then said it again: "People need to hear about Jesus."

John then told us what it was like to be a missionary under the reign of Idi Amin. He said it was a world of constant military oppression, killings, and sleepless nights when gunfire would shatter the quiet of night and screams would echo through mountains and valleys. It left him no stranger to poverty, life without a constant flow of electricity, clean water, access to health care professionals, let alone medicines, transportation to town, or a solid metal roof overhead to protect his family from seasonal rains.

He knew what it was like to face death, more than once, simply because he confessed to his extremist Muslim captors that Jesus Christ was his Lord. And like Festo, he knew how, by God's grace and miraculous love, to forgive them. It was only possible, he told us, because Jesus is able to save us and, by His almighty power, change the feelings and attitudes of our hearts for those who hate us.

With that, he prayed for us and sat down.

Some said they could not understand him that first Sunday because of his accent. But I did. To me, it was as if Bishop Festo himself were standing there, or Bishop Hannington, or Archbishop Luwum, or the young Ugandan children who went into the fire. He had inside him the same depth of tested faith. It was strong, courageous, bold, almost fearless; and yet it radiated a certain gentleness and humility that was unwilling to attract attention to itself. His words, his tone, were laced not with heroism on his part but surprising grace and abundant mercy on God's part.

And yet, as John pointed to the glory of God, who alone gave him the strength to face the thunderous powers of evil, I could see the scars left on him. Scars I didn't have on me. He had known suffering like I never had.

The apostle Paul said, "we also rejoice in our sufferings, because we know that suffering produces perseverance; perseverance, character; and character, hope" (Rom. 5:3–4). What did I know about perseverance, character, and hope as compared to this man? What had I missed in Christian discipleship simply because I was born in an affluent and peaceful land where being a Christian requires little risk, low cost, and no sacrifice? The difference between us, his towering faith—his readiness to die for the Lord Jesus—and mine, was like day and night.

I look back at that Sunday in December 1988, amazed at God's own orchestration of events. No one can take credit for it. John didn't plan it, and neither did I. As it happened, at just the right time, I was reading a little book by Festo Kivengere and feeling the lack of depth in my relationship with Jesus Christ. Just as I was preparing to share its message in the morning sermon, a miracle happened. That little book came to life before my very eyes. The office door opened and there he stood, an African priest, brushing the snow off his borrowed winter coat.

CHAPTER 2

MISSION-FIELD AMERICA

I came to faith in Jesus Christ during the renewal movement of the 1970s. I got my degrees—first a bachelor's in religious studies at the University of Michigan and then a master of divinity at Yale. I was ordained an Episcopal clergyman and gave myself to ministry in the American context. What I did not have, and what no theological textbook could give me, was the kind of Christian faith that was tested on the anvil of suffering and persecution.

Standing next to John, I felt like the classic 1980s couch-potato Christian with my belly hanging out, ketchup stains on my T-shirt, exhausted from an uneventful day, and flicking the channel-changer from station to station for my personal entertainment. He, on the other hand, was like a seasoned athlete in constant training for the world Olympics—the fit frame, flexed muscles, focused mind, disciplined lifestyle, and the intense desire to do better and be better for the glory of God and the spread of His kingdom.

I belonged to a church in the global North, where compromise (the act of challenging, even opposing, essential Christian teaching) was an accepted practice. In some academic circles, it was heralded, and still is, as the high doctrine of "Openness."[1] John belonged to a church in the global South, where compromise was totally unacceptable. It was simply called for what it was—sin. To them, the Bible was the authoritative Word of God. When that Word was preached, people came to faith in Jesus Christ.[2] To challenge the Bible was to challenge God Himself. They were therefore quick to stand with the apostle Paul, who said, "I am not ashamed of the gospel, because it is the power of God for the salvation of everyone who believes" (Rom. 1:16). This unwavering resolve led to both unprecedented growth in the African church during the last century and to untold persecution from their opponents.

From the start, I knew John would not, could not, compromise his faith in the Lord Jesus Christ. He had personally experienced the "power of God for salvation" through the faithful preaching of the gospel. He had spent years preaching the Bible throughout East Africa and witnessed firsthand the same saving power of Jesus Christ in countless lives. No academic courses or theological textbooks would persuade him otherwise. How could they? The Lord had confirmed the authority of His Word in the daily administration of John's ministry over many years.

Yet, at the same time, John had a deep thirst for academic knowledge. He had come to the States to study and earn a master's degree. But he would not have come unless he knew that it was an evangelical seminary, basing its curriculum on the authority of Scripture. He found just the right place in Pittsburgh.[3] The reading, lectures, discussions, and research both challenged and excited him. For two years, from 1988 to 1990, John was in his element.

But he was so unlike the rest of us. On the one hand, he was this poor, short African man with a quiet, humble personality—hardly noticeable. On the other hand, he possessed this golden faith, tested by fire, far surpassing his American counterparts. I couldn't help but think, *What irony that he should be studying from us when, in truth, we should be studying from him.*

• • •

We began working together. Our first project was to raise funds for his wife and two youngest children to come to Pittsburgh for the last year of his studies. The second project was more complicated. We had the vision of shipping a container full of medical supplies, clothing, fabric, furniture, seed, tools, schoolbooks, toys, art supplies, bicycles, and various household items to benefit the poor in John's community. In addition, before leaving for Uganda in June 1990, his bishop had given him a new assignment to coordinate all mission activities in the region. Up to that point, John's means of transportation had been a bicycle. This new position required a car. Joined by the missions committee of our church, we carefully put together a budget for the whole project. We soon realized our church was not able to fund the entire shipment. We needed to get the word out, telling more people, especially clergy and their churches, about this effort.

As we prayed, the answer became obvious. It seemed right for us to ask the Lord to open opportunities for John to preach in churches across America. All of us involved in the project were convinced that his message needed to be heard—and that's exactly what happened. Invitations began coming in. John would do his schoolwork during the week and travel on the weekends mainly to the East Coast, south and midwest. It was the perfect solution for raising the funds needed for the shipment.

He had only one stipulation: "I will only preach the gospel. I will not raise funds."

"But, John, maybe you could carry a brochure on the project with you and hand it to the minister. Let someone else talk about it on your behalf."

"No, we must be clear. I am there to preach the gospel only. No mixing."

"But if this project is going to be successful, we need to get the word out. These invitations are a perfect opportunity for people to give to something tangible."

"My brother," he said, wanting me to understand, "this project is for the poor in my country. The Lord will do it. All the funds will come in because we are doing this for His glory and not for ours. You must have faith in what He is calling us to do."

I paused a minute, trying to take it in. "So, you're not going to mention it at all?"

"When I step into the pulpit, I must tell people about the Lord Jesus Christ and what He has done for them. Full stop! Nothing more!"

John knew the danger. It was too easy for poor Africans to come to America with their hands out, asking for money, and not be faithful witnesses of the Lord. At first, I did not understand the nature of his resolve. But the more time I spent with him, the more I understood.

"What can I do for you?" a man once asked John after a church service where he had preached. The man seemed quite ready to make a financial contribution.

"You can be in relationship with me and my family," John replied quickly. Then he smiled and reached out his hand to him. "It is the Lord's blessing to stand at the cross of Jesus where we can fellowship together and pray for each other."

The man agreed, though he looked puzzled. Clearly, he expected John to give him a litany of the tremendous needs back in Uganda and ways he could help pay for them. Instead, John took the opportunity to give his testimony.

The man was deeply moved by John's story and, in turn, shared how the Lord Jesus had met him and how his life had been completely changed. They talked for the better part of a half hour, rejoicing in the goodness of the Lord, never once mentioning the needs back home in Africa.

For me, it gave deeper insight into John. He was not first a poor African man in need of American money. He was not someone to look down on, deserving our pity and begging for our charity. He was first a Christian man, a sinner saved by grace, one for whom Christ died and rose again. He had come to the United States to share Jesus and all the life-changing spiritual blessings that come in knowing Him as Savior and Lord. For John, this spiritual wealth far outweighed anything we could give him and his country in material wealth. Nothing else had priority for John.

Yet, I wondered, was there a way to stand at the cross, brothers in Christ, and work together sharing our different kinds of wealth? It was, I believe, what Paul meant in Romans 15:27: "For if the Gentiles have shared in the Jews' spiritual blessings, they owe it to the Jews to share with them their material blessings."

On our part, there was much work to do in bringing "material blessings" to his people. On his part, there was a gospel of "spiritual blessings," deepened through the persecution, trials, and suffering from his life in Africa that needed to be heard by American Christians.

The question for me was practical: How do we do this?

Obviously, we honored his stipulation that he would not raise funds. But I personally did not hold out much hope for the success of the shipment project. I was grateful for the opportunity for John to preach across the country, but I had no idea where the money would come from to complete the work—and it concerned me.

One weekend, John came back with a $5,000 check for the shipment.

"What happened?" I asked, elated. "Did you tell them about the project?"

"No!" he said, with a smile on his face. Then he raised his index finger, ever so characteristic of John when making an emphatic point, and declared, "People's hearts were moved by the Lord, and they gave spontaneously. My job was simply to preach the gospel so that people could hear about Jesus! My brother, I told you this was going to happen. The Lord will take care of this project for the poor in my country."

And He did. We actually received more than we needed, weeks ahead of schedule.

The shipment arrived three months after John returned home, everything intact and in good order. As our church gave thanks to the Lord for the abundance of His provision, I marveled at my lack of faith and my inward desire to make this project happen in my own strength. But I also knew that the Lord had given me a great gift of extraordinary value. I got to stand beside John and watch his faith at work. I saw him put the Lord Jesus Christ first, both in principle and practice. He remained true to his calling of preaching the Bible, without any pretense of raising money. He trusted the Lord to handle all the details; and when the work was completed, he gave glory to God, who alone performed the miracle of the shipment project.

I had never seen anything like it before.

• • •

Over the years, all kinds of projects were begun through the generous donations of many people, churches, and foundations. In the early 1990s, we began planning for an orphanage in Hoima, Uganda, near John's home. On July 1, 1994, the Mustard Seed Babies Home opened its doors to forty children whose parents had died of AIDS.[4] After that, a school was built—costing over a half million dollars—in the northwest of Rwanda.[5] It opened in September 2001 with the capacity to educate more than 350 students and sleep two-thirds that number of children, most of whom were orphaned by the genocide of 1994. At regular intervals, more shipments were sent over. Other projects were launched—starting poultry farms, various building projects, funding evangelistic campaigns, assisting with medical needs—especially as many of us, since 1991, traveled to Africa to meet with John and Harriet. They graciously opened their home and allowed us to join their ministry of reaching the African people, both spiritually and physically, for Jesus Christ.

In turn, John came back to America every year. In 1991, he returned for a six-week preaching mission to churches he had visited while at seminary. From 1992 to 1994, with more invitations, we had to expand the yearly mission to eight weeks. In 1995 and 1996, he had more invitations than we could handle. John limited his time in the States to three months.

It didn't always go well for John. I remember attending a conference where he was giving an address. During his presentation, an Episcopal priest in the congregation leaned over to a fellow clergyman and whispered, "These Africans are basically ignorant people, aren't they? They believe every word of the Bible. You know what it is, don't you? It is the simple faith of the uneducated. That's all. If only they would come to our seminaries, get a decent education, read the modern theologians, broaden their horizons, and then take it back to their people. What a difference it would be for all of us! This is absurd."

And then he smiled, shaking his head and rolling his eyes as if everyone who was anyone would completely agree with his analysis.

"That ignorant African is a friend of mine," the other priest whispered back coldly.

"Sorry?"

"The preacher—John Rucyahana. He's a friend of mine."

"I didn't mean to offend you. But you have to agree—"

"Wait a second," he said, interrupting. "I believe the gospel he is preaching. I believe the Bible is the Word of God, just like him. And here's some trivia for you: Christianity is exploding in his country. People are hearing this same message and coming to faith in Jesus Christ. In many places, they have to hold their services outside because they can't handle the number of people coming to church every Sunday. But here in the United States, Christianity is declining. Our own denomination has lost a third of its membership in the last thirty years. Do you think it's because we're too educated to hear the gospel?"

"Our theological education is better today than ever before!" the man retorted.

"Well, let me tell you something about John. He was actually educated in the United States. He went to seminary in Pittsburgh and received a master's degree, just like us. But, thank God, it didn't change him. He is still preaching the gospel message that first changed his life."

He paused a moment, listening to John preach, and then added, "And it changed mine. I think you should listen to him."

The other man fell silent. Afterward, the two men greeted each other cordially and went their respective ways. But what happened between them was not uncommon. The racial prejudice and arrogant tone of the American churchman toward the African Christian surfaced more times than I want to remember.

Once, a religion writer for a local newspaper in the Midwest interviewed

John on one of his visits in the early 1990s. They met in a local coffee shop. She had done some initial homework on John's story and opened the interview with what she thought was a completely neutral question.

"You came to the States in August 1988 to earn your master's degree," she stated. "How has it helped the primitive African church, plagued by ignorance and a lack of proper theological education?"

"Well," John said quietly, deliberately, as if he expected the question, "if my people are ignorant, then I will stay with them and be called ignorant with them. I don't mind."

She gave a stunned look back and said, "No, that's not what I meant. You do agree that most African clergy don't have access to modern theologians and the higher standards of academic training. What they presently have is, well, like I said — primitive!"

"You see, in my country, people are coming to a living faith in Jesus Christ. It is where I met Jesus. I didn't meet Him in seminary or in a theology classroom. Let me tell you that the East African church has been experiencing revival since 1934. The church continues to grow to this day. Did you know in Uganda we have many more Anglicans attending church on Sunday mornings than Episcopalians in your big country? You should check your facts. So, if you call us Africans ignorant and primitive, simple and uneducated, then I would be happy to give my seminary degree back and be called those names with my people."

The reporter was stunned. After a moment of scribbling on her pad and trying to regain her composure, she simply moved on to another subject.

As much as John prized education, he knew our tendency in America to idolize it and look down on those who don't have it. Moreover, he knew that proponents of an extremely liberal gospel in US mainline denominations had built their conclusions on an academic foundation. They depended on modern theologians who vigorously and systematically disproved the authority of the Bible. Worse yet, and beyond John's comprehension, was how these radical church leaders used this new, advanced scholarship to justify positions that the Bible — and, for that matter, two thousand years of church history — openly renounces as sin and immorality.

"I tell you, my brother, this is a great danger for us in Africa," he would tell me many times over the years.

"In what way?" I'd ask.

"Because these people see us as their mission field. They believe we are primitive and in need of their education. I am telling you, their gospel will eventually come to us."

"But the African church is strong. It will not tolerate the American gospel."

"Maybe, for now. But when their gospel comes in one hand and their money in the other, it becomes a great temptation to us who are poor. It is hard for church leaders to say no! They need the money — so they allow these heresies to take root. It's very seductive and dangerous."

Being "ignorant" and "primitive" were only two of the accusations John received over the years. Some critics said John came to the United States only to secure money for projects back home and, secretly, money for himself. Some said it was all about John's desire for power, personal reputation, selfish gain, and the hope of someday gaining a prestigious position in America. Others said he was nothing more than a pawn manipulated by political conservatives in the church to further their agenda against radical liberals. In the pews, some would whisper their amazement that an African had the nerve to come to the States and preach to Americans.

"Who does he think he is?" a parishioner once told me after a service where John preached.

"Do these Africans think they have something to teach us?" another said piously.

"He has no right talking about the sins of Americans and calling us to repent," one woman lashed out. "He should go home and talk to his own people about their sins!"

Most of it was said behind his back. But he knew what people were saying. Sometimes, he heard it in casual conversations at coffee hour after church or at special dinner parties held in his honor. Other times, he read about it in newspapers as reporters covered his church visits and interviewed parishioners. It always amazed me that he never ignored the comments or brushed them harmlessly aside. Nor did he let the words take root in his heart. Instead, he did what African Christians do, especially those who have experienced physical opposition and life-threatening persecutions because of the gospel.

"It is a requirement of Christians," he taught me. "We must forgive those who offend us."

I remember mornings when John and Harriet would come to breakfast during their US trips, neither of them having slept.

"Is everything alright?" I'd ask.

"You know," John would say, "there are times when the Lord does not give us sleep. He calls us to pray." After a few more questions, I'd learn they had been praying for their accusers. I'd think, *If only these American people knew that this African clergyman and his wife—poor, ignorant, and primitive—were actually on their knees during the late-night hours praying for them and forgiving them from their heart!* Maybe to them it would be laughable. But for John and Harriet, it was part of following Jesus daily.[6]

"He's a hard man to see," a priest once told me at a church reception.

"What do you mean?" I asked.

"Well, look at him," he said, pointing to John, who was lost in conversation several feet away. "He doesn't exactly fit the American stereotype of what a strong church leader should look like. He's quiet, short in stature, a peaceful man—humble. In appearance, he's mostly lamb, not lion. He doesn't 'light up the room.' We need tall, handsome, outgoing, mover-and-shaker types who turn our heads when they walk in the room and attract us by their charm and charisma."

I nodded.

"I hate to admit this," he went on, "but during his two years at seminary, I hardly noticed him. I remember going to hear him preach in chapel once—but I didn't really listen. I think we sat next to each other at a couple of lunch meetings on campus. We talked once in a while—but that was it. If you told me this little African priest was going to impact the American church in a dramatic way, I would have said, 'You've got to be kidding!'"

"None of us knew," I came back.

"Yeah, but why? Is it because he's an African student, here for two years and then gone? Or is it because we don't pay much attention to people from the Third World with different color skin and funny accents? Maybe we look right past them because we think we're more advanced and they have nothing to offer us. All I know is that when he was here, I totally missed him."

"In all fairness," I said, "if he hadn't come to our church, I would have missed him too." Then I told him about that snowy Sunday morning in December 1988 when John first came to the church, ready to serve as a priest, and how he ended up speaking to the congregation. I wanted him to know how this African had impacted our church and my life from that day on. I didn't get very far. Someone came up to us at the reception and interrupted. I never did finish the story.

Actually, it's not an easy story to tell.

It requires a dramatic reversal in thinking. Over the last century, the First World has led the way in sending missionaries to Africa. We have grown accustomed to the mind-set that we are stronger in faith, the light bursting down upon the dark continent. Who would ever, in their wildest imaginations, suppose that maybe, just maybe, we were the ones in need of a missionary?

And what if that missionary came to us from Africa?

His name is John Kabango Rucyahana. (The last name is pronounced roo-CHA-ha-na, which means, in his native tongue, "to rebuke, to correct"—a meaning as vital to this story as it is to his character.) He was born in the northwest of Rwanda on November 14, 1945. At the age of fourteen, due to civil unrest, he was exiled from his country and spent the next thirty-five years in Uganda. From August 1988 to June 1990, he lived in the States simply to study. He never saw himself as a missionary to America.

But from the first day I heard him speak, I knew it. If nothing else, he was a missionary to me. I wanted John's boldness, faith, and courage in the Lord. I wanted his ability to surrender fully under the almighty hand of God even when, in those terrifying moments of being oppressed and beaten down, he had lost control over his situation. I wanted the humility and perseverance that God seemed to etch into his character through the pain of suffering for His name's sake. I wanted John's passion to live first and always for the glory of God alone.

But he didn't come just for me.

It was the Lord Himself who opened a door for John to preach in America. During his years at seminary, he traveled across the country preaching a message of "real biblical repentance and faith in the Lord Jesus Christ, which requires everyone to follow Him fully, without counting personal cost." The more he preached, the more people wanted him, and the more the circle expanded. In 1991, after he returned home to Africa for a year, people wanted him back. So he came that year, and the next, and the next. And the circle kept getting wider.

This is his story. It's how an African became a missionary to America.

CHAPTER 3

THOSE WHO WAIT

In July of 1997, my wife, Erilynne, and I walked the Litchfield beach nearly every morning. The tourist season was in full swing, and in South Carolina, in the humidity and heat of high summer, there is hardly a better place to be. On any given day, we'd see the sun rising like a hot fireball over the ocean, porpoise fins gently rising to the surface then disappearing again, and pelicans flying together, sometimes skimming the waves in such unison that each movement looked professionally choreographed. This is the low country, where the waves are big enough to surf, the sand firm enough to bike or jog, and the breeze off the shore just cool enough to stay for the whole day.

Even as the crowds filled the beach and played in the sun and surf, Erilynne and I kept our brisk pace near the water's edge. This was not a vacation spot for us. It was home, and we didn't know why.

In February we had moved to Pawleys Island, some thirty miles south of Myrtle Beach. After nearly nine years of planting and nurturing a new church in Pittsburgh, we had come to work for an organization that helped start new congregations across the country. We had prayed. We had sought the counsel of colleagues, church elders, family, and friends. All the pieces seemed to be in place, and it appeared that God was calling us to this new work. Of course, the location was fabulous. Our home was less than two miles from the beach in one direction and a half-mile from the Intracoastal Waterway in the other. But more importantly, there was a vibrant church in Pawleys Island in our Episcopal tradition called All Saints Church, Waccamaw, a historic congregation dating back to the mid-1700s. Under the leadership of the Rev. Chuck Murphy, who came in August 1982, the church had soared in attendance with people's lives being changed, often dramatically, by the

Lord. Chuck was committed to biblical preaching, excellence in worship, and a relentless devotion to the belief that "things happen when God's people pray." And things were always happening at All Saints—another building project, leadership conference, mission trip to Haiti, or famous guest preacher coming from some part of the world to this little seaside resort community. By 1997, nearly a thousand families a year would come through the doors as visitors just to see what the Lord was doing at All Saints Church.

"There was only one traffic light when Margaret and I came in '82," Chuck often says, "and it blinked yellow most of the year when the tourists were gone. The population of zip code 29585 was only a couple thousand." To this day, he loves to call Pawleys Island "Hooterville."

But in little old Hooterville, Chuck constantly set forth a challenge to churchgoers to "stand up, step out, and risk boldly to follow the cloud of smoke by day and the pillar of fire by night" just as the Israelites in the Old Testament followed the Lord in the wilderness.

Expectation was always in the air. In 1995, the elected leadership of the church adopted a vision statement that clearly stated their intent: "To become a people who risk boldly in sharing the Full Counsel of God, bringing encouragement to the Church and to the World." In a relaxed, oceanfront setting, where most people retire to play golf and enjoy the warm southern climate, these were serious Christians with big vision and deep conviction that the Lord had a mighty work to do through them. It was so evident that, for nearly seven years, clergy from around the country would bring their lay leaders to All Saints for weekend conferences just to experience all that the Lord was doing at this church.

"What an amazing place to be!" our friends would tell us, with a hint of jealousy.

We would simply nod and smile.

"Yeah, I can see you're really suffering for the Lord in a spot like that!" they'd joke, and we would all laugh. For many people, we were living a dream come true. But after six weeks in the new job, we knew we had made a big mistake. It wasn't the right fit. We weren't in the right place. Neither of us were doing what we were gifted to do. Both of us needed to be back in parish ministry. The organization that hired us was top notch. The people at All Saints welcomed us with open arms. The coastal surroundings were unbeatable. But somehow, at some point, we had missed the Lord's call on our life and we knew it. We had stepped out of His will and we didn't know why, or how we did it, or how to find our way back. We felt like Abraham holding Ishmael, the son who had come through his own efforts, and not Isaac, the son God had promised. We felt like the winds had been stolen from our sails and the rudder lost somewhere at sea. And so we walked the beaches, talking, praying, reviewing each decision of the past months step by step, again and again, wondering "what if" or "if only." We were miserable. The sand under our feet, the wind in our faces, the sun dancing on our skin, the sound of the ocean pounding the shore, and even the delight of being part of All Saints Church could not satisfy our deepest need.

We wanted to be back in God's will for our lives.

That summer, the heavens were silent. I quietly put my name out for other work while still being faithful at the office every day. On occasion, we'd sense a moment of peace inside as if the Lord were quietly saying, "You're right on schedule; you haven't missed a step." But then there were other days, most days, when we felt the exact opposite. The Coach had yanked us from the game and told us to sit on the bench with no explanation whatsoever. Just sit, wait, and be still. I didn't like it. Nearly my entire Christian life I had been active in ministry of some kind. Out there, on the field, I got to do what I loved to do best—what I felt God had called and gifted me to do. Not to do it, to be sidelined, to feel pushed aside like a book on a shelf gathering dust, like a candy wrapper ripped open and tossed aside, made me restless.

Benched!

"We messed up somewhere," I said to Erilynne for the millionth time on one of our walks on the beach in mid-July. "We turned left when we should have gone right."

"Even if we did, there's nothing we can do about it."

"I know that. But I keep feeling that maybe it's over. We're done—washed up."

"But what if that's true?" she prodded.

"What do you mean?"

"What if the Lord wants us to stop for a while? Maybe He wants to get our attention, get our focus off ministry and back fully onto Him."

"It makes sense," I said, thinking about it. "If I knew He was intentionally putting us on the bench for that purpose, I'd feel a whole lot better. I think we'd have the grace to use this time differently. Instead, I'm constantly wrestling inside simply because I can't shake the idea that we've done something wrong and—I don't know what it is!"

"I know. I do the same thing."

"These last few months have been confusing. We keep asking, what are we doing here? Is this really where He wants us? We keep praying, and there doesn't seem to be a clear answer. For me particularly, it's *not knowing* that's so hard. I wish I felt better about all this."

"Well, what we do know is this," Erilynne said, going back to principles that have helped us down through the years. "We have to wake up in the morning. We have to do what our hands find to do. We offer ourselves, like the Bible says, a living sacrifice, holy and acceptable to the Lord. The rest is up to Him. It's His call. If we've done something wrong, He will show us. At the right time, He will tell us where to go and what to do next. I don't know what else to say. I think we'll look back on this time and understand it. But for right now, I think we sit on the bench and love Him with everything we've got."

"I like that. And in the meantime, we pray for the Lord to show us the big picture."

"Absolutely!"

"So, what are we saying? Really, we've got to trust Him and the plan He has for our lives. That's it, isn't it? Eventually, He will make it clear."

"Yeah."

"I wish it got easier."

"Me too."

Little did we know, but God had begun answering our summer prayers long before we even prayed them.

•   •   •

A fax came into our office. It was February 19, two days before we made our long drive out of the north to Pawleys Island, South Carolina. We were packing the car, visiting with friends, and finishing up last-minute details before heading south. The fax was from John. Near the end, he wrote, "We have been asked to consider working in the northern diocese of Rwanda as one of the candidates for the new bishop. So we accepted and we have let our name go on the list. . . . Soon there will be an election going on . . . so please pray for this."

John and I were in the same Christian denomination. As an Episcopal priest in the United States, I was a member of the worldwide Anglican Communion, as was John, serving as an Anglican priest in Uganda. In its simplest form, Anglicans hold to four basic essentials as stated in the Chicago-Lambeth Quadrilateral of 1886 and 1888. First, we believe in the "Holy Scriptures of the Old and New Testaments as the revealed Word of God . . . as 'containing all things necessary to salvation,' and as being the rule and ultimate standard of faith." Second, we hold to the "Nicene Creed as the sufficient statement of the Christian Faith." Third, we agree in the "two Sacraments—Baptism and the Supper of the Lord—ministered with unfailing use of Christ's words of institution and of the elements ordained by Him." Last, we are committed to the "Historic Episcopate, locally adapted in the methods of its administration to the varying needs of the nations and peoples called of God into the unity of His Church."[1]

It was this fourth point that now faced John. The word *episcopate* means bishop.

Generally, a bishop presides over a region called a "diocese." In Rwanda, there are nine such dioceses. The office of bishop in the northwest was now vacant, and John's name had been selected for candidacy. For John, it was an invitation to return home, since he was born in Rwanda's northwest, just outside the town of Ruhengeri, in the Butete, Kidaho Commune. But there was a specific reason the position was now open. The former bishop did not retire, nor had he died or become ill and incapacitated. Rather, he had fled the country and vacated his see. Tragically, his name had been directly and publicly linked to the genocide in Rwanda in the spring of 1994.

On March 5, another fax came from John, this time to our new office in Pawleys Island. It turned out that on February 20, the selection committee of the diocese had voted:

> The elections have started in the Diocese of Shyira. There were nine candidates examined by a selection committee. . . . those who supported my candidacy (out of 110 members) were 86. Those who did not were 16. Those who did not vote were 8. . . . The Council of the National Episcopal Church in Rwanda will meet on April 1–3. . . . pray for these meetings.

The diocese had selected John as their lead candidate for bishop. His name was submitted to the national office, the provincial headquarters, for final approval in early April. As it turned out, this was the exact time Erilynne and I would be attending a missions conference in western North Carolina.

It was there that we saw Emmanuel Kolini, an African bishop from southern Zaire (present-day Congo). He and John Rucyahana were the closest of friends. They were born two weeks apart with only seventy miles between Emmanuel's hometown of Goma, at the very eastern edge of Zaire, and John's hometown of Ruhengeri, Rwanda. They first met as students attending the same secondary school. But in the mid-1960s, both exiled to Uganda, they met again as budding young teachers at the Kinyara Primary School, located some forty miles north of a little town in the west of Uganda called Masindi.

In those days, the East African revival was in full swing, and Emmanuel gave his life to Jesus Christ in 1965. A year later, John became a Christian, and his life also was radically changed. Both men experienced the Lord's call to ordained ministry and, at different times, attended Bishop Tucker—a theological college in Mukono, near Uganda's capital city of Kampala. Emmanuel was ordained first as a priest in the Anglican Church of Uganda and then John, a few years later. Together these men served side by side as evangelists, pastors, and preachers, priests together in the same diocese of Bunyoro-Kitara. On December 20, 1969, Emmanuel performed the service of holy matrimony for John and Harriet Rucyahana.

Their lives were providentially intertwined.

They served together for the next ten years, as new husbands, young fathers, and brothers in Christ. They were the most trying years imaginable. It was Uganda in the 1970s, when extremist Muslim dictators by the names of Milton Obote and Idi Amin came into power.

In 1980, Emmanuel was elected bishop of the diocese of Shaba in southern Zaire—thousands of miles from western Uganda. The new bishop, his wife, Freda, and their eight children made the long journey as missionaries to a region in Zaire they had never known. Their separation from the Rucyahanas would last ten long years. The distance between them, in the context of the Third World, made travel and communication, either by phone or mail, nearly impossible.

It wasn't until January 1990 that the two couples reunited.

John and Harriet were in Pittsburgh, Pennsylvania, at the time. John was beginning his last semester of study at Trinity Episcopal School for Ministry. He was at home in his office, on a cloudy winter day just below freezing, preparing for his morning classes, when the phone rang.

"John, Alden Hathaway here." It was the bishop of Pittsburgh.

"Yes, Bishop, how are you doing? It is a joy to hear from you."

"John, I'm fine, and it's good to talk to you. I hope you and Harriet are well."

"Yes, we are. Thank you for asking."

"Listen, I need to ask you something. I have an African bishop and his wife visiting this weekend and my wife is not feeling well. She has caught a bug of some kind and I simply cannot accommodate them. And so, I thought of you. Would you mind having them in your home?"

"No, Bishop. Thank you very much. It would be an honor for Harriet and me to have them stay with us. But tell me, where in Africa do they come from?"

"I think it's Zaire, John, but I'm not sure."

"Zaire?"

A few days later, in a little town outside of Pittsburgh called Ambridge, John and Harriet stood in the seminary parking lot, bundled in layers of winter clothes, waiting for their guests to arrive. They watched in complete shock as Emmanuel and Freda Kolini stepped out of Bishop Hathaway's car with an African cry of greeting. What miraculous surprise! What indescribable joy! They were suddenly embracing each other after all this time in a cold and foreign land. They kissed both cheeks and immediately exchanged English for their native tongue of Kinyarwanda. Amid the laughter, tears, and rapid conversation, it was not hard to see that the sovereign hand of God had brought them together again.

Providentially intertwined.

• • •

Erilynne and I first met the Kolinis that weekend. Bishop Emmanuel graciously came to our church that Sunday morning and preached on Isaiah's call to ministry: "Here am I. Send me!" It was an unforgettable sermon calling each of us to offer ourselves fully and willingly into the service of almighty God.

The bishop's tall and noble stature, combined with a slow, deliberate speaking style and a gentle yet commanding presence, dramatically heightened the importance of his challenge to us from Scripture.

Afterward, I could tell that the Kolinis and Rucyahanas were extremely tired.

"John, are you okay?" I asked him privately.

"My brother, we have spent all our time talking. Since Friday, we have not slept at all. There has been too much time apart and we are very happy to be together again." I could see it in his eyes and hear it in his voice. Behind him, I caught a glimpse of Harriet and Freda holding each other's hands as they talked with parishioners. They were inseparable.

"It must have been so hard for you not to see them for such a long time."

"But it happens. In Africa, sometimes we are forced to live for years without seeing people we love, even our own family members. Communication is impossible. So we don't know if we will ever see them again. Sometimes we think, *Are they alive? Have they been suffering? Are there wars, famine, sickness, hardships? What is happening to them? How are they doing? How are their children? Is the Lord blessing their ministry?* We even wonder what they are doing that very day. But all we have are questions. We don't know. But we know God knows. So we pray for them. They pray for us. And we hope one day the Lord will bless us to see each other again in the flesh. If not, we wait for heaven."

"And He has, John."

"Oh, my brother, it is a real miracle."

●   ●   ●

At the missions conference in North Carolina, Emmanuel Kolini found Erilynne and me sitting outside on patio chairs between lectures, enjoying a cup of coffee. It was midafternoon on April 3, 1997. He pulled up a chair, sat down, and rested his hands firmly on the arms of the chair. For a brief moment, a smile lit his face. But his look turned abruptly serious.

"Well, I have some news," he began. "John was elected today to the office of bishop in the diocese of Shyira in the northwest of Rwanda." He paused, making sure we were listening carefully, and then he told us about the ambush that had nearly taken John's life.

I wrote in my journal that night.

Bishop Kolini has told us of John's election. He will be consecrated in the early part of June. But in nearly the same breath, he told us that the northwest region is unstable. There are "retribution killings" going on day and night. Rebel forces are crossing Zaire's border into Rwanda, often disguised in everyday clothing. Then he told us, just before his election, an ambush had been set against John's life and that he survived. He said there were now military guards surrounding him and his family. What is more, the election was altogether "God's own doing." The Hutu ethnic group dominates the northwest. They are the ones that planned and executed the genocide in 1994 against the Tutsis. John is a Tutsi. They have elected him, not on the basis of his national and ethnic grouping, but for the strength of his faith and leadership in Jesus Christ. Emmanuel said that this shows people's hunger for forgiveness and reconciliation and not for politics.

John sent us a fax on the day of his election.

We want you to join us in thanksgiving. The election of new bishops is over. I was elected Bishop of Shyira Diocese by the Electoral College of the Episcopal Church in Rwanda today, April 3. My consecration will be on June 8. Thad, I want to thank God that He, in His divine means, has led me into this office without friction or struggle. . . . I have been called to be a preacher and a witness. . . . I need your prayers because I am to face higher challenges. Keep in prayer that the name of Jesus be glorified. My diocese is the biggest and most hilly. . . . We are continuing to pray for the insecurity in this area.

Typical of John, he mentioned nothing of the ambush. I responded with a fax expressing both joy and concern. I told him I needed to know about the attack on his life and how he viewed the instability. I wrote,

Bishop Kolini told us about the ambush—what happened? How can you live in the northwest if infiltrators are still fighting and killing Tutsis? Why not wait until the region has stabilized? The image of military guards around you is frightening. John, please take every precaution. We don't want anything to happen to you, Harriet, or your family.

He sent back his answer in a fax on April 16.

I am convinced beyond doubt that Jesus is the answer to Rwandan problems of economy, social discrimination, [and] insecurity. People need to know, love, and respect God before any significant transformation takes place. So God will always use us as His agents in such circumstances to cause changes. Keep in prayer for we feel [we must] respond to the call and meet the need. . . . The ambush which we survived was not intended to hurt me in particular. It was a general ambush which took place before my election.

On May 1, another fax came in. John reported that on April 27, rebel forces attacked a girls' high school in his diocese in the town of Rambura. The infiltrators demanded the girls separate into their ethnic groupings—Hutus on one side, Tutsis on the other. John wrote, "They were trying to finish the work of the genocide and kill off all Tutsis. But these girls refused to separate. They had borne the pain of the war in their hearts. They had lost too many family members. So they decided to stand together as fellow Rwandans and not let their captors identify themselves either as Hutu or Tutsi." With that, John said, the rebels randomly opened fire, killing seventeen girls and one white missionary who worked at the school. Several were wounded.

"We are not despaired by evil," John wrote later. "These girls made a stand. No one would expect young girls to face death and stage a real challenge to their killers. They have told the country and the world that Rwanda is living in a new day. We will not be separated anymore. We are a united people. It is time to move forward. I am telling you, we shall never forget these brave girls."

CHAPTER 4

SILENT ONLOOKERS TO HELL

R wanda, one of Africa's poorest countries, with a population of eight
million, is a nation the geographic size of Vermont. Known for its
beauty as the "land of a thousand hills," it sits nestled in Central Africa with
Congo to its west, Uganda to the north, Tanzania to the east, and Burundi
to the south. In principle, Rwandans all share the same language and culture.
Gerald Prunier wrote in his book *The Rwanda Crisis*, "They had none of the
characteristics of tribes, which are micro-nations. They [the Hutu and Tutsi]
shared the same Bantu language, lived side by side with each other without
any 'Hutuland' or 'Tutsiland' and often intermarried. But they were neither
similar nor equal."[1]

In November 1959, Hutus came into power, driving many Tutsis to flee
their homes. Prunier stated that the violence that year had "irremediably split"
the Rwandans into "mutually hostile Tutsi and Hutu groups."[2] He added,
"there are at most 700,000 *refugees*, i.e. people (and their children) who left
Rwanda because of political persecution between 1959 and 1973 and who
still identified themselves as refugees in 1990."[3] It was all the more extreme in
Rwanda's northwest "where the Tutsi were most relentlessly hunted down."[4]
For John, at the age of fourteen, and his family, the Social Revolution of 1959
meant immediate exile from their homeland. They crossed the border into
Uganda, having no idea they would remain in exile until 1994.

On several occasions, Tutsi refugees organized and attempted military
operations to overthrow the Hutu government. From December 1963 to
January 1964, for example, Tutsi forces tried to regain control of the country.
Their attempt failed—with roughly ten thousand Tutsis killed in battle with
all "surviving Tutsi politicians still living in Rwanda" executed.[5]

The Hutu hatred against Tutsis only intensified.

"The notion of a genocide had become common talk in Kigali (Rwanda's capital city) during 1993–4."[6] The Hutu-led government had developed a plan for the complete and systematic annihilation of all Tutsis in the country. Strategically, they had kept Rwandans illiterate — "60% of the population could not read or write."[7] They had demanded the highest respect from a people already "bent towards obeying authority."[8] With a government-controlled radio network and years of describing all Tutsis as evil people, the stage was set for an all-out and immediate holocaust. All they had to do was give the order to kill.

On the evening of April 6, 1994, the dark clouds of civil war descended on Rwanda. What took place in the next three months is beyond human comprehension. Philip Gourevitch, in his book *We wish to inform you that tomorrow we will be killed with our families*, wrote,

> Decimation means the killing of every tenth person in a population, and in the spring and early summer of 1994 a program of massacres decimated the Republic of Rwanda. Although the killing was low-tech — performed largely by machete — it was carried out at dazzling speed: of an original population of about seven and a half million, at least eight hundred thousand people were killed in just a hundred days.[9]

The order went over the radio. All Tutsis were to be found and killed at once. Each Rwandan had an identification card saying HUTU or TUTSI or TWA. "To be identified on one's card as a Tutsi or to pretend to have lost one's papers meant certain death."[10]

But who would do the killing? It was perfectly clear that the government expected the ordinary Rwandan Hutu peasants to pick up a machete and kill their Tutsi neighbors or, in cases of intermarriage, their own family members.[11] By government order, all Hutu citizens were now part of the military, forcing them to kill just to stay alive. They gave no options. Either "you took part in the massacre or else you were massacred yourself."[12] For example, in one situation, a Hutu family demonstrated an act of kindness by covering up the naked body of their dead Tutsi neighbor with banana leaves — and was killed for it.[13]

For the Tutsis, it was said, "few of those marked out to die had a chance to hide."[14]

In the northwest, the war ended quickly: "We never had many Tutsis here and we killed them all at the beginning without much of a fuss."[15]

It is called *ethnic cleansing.*

It happened quickly, violently, to the young and old, men, women, and children, from the well-known and highly educated doctors, lawyers, politicians, and successful business entrepreneurs to the poorest of the poor. People were hacked to death in broad daylight—often by people from their villages whom they had known all their lives. In less than three months, some estimate, one million people were brutally slaughtered. The "daily killing rate was at least five times that of the Nazi death camps."[16]

"There are no devils left in Hell," a missionary told reporters a few weeks into the bloodshed. "They are all in Rwanda."[17]

The war was officially over on July 19 as a new government (led by Tutsis but intentionally including Hutus) was sworn in. The RPF, the Rwandese Patriotic Front, "an offensive political organization dedicated to the return of exiles to Rwanda,"[18] had taken the capital city of Kigali by force, ousted the old regime, and generally secured Rwanda's borders. The country's infrastructure was in shambles. Tens of thousands of dead bodies were heaped in piles and left unburied. Thousands more were thrown into lakes and rivers. Sickness and widespread disease threatened to prolong the untold misery and take more lives.

How was the new government going to bring justice to those who committed the genocide? What would they do about the long-exiled Tutsis who were pouring over the borders from neighboring countries in an attempt to return to their long-lost homeland? What about the people themselves who experienced the genocide—who saw their loved ones killed—who were hacked and maimed but did not die? What about the widows who were forced to run with their children and had no place to go, no ability to feed the children, and no means of handling the trauma? What about the thousands upon thousands of children who roamed the streets and countryside without father, mother, family, or home? Prunier wrote,

> The place was full of the walking wounded; traumatized Tutsi survivors who had lost everything—their friends, their relations,

their houses — and were wandering around like ghosts, and traumatized Hutu survivors who could not believe what they had done to them.[19]

The war was over — except in the hearts and minds of those who physically survived.

• • •

Two more unspeakable horrors of those days in Rwanda need to be mentioned. The first strikes at a despairing, almost incomprehensible, reality. The world community knew what was going on — and did nothing about it. General Romeo Dallaire, appointed to command the United Nations Assistance Mission in Rwanda (UNAMIR), sent the famous "Dallaire fax" in January 1994 warning the world that Hutu extremists "had been ordered to register all the Tutsi in Kigali," believing it was for their extermination.[20] This only confirmed earlier reports from the CIA that "warned of the likelihood of large-scale ethnic violence."[21] Two days after the genocide began, General Dallaire sent a cable to New York describing "a very well planned, organized, deliberate and conducted campaign of terror." Major media outlets were already describing "the widespread targeting of Tutsi and the corpses piling up on Kigali's streets."[22]

In December 1948, at the "international convention on the repression of genocides," it was made "mandatory for any of its signatories to take immediate action once a genocide had been clearly identified."[23] But what happened was the exact opposite. The UN Security Council, on April 21, pulled most of the UN peacekeeping forces out of Rwanda.[24] President Clinton acknowledged, four years later in March 1998, at the airport in Kigali, that "We in the United States and the world community did not do as much as we could have and should have done to try to limit what occurred."[25] Samantha Powers, in her convincing article in *Atlantic Monthly*, "Bystanders to Genocide," stated succinctly that "staying out of Rwanda was an explicit U. S. policy objective."[26] And Prunier wrote, "But the symbolic impact of the UN withdrawal was nevertheless disastrous. The message to the killers was that the international community did not care and that they could go on with their deadly business without fear of intervention or even disapproval."[27]

The unimaginable conspiracy is that the world knew what was going on and chose to stand on the sidelines, watching in silence as dark, barbaric forces of evil slaughtered nearly eight hundred thousand people.

It is one thing to say that you didn't know. It is quite another to know—and do nothing.

There is a second horror to mention, and it concerns the role of leadership in the church. During the war, courageous men and women risked their lives by choosing not to obey the Hutu government and kill their neighbors. Many Hutu Christians, lay and ordained, gave their lives in helping rescue the hunted Tutsis.[28] *But where was the church? What were the religious leaders saying to the public? What were they doing to stop the genocide?* In the critical hour of complete national devastation, both Catholic and Anglican church leaders were tragically found "in total support of the regime." The Catholic Church of Rwanda had "always solidly supported [the Hutu] President Habyarimana."[29] The Anglican Church was also "too closely aligned with the [Hutu] government. The Archbishop spoke openly in support of the President and his party . . . and all the Anglican diocesan bishops were Hutu."[30]

In other words, the church did not stand against the government and its policy for ethnic cleansing. Nor did they stand helplessly by, watching in silence. It was worse than that. Top church officials openly supported the government. Some of them, the world would later learn, actually participated in the genocide itself. The demonic evil of a government gone mad, like a fierce deadly disease, had fully infected the church.

The people knew it. They experienced it.

In the town of Nyamata, as in many such villages across Rwanda, Tutsis ran to their local town church, locked the doors, bolted the windows, and believed that the church was the only safe place left in the country. "There could be up to 4,000 people huddled together in some of the larger churches."[31] What they did not know, what remains beyond the human ability to understand, was the most horrible and devastating deception possible: *The church was not safe.* In Nyamata, for example, mortar shells and hand grenades broke through the roof of the church, shattered the windows, and all the people died.

The world outside Rwanda had turned its back. The church inside Rwanda had blood dripping from its machete. In the aftermath of genocide, where could survivors turn for help? How would they ever find peace and reconciliation with the nations of the world, the church—let alone God Himself—in light of such complete betrayal?

● ● ●

In early August 1994, some three weeks after the new government took office, John Rucyahana reentered Rwanda for the first time in thirty-five years. With him were nine clergymen from Uganda, some Rwandan refugees, and some with Ugandan citizenship. They drove straight to the capital city of Kigali. Their first stop was to ask permission from the new government to tour the country and assess the devastation. Once they received it, John traveled with the team of clergy through the major regions, towns, and villages of their beloved Rwanda.

"We had to see the brokenness of our country," John told me on his US visit that next fall, "and to see the faces of the people for ourselves. It was very important that we allow this tragedy to come into our own experience. We needed to get the feel of it in our hearts and let it roll in our minds."

During the war, John read the daily news briefings from his home in Uganda. He watched as fellow refugees slowly received word about family members back home. At one point, he traveled to Nairobi, Kenya, on church business and stayed with old Rwandan friends. One night while he was there, his friends received a call from their son still living in Rwanda. Infiltrators had just stormed his village. Everyone was running, trying to find someplace to hide. This young man had picked up the phone to call his parents. He wanted to say good-bye. During the call, the parents heard the attackers enter the room—their voices raised, their son's plea for mercy, and then—disconnected. They tried and tried to call back, but no one picked up.

No one was there to answer.

Now John was physically in Rwanda, at the scene of a million crimes. All the stories that had come across the Rwandan border, all the newsclips that had flashed on local television stations and then echoed across the globe by CNN satellite were suddenly coming into full view. And it was more, a thousand times more, than he could have ever imagined.

"It was too much," he said, cringing with disgust. "It was beyond the scope of what the human mind can take in. We thought—no human being could do this to another human being. We saw mass graves containing more than twenty-five thousand dead bodies, all heaped into a big ditch, with the rancid smell of human decay. We saw others where heavy machinery had already filled the graves in with dirt. But it was just as bad. The land was settling; bodies were swelling; elbows,.heads, and feet were cracking the soil. It was a terrible shock—real trauma. We were all in tears. We sat down with the life drained out of us."

As he talked to me, the pain set deeper into the crease of his brow, as if he were physically still there. He reached into his black briefcase and pulled out several rolls of film taken during the trip. He wanted me to see them, so I could try to understand. At certain points, he'd stop and hold up a picture. One was in a medical clinic. A patient was sitting up in bed, his left leg cut off, a huge gash across his cheekbone from a machete. Behind him were rows of beds, all full. John told me his name, the story of how he survived, the number of people in his family who were now dead—including most of his children—and the big question concerning his future: *Who would take care of him?* In another picture, a woman in her midthirties stood ten feet away, staring blankly into the camera. She was outside, under a lush canopy of trees with perfectly terraced hills behind her. At her feet was commotion—cans, shoes, sticks, a rooster, a water jar, a small campfire with a pot resting on top of it. Off to the left was a small ditch, not yet filled in with dirt, that held skeletal remains of people from her village. Once again, John remembered her name, her story.

She was alone. Everyone else—including her husband and her four children—was dead.

"By the end of the first day, some of the clergy got mad at me," John stated, as a matter of record. "The suffering was unbearable. The tears were too many. They couldn't understand why I brought them to see such excruciating pain. One of them broke down. He could not take in any more. A number of them left me and went back to Uganda to recover."

"So what made you go on?" I asked.

"In my heart, I knew God was calling me to be part of the healing and reconciliation of my people. How could I do that if I didn't go to them? I needed to get a feel for their suffering—both the torture of their memories and the realities of their present conditions. I needed to pray with them. It was a terrible blow for me personally to be there. But it was very important. The Lord has a purpose for them. I knew beyond any doubt that the Lord was bigger than their brokenness. He is the only One who can bring about real and lasting transformation. This is what they needed—desperately—in every area of their lives. It is what the country needs."

As I held his pictures in my hand that fall of 1994, listening to every detail of his story and watching the tears fill his eyes, I knew enough to ask him, "John, do you see yourself going back to Rwanda to stay?" He paused a moment with a hint of uncertainty in his eyes.

"I know that God can use us. What I don't know is the approach. What approach—or, maybe, what strategy—does the Holy Spirit want us to take in the healing of this country? That is my question."

• • •

From that time on, John went back and forth between Uganda and Rwanda. The Consortium of Anglican Provinces of Africa (CAPA) asked both John and Bishop Emmanuel Kolini to serve on a fact-finding team. Their job was to research the Anglican Church's involvement in the Rwandan war—to find out which bishops had fled the country; to ascertain the immediate needs of the provincial headquarters in the capital city of Kigali, as well as the eight other dioceses; and to make a proposal, based on facts, in how to help the Anglican Church of Rwanda recover.

Once again, John and Emmanuel were reunited. As they, and other colleagues, began their work together, it was immediately clear that the clergy were suffering from both physical and spiritual depression, apathy, lethargy, fear, grief, and confusion. It left them ineffective in carrying out their pastoral duties at the local church level and in the larger context of their communities. Immediately, John and others planned a national clergy conference in 1995.

"How can the churches recover if the clergy are not cared for?" John asked me in January that year. "They need to confess their embarrassment and shame. Many feel lost. Many fear each other. They need the grace to repent and to forgive in the name of Jesus. They need to see the vision that God can use us again for His service. He can take our hurt and our brokenness if we surrender it to Him. Then He will use us for His glory and for the restoration of Rwanda. This work must begin in earnest for the leaders."

In 1995–96, a series of conferences was launched, aimed first at ordained clergy and then lay church leaders across the country. African Evangelistic Enterprise held a nationwide crusade in Kigali in 1996 that called nearly ten thousand Rwandan Christians to stand courageously for Jesus Christ and to work hard for the recovery of the Christian witness in all the churches of Rwanda. Each event seemed to leave in its wake "the taste of hope," as John called it, "that the Lord has not abandoned us. He loves us. He has made His promise clear to us—'Never will I leave you; never will I forsake you'" (Heb. 13:5).

● ● ●

"It begs the question," Mark Elfstrand said to John on a live radio broadcast in Pittsburgh in the fall of 1995. Mark hosted a daily afternoon talk-show program from three to six o'clock. "Rwanda is basically a Christian nation. The majority of people are affiliated with a Christian church. How could a civil war of this magnitude happen to a people who supposedly believe in Christ?"

John sat up and spoke directly into the microphone.

"You know, Mark, this is a very important question for both of our countries. It is possible, isn't it, for a person to become converted to the church and not be converted to Jesus Christ as their Lord and Savior."

"Yes, of course it's possible," Mark responded.

"Many times people convert to Christianity for social reasons, but their hearts are not changed by the power of almighty God. The people of Rwanda and the people of the United States need Jesus desperately. The church must be a place where the gospel is preached and people come to real repentance and a saving relationship with the Lord Jesus Christ. You see, Mark, it doesn't matter how many people attend church if it is for the wrong reason."

Mark agreed, first to the principle and then to the almost jolting comparison that what happened in Rwandan churches was happening here, in our own country. As the interview went on, I kept going back in my mind to John's answer. Later, others would argue this exact view concerning the effect of Christianity in Rwanda in 1994. One writer said, "After a century of Christian proselytisation, the country was catholicised but not christianised. Ritual was generally followed but the spirit was missing." Prunier wrote, "the reasons for converting to Christianity were fundamentally social and political."[32]

But there was something in the sound of John's voice as he spoke. It was more than a public defense of what took place in his country during the genocide. He spoke with a certain fire in his belly, as if he were not a man looking back, rationalizing the past — but a man looking forward, seeing the vision of what was ahead. He knew what the people of his country needed most.

Then it clicked. I knew John had found the approach he had been praying for. He knew that reconciliation would begin in Rwanda if the focus switched away from doing church to being church. It was time for true biblical preaching — "real repentance and a saving relationship with the Lord Jesus Christ." It was time for Christian leaders "to contend for the faith that was once for all entrusted to the saints" (Jude 3). This was John's heart — that God in Christ would reconcile Rwandans to Himself and to each other (2 Cor. 5:18–20).

From that moment on, I knew John and Harriet would be returning home.

• • •

Emmanuel, John, and the team assigned by CAPA finished their report and requested that the Episcopal offices vacated by the exiled bishops be declared vacant and that formal elections take place at the earliest possible time. It was clear to both John and Emmanuel that post-war Rwandan Christians would no longer tolerate political ambition in their clergy or their elected officials. One Anglican bishop, for example, who remained in the country, active in his duties, was publicly shunned everywhere he went. At church services, he was not allowed to speak. The moment he tried, the congregation would start singing a hymn or praying out loud. Even standing in front of the congregation was a problem. Church leaders would come forward and surround him, forming a human wall, so that the congregation would be spared from seeing his face. He had aided the genocide, and everyone knew it.[33]

The next wave of leaders would have no association with the former government. They would be called by God and selected through the careful discernment and prayers of the people. They would be filled with the love of God for all Rwandan people, no matter their ethnic grouping. They would stand in the full conviction of the Bible as the Word of God and believe, with all their hearts, that through preaching repentance and faith in Jesus

Christ alone, what seemed utterly impossible would be made possible—the recovery of a shattered nation.

On May 1, 1997, about a month after he was elected bishop in the northwest, John sent a fax to my office in South Carolina. In reading four short sentences, I realized that one of Rwanda's new wave of leaders had emerged.

God is clear in His call to us.
We are to be used in the transformation of this nation.
God will do it with His gospel.
Please pray for us.

On May 12, another fax came in. It was the news I dreaded. I had hoped John would not live in the northwest while rebels were still breaking across the border and killing innocent people. Maybe, I thought, he'd stay in Kigali until the region settled. He was thinking otherwise: "We are hoping to have a hired house in Ruhengeri town. Pray continually for our protection. We are bound to serve Jesus in all places."

On June 8, John Kabango Rucyahana was consecrated the second bishop of Shyira diocese in Ruhengeri, Rwanda, before twenty-five hundred people. The archbishops of Uganda and Burundi were present, as well as dignitaries from other denominations, the national government, the local community, and longtime friends from Uganda and the United States. The service lasted nearly four hours. Choirs from all over the northwest sang. Church leaders stood to speak. A retired bishop gave the sermon from a text in Nehemiah, the story of rebuilding the fallen city of Jerusalem. Scripture was read, prayers offered, Communion distributed, and gifts were given. In the midst of the celebration, hardly anyone could believe the most extraordinary miracle of all: The Lord had raised up one of their own, a native son, a Tutsi in a land dominated by Hutus, to lead His church. A few years back, it would have been unthinkable.

Near the end of the service, John gave his first formal address as bishop. His message had one resounding theme that echoed over and over again:

The gospel of our Lord Jesus is the imperative.

In the midst of "experiential poverty" and under the strain of continued war, John said, "We are called together to respond to the needs of our people."

He spoke openly about the "need to rehabilitate people's attitudes toward each other." Without reconciliation to God and to each other, he said, nothing would dramatically change—and the needs were endless. Outside the church walls were homeless people, widows, orphans, men roaming the streets without work, families locked in their homes afraid to go into their fields for fear of being killed by infiltrators. People needed food, clothing, medical treatment, a proper education—including how to read and write—vocational training, personal and family counseling, and a tiny flicker of hope that peace and stability were close at hand. Nothing was clearer to John. It was time for the church to impact the daily life of the people of the northwest.

> It is the will of God that in this present time, I serve my country of origin. God has called us together to build a community much stronger than it is now. . . . We are faced with great challenges spiritually, socially and economically . . . but with trust in Him who calls us, His promise and His presence among us, we must bow to His will and take up this work. . . . He has called us to preach effectively in this nation for results that may glorify Him.
>
> This call requires a commitment in obedience to the will of God [and], by the guidance of the Holy Spirit, . . . to preach the gospel and teach Christian principles. . . . Admittedly, we need to work very hard to have a church which observes what Jesus commanded us in the Bible.

Bishop John called for a new day. If change was going to take place in Rwanda, it had to start with church leaders modeling the Christian life, obeying God's Word, and living what the Lord Jesus Christ had commanded. How else could Rwandan survivors put their trust in God again? This was John's challenge, and he spoke as a man who knew what it meant. This was not merely a preacher emotionally stirring up his congregation or a campaigner making empty political promises. He spoke with authority—and everyone knew it. John was already modeling the Christian life. He had obeyed the call of God and, by faith, moved to Ruhengeri. He knew that Hutu rebel forces were roaming the countryside, hunting down and killing Tutsis. He knew the personal risks to himself and to his family. He never mentioned these things in his address. He didn't have to. Everyone could see that their new bishop was willing to follow Jesus, no matter the cost.

It wasn't just talk. He was actually doing it.

"We have just started," he said in closing. "The journey is long, but the Lord is near. Please keep us near your hearts and minds. We need each other in the Lord Jesus and more so in this challenging world."

•   •   •

In July of that year, Bishop Emmanuel Kolini was elected to serve as the new bishop of the diocese of Kigali. After much prayer, Emmanuel and Freda accepted the new call and, late that summer, moved their family from southern Zaire to the capital city of Rwanda.

For Emmanuel and John, the task at hand was incomprehensible. After nearly a lifetime in exile, they had come home only to find their people reeling from the unending wake of what the world now recognized as "the fastest, most efficient killing spree of the twentieth century."[34] The severity of the problems only multiplied amid the rubble and ruin of a church that had failed to respond in the country's darkest and most critical hour. These men, now both bishops, leaders in the Anglican Church, knew there was nothing in themselves that could revive their country. Only God, in His sovereign grace, could do that. By moving home to Rwanda, by accepting their respective calls, they demonstrated their belief that God still had a purpose for the people of their country.

This belief was altogether confirmed when the Anglican bishops of Rwanda, both the newly elected and those who had remained faithful during the war, met together for the first time. It was in that meeting, and all the rest that followed, that they knew something miraculous was at work. These were not political bishops striving for the approval of the government or basking in their high positions of leadership. Nor were they first religious men, more concerned for the traditions of the church than for the eternal destiny of the people inside and outside the church. These were men of humility and prayer, sinners saved by the grace of Jesus Christ, and committed to taking up the work He had given them to do, even if it cost them their lives. By God's own mighty power, these bishops were united in their resolve and, with one voice, echoed the words John had already spoken weeks before his consecration:

God is clear in His call to us.
We are to be used in the transformation of this nation.
God will do it with His gospel.
Please pray for us.

And that's what we did back home in South Carolina. We committed ourselves to prayer, joining with a strong network of people across the United States who were also moved by God to pray daily for these Christian leaders in Rwanda. The serious nature of these prayers was a new and painful reality for us. We were deeply aware of the constant danger that faced them — especially John, Harriet, and their family in Ruhengeri. We read the weekly reports over the news wire of rebel activity in the northwest — ambushes, fighting, killings — and, each time, we couldn't help but think, *Was it them? Are they safe? Did they know the people who died? Were they nearby when it happened? Were they scared?*

It was mid-July 1997.

John was now a bishop in Rwanda and engaged in the most challenging call of his life. Thousands of miles away, on the coast of South Carolina, in a little seaside town called Pawleys Island, Erilynne and I walked the beach, worked at the office, and kept in constant communication with John by fax. Unlike John, we had lost the call of God on our lives. We seemed to be wandering aimlessly, wondering how and when all the mixed-up pieces of the puzzle would fit together.

CHAPTER 5

RWANDA CALL

On May 1, 1997, before John's consecration, a fax came: "We feel strongly that being bishop would not stop my coming to share and preach the gospel. So I am coming this fall. It may be shorter than usual."

Less than a month after his election, John knew "strongly" that the Lord's call on his life as a missionary to the United States was not yet over. I got on the phone, contacting those who help me set up his yearly preaching schedule, appointments, and travel arrangements. As the summer passed, the details gradually fell into place. For the most part, little had changed. A reduced schedule simply meant more midweek services and meetings. We added a conference in Dallas for national and international Anglican bishops in late September. His home base, typically with us, was now Pawleys Island, South Carolina. John seemed pleased with the itinerary, and we headed into the fall thinking it would be a normal year.

Instead, something unexpected happened.

A significant shift had taken place in the Episcopal Church. Like many mainline denominations, the permissiveness inherent in a wealthy, advanced culture had seeped into the political machinery of the church and its seminaries. Compromises in generally accepted policy, in canons and constitutions, and in the character, conduct, and beliefs of its elected leadership were being sanctioned at the highest levels of the church. These were but symptomatic of the most deadly and critical compromise possible—*a denial of Christian, biblical faith*—"the faith that was once for all entrusted to the saints" (Jude 3).

Clergy and lay delegates at the 72nd General Convention of the Episcopal Church, held in Philadelphia in late July 1997, by majority rule elected as its next leader a bishop who championed the compromises. For nearly thirty years, this new cause—in fact, this new gospel—had advanced slowly and methodically, both in political resolutions at local and national conventions as well as in overt actions, without disciplinary correction. Over the years, many leaders, lay and ordained, opposed the new direction by raising their voices, educating churchgoers, and amassing names, money, and support for resolutions that countered the drift into modernism and heresy. But amid all the good effort, no leader or movement was able to stop the momentum or turn the church back to its biblical foundations.

In the summer of 1997, what had once been the rebellious beliefs and actions of a few had now become the driving force of the many. In direct opposition to the plain teaching of the Bible—and to thousands of years of Judeo-Christian history, morality, and ethics—the Episcopal Church enthusiastically gave its endorsement to the ever-changing cultural values and beliefs of the American society.[1]

Into this setting, six weeks later, John Rucyahana stepped off the plane in Myrtle Beach. We did not know that day—none of us did—that the arrival of this Anglican bishop from the global South would mark the beginning of a massive correction in the United States that would eventually impact the Anglican Communion worldwide. All we knew was that a significant shift had also taken place in John.

I could see the physical change. He bore the suffering of Rwanda's war-stricken northwest on his face, in his bloodshot eyes, and in the weary tone of his voice. He reminded me of a soldier in battle—focused, tense, driven, concerned—coming off the front lines but not for one second, in his heart, leaving the battlefield or his fellow soldiers. John knew all about the poisoned fruit of gospel-compromise among church leaders. He had witnessed first-hand its devastating effects on the Rwandan people immediately following the genocide. When we told him about the severity of the crisis that had befallen the Episcopal Church in recent days, he knew the deadliest response of all was to stand idly by and do nothing.

This, he said, *must not happen.*

But why did he care, especially now of all times? He had enough problems back home. Yet, he did care—intensely. As we talked, he listened carefully, strategically, to the complicated nature of our situation, and offered timely and godly counsel. What was it inside him that insisted we take immediate action? Why did he offer himself, if necessary, if worse came to worst, to join us in that action? *You are willing to help us?* Why not leave well enough alone, go back to the hardships and suffering in Rwanda, and simply commit us to prayer?

I asked John these questions. But he wouldn't answer me. I soon learned that these were the kinds of questions not to be answered in simple conversation. If I really wanted to know, he told me, there was only one way to find out: "You must come to Rwanda, my brother. You must come to my diocese in the northwest, and see for yourself."

•   •   •

My first glimpse of daily life in the northwest came through John's stories of that first year—phone calls, faxes, and e-mails.

"Yesterday," John wrote, "many people were killed on one of the university campuses in Mudende: 144 perished at the hands of infiltrators. Many homes were destroyed, churches, and other valuable properties. As a result of the confrontation between these attackers and the soldiers, many other people died—and displacement continues to take place. Hence, we have over 200 refugees at one of our churches in the area. We are in a crisis. We need you to pray because we are faced with the practical problem of feeding these people and giving them shelter. This is so in many other places in the diocese."

Another letter said, "We lost five people at the hands of infiltrators who attacked Shyira . . . killing the principal of our high school, a lady who worked for the school and her two teenagers (who are related to me), and another person near the school. These incidents are happening more often in different places in the diocese. It seems that the rebels lost the war and have no political line but just to disturb people's peace and hinder development."

Often his writing moved from general, big-picture vision to vivid detail. "The issue of orphans is getting out of proportion," he noted. "Please pray for healing miracles in our society. Our people's minds, hearts, and continued pain need the mighty hand of God." In the same letter he announced, "We lost one of our pastors, who left a widow and seven orphans." Sadly, this would not be the only time. John had 486 congregations under his charge with only 39 ordained ministers. Lay pastors, accountable to one of the clergy, ran most of the weekly services. By midsummer 1998, he lamented, "Three of my clergy and many lay pastors were killed along with their families. Many of our dear Christians also died in the violent attacks of my first year."

On December 12, 1997, he wrote that eleven of his priests and their families were physically displaced from their homes by rebel forces. In addition, another attack on a Mudende refugee camp had killed three hundred. Finally, fourteen others were murdered a few miles from John's home. He asked us to pray for "miracles in this dark time of our country. . . . We hope that the war will end soon."

Perhaps nothing was more personally devastating than the story of his niece.

A few months after my consecration, my niece, Madu, came to visit. She was sixteen years old, a high school girl. She had come to tell me that she and her mother, her sister and brother wanted to move from their town to near where we lived. They felt unsafe. Ethnically, they were a mixed family. Her father was a Tutsi, her mother a Hutu. She wasn't sure if the rebels would pick them out—so she was scared. I was able to reassure her that the provisions for the move were cared for and that they should come immediately. She went back home and made preparations.

But that same evening, infiltrators attacked them and they stripped her naked, raped her, took their machetes and peeled the flesh off both arms from her shoulder to her wrist and hands—while she was still alive. Then they slaughtered her and cut her neck. Early the next morning, some of our Christians from that town came out of hiding and brought the news to us. We had to make burial arrangements for her, her dead mother, her dead brother and sister. The soldiers would not let me attend the burial of my family. They told me, as a bishop coming to this town, I would attract public attention and many more people would die. It was a tragic and devastating moment in our lives. We had to mourn them in silence. It was very painful for my children, especially my daughters who were near her age and very close to her. They could not conceive—none of us could—the pain this dear girl went through. To this day, we deeply grieve their loss.[2]

That first year, John and Harriet rented a home in the center of the town of Ruhengeri. Surrounding the house was a ten-foot wall made of brick, on top of which, cemented into the wall, were large pieces of cut glass. Dogs circled the house, mostly at night, keeping watch for intruders. Often government soldiers—dressed in fatigues, black boots laced to the calf, carrying a rifle loosely in one hand—came in and out of the compound through a large metal door that, when opened, was big enough to drive through. The house was locked down at night. The situation demanded it. Having a Tutsi bishop in the midst of an extremist Hutu war zone was like putting a lamp outside on a summer's night to attract bugs.

Amid all the security, the attacks kept coming. Archbishop Emmanuel Kolini[3] commented to the Rev. Dr. John Rodgers in the summer of 1998 that he believed it was a miracle John and Harriet Rucyahana were still alive. No one knew this better than John Rucyahana. There were too many close calls, too many times when a matter of minutes, even seconds, made the difference. John was always reluctant to tell the stories. But I kept insisting, asking more questions than he wanted to hear or answer. Following are three reports from excerpts of his writings and interviews.

> The infiltrators, standing by the road between Ruhengeri and Gisyeni, shot eight bullets at us, but God delivered us. . . . They bombed a number of mini-buses, which were just ahead of us, and they killed twenty people. Our car came onto the scene seconds after that. We found warm, bleeding dead bodies and others at the verge of death. Blood was fresh flowing in the middle of the road. One of the mini-buses was still burning and the flames were high. We nearly perished with them.
>
> I could see some men coming down the side of the hill toward the road with military guns in their hands. They looked to me to be infiltrators. I told the priest driving the car to speed up. We were able to drive past them before they got settled. The van behind us got intercepted. Five people were killed.

A few days before Erilynne and I arrived in Ruhengeri, in the spring of 1998, Bishop John was headed home after a day's work at the cathedral offices. Just as he got in his car, some workers asked him for a ride. They didn't want to walk home due to an impending storm. He agreed, they got in, and off they went to the section of town where they lived. John dropped them off and headed to his house. Twenty minutes later, the phone rang. One of the workers reported that rebel forces had just attacked their street, killing a number of people.

"Had we walked home, Bishop, we would have most certainly died today."

John put the phone down. He went back over the scene in his mind, step by step. Had he left the office a few minutes later, if anything had delayed him—one more note to write, one more call to make, a meeting that went a few minutes longer—he would have turned down their street to drop them off at the moment the gunmen opened fire.

His emotions were mixed. On the one hand, again, by the providence of God, his life and the lives of the workers had been spared. On the other hand, people had just died. Their families and neighbors were now in tears, mourning their loss. Fear would soon spread to towns and villages as word got out of more killings, like ripples on water after sudden impact. For John, it was another day in a long, wearisome string of days to beg God for His mercy and to ask that He would end the violent aftershocks of a war that had supposedly ended in mid-July 1994.

•   •   •

We stayed at John and Harriet's home. At first, it seemed quite peaceful. The house was full of people when we arrived, warmly welcoming us to Africa and to their beautiful town of Ruhengeri. After settling into our room, we were given a tour of the house and grounds. A buffet dinner had been set on the table, and during the meal Erilynne and I had the opportunity to sit and talk with most of the guests. What surprised us was how many spoke English fluently, and to find them smiling, even cheerful, and quite busy with their lives. It made us feel hopeful, as if the destructive and thunderous storms of recent days had already passed overhead and were now faintly heard in the distance somewhere.

But nighttime more than told the story.

Lying in bed, we could hear the occasional whispers outside our window of men guarding the house and the constant, frenetic movement of the dogs going back and forth, as if they had caught a scent of some kind. Beyond them, just past the large barricade of walls, we could hear sounds coming from town like a thousand echoes bouncing off the hills behind us, all converging at the same time. There was music—was it the sound of radios blaring or live musicians playing in different places? There were voices—but we couldn't understand them, not from a distance, not in a foreign tongue. Then a man's voice stood out. It was raised, impassioned, and brief. Then another, as if he were responding. *Why were they yelling? Was it an argument between them? Or was something actually wrong? Maybe they were calling for help or trying to warn us? Maybe they had seen infiltrators?*

No, it couldn't be, we told ourselves. It was our imaginations running wild. We were tired from the long trip and the time change. We had heard too many violent stories from Rwanda's northwest and they were playing havoc with our minds. It was best to tune it all out, roll over, and go to sleep.

Then—*Bang! Bang! Bang! Bang!*

Gunfire. Shots, real shots. We both sat up, eyes wide open. *Did you hear that? How close was it?* It could have been miles away, given the mountains around us. It could have been down the street. *What are we supposed do? Where are we supposed to go?* There was no movement in the house—were John and Harriet awake? Did they hear it? *Maybe it was from military soldiers, protecting the peace. Yes, but what if it was from attacking rebels?* We wondered if people had just been killed, if others were running for safety, if children were waking up scared and crying for their parents—*if they were coming for us.*

We waited for more, but nothing.

Some time passed, maybe an hour or two, and it happened again—three times that first night. Each time, we sat up in bed, fearing the worst. Slowly, we'd put our heads back on the pillows, our hearts racing, the adrenaline flowing, our imaginations tormenting us. *What would stop the infiltrators from coming tonight?* The dogs could warn us, the men outside could handle a few of them—maybe. But if they stormed the compound with a dozen soldiers and a clear plan in mind, there would be little to stop them. It would happen just like that, in a flash of time, and what could we do? Where could we hide?

We would not escape.

In the long hours past midnight, such thoughts only multiplied and played like a movie clip over and over again. For me, all night, I kept seeing the jet-black African face of Archdeacon Ephraim, one of John's clergy. He was the one who had picked us up at the airport in Kigali that afternoon. He had a round, gentle face with brightness in his eyes, a gracious smile, and a warm, pastoral disposition that seemed altogether kind. He greeted us with a handshake and an apology that English wasn't easy for him. He immediately handed us a note from Bishop John:

> You are most welcome in Rwanda. . . . I am very sorry for not being at the airport to meet you. I have an important national meeting to attend. I was asked to give a talk. I will explain on arrival. . . . I have sent Archdeacon Ephraim Semabumba to meet you. The way is well protected. Be at peace.
>
> *Yours in Christ,*
> *Bishop John Rucyahana*

I put the note in my pocket and we followed Ephraim.

We got in the car, drove out of Kigali, and took the major roadway to the mountainous northwest. For an hour and a half, we had front-row seats to witness the magnificent beauty of Rwanda's lush terrain, the meticulous architecture of terraced hills and cultivated valleys with rivers, cut deep into the landscape and still lit by the midafternoon sun, meandering gently on their courses. Every parcel of land, even the steepest of hillsides, seemed groomed and eager to produce crops. At nearly every bend in the road, we could see workers scattered everywhere, women carrying produce on top of their heads, often with babies slung on their backs, men hauling debris, others in the fields working, and still others, near the roadside, standing around, watching us pass. It would have been a sightseer's dream come true had we not known about this particular road.

This was where, several months before, John had nearly lost his life in an ambush. Only a few weeks ago, I had read over the Internet that infiltrators had attacked a mini-bus, setting it on fire, looting and then killing everyone on board. It happened on this road—and we knew it. We wouldn't have worried nearly as much if Ephraim had been more confident and relaxed. But he was definitely and noticeably nervous. He barely said a word the entire trip. He held the wheel tightly in his hands, his body leaning slightly forward in the seat, his eyes moving back and forth from the road to the mountainside in an unending and annoying rhythm. I knew he was watching for infiltrators. I kept looking at him in the rearview mirror, convinced he was just as frightened as we were. He knew what could happen. He also knew he had, in the backseat of his car, two white Americans—a perfect catch for enemy forces. Ephraim was focused. He had to get to Ruhengeri—that was his job—but any minute, any second, he knew how quickly it could change.

That face, those ever-moving eyes. I kept seeing them all night long. I kept hearing the words Bishop John had written to us: *The way is well protected. Be at peace.* I kept waiting for that moment, that sudden terror. The drive couldn't have ended soon enough. The first light of dawn couldn't have come fast enough.

• • •

Sitting down to breakfast the next morning, having had little more than catnaps the night before, Erilynne and I asked John and Harriet how they had slept, assuming they were somehow used to it all.

"Not very well," John told us, looking as tired as we felt. "No one ever gets used to it. Never."

"There were shootings last night," I said.

"I know, three times. Actually, it is getting better. We are seeing some improvement. The Rwandan military is doing a good job. We believe peace is soon coming to the northwest."

"But for now," Harriet added, "we have to trust the Lord. We ask Him to stop the killers from hurting our people and causing us to be frightened in our homes at night. This is how we pray."

The family had gathered around the dining room table and taken their seats, along with those who work or stay in the house. The table was spread with an abundance of fresh fruits—mango, papaya, and banana—plus scrambled eggs and toast, sweet and Irish potatoes from the night before with lightly fried, steaming hot African matoke, side dishes of butter, jellies, and honey, along with fruit juices, coffee, milk, and tea.

John asked if we'd all bow our heads for prayer. He prayed, "Gracious, loving Lord and Father, we come before You in humility to thank You for keeping us safe last night. We remember those who were physically hurt and traumatized by the shootings and who feared for their lives. They need Your divine touch. Our country needs peace, Lord. We ask You to intervene. We remember the rebels who have lost their senses and hardened their hearts against You. Reach out to them. Stop them in Jesus' name. Lord, we bring before You the many homeless widows and orphans in our communities who are waking up with no place to go and nothing to eat. We pray You would extend Your kindness to them and Your hand of mercy even now, that today they might have food and shelter. Watch over them, Lord, we pray, and bless them. Most Holy Father, we know You alone give the gift of security. You alone provide for our needs. Without You, we have nothing. This morning, we thank You for the food set before us and for each person at the table. Our hearts are full of praise for Your kind and redeeming love given by our Lord Jesus Christ, who laid down His life for us on the cross. Help us, Lord, and forgive us that we might serve You today with all our hearts. We need You, Lord, and we love You. We turn to You and seek Your face. Be with us, we pray. We ask this in the name of Jesus. Amen."

This was like no world I had ever known. All my life I prayed the Lord's prayer — "Give us this day our daily bread . . . deliver us from evil" — in the context of my American home. Our kitchen cupboards were always full, like our bellies, and the grocery stores always open. At night, we slept with locks on our doors and security systems armed, even though we lived in peaceful suburban communities that knew nothing about enemy fire and mass killings at night. In my world, provision and security were a given. We woke up expecting to wake up. We ate expecting to eat. It never dawned on us that we, as a family, should stop and give thanks to the Lord who made possible a safe night's sleep, or honor Him for His gracious gift of a new day with food on the table and the opportunity to be together again.

I was clearly not in America anymore.

Over the next few days, we traveled to different parts of the diocese, and even back to the capital city of Kigali, with military soldiers surrounding us at all times. They did not make me feel safe. It was the exact opposite. They were a constant reminder that this world was at war and insecure, and insecurity—whether it's political, emotional, physical, marital, economic, or any combination—always introduces chaos. Things so easily taken for granted are suddenly called into question. Just getting out of the van to walk in the countryside, or to talk with people John knew, or to go into a school and visit the children and their teachers, or to stop in one of the churches —felt unsafe. I found myself constantly looking around, as if something were about to happen. It felt like evil forces outside myself were staring at me, waiting for me, ready to pounce. I was vulnerable, with nothing in my American arsenal that could rescue me. There was no magic 911 number to call on my cell phone. It didn't matter that we were born into the right families, schooled at the finest academic institutions, or that we were successful as doctors, lawyers, clergy, politicians who knew the right people at the top who could pull strings. In this world, there were no strings. There was nothing, absolutely nothing, that could immunize us from the real possibility of a rebel attack at any given moment.

This was a world where I was not in control. This was John's world—every day, every night.

During these days, we watched the African Christians live their lives and say their prayers in an attitude of humility and complete surrender to their almighty God and Father. They felt what we felt and a thousand times more. But they knew where to go and who to turn to. They trusted the Lord as they walked the streets of town to buy food at the markets or visit a friend or attend church. They trusted Him as they tucked their children into bed at night. They turned to Him when the memories of war would physically grab their insides. They turned to Him when they were forced out of their homes—and, night after night, slept on mats in a church sanctuary with their children beside them, with people sleeping everywhere, and with no sense of where tomorrow's food and water would come from.

These were Christians, changed by the saving power of the Lord Jesus Christ. They loved Him, and that love radiated from their faces. He was their security, their daily bread and clean water, their protection from sickness and disease, and their Everlasting Father watching over them and their children. He was their everything, their "all in all." Jesus had promised to be with them "until the end of the age," and He was being faithful to that promise day in and day out. They knew that even if famine or disease struck them down—even if rebels attacked and killed them—He would still be faithful to the end. He would save them in their darkest hour. By His extreme suffering, death, and resurrection, He had prepared a place for them, an eternal home in the glories of heaven. They knew it. They sang about it. They longed for it.

Every day, every night, He was all they had.

"John, this place is not safe," I said to him, driving out of the northwest toward Kigali.

"I didn't go in for this because it was safe. I knew it was dangerous, but I knew—even in danger, in life and in death—God saves. God sends His workers to be able to make a difference in a situation. We have talked about this before."

"But you're a Tutsi. It's even worse. You're like a lightning rod."

"Did you know," he said slowly, "that at the time of my consecration, soldiers, politicians, fellow churchmen, and people who loved me told me they thought I was going to die in less than a month's time? But my conviction was that I needed to make a difference and preach the gospel of our Lord Jesus, which is never Tutsi or Hutu, but is the only remedy to heal a nation racked with division and pain."

I sat back and stared out the window. I tried to imagine myself going back to stay in Ruhengeri during these days of insecurity. Instead, I felt both guilty and relieved I was leaving. The next few nights, we'd stay in a hotel and then fly home. John would head back to Ruhengeri, his life constantly at risk. *Could I do that? Could I go back and live my life there?* A soldier sat between Erilynne and me, his eyes glued to the road straight ahead, his rifle securely at his side standing straight up. John, sitting in the front passenger seat, spoke to the driver in his native tongue and then, after a few minutes, turned back to me. His words were so familiar. I had heard them a thousand times—whether it was in everyday conversation, in various sermons over the years, or in talking about the many times he nearly lost his life in Uganda or, in recent days, Rwanda. But this time, it was different. Having experienced the briefest glimpse of his life in the northwest, I realized this was the testimony of his life. He said it because he lived it.

"The Lord calls us to follow Him," he said. "We must do it. It may not be easy. We may not feel comfortable. It may mean we lose things we hold dear. But we do it. We take action because we love Him."

I nodded, like I had done so many times before when he had said it. But this time it hurt. I heard it not in my head, agreeing with the biblical principle, but in my heart—where I just wasn't sure whether I could "do it" or not. Why didn't I have what John had—the resolute passion to follow Jesus, no matter what it cost in personal suffering, just because I love Him above all else? I hated the feeling, but it was there. I wanted to go back home where it was safe, where shots don't ring out in the night, where people aren't afraid for their lives every minute of every day, and where the basic provisions of life aren't in jeopardy. I wanted to go back to where it was easy and comfortable.

I turned toward the window, aching inside. I did the only thing I knew to do.

I told Him I was sorry.

CHAPTER 6

SILENCE OF SCREAMS

Upon arriving in Kigali, we picked up the Rev. Chuck Murphy, rector of All Saints Church, Pawleys Island, at the airport. We were scheduled to have three days of meetings with Bishop John Rucyahana and Archbishop Emmanuel Kolini concerning the crisis back home in the Episcopal Church. That night, we ate dinner together at the hotel. Tables were set outside on a stone patio overlooking the city, partially covered with a deep green-and-white striped awning. Over to one side, near the bar and cash register, a television set was broadcasting local news and was just audible enough for us to hear the reporter speaking in the native language of Kinyarwanda. As we were being served, John turned toward the set.

"Oh no, that's terrible," John said quietly, cringing as he overheard the news.

"What is it?" I asked, not understanding the reporter.

"A man turned himself in to the police today. He couldn't sleep at night. He had nightmares and cold sweats. He killed his neighbor during the genocide in '94 and, when he sleeps, he sees that dead man's face come alive, he hears his voice screaming at him, saying, 'Why did you kill me?' Finally, he gave up. He couldn't stand it anymore. So he dug the man up and took his bones to the police station. He laid them on the desk and said with tears running down his cheeks, 'Here! I am guilty! I killed this man! Arrest me! Put me in prison!'

"You see," John continued, "many Rwandans live like this man. The government told them to kill and they did it. But they remain traumatized to this very day. They don't know what to do with themselves. They are desperate and hurting. They are guilty of their crimes, but no one brings them to justice. It is a very sad case. But it shows you what we must do in preaching the gospel in the Rwandan setting. People need Jesus desperately. Whether they were perpetrators or victims, they need to hear the Lord Jesus say from the cross, 'Father, forgive them, for they do not know what they are doing.'[1] They need to experience His saving power that transforms lives and works miracles of healing and reconciliation in their hearts. This is what we preach in our churches. We are seeing many people like this man changed by the gospel. They are coming to meet Jesus Christ in tears. They are hugging their neighbors. It is a sovereign work of God. This is what we pray for. What else could save a man like this one? Do you think he will find peace in prison?"

He paused, and then answered the question.

"No! But this gives you a taste of what we face every day in Rwanda."

The image stuck. The man digging up the bones, carrying them to the police station, and turning himself in — four years after the crime.

It set the tone for the next few days. As much as we wanted Emmanuel and John to understand the nature of the problems facing the American church, they wanted us to experience the present sufferings of the Rwandan people. It wasn't enough to talk about it. We were on their turf, and they wanted to show us firsthand. So, on the second day of our meetings, they asked if we would like to visit two memorial sites of the genocide. Both were churches. We agreed, and after a light lunch, John and Harriet, Chuck, Erilynne, and I drove some thirty miles south of Kigali. We were not prepared for what we were about to see.

The first church was in a town called Nyamata.

From a distance, the orange-brick building looked altogether normal, ready for Sunday services. A round steeple with a simple metal cross on top of it rose into a partly cloudy sky above the sanctuary. The grounds were neatly manicured, with flowering bushes and old towering trees scattered about. A tall red-iron fence outlined the perimeter of the property with a gate standing open at the front and a sidewalk easily pointing to the entrance, where a small group of men and women were gathered.

As we got out of the car and approached the church, an African man in his midthirties stepped away from the others to greet us. He said, through John's translation, that we were most welcome to Nyamata and to the church, which he called a historic landmark of Rwanda. He wanted us to know some facts about the church — when it was built and a variety of significant events that had taken place down through the years. Then he informed us that somewhere between April 9 and 14, 1994, five thousand people were killed inside.

"Did you know any of them?" I inquired.

"All my family," he said in broken English, looking straight at me. Then he turned to John, asking in Kinyarwanda if we were ready to go inside. John nodded, and the man opened the door.

The church was swept clean. The wooden benches were placed around the altar in a half circle. On the altar, a cloth frontal piece depicted the Last Supper. Behind it and to the right were two contemporary stained glass windows dug into the back wall, one above the other—both a few feet tall and rectangular. On the bottom pane, in bright cheerful reds, yellows, whites, and blues, was a man standing, looking up, with his hands raised, giving praise to God. The top pane, with the same colors, had a half dozen people, dressed in robes, kneeling. Their heads were also raised and, coming down from heaven, were the "tongues as of fire"—remembering the day of Pentecost. Below both was a clear window, the same size, letting sunlight flood into the sanctuary. Ten feet in front of the windows was a round, almost ivory-looking baptismal font with hand-painted Christian symbols drawn around the side.

It all looked so peaceful.

But the moment we looked up, the story changed. The ceiling was raised, angling up and peaking in the middle of the sanctuary. It was made of iron sheets, and in it were a thousand and more tiny holes scattered everywhere, with the light of day pouring through them, evidence of shrapnel spraying from the grenades—proof that this church had become a place of unspeakable terror.

A room off the sanctuary had a table stacked high with bones, another table with rows of skulls, and another with a woman's body still in a state of decomposition. Our host told us that she was raped, then bludgeoned, then thrown into a pit with bodies piled on top. She had just been recovered. They were surprised to still see flesh on her. They were building an undercroft below the sanctuary that would serve as a museum. Her remains would lie in state for public viewing. Her husband and twin children died with her.

"She will be remembered," the man said. "Her story belongs to our country."

Behind the church, underground, sixty-four square rooms housed the dead. The work was not yet completed. One day these catacombs would be lighted for the public to visit and mourn. But for now, we stood at the top of the steps looking down on the first room exposed by sunlight. It was maybe ten feet wide, about the same deep, made of concrete, with large wooden shelves spanning the three walls. Like before, the bones were neatly stacked in rows, the skulls separated. One skull in particular, in the front row, had wrapped around it a silver chain with a cross hanging down over the shelf. I slipped down the stairs and saw that the rooms were actually set back a few feet, creating a hallway on either side for people to walk past each room. It was completely dark, the air stale, the place still. I stayed for a moment, realizing that this massive crypt, with its twenty thousand bodies, was like an oversized lighthouse in Rwanda with a bellowing foghorn wailing out to the world, and to generations yet born, to come, see, and never forget.

This is the proof of genocide, these bodies—these people and their untold suffering.

We walked the grounds in silence, trying to take it all in. As we drifted back to the van, a group of thirty schoolchildren passed by with their teachers. They stopped to talk to us with John, again, interpreting. The children were fascinated with our white skin and my wife's blonde hair and blue eyes. One of them, a young boy of nine, stood in front of me. He had a big smile, a playful, even mischievous look in his eyes. As I looked down at him, I saw on the left side of his head a six-inch scar that had indented his skull nearly a half-inch. I caught Harriet's eye. She came over and put her hand on the boy's shoulder and talked with him. He was very articulate and expressive, his hands telling the story.

"It happened during the war," she said to me. "This is a machete wound. They tried to kill him with the rest of his family, but he survived. Now he lives with relatives. He attends school and is happy." With that, he looked up at me, wondering if I understood. He reached for my hand, shook it, and held on tight while his teachers continued to talk. Every once in a while, I looked again at his scar, amazed that he had survived. I squeezed his hand back, as if I were holding on just as much as he was. After all, here was a boy who was alive—*thank the Lord, he was alive*—and not one of the dead I had just left behind in the crypts.

But so many kids his age did die.[2]

The second site was harder than the first. The church in Ntarama was smaller, rectangular in shape and simple in design. The front entrance was at the back of the church, on the lefthand side, and open. There was no door. Along the side of the building were windows not made of glass but squares of white concrete block with an artistic design in the center of each, allowing air to pass through easily. We parked the car off the road and walked to the church a few hundred yards up a dirt driveway, set under a dense canopy of trees.

As we approached, we saw a large hut with a thatched roof off to our left, adjacent to the front of the church. It was built to house the bones of those who died on church grounds that day. "Many fled the building, trying to escape, and did not make it," John told us. "Their remains are in there." We went over and looked in. Once again, the bones were on tables, neatly stacked, with the skulls on other tables, laid out in rows.

It was very different inside the church. This memorial site, it was decided, would remain as it was on the day the people were killed. Nothing would be touched. The bodies lay where they had fallen.

We were not allowed in the church, only at the door. When it came to my turn, my eye first caught the gaping hole on the side of the building opposite me. "A grenade blast," John said. The pews were nothing more than old wooden benches running up both sides of a center aisle. On them, under them, was a church packed with charred bodies, clothes, books, glasses, and other personal possessions, scattered in complete chaos. The walls were bloodstained and chipped by gunfire. Up front, on the altar, I could see remains strewn on top. The fire was out, the smell of death gone, the bodies decomposed but, immediately, I felt an adrenaline rush, as if it had happened just hours ago. I could feel my heart starting to pound and my mind racing—*What should we do? Were the murderers still around?* No, of course not. But this was it—the crime scene as it was on that fatal day. This was what they had done and we were there—transported back in time to the days when the blood of genocide flooded the land of Rwanda. The terror felt all too real, all too physically present. The "dark powers of this world," the "spiritual forces of evil" hung palpably in the air so we could feel it, we could breathe it.[3]

I want to do something.

"You can almost hear their screams," John said quietly.

It would have been easier if they had cleaned the church, gathered the dead, and carefully ordered their bones on wooden shelves. But to leave the church as it was on the day the people died forced us to be like those who witnessed the crime. John was right; we could almost hear their screams—begging for mercy, crying out to their tormentors, praying for God to spare them, and then perishing in sudden, unspeakable horror. This was not a step back into the past, remembering those who died in the war—this was the past assaulting us, forcing us to stand alongside these people when all the powers of hell descended and no one came to their rescue.

I had never expected this—or the waves of grief that kept crashing down on me.

We walked the grounds for nearly an hour. At one point, Harriet came over and said quietly, slowly, "This is just one place. What happened here—happened all over our country. It was terrible. Nobody can believe it, even to this day. It is a sad time for us. It is even worse because it happened in our churches. You must pray for us."

• • •

We were back in Kigali by five o'clock. Archbishop Kolini came out of his office to meet us as our car pulled into the cathedral parking lot. His words were memorable: "You had to go there. It is part of who we are. Otherwise, you would not understand our tears."

• • •

At the second church, John and I had some time to talk. He wanted me to hear more than their screams. There was another sound. I had read about it in books, magazines, and news articles. In fact, John and I had talked about it extensively before. But it was academic in comparison to being there, at the two churches, in front of the thousands dead. It was, just as John said, even worse than the screams and, strangely, just as loud. There was no way to avoid it.

The silence.

These people cried for help and no one responded. It wasn't as if no one could hear. If only that were true. Then the silence would be understandable. But the fact is, we all heard it. The media blasted the images of carnage from one corner of the globe to another, so that no one could say, *We didn't know.* The fact is, we knew what was going on—from presidents and heads of state, to policy makers at the United Nations, in Washington, DC, to common people watching the nightly news or reading their daily paper. And the response was the same: *silence*. Who can imagine what that would feel like—*the betrayal! the utter despair!*—to cry out for help, to know people have heard you, and then to see them turn and walk away? *They don't care enough to respond?* No one did. No one came to their rescue—not even my country.

This silence was a global silence and an American silence.

History would later record that "President Clinton did not convene a single meeting of his senior foreign policy advisers to discuss U.S. options for Rwanda. His top aides rarely condemned the slaughter. . . . the United States again stood on the sidelines."[4] The Senate minority leader, Bob Dole, held the same opinion, stating, "I don't think we have any national interest there. The Americans are out, and as far as I'm concerned, in Rwanda, that ought to be the end of it."[5] As a result, "during the entire genocide the possibility of U.S. military intervention was never even debated. . . . Rwanda was never thought to warrant its own top-level meeting."[6] The operative word, confirmed by the secular press, was that "the Clinton Administration was largely silent."[7]

After the genocide, Samantha Powers, in an article in *The Atlantic Monthly*, reported that the new president of Rwanda, Pastor Bizimungu, flew to Washington and met with US government officials. While there, in a meeting with Prudence Bushnell, the deputy assistant secretary of the State Department's African Bureau, he "leaned across the table toward her, eyes blazing, and said, 'You, madame, are partially responsible for the genocide, because we told you what was going to happen and you did nothing.'"[8]

We told you . . . and you did nothing.

The United Nations Secretary-General Boutros Ghali confirmed the president's charge: "We are all to be held accountable for this failure, all of us. . . . It is a genocide. . . . I have failed. . . . It is a scandal!"[9] Then Vice Secretary-General Kofi Annan testified, "Nobody should feel he has a clear conscience in this business. If the pictures of tens of thousands of human bodies rotting and gnawed by the dogs . . . do not wake us up out of our apathy, I don't know what will."[10]

It was Canadian Army General Romeo Dallaire, commander of the United Nations peacekeeping forces in Rwanda, who had warned the UN before the genocide broke out. "Not one country on Earth," he said in a recent interview, "came to stop this thing. The Western world provided me with nothing."[11] In June 2000, he was "found unconscious on a park bench in Hull, Quebec, drunk and alone. He had consumed a bottle of scotch on top of his daily dose of pills for post-traumatic stress disorder. He was on another suicide mission." The Canadian news picked up the story. Dallaire would simply say in reply, "There are times when the best medication and therapist simply can't help a soldier suffering from this new generation of peacekeeping injury. . . . My soul is in Rwanda. It has never, ever come back, and I'm not sure it ever will."[12]

We told you . . . and you did nothing.[13]

Tragically, a journalist said, "The only noise that could be heard was the sound of machetes slicing their way through Rwanda's Tutsi population."[14]

I heard the silence that day, walking the church grounds.

I learned that this kind of silence is not a peaceful, quiet sound. Actually, it is the exact opposite. It roars like thunder overhead, shaking the ground beneath, shaking every fiber of the human heart, because it never allows us to forget the people who cried out. It always reminds us of the decision not to act in a time of crisis.[15] It forever demands that we bear the guilt and culpability for those who died without our intervention. *There is a sinful, evil silence.* I could almost hear it that day between the screams of those perishing—the silence of a world turning away—and the images playing over and over in my mind of skeletal remains that lay still on the floor of the church in Ntarama.

John wanted me to understand the nature of this silence. So, at dinner that night, with everyone at the table, I asked him if he would tell the story of his little sister one more time.

● ● ●

Her name was Adela.

It was a midsummer afternoon in Rwanda in the early 1950s. Their house and farmland sat at the eastern base of the mighty Mhubura Mountain, which stretched so high into the air that, on most days, its summit would be completely lost in the clouds. John was eight or nine years old at the time. School was out. His chores were done. For whatever reason, he came on the scene at just the wrong time.

Adela knew she was not supposed to ride the bicycle. Her father had made it very clear to all the children. It was the family's only means of transportation. It was dangerous for the bicycle to be treated as a toy and dangerous for the family not to have a means of transport. So it was something they never did. But that afternoon, when she thought no one was looking, she went over to the bicycle, lightly touched the handlebar, and imagined herself riding it. She looked again and still no one was around. She gently pushed up the kickstand and walked the bicycle to the back of the compound, where she could ride in secret. Once there, Adela got on the seat and began to push the pedals down with her feet. She had no idea her older brother was watching. Like all young children, it was wobbly at first. She couldn't coordinate the movement of her feet and the steering of her hands with the weight of her body. She started and stopped, nearly falling a few times, but slowly she got the knack of it and, after a while, still unsteady, she was actually riding it. A smile lit her face — nothing could be more fun than this, the wind in her hair, and the ground moving below her. It lasted only a few minutes.

Neither John nor Adela heard their father approaching. Suddenly he was there and she was caught. He spoke to Adela with a stern voice and, as John said, "gave her serious punishment and discipline. But when he finished with her, he did the same to me. I received no less punishment, even though I didn't do it. I was held responsible because I did not speak to my younger sister and stop her from doing what was wrong. I fell into the trap of thinking that since I wasn't doing it, I was innocent. This was the lesson my late father taught me: *We never keep quiet when something is going wrong.* I was taught this principle many times growing up. The one who commits sin and the one who stands by in silence, doing nothing about it, are guilty of the same crime and deserve the same punishment."

• • •

This was John. It was more than a lesson quickly learned and easily forgotten. This principle dug deep into his soul and permeated every fiber of his being. He lived by it and, at times, nearly died because of it. As early as nineteen, when John was a refugee in Congo during the 1964 Mlele War, two soldiers came into the camp to abduct a young woman and rape her. They literally pulled her from her stepfather and mother as she cried out, appealing for someone to do something. The soldiers had guns. No one else did.

But John knew he could not keep quiet. He got three other men. Together they confronted the soldiers, with guns pointed at them, and told them to hand over the young woman. They were ready to fight and, even if one or two got shot, the others would do everything in their power to win the woman back. The soldiers cursed the young men, assaulted them with the butts of their rifles, and threatened to kill them on the spot. But the men didn't stand down. They stepped closer, demanding her release.

The soldiers raised their voices, laughing at them.

But it worked. The persistence of the young men paid off. The soldiers let the woman go.

This was John. He could not remain silent when wrong was being committed. It's what made him stand up to Idi Amin's soldiers as a young priest in Uganda. It's what drove him to return to Rwanda to be part of the recovery of his homeland in the northwest, even while it was still at war. It's what lay at the heart of his faith in the Lord Jesus Christ.

"You know, it's biblical," John told us that night. "The Lord heard the Israelites' cry in slavery in Egypt, and He responded. To this day, He hears the cry of all of us in our sin and, out of love for the world, He sent His only begotten Son, Jesus Christ, to save us. This is what He does. He hears us and, in His love for us, He acts. He cannot stand back and watch in silence, no! He comes to our aid and He expects us to do the same. When His love is poured into our hearts by the Holy Spirit, we must never keep quiet. You must always remember this — it is a biblical principle. It is the nature who God is and it's what He always does."

We must never keep quiet.

"In the war," Emmanuel said slowly, deliberately, "there were three sins. There were those who planned the genocide. There were those who committed acts of genocide. And there were those who stood back and watched it, but did nothing about it. In Rwanda, all three sins are one. They are the same. If a person is rich or poor, a politician or a doctor or a common farmer or a church leader — it doesn't matter. We don't care. If they saw an act of violence and turned their head as they walked by, they are equally guilty."

He paused for a moment, sitting back in his chair, letting his words sink in.

"The same is true in the United States," he added, "and in the American church."

That night, the torch passed. In these few words of Archbishop Emmanuel Kolini and Bishop John Rucyahana, coupled with the experience of visiting the memorial sites, we understood our orders. These men were challenging us to follow their lead. *We were not to stay quiet.* The time had come for us to stand strong against the problems facing the Episcopal Church back home. Chuck Murphy had carefully presented the case to our Rwandan friends, stating that the majority of bishops and elected leaders in the church had subscribed to a new gospel that openly embraced the tolerant nature of our American society and equally challenged the authority of the historic Christian faith. Chuck made it quite clear that if something were not done, the apostasy itself would be the ruin of the Episcopal Church and eventually metastasize like a cancer throughout the Anglican Communion as a whole.

This was not a time for silence.

"What about the evangelical bishops in the Episcopal Church who do not believe in this new gospel?" John asked. "What are they doing to stop it?"

"Quite frankly," Chuck responded, "they have spoken out, but they haven't done anything to lead us out. Here's the problem — they are bishops and we're not. We are just clergy and laypeople. We have no clout. But to sit back and watch this drama unfold isn't a preferred future for me, for my church in South Carolina, for many clergy and leaders across the country, or for the future generations of our children and grandchildren. What I'm hearing you say is that we shouldn't sit back, remain silent, and pretend this thing is going to work out someday."

"Exactly," John interjected.

"Yes," Emmanuel said. "You have to take action."

It was then that we asked for their help.

The next day our meetings came to an end. They drove us to the Kigali airport to make the long journey home to the States. Just as we were leaving each other, the archbishop made one last comment.

"You know, physically, Rwanda is the smallest province in the Anglican Communion. Because of the war, we are the weakest, and possibly the poorest. Yet, we are not willing to see you suffer and do nothing about it. If we are needed, we will stand with you.

"But first," he continued, "you must be willing to act. It may cost your jobs. You will be called names. You may lose your church properties. But when the church fails to preach the gospel of the Lord Jesus Christ, everybody suffers. The Bible teaches us that people perish. It may not be a physical genocide like we know in Rwanda, but it is worse. It is a spiritual genocide. People die spiritually from God—and eternally. You must never forget that. This must not happen in your country. You cannot sit back and do nothing. You are responsible."

With that, he shook our hands and sent us home.

PART 2

WAR
OF TRUTH

CHAPTER 7

KUALA LUMPUR'S PROMISE

What happened next, in the late summer of 1997, can only be described as a sovereign act of God. Even then, it was only in hindsight that we could see it. He was doing something far beyond our best efforts and clever scheming. It was during these days that Erilynne and I realized the Lord had brought us to Pawleys Island for a reason. And it was here, on the remote banks of the Atlantic, in a place known mostly for its manufacturing of hammocks, that the Lord began a reforming movement inside a mainline denomination that had, over many years, abandoned the heart and soul of the Christian faith.

I am talking about the Episcopal Church.

But our story reaches into the heart of every denomination in the United States, every church structure, every pastor, board of elders, and person attending Sunday worship. We are all wrestling with the same cultural demons. We, in the global North, are living in what is now classically called "an emerging post-Christian society."[1] It is best characterized as a mind-set where there is little acknowledgment of absolute truth.[2]

This is our story. Although it takes place nationally in the Episcopal Church and globally in the Anglican Communion, it is a story that leaps over denominations and gives hope to Christians across our great land that a reformation in the American church is — in a small way — just beginning.

I wish I could say we planned it. But we cannot take credit for strategically organizing the course of events that follow. This work belongs to God. In His rich and abundant mercy, He sent us an African missionary whose heart was aflame with passion for the Lord Jesus Christ and His gospel. Then He sent us others just like him — from Africa and Asia — who, in hearing our cry and seeing the deplorable state of our church, cared enough to come and help us—and that has made all the difference.[3]

● ● ●

Every denomination has its own structures and practices that govern its daily life. In the Anglican Communion worldwide, there are thirty-eight provinces—or jurisdictions—each of which has a senior bishop (called an archbishop, or presiding bishop) elected by the province to lead. The archbishop of Canterbury presides as the primary leader of the Communion—a tradition dating back to Augustine, the first archbishop of Canterbury in 597. In one sense, each province is autonomous and self-governing, yet it is connected to the worldwide Anglican Communion through basic, essential principles of Christian faith and historic church order that have forged a solid, seemingly unshakable unity that has lasted for centuries.

It is therefore a rare moment when one part of the Communion lifts up its voice in loving, concerned protest against the decisions and actions of another part. To call for correction presumes that a legislative system of mutual accountability and interdependence is both intact and able to negotiate the presenting issues. But that presumption, quite honestly, is the problem. Most of the international meetings between provincial leaders have been, as an African archbishop once mused, "like a grand English tea-party, most cordial and proper." What happened in Kuala Lumpur on February 10–15, 1997, proved beyond a shadow of doubt that accountability between provinces, either relationally or legally, is nonexistent.

The meeting was called the "Second Anglican Encounter in the South."

Archbishops, bishops, and leaders from the global South had first met in Kenya in 1994 to discuss matters specifically concerning their regions. But at this second meeting in 1997, with eighty delegates present, the focus of conversation shifted to the global North—and, in particular, the unbiblical and irregular actions of the US Episcopal Church in the area of human sexuality.

The facts alone were startling.

In 1988, the General Convention of the American Episcopal Church —held every three years—passed a resolution reaffirming the "Biblical and traditional teaching on chastity and fidelity." The vote surfaced an opposition party. It was by no means unanimous. Twenty-nine bishops voted against it. One year later, an Episcopal bishop ordained "an avowed, non-celibate, homosexual man to the priesthood."[4] This bishop was not disciplined, tried before an ecclesiastical court of his peers, or removed from office. The inability to admonish him not only condoned his actions publicly, but it also quickly opened the door for other bishops to do the same. One year later, another bishop followed suit. This time, this particular bishop had the support, blessing, and counsel of the presiding bishop.[5]

By 1991, another resolution appeared before General Convention stating that "all clergy of this Church shall abstain from genital relationships outside of holy matrimony." What once seemed obvious, a commandment given by God Himself, was now subject to rigorous debate. When it came time to vote, in an unprecedented moment in church history, the majority of bishops turned it down.

A new and terrifying day had dawned in Christendom.

By Convention 1994, there was no stopping what had begun. It was a known fact that bishops were ordaining practicing homosexuals and either boldly encouraging or quietly tolerating their clergy to bless same-sex marriages. In those days, it seemed the only hope for true, godly, and biblical repentance was the election of a new presiding bishop who, refusing to compromise the Christian faith, would turn the church back to Jesus Christ. But that election would not happen until the next General Convention in July 1997. In the meantime, evangelical Episcopalians coalesced from all across America—laity, clergy, and bishops—and produced a document called "A Place to Stand," which confessed adherence to the ancient gospel faith and a refusal to accept the rebellion that had mutinously taken over the Episcopal Church. The statement ended with a promised course of action if their voice was not heard:

When there arise within the Church at any level tendencies, pronouncements, and practices contrary to biblical, classical Anglican doctrinal and moral standards, we must not and will not support them. Councils can err and have erred, and the Church has no authority to ordain anything contrary to God's Word written. . . . When teachings and practices contrary to Scripture and to this orthodox Anglican perspective are permitted within the Church — or even authorized by the General Convention — in obedience to God, we will disassociate (Adopted August 7, 1996).

Thousands signed the document.

By February 1997, at the Second Anglican Encounter in the South in Kuala Lumpur, the leaders from the Anglican provinces of the global South, having heard all that was taking place in the Episcopal Church, decided unanimously to add their voice of opposition. They knew (as we have seen from Christian leaders in Rwanda) that it was wrong to witness an act of sin and do nothing about it. They also knew that if nothing was done, the leaven of this heretical teaching would seep into all parts of the Communion. "When America sneezes," one African bishop said, "the whole world catches a cold."[6]

The Kuala Lumpur statement echoed throughout every part of the Communion, and some within the Communion were taking steps to disassociate themselves from those who didn't "stand with this statement."[7]

The moment was poignant. Global South leaders were gently but firmly calling the wealthy, powerful Episcopal Church to account. At home, evangelical Episcopalians were giving the same message in their document "A Place to Stand" — "we will disassociate." It was five months before the General Convention reconvened in Philadelphia. There was no way for the leadership of the Episcopal Church to miss the message.

They would have to respond one way or the other.

• • •

Chuck Murphy did not go to convention that year.

In one sense, he didn't care. He loved being the rector — senior pastor — of All Saints Church. After fifteen years, he couldn't shake the deepening sense of God's call. "I think about what Jesus said: 'to whom much is given, much is required.' The leadership in this church demonstrates a continued willingness to follow Jesus Christ and take risks for the kingdom. I am not looking for another project. I think I have a job. I want to stay the course at All Saints and keep on keeping on." That was Chuck's style — steady, deliberative leadership in the same direction over a long period of time. In early August 1997, there was a certain joy in Chuck's heart. He was in the center of God's best for his life, and he knew it.

On staff, he had an assistant named the Rev. Thomas "TJ" Johnston who was a mover and shaker, a leader cut from the same mold as Chuck. TJ had given up a lucrative career as a lawyer in Charleston, South Carolina, to follow the Lord's prompting into ministry and to apprentice his first few years under Chuck's leadership. Another priest, the Rev. Dr. Jon Shuler, was also located in Pawleys Island. Jon was a seasoned clergyman who had stepped down as rector of a large church in Knoxville to start new churches throughout the world that had a singular passion for the lost. In the mid-1990s, Chuck and Jon believed the Lord would use All Saints Church as the headquarters for that missionary work.

There was also a retired Episcopal bishop—Alex Dickson—who had just moved from Memphis. He was coming to All Saints at Chuck's request to oversee the beginning years of a parish-based seminary, which he was glad to do. Even in retirement, Alex felt deeply called of God to be a strong voice urging his fellow Episcopal bishops to remain true to the authority of the Bible.

These three men—TJ, Jon, and Alex—knocked on Chuck's office door the second week of August 1997.

"Chuck, we have got to talk," TJ said, opening the door and stepping into the room.

"Come on in and let's huddle," Chuck replied. He came from around his desk and in characteristic fashion invited them to sit in his padded rocking chairs—the trademark of Murphy's office. Then he added, "So tell me what happened at General Convention. Are you guys smiling?"

"Chuck, it was bad. Real bad," Jon said with genuine sadness. He had been to General Convention in 1994. He knew, without repentance, the Episcopal Church was moving toward a formal rejection of the historic Christian faith. Shortly after that convention, Jon had a vision for "First Fridays." On the first Friday of every month for nearly two years, he traveled from city to city calling Episcopalians everywhere to pray and fast for a spirit of repentance to fall on the Episcopal Church at the 1997 convention. He felt the Lord's urging that something must be done to "contend for the faith that was once for all entrusted to the saints."[8]

It was a bitter, painful moment for Jon. He was now on the other side of the 1997 convention and there was no repentance whatsoever.

"So here's what happened." TJ stepped in. "First of all, the Kuala Lumpur

Statement was brought to the floor of the House of Bishops for endorsement. By a two to one vote, the bishops declined to affirm it.[9] They are simply not going to take correction from their Anglican colleagues in the global South. Second, Convention elected Frank Griswold as the new presiding bishop—a man who has publicly admitted to ordaining avowed noncelibate homosexuals.[10] So the beat goes on. He is clearly not God's anointed leader to turn this church around. Third, the leadership of the Episcopal Church not only refused to require a biblical sexual ethic for the clergy, let alone the people in the pews, but it proactively passed a resolution extending health coverage to the unmarried lovers of church employees."[11]

"You have got to be kidding!" Chuck said, appalled.

"No. I'm telling you, it's over," TJ responded.

"This is unbelievable," Chuck said. "In all church history, it has never been done before. Never."

"Let me say something here." Alex jumped in with his characteristic Mississippi drawl. "There were a number of disappointments for me at convention.[12] But, personally, the most difficult goes back to the vows we bishops made before the Lord. We promised at our consecrations, 'with all faithful diligence, to banish and drive away from the Church all erroneous and strange doctrine contrary to God's Word.' Then we vowed, 'both privately and openly to call upon and encourage others to the same.'[13] I know many bishops who refuse to compromise the Christian faith in the pulpit and in practice. I consider some of them to be my close personal friends. But at this moment in history, they are simply not able to take a stand in the councils of the church. I think we have to face some hard facts here. We can no longer expect these bishops to lead us out of this crisis."

"Alex is right," Jon said. "If one bishop had stood up in Philadelphia and said, 'The actions of this convention are heretical. They are contrary to everything we hold dear, everything we vowed and promised to God; I'm walking out and I'm reconvening across the street with anyone who will meet me for prayer,' I would have stood up and walked out. If it was only two people, I wouldn't have cared. To me it would have been a sign of leadership—a ray of hope that this thing isn't over yet. But nothing like that happened, and that's when it hit me. Chuck, I came away convinced that if we wait another day for the bishops of the Episcopal Church to lead us in a day of repentance and reformation, we will have to give an account to Jesus about why we waited.

I'm serious about that—we will have to give an account."

"That's right, Jon. No question about it," Alex commented.

"Chuck," TJ interjected, "I believe with all my heart that these men are right. This is a matter of *leadership*. Our church is being hijacked, and evangelical, orthodox bishops simply have no vision and no strategy to counteract the opposition. I agree with Bishop Alex. There are a lot of faithful men but, for whatever reason, they seemed just totally immobilized at this moment in church history. And I agree with Jon. We can't wait. Something has to happen."

Chuck sipped his coffee, reflecting on all that had been said. "I can't remember a time in history when a reforming movement began with a resolution at a convention in a mainline denomination. I think when God moves, He starts where you least expect it. It's my sense that y'all are on to something. It's time to act—and the best place to start is with strong clergy with strong flagship churches that have made a difference and can make a difference."

With that, the conversation took on a whole different tone.

These four men began to brainstorm a possible meeting of senior clergy from across the United States who were proven leaders, successful in ministry, solid in their proclamation of the gospel, and supported by lay leaders who wouldn't blush or blink in the face of controversy. The more they talked, the more confident they became that something had to be done—and this was, at the very least, a way forward. By the end of the meeting, they had come up with more than forty clergy names. It was decided that Chuck and Jon would make the calls. A date was set, September 8–9, and the place, All Saints Church, Pawleys Island, South Carolina.

Ten days later, after all the calls and conversations, thirty senior clergy had agreed to come.

"It just amazed me," Jon Shuler told me later. "Murphy didn't want to take the lead on this thing. But I'm telling you, for me, it was clear from the beginning. Not one person Chuck called turned him down. I think half the people I called came. I know that surprised him. But it didn't surprise me. It was so obvious to TJ, Alex, and me. The Lord Jesus had called Chuck to lead this movement right from the start."

The meeting was set, but not the strategic plan ahead. The question that faced these four men was this: What could thirty senior clergy of large US Episcopal churches do in a wealthy mainline denomination where legal structures, geographic boundaries, an archbishop, and bishops lead the way?

TJ recounts that the morning of the conference was invested in first updating all the pariticpants, and then in a time of powerful prayer.[14] Later in the day, after a great deal of discussion, it became evident that two major principles had surfaced.

First, they based their response on the first promise made at their ordinations: namely, to "be loyal to the doctrine, discipline, and worship of Christ as this Church has received them."[15] This critical issue led to their titling their statement "The First Promise." Their ordination vow bound them to "a most sacred trust" and that "this trust is incapable of compromise or surrender by those who have been ordained."[16] Consequently, they declared the authority of the Episcopal Church impaired.

The second principle that emerged was to align themselves directly to the Kuala Lumpur Statement and those bishops and archbishops of the global South who were boldly correcting the heresy of the global North and modeling loyalty to the "doctrine, discipline, and worship of Christ." It had become imperative that they acknowledge the global South bishops' voice—which was not heard in Philadelphia at the convention—and stand with them in their defense of the gospel. By the end of the conference, the statement was formed and signed by all.

The leadership of the global South was also showing that to take a stand means action, and action has a cost. They had laid steps for the reformation of the church, but it was becoming increasingly evident that these steps could very well cost people their careers.

Indeed, some of those heading home weren't even off the plane when the story hit the Internet. They never had a chance to set up planned meetings with their vestries or bishops. Major media outlets—religion writers from newspapers and magazines, and radio talk show hosts—were picking up the story and calling their homes and cell phones for interviews. Within forty-eight hours, "First Promise," and the names of those who signed it, had become public knowledge.

Immediately, a number of the ministers were suffering a great deal of pressure both from their vestries and bishops. Within a couple of days, a handful of the signers were making phone calls and sending e-mails insisting that, after reflection and prayer, they wanted their names off the First Promise Statement.

TJ remembers well the sacrifice:

It was a costly moment. . . . But here's the home run: We were calling the church to biblical repentance. We were willing "to risk our jobs to do our jobs."[17] It was clear that the church was in trouble and that the evangelical bishops were either unable or unwilling to lead. Now, twenty-plus senior clergy from around the country—with little or no legislative authority in the church—stepped up to the plate and hit the ball.

• • •

Erilynne and I were on a preaching mission in Council Bluffs, Iowa, the week First Promise was born. For whatever reason, that week was a terribly low point for us. The weight of being out of God's will for an extended period of time was taking its toll. Both of us felt the grace to handle our situation weakening, leaving us more confused and feeling more isolated. The good news, it seemed like the only good news, was that our flight back to South Carolina arrived at the same time John's did from Africa.

It was time for his annual visit.

He was in more demand than ever. He was three months a bishop, and from the time he entered our home, it seemed like the phone never stopped ringing. Those who knew him and loved him were deeply concerned for his safety and the safety of his family. Just having him in our home and spending late nights and long hours in conversation and prayer blessed and revived our weary hearts.

In the few days we had together, before starting his US travels, we introduced John to All Saints—to Chuck Murphy, Jon Shuler, TJ Johnston, Alex Dickson, the church staff, and friends who had kindly welcomed us in our first seven months in Pawleys Island. Amid the cordial greetings and gracious conversations, it was clear that none of us made the connection between John Rucyahana and First Promise. We simply could not put two and two together. But in hindsight, it was nothing less than the impeccable timing of a sovereign act of almighty God.

First Promise wasn't even a week old. Reactions were pouring in to the All Saints' office from all over the country—many shocked that clergy would call the leaders of the Episcopal Church to repentance, and then have the audacity to appeal to Anglican bishops overseas for support and assistance.

In the frenzy and commotion of that week, suddenly, surprisingly, the Lord sent us a gift from heaven. A newly consecrated African Anglican bishop walked into our office, greeted the staff, talked with the clergy, and was given a guided tour of the campus.

At the time, we just didn't get it.

John had asked us to schedule him in Dallas from September 20 to 24. For the second time in a calendar year, Anglican bishops and archbishops, primarily from the global South,[18] were meeting to discuss the major issues facing the Anglican Communion. It was the first time for John as a new bishop to attend such a meeting. He was less than quiet.

"I told them plainly," he said to me over the phone, "that our collegiality as Anglicans is not around institutional unity. No! Any unity that does not recognize Jesus Christ as Lord and Savior, and does not recognize the Bible as the authoritative Word of God, is an idol. And that idol must never be worshipped." In this setting, John was among friends. By the end of the conference, another statement was issued. Once again, global South leaders were calling their colleagues in the North to repent and stop their rebellion against God and His Word, and asking for a response before the end of the calendar year.[19]

To the best of our knowledge, a reply was never given.

Bishop Alex Dickson attended the Dallas conference, as did Jon Shuler and TJ Johnston. Once again, they were to meet Bishop John Rucyahana.

John left Dallas and continued his travels that fall, as usual, visiting churches and conferences where he was asked to preach. In every diocese, he always made an effort to meet with the local Episcopal bishop. Some met with him — others did not. Still others urged him not to come at all, forcing their clergy to rescind the invitation for John to preach in their churches. It wasn't until the second week in October that John was back in Pawleys Island.

That's when it all came together.

It happened at a dinner party. Jim and Acton Beard, both in lay ministry at All Saints, hosted an evening for Bishop John with a handful of people from the church. Among them was Alex Dickson. During dinner, we were all seated at the Beards' dining room table engrossed in numerous conversations. Bishop Alex was seated across the table from Bishop John. Jim Beard, Anne Harvey, Erilynne, and I were seated around them and talking among ourselves when Alex introduced a new subject.

"Now, John, I'm sure you've had time to read the First Promise Statement by now. Am I right?"

"Yes, I have."

"Well, tell me what you think."

"It's okay—it's a pretty good document." John responded with hesitancy in his voice.

"Now, come on, you have to tell me what you mean by 'pretty good.'"

"Bishop Alex, quite honestly, I believe it is not strong enough."

The expression on Alex's face was worth the cost of dinner that night. He was absolutely startled. He immediately began to defend the statement as the strongest call for repentance by gospel-believing Episcopalians to date. Nothing else had championed a plan of action for clergy and lay leaders if their bishops and the leaders of the national church continued their opposition to the clear teaching of the Bible. What more could be said than that?

"I give up, John. I don't know how that document could be any stronger than it is!"

"It's actually quite simple. Have ten Episcopal bishops sign it."

"Excuse me?" Alex said, trying to take it in.

"Get ten of your colleagues to stand with you and the clergy of First Promise."

"Ten?" Alex replied. We could almost see his mind racing through the names of his friends. "I have to tell you, I feel like Abraham standing with the Lord before Sodom and Gomorrah was destroyed. John, I don't know about ten—what about eight? I'm afraid most of these guys are with me right up till the time they have to do something or sign something. That's when I lose 'em. What if I got six bishops—maybe I could get six retired bishops to sign it? Actually, I'm not even sure I could do that."

"You know, Alex, this is an American problem. You need to motivate these American bishops to see the reality of the problems facing the church and to do something about it. Take action! It's their job and divine calling. We cannot come to your support as bishops from overseas unless you ask us to. But first, you must be willing to do something yourselves. So get them to sign on. If you do, we will come and support you!"

"You think you'd come support us if a number of us bishops invited you?"

"Yes, we will!"

"Oh, my brother," Alex said, pausing, taking a deep breath, and sitting back in his chair, "this is good news."

A felt silence came upon on our side of the table. Anne Harvey, a long-time member of All Saints and a leader in the prayer ministry, began to tear up. "This feels like church," she said. "The Lord is here. I'd call this a God moment." Alex quietly nodded toward Anne, and then spoke directly to John. "Well, you have challenged me here tonight, my friend. It looks like I have my work cut out for me."

John put his head down and then looked up, peering over his glasses.

"You know," he said, "you should have no problem getting ten bishops to sign First Promise. If they don't, it will become an embarrassment to them. It will tell the whole world that they refuse to do their job, forcing their own clergy and church leaders to do what they refuse to do! No, I'm telling you, they will sign it. They cannot afford to have egg yolks splattered on their faces. You must call them together, give them a plan of action, and then let them sign it!"

"Well, John, I hope you're right," Alex said, his expression alternating between wonder and doubt.

"I tell you, they have no choice. Their shame would be too great."

I sat there, lost in the surprise of the night. It was the first time any of us dared to believe that our dreams might come true — that we in the North would be dynamically connected to Christians in the South. That night, the link was made between John Rucyahana, Alex Dickson, and First Promise. Erilynne and I saw it with our own eyes.

"I am sure grateful to the Lord that this night happened," Alex said at the close of dinner. "He has clearly shown us a way forward."

I couldn't have agreed more. This night — this conversation — had been a gift from God. On the drive home, John told us he thought the evening was providential. "You know, it is a real miracle," he said. "We don't always know the Lord's plans for us. But then, later on, He shows us. You and Erilynne came to Pawleys Island last February. You didn't know I was going to be made a bishop. You didn't know First Promise would happen here. You didn't know we'd be having this dinner tonight. But the Lord did. He had this night in mind. So we must praise Him and give Him glory for leading us when we don't know where we're going!"

Then he smiled and laughed — we all did. This incredible joy filled the three of us. After months of thinking we had completely lost our way, now, suddenly, that night, we knew. The Lord had sovereignly orchestrated the events of our lives far beyond our understanding. *No, we had not disobeyed. We were not out of His will. We were right on schedule.* The Lord had taken our relationship with John Rucyahana over all these years and given us the gracious privilege of introducing him—at just the right time—to Alex, Chuck, TJ, Jon, All Saints, and the emerging leaders of First Promise. We had no idea what it all meant for the days ahead—but it really didn't matter. This was His doing, not ours, and we knew it.

That night, in the car, the three of us worshipped the Lord, giving Him all the thanks and praise for His mighty power that does "immeasurably more than all we ask or imagine" (Eph. 3:20).

• • •

Bishop Alex went to work immediately.

On October 16, 1997, he wrote twenty-seven bishops to see if they would be willing to meet in Jacksonville, Florida, December 16–18. "To my dear brother bishops: I feel the time has come for us to act!" he wrote. He followed up with phone calls. He wrote another letter on November 11 that outlined a plan of action for bishops to both sign the First Promise document and form a council of orthodox bishops. He assured them that if they took this step of faith, risking presentment for ecclesiastical trial and probable conviction, the global South bishops and archbishops would not abandon them. "I am convinced they will participate in this council with us." Once again, he was pleading for his fellow bishops to take the reins of leadership, to stand against the onslaught of false teaching, and to provide episcopal oversight to distressed clergy and congregations who could no longer, in good conscience, submit to ungodly leadership.

"If not us," Alex wrote, "who?"

Of the twenty-seven, eighteen agreed to come and seventeen showed.

In November that year, leaders in the Episcopal Church were boasting in their great win at the Philadelphia convention. One of their bishops by the name of John Spong wrote a letter to the archbishop of Canterbury stating that for "the first time we achieved a statistical majority . . . in favor of blessing same sex unions. . . . the wave of the future seems clear."[20] In other letters to the archbishop, John Spong wrote, "the external standards of the past, like the literal Ten Commandments and the literal Bible, can clearly no longer be held as authoritative." The "new insights," "new revelations," of recent biblical scholarship could no longer allow the Bible to "govern our ethical behavior for all time."[21] Bishop Spong, a masterful leader and politician, made sure his letters were published openly on the Internet.

There were other surprises that fall.

First Promise was gaining strength. A month after the public release of the First Promise document, close to one hundred Episcopalians from around the country had signed on. Chuck Murphy, and the early leaders surrounding him, decided to hold an open meeting in Atlanta on December 1 for all interested parties. Seventy-two attended—mostly clergy. By that time, not only had more signed the document, but also one hundred twenty-five Episcopal clergy from twenty states and thirty dioceses had now taken courage to affix their names to First Promise. Momentum was building.

First Promise was becoming a movement.

It gave Bishop Alex all the more confidence to believe that John Rucyahana was right—ten bishops would step up, sign the document, and lead this new work. Maybe more than ten. If the clergy were willing to pay a price, how much more the bishops. The stakes were high—but the timing was perfect. John Spong and his colleagues were laughing, mocking both the Bible and the God who wrote the Bible. If these bishops in the Jacksonville meeting would simply rise to the occasion, sign First Promise, and form a council of orthodox bishops, they would have a deluge of clergy, lay leaders, and Episcopalians rushing to stand with them. With the Lord God Almighty as their strength, this could be a time of reformation to recapture the Episcopal Church for the gospel of Jesus Christ and call the "statistical majority" of its leaders to biblical repentance. If these bishops would just act, Alex thought, the Lord would work through them in a mighty way. It could literally be a new reformation that would evangelize our nation.

Bishop John was back in Africa when Alex wrote him. It was December 19. The meeting in Jacksonville was over.

John, my dear brother in Christ:
I was very much aware of your prayers and the presence of the Lord during the deliberations of the bishops in Jacksonville. We had

seventeen bishops attend our meeting. . . . I was pleased to have at least seventeen. I had sufficient time to present my plan for action. We then had good honest discussion for several hours, but my plan was too bold for most of them. . . . I feel I challenged the bishops in Jacksonville. They are still struggling with this challenge. I pray that God the Holy Spirit will bring this Council into being. For now, I will just wait to see what He will do. John, it may be that we will have to ask an African or Asian bishop to provide episcopal oversight to clergy or congregations in [troubled areas]. . . .

I continue to pray daily that our God will protect you and Harriet and the people of your diocese and your country. God grant you both a blessed Christmas.

In Christ Jesus,
Alex

Not one bishop signed the document.

Bishop John wrote back on December 26. It had been a bleak December in the northwest of Rwanda with more killings and personal threats against his life. "I am stationed in Ruhengeri," he wrote, "not because it is the best office and area for me but because we are engaged to preach the Gospel of Jesus in all places—even through risks I suffer to this day." Then, in sharp contrast, he responded to the news that came out of Jacksonville: "It is very sad that the leadership of the Episcopal Church in the USA continues to persecute Jesus and those who serve Him." Then he said that he feared our bishops were more concerned about being "comfortable in their flesh, minds and pockets" than risking their jobs to stop the devil from destroying the body of Christ. He said the Anglican bishops of Rwanda would never "embrace anything which denies the deity of Jesus or the holy, active authority of the word of God."

He closed this section of his letter with these words:

I am sure God has a plan for His Church both here and in the States. We only need to speak the truth and go by it. I am praying for First Promise not only as a philosophy but as a living and believing movement in the USA . . . Keep us informed and suggest every possible thing you want us to do to uphold the gospel and the Lordship of Jesus.

In those last words, we found hope. As 1997 came to a close, there was one active bishop willing to sign the First Promise document—just one—and he was from the global South. If the "Jacksonville bishops" refused to hear the cries of the clergy and congregations across the Episcopal Church and act on their behalf, then this African bishop would do it. He would speak to his fellow Rwandan bishops. He would pray with his archbishop. He would do "every possible thing," because what happened in Jacksonville was simply wrong.

"Never remain silent in the face of sin—never," John would say. "You must take action."

His signature came at just the right time. On December 28, 1997, an interview came out in the *Philadelphia Enquirer* with the newly elected presiding bishop, Frank Griswold. He stated publicly, without blushing and without shame, that the Episcopal Church was intentionally, and by God's decree, living in contradiction to the words of the Bible.

> Broadly speaking, the Episcopal Church is in conflict with Scripture. The only way to justify it is to say, well, Jesus talks about the Spirit guiding the church and guiding believers and bringing to their awareness things they cannot deal with yet. So one would have to say that the mind of Christ operative in the church over time . . . has led the church to in effect contradict the words of the Gospel.[22]

The rise of heresy had found its way to the top. The old adage from the early church fathers still rings true: "He is no true bishop who departs from the teaching of the apostles." In our day, the saying is greatly enlarged: "They are no true bishops—nor is it a true Christian denomination—which publicly departs from the teaching of the apostles."

So what do we do?

In Little Rock, Arkansas, a new bishop was elected, as well as a new dean for the downtown cathedral. Both men walked in the ways of the presiding bishop, defiantly preaching against the gospel "once for all entrusted to the saints." One Sunday, it just happened. Quietly, and without fanfare, a number of key leaders and committed members of the cathedral slipped out of their pews, left the cathedral, and never came back.

CHAPTER 8

LITTLE ROCK

On November 30, 1995, US Magistrate Judge H. David Young voted against the election of Henry Hudson to be the new dean at the cathedral in Little Rock. He was the only one. He raised his hand in protest in front of the committee and his bishop. A number—including Dabbs Cavin and Jeff Rawn—abstained. The majority of the search committee passed the motion, in unison with their bishop's counsel.

After the meeting, David Young, Dabbs Cavin, and Jeff Rawn met in the cathedral courtyard. These men had every reason to be discouraged. Their beloved church had just been hijacked by the radical liberal agenda sweeping across the Episcopal Church. But, for whatever reason, these men saw a moment of opportunity. Dabbs had been thinking about it off and on for six months. It had been in David's prayers since the early nineties. Neither had uttered a word about it to the other—until now.

"Maybe the Lord wants us to plant a new Episcopal church in Little Rock," one of them said. "We need to be doing mission—reaching people in Little Rock for Jesus Christ—not fighting against the doctrinal errors in the church. Let someone else do that." They all agreed. These last months had exhausted their spiritual resources. It was time for a positive way forward, and the election of this new dean was just the right incentive they needed to step out and respond in faith to the Lord's call.

That day, on the cathedral grounds, a vision took flight. In less than three years, that new church would be the subject of heated debate among the highest officials in the Anglican Communion. It would force church legislators to put forward a resolution at a meeting of Anglican bishops worldwide in the summer of 1998—creating international media coverage. It would do what few had the courage to do: to shake the foundations of one of the most sacred doctrines in Anglicanism—the doctrine of unity, or at least, perceived unity—to its very core.

• • •

The first meeting convened in early February 1996. The Honorable David Young was the natural leader—he was a federal court judge, highly respected in the Little Rock community, and the former senior lay leader at the cathedral. Several families—mostly from the cathedral—gathered to hear David, Dabbs, and Jeff put forward their vision for a new Episcopal church in Little Rock.

"It's about mission," they told them. "It's about reaching the unchurched with the gospel."

"But I think," one of them said, "we need to be a home for traditional Episcopalians."

Patty Gould and Janet Hedges saw the danger immediately. It had to be clear from the start, they said, that this church was positive in nature, not negative. They would have no interest in starting a church that had, as its missionary strategy, to challenge or compete with the Episcopal Church.

"Therefore, we shouldn't target disenchanted Episcopalians," commented Mark Millsapp. "If they come, fine. But our objective has to be gospel driven. Otherwise, I think this mission will fail."

Everyone agreed: *Keep it positive. Reach the unchurched.*

There was a tangible excitement in the air for the first time in a long time. By the end of the night, they decided to meet regularly. They needed more time to talk, study the Scriptures, pray, and discern whether God was truly calling them to start this new church. David Young closed the meeting with prayer.

Over the next few weeks, the questions became more focused: Was the Lord calling them to begin an evangelical, liturgical witness to the gospel of Jesus Christ in Little Rock? Would it be a church honoring the great commandment to love God and their neighbors? Would their first priority be the great commission to evangelize and make disciples? Would they commit entirely to the authority of Scripture and its proclamation? Would they remain fully within the Episcopal Church and submit to their local bishop?

By April, they thought they had some answers.

David Young was appointed by the group to meet with Bishop Larry Maze, which he did that same month. Sitting in the bishop's office, engaged in a polite, cordial conversation, David set forth the vision. He told the bishop that a core team of lay leaders had sensed a call to start a new Episcopal church that "would reach new people for Jesus Christ as well as renew the faith of others that were otherwise no longer attending or being discipled by any particular church."[1] He went on to say that it "was not a comment on the effectiveness of any other Episcopal church in bringing people to faith in Jesus Christ."[2] This call had a positive focus—a missionary focus. This church had in mind the vast numbers of people lost without Christ in Little Rock. It was time to throw another net in another place—as fishermen might do—to reach a new generation. The core team seemed ready and called to do just that.

Not one word was said about the controversial sexuality issues dividing the church. Not once did David describe himself as representing conservative Episcopalians.

Bishop Maze responded by saying there was a diocesan strategy for the planting of new churches and that the diocese (his area of supervision) could not financially afford another small mission project.

David assured the bishop that they did not plan on being a "small mission project" and that from the start they would be a financial blessing to the diocese. No monies would ever be needed. They simply wanted the bishop's blessing to begin the new work.

The bishop didn't give it. He was clear, firm. There would not be a new Episcopal church at this time. He urged David—and the others—"to stay within the ranks of the larger Church"[3] and said he would do all in his power "to help this group find a home in one of our existing congregations."[4] If they were being called by God to plant a new church, the bishop warned, they would be on their own. "But you can't make it an Episcopal church simply because you call yourself Episcopalians—that's not part of Episcopal polity."[5] Bishop Maze made it quite clear that he had a mission strategy for starting new churches and "anything outside this diocesan strategy is not acceptable."[6]

David Young accepted the bishop's statement but told him that a new church might still be in the works.

• • •

The bishop's opposition confused the group. They still believed the Lord had called them to start the church in the Episcopal tradition. David Young decided to call Bishop Ed Salmon for counsel—his former pastor in Fayetteville, Arkansas, and the Episcopal bishop of South Carolina. During the phone conversation, Ed suggested David contact the Rev. Dr. Jon Shuler in Pawleys Island, South Carolina. In those days, Jon's ministry was primarily focused on starting new Episcopal congregations in the US.

David took Ed's advice and made the call.

Jon was hesitant at first. He had never worked in an area where the local bishop had withheld his blessing. He agreed to come to Little Rock in early July, but, in David's words, it was an act of "compassion for our situation. I could tell Jon had no intent of actually supporting the start of this new congregation."[7] That all changed after the July visit.

That summer, after much prayer and more conversations with David, Jon made the strategic decision to "assist this group of people to build a healthy, growing, disciple-making congregation in the Episcopal tradition, even if, for a season, they find themselves outside the Diocese of Arkansas."[8] In a private meeting with Bishop Maze that next October, Jon communicated this resolve. As a result, the chasm between the new church and their local bishop widened. Jon wrote the bishop shortly after his visit, and in the ensuing dialogue and subsequent media coverage, Bishop Maze clearly staked out his stance that he viewed the proposed new congregation as no more than a special interest group, forming solely for political reasons.[9]

From its earliest days, the founders faced heated opposition. Rather than strengthening their resolve, it gave rise to persistent doubts—should they go on? Were they politically driven? Had the Lord called them, or were they secretly trying to challenge the direction of the Episcopal Church? Should they concentrate their energies on fighting their opponents, or should they do what God had called them to do?

It's about mission. It's about telling a new generation about Jesus Christ.

Jon Shuler helped set a course with the leadership of the new church. They began hosting several fellowship/Bible study groups in their homes on a weekly basis. Then, once a month, all the groups would meet together for corporate worship. Jon helped them find a church-planting "coach" who came alongside the fledgling congregation for counsel, encouragement, and direction. During the course of the next year, from October 1996 through November 1997, gifted evangelical clergy from all over the country flew into Little Rock to preach, celebrate Communion, and lead their monthly service.

In March 1997, TJ Johnston flew in for the service. David Young capitalized on the moment. He knew TJ was a passionate man, a former lawyer, and trained under Chuck Murphy as priest and leader. In David's mind, he was a perfect candidate to lead this young church as their first senior pastor. TJ found himself in an interview for a job he didn't want.

On November 18, 1997, Bishop Larry Maze had a message left on his answering machine: *The new church has called its first senior pastor.* The clergyman left his name. He said he was an Episcopal priest in good standing in the diocese of South Carolina. He had just accepted the call and wanted the bishop to know. He and his family were moving to Little Rock at the beginning of the year—with or without the bishop's permission.

•   •   •

TJ sat across from me, trying to explain how God had led him into this leap off the ledge. He is fit and thin, with a strong chin, and auburn hair tinged with silver. He has a warm, open gaze; and yet for all of his southern charm, TJ can be intense and focused when needed.

"It started that July." TJ's intensity kicked in as he recalled the details. "My family was given a week's vacation sailing in the Caribbean. About the fourth or fifth night out, we were nearing St. Thomas. I was lying on the deck of the boat looking at the stars when I had a clear sense that God was speaking to me. It was so simple: *You are going to be part of a new work.* I didn't understand it exactly. But the words spoke to my heart. At that moment, I knew something incredible was about to unfold and I was going to be part of it.

"Within two months, two major events happened in my life. In September, we signed the First Promise Statement in Pawleys Island. Later that month, I was in Dallas meeting Third World Anglican bishops—including John Rucyahana from Rwanda. In both meetings, I kept sensing the same thing in my prayers. I was being called out. There was going to be a new work. I knew my life and the life of my family was going to change dramatically. I didn't understand the details exactly—but I had a real sense of peace, a real sense of direction, and a real sense of energy.

"Before I knew it, I was on the phone calling David Young.

"You have to understand," TJ continued. "I didn't want to leave South Carolina. Our home was one hundred yards from the beach. I loved my job. I loved working with Chuck Murphy and All Saints Church. I had no intention of ever leaving."

"So," I interjected, "what exactly happened when you went to Little Rock?"

"Halfway through the service, I was preparing the table for Communion. There were only thirty people that night gathered in the basement of a Roman Catholic seminary. We were singing what we call the offertory hymn. Halfway through, I knew the Lord was speaking to my heart.

"He said, *I want you to give Me two things.*

"Silently, I asked, 'What two things, Lord?'

"*I want you to give Me your love for South Carolina and your love for All Saints Church.*

"He hit the nail right on the head. If there were idols in my heart—these were the ones. If there were obstacles blocking me from responding to the Lord's call on my life—I'm telling you, these were the ones." TJ glanced away and laughed quietly, shaking his head. "I love South Carolina. I love All Saints parish. I wanted to spend the rest of my life right there. My family was happy. I was happy. It was the best of all scenarios. But that night, at the Lord's Table, I knew Jesus Christ was asking me to lay them down at His cross. He was asking me to love Him first—above everything else. He was calling me to follow Him and Him only."

"What did you do?" I asked.

"I did it. I surrendered these two specific areas of my life."

"That night?"

"Yes, that night—before we had Communion. By the end of the service, I knew I was going to Little Rock."

The formal invitation came on November 12, 1997.

• • •

TJ finally talked to Bishop Maze in person for the first time on November 25. During the conversation, the bishop was polite but very direct. He made it clear that he was the Episcopal bishop of Arkansas and that no Episcopal priest would function in his diocese without his blessing. The canons — or laws — of the church allow sixty days of grace. After that, formal charges would be made against TJ, and he would be legally and immediately deposed as an Episcopal priest.

The message was clear: Don't come. Don't risk your career. The new church is not, and will never be, an Episcopal church. If you come, I, the bishop, will do everything in my power to keep this work from moving forward.

They talked again on December 18.

TJ restated that he and his family were moving to Little Rock in early January. Larry urged him to reconsider, saying again that political issues were not the grounds for starting new churches. TJ's quick legal mind couldn't refuse the moment. He asked Bishop Maze if he had publicly signed the "Koinonia Statement." This statement was the first major declaration of support for the gay movement, penned by Bishop John Spong of the Episcopal Church. Some ninety bishops, active and retired, had signed it.[10]

Bishop Larry Maze said yes, he had signed it. TJ told him that he and the leaders of the new church stood in profound disagreement with him. Even then, TJ said with utmost clarity, the issue of human sexuality was not the motivating or directing purpose for the new work. They were about mission. It's why TJ was coming to Little Rock.

TJ could have said it right then: *Bishop, we have every reason to start this new church. You have publicly betrayed your commitment to defend the historic Christian faith, to honor and uphold Scripture as the Word of God, and to stand in the mainstream of two thousand years of Christian tradition. We are not leaving the Anglican Communion. But you, by signing the Koinonia Statement, have already left it in principle and in practice. If anyone is Anglican in Little Rock — it's us, not you.*

But he didn't say it. He let the moment pass. He wanted to honor the leaders of the new church. They made a strategic decision at their first meeting in the winter of 1996 and had stuck to it: They didn't want to fight the doctrinal errors in the Episcopal Church. They were called to reach a new generation for the Lord Jesus Christ. That meant they chose to stay positive, keep the focus, steer away from controversy, reach the unchurched.

TJ and the bishop agreed to meet in Little Rock at the beginning of the year.

• • •

Bishop John Rucyahana understood the situation perfectly: TJ was going to Little Rock, and in sixty days the bishop of Arkansas would depose him. I think it caught John by surprise that TJ, an American Christian, would willingly allow himself to be persecuted for the sake of the gospel. On the day after Christmas, John sent Erilynne and me a fax:

> If TJ gets in Little Rock, the Lord will be with him. This will be the starting point of a spiritual revival in the US Episcopal Church. . . . We are together in Jesus and in prayer. . . . If you want that congregation to be the 45th parish of my Diocese—study it and tell me! We are praying for your suggestions. Maybe we shall have American missionaries licensed from Rwanda![11]

John had done his homework. In the late fall, he had intentionally met one-to-one with several evangelical US Episcopal bishops and asked them to cover TJ if Bishop Maze deposed him. Each one said no, stating the risk of disciplinary action against them, ecclesiastical trial from their peers, and the near certainty of being removed from office. Their refusal to act on TJ's behalf stunned the African bishop. How could they not care for one of their own—whether it cost them their office or their life? Isn't that what shepherds do for their sheep? Isn't it what the Savior did for us?

On the flight home, John knew the Little Rock church had no hope of remaining Anglican. If the US Episcopal bishops would not come to their rescue, who would? Something had to be done. Maybe, he said in his fax, with a vision as wide as the oceans themselves, Little Rock could belong to Rwanda.

• • •

On December 31, 1997, TJ wrote the clergy who had signed First Promise:

> The boxes are being loaded even as I bang out this note to you—as of Saturday morning I will begin a new work in Little Rock, Arkansas. By the grace of God I pray this new church will be a

strategic Kingdom work within the Anglican Tradition. I will share the name of the church with you as soon as it has been decided on. . . . I ask for your prayers and support.

Linda Caillouret covered TJ's first service for the *Arkansas Democrat-Gazette*, referring to them as "a group of 'renegade' Episcopalians" and objectively describing their first meeting.[12] Larry Maze wasn't happy with the public coverage in the newspaper. On the next day, January 16, 1998, he put out a public statement in which he insisted that church law—not biblical faith in Jesus Christ—"ordered" and "provided boundaries" for the unity of his diocese, the Episcopal Church, and the Anglican Communion. For Maze, and those like him, breaking church law had become a greater offense than breaking the laws of God as revealed in Holy Scripture.

"TJ, why doesn't Larry Maze understand?" Rucyahana once asked him. "The Koinonia Statement is in direct conflict with the Bible." And then he said, as a persecuted African Christian who has more than once risked his life for the name of Jesus Christ, "When he denies the gospel, I have no meeting place with him. We do not meet on social grounds. We do not meet because of church law. We can only meet in the Lord Jesus Christ as He is revealed in the Bible and whom Maze openly and publicly denies."

For Bishop John Rucyahana, the lines of battle had been drawn, the points of disagreement firmly established. Two bishops—one from the First World, one from the Third—engaged in an ancient conflict between those who hold fast to the traditions of the church and those who hold fast to the commands of God. (See Matt. 15:1–3.)

TJ was not going to make it easy for Bishop Maze. On February 10, TJ wrote Larry and informed him that the new church had incorporated as an independent church by the name of St. Andrew's. This news would please the bishop. However, TJ also told him plainly, "I am not, however, willing to renounce my vows."[13] TJ would remain an Episcopal priest until the time Larry Maze formally deposed him. This did not please the bishop. He wrote TJ back, urging him to renounce his vows.[14]

Time was running out, the sixty days nearly passed. Once again, Bishop John sent a fax: "You are aware that I am prepared to go in for the missionary venture in the USA. We cannot sit back and watch the Church of Christ sinking."[15]

Amid all his struggles in the northwest of Rwanda, the Little Rock story weighed heavily on John. He later told me, "It pained my heart, and I went into times of prayer for TJ and the church. I knew Larry Maze protected his geographic boundaries as a bishop. But the Lord made it clear to me that if a bishop renounces the supreme Lordship of Jesus Christ and signs documents rejecting the authority of Holy Scripture, then there is nothing sacred about his geographic boundaries. He is no different than a Muslim to me, and I do not ask Muslims permission to come to their town and minister to Christians. No! I have no boundaries with Maze if he refuses to hold fast to the primary boundary—faith in the Lord Jesus Christ!

"That is when I felt an urgency from the Lord that I must step out and take action. I needed to stand for them and for the gospel. These Christians were being unfairly treated. They were being denied their rights to remain true to the faith as Anglicans. I had to do it in obedience to the Lord. Of course, I knew my actions would stage a challenge to the whole Anglican Communion. I could lose my office and cause trouble for my fellow bishops in Rwanda. But it had to be done to expose the heresy to the world.

"I went to my archbishop, Emmanuel Kolini. He asked me to prepare a presentation to our House of Bishops in Rwanda, which I did. They listened to me and adopted my proposal to cross diocesan and provincial boundaries for the sake of defending the Christian faith. We were together. This was our conviction. We knew we could not sit by. We needed to witness to Jesus. That is when I sent you the fax saying I was ready to go in for the Little Rock mission."

I got the fax and called TJ.

TJ had gone to Little Rock by faith. He knew he had sixty days before being deposed. He knew there wasn't one Episcopal bishop who had promised to stand with him against the fervent opposition of Larry Maze and his team of lawyers. But one thing he did know. Early on Bishop John had given him wise and godly counsel: "Walk faithfully in the way God has called you, TJ. We do not know what the moment will require until we get to that moment."

The moment had now come.

It was late February. TJ was encouraged by the news that John was willing to talk. He picked up the phone and spoke to Bishop John and then later to Archbishop Kolini. They asked him to send a letter explaining his situation and requesting their assistance. TJ did just that.[16]

TJ explained the process for transfer in his letter. He was a priest in good standing in the diocese of South Carolina under Bishop Ed Salmon. According to church law, if Rwanda accepted his proposal, then TJ would request Bishop Salmon to send his formal papers to Bishop John in Rwanda. This was the routine procedure for transferring clergy around the Communion. However, there was a small glitch. Such a transfer implied that TJ was physically moving to Rwanda. In this particular and irregular case, TJ would be living in Little Rock as a missionary Anglican priest from the province of Rwanda. He would be serving in Larry Maze's diocese, but Larry Maze would not be his bishop nor have any legal authority over him.

It was risky at best. Would Rwanda go for it? Would Bishop Ed Salmon make the transfer?

On March 9, while waiting for a response from Rwanda, TJ decided to write Bishop Maze one more time in the hopes of a peaceful reconciliation. TJ refers to it as the "Gamaliel letter."[17] TJ sent the letter and filed a copy of his own. At a later date, he took the letter out, grabbed a pen, and wrote on the bottom of the page, "Bishop Maze never responded to this letter."

●　●　●

On March 12, Bishop John responded with a handwritten fax to me.

> We have been in prayer and consultation with Archbishop Kolini on the case of TJ and the whole Episcopal Church. We have resolved that TJ may send his Canonical application to me for consideration so that TJ may be on the list of our priests. Pray and fast.[18]

Ten days later, TJ sent a letter to his bishop, Ed Salmon. "I am writing to you to request that you send my letters . . . to the Rt. Rev. John Rucyahana, Bishop of the Diocese of Shyira, Province of Rwanda."[19] Ed knew he did not need permission to transfer a priest in good standing to another part of the Anglican Communion. But this case presented a number of complications. He picked up the phone and called Frank Griswold, presiding bishop (archbishop) of the US Episcopal Church. Frank was on retreat in Iowa. The Rev. Carl Gerdau took Ed's call, heard the story, and passed the news on to the presiding bishop. Ed made it clear he would not transfer TJ if Frank objected.

A few days later, Carl called back. Frank Griswold had no objections.

Ed Salmon was pleased. It meant South Carolina and Arkansas would avoid an ecclesiastical legal battle over deposing TJ, which would have been a nightmare—especially with the press. Now it was simply a stroke of his pen and case closed. On April 6, 1998, Bishop Salmon formally transferred TJ Johnston, a priest in good standing, to the episcopal oversight of John Rucyahana in the diocese of Shyira, Rwanda.

Larry Maze got the news. He called Ed Salmon, "expressing surprise and upset at the transfer." Ed made two points clear: one, "it was my call to make" and two, "I had gotten a position of no objection" from Frank Griswold, presiding bishop. Maze was dumbfounded. He had just called Frank, and Frank said he knew nothing of the transfer.

But he did—only a few days ago.

Ed immediately called Carl Gerdau and reminded him that Frank had given his blessing. Carl remembered. He talked with Frank, and Frank remembered. Ed wrote the presiding bishop a letter, making sure everything was properly written down. He kindly gave Frank Griswold the benefit of the doubt, saying, "I am certain that with all the things that come at you in telephone conversations, much will pass out of mind. It is true with me."[20]

The deed was done.

The sixty days came and passed, and there was little Larry Maze could do about it. TJ Johnston was a full-fledged Anglican priest residing as an African missionary in Maze's geographic diocese.

"It was a real miracle," Bishop John said later, after hearing the full story. "Ed Salmon transferred TJ to me, and Presiding Bishop Griswold consented! I am eternally grateful to Ed for doing that."

It happened in April of 1998, on Frank Griswold's watch and somehow, mysteriously, with his blessing. An African Anglican bishop now presided over an Anglican church and its priest on US soil.

●　●　●

A month after the "Gamaliel letter," TJ informed Bishop Maze of his transfer to Rwanda. Maze, in turn, wrote a letter to the members of his diocese, clearly outraged by the "failure to respect diocesan boundaries."[21]

The *Arkansas Democrat-Gazette* picked up the story and interviewed

Jim Solheim, news director for the Episcopal Church. He commented: "I've never seen a similar situation within the church where a bishop outside the country claims oversight of an American priest. There's no precedent for it, and no one knows what it means. . . . We've never been here before."[22]

Maybe if Larry Maze had deposed TJ on the sixtieth day, instead of lingering for a month, these headaches would never have come.

It was time, he reasoned, to write Rucyahana the African—bishop to bishop. He needed to state his argument simply—this "issue with Mr. Johnston is not one of ideological differences as much as it is a clear issue of whether or not diocesan boundaries will continue to be respected by all members of the Anglican Communion." This was not a matter of liberal bishop versus conservative. It was a matter of law—church law. Surely the African could see that, and he was saddened that Bishop John had been brought into the matter.[23]

He wrote it on April 27 and sent it by ground. John would not receive it until June 10. Nine days later, he responded by sending a fax to Bishop Maze's office. John wanted Maze to know that his "simple but clear concern and commitment is to give St. Andrew's and Rev. Johnston spiritual asylum":

I am saddened even more that you got at a point where Church leaders force people to schism. I pray that this congregation remains Anglican up to a time you resolve your differences.

John didn't buy Maze's argument, and he said so. The issue between them was not about church law, but upholding and defending the essential matters of the Christian faith, without which the church ceases to exist.

A few weeks later, after consultation with Archbishop Kolini, John wrote George Carey, the archbishop of Canterbury. Among the thirty-eight archbishops worldwide (overseeing the thirty-eight provinces in the Anglican Communion), he is regarded as the "primary among equals." John believed Archbishop Carey would be sympathetic since he was, by reputation, an evangelical, and so he was calling the archbishop of Canterbury and the Angican Church to take action—to stand for the apostolic faith in the Lord Jesus Christ.

John expected a swift, positive response. He was shocked to find Archbishop George Carey's swift response in the negative. Evangelical or not, the archbishop sided with Larry Maze and the argument from church law, urging John to "quickly disentangle yourself" from the matter.[24]

John later reported, "Archbishop George Carey was telling me to back off, to let that congregation get lost and be whatever it wants to be. But I felt the same reaction as Peter and the other apostles did when they faced persecution from the rulers of the Jewish community: 'We must obey God rather than men' (Acts 5:29). I took them by conviction and in obedience to the Lord. It was high time to challenge the apostasy that is choking the church. When the American Episcopal Church repents, I will return St. Andrew's back to their care. But they have not yet repented. Until then, how could I let them go?"

The African's resolve was unwavering. And yet, at the same time, John knew the significance of the moment. The archbishop of Canterbury had spoken.

• • •

Every ten years, all the bishops and archbishops in the Anglican Communion meet together in a conference called Lambeth. The next meeting was set for that summer, July 18–August 8, 1998. Momentum was escalating in defense of Larry Maze's position. Laurie Pierce at the *Arkansas Democrat-Gazette* captured the mounting evidence from two prominent dignitaries. Frank Griswold, US presiding bishop, firmly believed in "the long established Anglican principle respecting the territorial integrity of dioceses and appropriate episcopal ministry." Archbishop of Canterbury, George Carey also affirmed, "I do support the honoring of diocesan boundaries."

In addition, in a surprising turn of events, the blame for the rescue of St. Andrew's by an African bishop was not being laid at the feet of Bishop John Rucyahana, Archbishop Emmanuel Kolini, or the House of Bishops in Rwanda. The finger was pointing back to evangelical Episcopalians in America who, it was argued, were grossly misusing and manipulating the Africans: "The Arkansas bishop said he believes that Rucyahana has been misled by St. Andrew's. . . . 'Our basic difference is whether this is a question of theological differences or a question of order,' said Maze."[25]

The *Church of England Newspaper* reported that many "liberal Americans argue that conservative Episcopalians are using more conservative bishops from the two-thirds world to further division within their own Church on issues such as homosexuality."[26] Specifically, Bishop Ronald Haines of Washington, DC, proved to be an example. Upon hearing of Rucyahana's intervention in Little Rock, Haines wrote, "I think that is very sad and unfortunate because it gives a strong appearance of an African Bishop being manipulated for your political purposes."[27]

The Africans found this argument to be both slanderous and filled with racial prejudice. Were they being manipulated because they were poor, ignorant, and easily bought with money? Had they no ability to reason with their minds, pray, and make the right choices before the Lord? This devilish attack produced in them a temptation to respond in kind, even though they knew it was nothing but a distraction. The issue at hand was about defending the historic Christian faith and the authority of the Bible.

Again and again, Rucyahana told reporters, "The work of the bishop is to defend faith. So faith comes first. Order and territory and other things are supporting to the first one. . . . *The Koinonia Statement* is in direct conflict with the Bible. . . . all American bishops who signed *The Koinonia Statement* should be declared 'out of the fellowship' with the Anglican Communion."[28]

TJ was saying the same thing: "I believe we're seeing the first wave of a coming reformation."[29] "Little Rock is no brush fire," he wrote to his congregation, already at 140 in Sunday attendance by Pentecost 1998. "To talk about order and respect for boundaries is meaningful only when the ground rules of Christian believing . . . are clear." To Kolini and Rucyahana he wrote, "We long for unity within the Anglican Communion, and within the Episcopal Church, but it must be a unity in Christ."[30]

Lambeth was coming. If it were a matter of power and wealth, the Africans would be silenced and defeated. If it were a matter of church law, the archbishop of Canterbury and the presiding bishop of the US Episcopal Church were already successfully lobbying for Larry Maze. But if it were a matter of biblical faith and godly discipline, as the Africans believed, then they were not alone. The Asians—and other global South Anglican leaders—had already spoken in February 1997 in the Kuala Lumpur Statement. The witness of Scripture itself, as well as two thousand years of Christian history, testifies to continuous reformations when men and women of faith, often little known and with few resources, triumphed over church officials who publicly denied God's Word. Even the history of Anglicanism was on the Africans' side. Bishop Stephen Neill wrote in the 1950s,

> Anglicanism is a very positive form of Christian belief. . . . Its chal-
> lenge can be summed up in the phrase, 'Show us anything clearly
> set forth in Holy Scripture that we do not teach, and we will teach
> it; show us anything in our teaching and practice that is plainly
> contrary to Holy Scripture, and we will abandon it.[31]

But times had changed. By the end of the twentieth century, the words
"Church law" had been substituted for "Holy Scripture." Men of great power
and wealth now led the Anglican Communion. These men knew how, by
politics and parliamentary procedure, to write, submit, and pass resolutions
that would govern and steer the Communion into the twenty-first century. It
seemed, at the end of July, before the Lambeth Conference opened, that they
would easily send this Little Rock story into a quiet oblivion.

Back at the First Promise office, Chuck Murphy sat behind his desk
seeing a different outcome.

For him, a new day had already dawned. All his life he had heard his
father say, "You're either a missionary or a mission field." In this case, leaders
in the global South had become missionaries to the mission field of the global
North. Chuck knew, as the Lambeth Conference approached, that it was not
merely a theological debate. Something had happened—an event of great
significance. On US soil, an African bishop now presided over an Anglican
church and an Anglican priest in Little Rock, Arkansas. The geographic lines
had already been crossed. This, he knew, was just the start. There would
be more churches, hundreds more, and the Lambeth Conference could do
nothing to stop it.

Little Rock was the wave of the future.

Chuck Murphy couldn't help himself. He stood in the pulpit of St.
Andrew's, Little Rock that year at the close of a gathering of several hundred
First Promise clergy and laity. Right in the middle of his sermon, at just the
right moment, he cast the vision in biblical terms for everyone to see.

"If you know the David and Goliath story," he said, pausing long enough
for us to remember, "David took on Goliath with—a little rock! In God's
hand, that little rock was all he needed."[32]

CHAPTER 9

THE LAMBETH LINE

Like a muddied spring or a polluted well is a righteous man who gives way to the wicked.

— PROVERBS 25:26

The phone rang in Pawleys. It was mid-February 1998.

"Chuck, I am telling you, this is bad news," John Rucyahana said, calling from his home in Ruhengeri. "The conference was scheduled for March, and it has been called off due to funding. Our leaders in Africa need to prepare for Lambeth."

"Tell me more about the conference, John," Chuck said. It was the first he had heard about it.

"Plans began some time ago to have bishops and archbishops from the Great Lakes region meet, pray together, study the Bible, and discuss issues before going to Lambeth. We are seven countries: Uganda, Zaire, Tanzania, Kenya, Rwanda, Burundi, and the Sudan. Twenty percent of Anglicans in the world are here as compared to the United States, which has about three percent. Most African bishops do not know what is happening in the US Episcopal Church. They are going to Lambeth ignorant of facts."

"Those are serious figures. You'd think it would give your region serious voice and vote," Chuck mused, knowing it was not the case. The Lambeth Conference, set for late July, meets once every ten years. When Anglican leaders gather, the agenda is historically set and controlled by the North.

"You know, Chuck, Lambeth is very difficult for Africans. English is not our first language. We don't know much about parliamentary procedures and the sophisticated political tricks of Americans and Europeans. They put us in small groups with other bishops from around the world so we are not together. Resolutions come to the floor. We miss opportunities. We end up remaining silent because we don't know what's going on. It's terrible. It's high time our people are exposed to the heresies of the Episcopal Church. We need to take precautions. We can't allow these lies to spread to our people. If we are going to be effective at Lambeth, if we are going to challenge bishops like Larry Maze, if we are going to make a stand together as Africans for Jesus Christ and the authority of the Bible, we need to be properly prepared."

"Indeed," Chuck responded. "Actually, John, I completely agree. The question is whether it can still happen before July and if we can secure the funds. Do you have any idea how much it would cost?"

"I don't know. I would have to meet with the archbishops of Rwanda and Uganda to see if it is still possible and then work on funding. Chuck, I need to say this. If you are able to secure the funds, it has to come with no strings attached. The Great Lakes Conference needs to be African — not American."

"In about two weeks," Chuck replied, "I'm headed to Atlanta for a meeting of First Promise clergy and laity. If you can find a way forward for this conference and find out how much you need, I will talk to those huddling in Atlanta, and we'll see what the Lord does — no strings attached."

"What are the dates?" John asked.

"March second and third."

"Let me see what I can do."

• • •

John could see two separate roads stretched out in front of his fellow Africans — one easy, one costly. Lambeth (which held its first meeting in September 1867) knew little about Africa. The archbishop of Nigeria, Joseph Adetiloye, once commented on his first experience at Lambeth: "In 1978 I waited at the microphone, and I was the first black African bishop to address the Conference. I told the assembled bishops that I was the first to speak, and it had taken until 1978 to be recognized."[1] Ten years later, at Lambeth 1988, the voice from Africa grew louder and more distinct. The question for

Lambeth 1998 was whether the North could regulate that voice and still chart the course for the Communion.

American bishop David Bell Birney was clearly concerned about the matter.

In early January 1998, he attended the installation of Emmanuel Kolini as the new archbishop of Rwanda. He went as a representative of the arch-bishop of Canterbury. Rucyahana was delighted to see him. Birney was a former professor at his theological college in Uganda. "He is a man I love," John told me. "I got excited to meet him and talk to him again." At the reception following the service, they had that moment to talk.

"David made it very clear he was disappointed in me," John continued. "He spoke with authority. He said he knew I was making a stand against the Episcopal Church. He knew there were many other Africans and Asians who intended to disturb the Lambeth Conference. If this happens, he told me, we would not be cared for financially. We would be marginalized — remain-ing poor with nobody helping us, nobody giving us money for projects and developments in our country. The bishops in the Episcopal Church will stop their funding. We could be certain of that. It was time for us to bow out and keep quiet.

"I said in response, 'Thank you very much, Bishop Birney. You've done your work to teach me. But now I've come of age. You are speaking your cause. I'm standing for the cause of my people. The means for their recovery is not your money. It is Jesus Christ alone. He will transform our people. I will not sell the gospel for your money. Keep your money and I shall keep Jesus. If we surrender our calling in order to get your money — and get your liberal theology of heresy — it will destroy our people.'"

The conversation, he said, ended abruptly.

John sent me a fax two days after the event with Birney. In it he reiter-ated his stand:

We are not going by threats. We will not bow down before our needs and betray the Lord Jesus. . . . We cannot have a share in sin which is clear and so destructive to the body of Christ.

It was here, at this very spot, where the two roads diverged. To make a stand was to risk financial resources flowing from the North to the endless needs of the African poor. The easy road, the broad path, meant stepping back, speaking softer, bowing out, and continuing their financial dependence on the North.

The Rwandan House of Bishops decided to risk the costly road. Three weeks after Bishop Birney left Rwanda, they elected to make their position clear to the Anglican world. They published an open letter to the Communion affirming the Kuala Lumpur and Dallas statements; their commitment and faith in the lordship of Jesus Christ; their belief in the Bible as the authoritative Word of God; their resolve that "homosexuality and lesbianism are clearly a deviation from the natural norm and divine order" and those who practice such are in sin; and their devotion to carry out their "pastoral role to . . . all who have deviated from God's law." In their mind, they had no choice. The northern gospel was coming south and they, at the end of their statement, recognized their responsibility as bishops to stop it.

We know that some [northerners] have introduced homosexual practices in the Great Lakes Region of Africa, but we, as Africans, repudiate the practice and do not wish it to be seen in our Province. We want to promote stable, monogamous marriage between a man and a woman within the love of God, "for better for worse, for richer for poorer, in sickness and in health until death us do part."[2]

Despite the threats, the Rwandan voice continued to speak. A few months later, they spoke again by taking oversight of St. Andrew's, Little Rock. In their mind, the timing for the Great Lakes Conference could not have been better. Their fellow Africans needed to be informed. They needed to know that the financial risk to the region was great. But this was their moment. As East and Central Africans, long persecuted for the sake of the gospel, they had an opportunity to lift their voice in unison and defend biblical faith in Jesus Christ to their wayward northern colleagues.

It was time to choose, as a region, which road to travel.

Then came the news: The Great Lakes Conference was cancelled. John knew that spiritual forces were at work to undermine the African resolve. He could not sit back and let that happen. Lambeth happens only once a decade, and they as a region needed to be ready. He prayed fervently. He set in motion a plan: Call Chuck Murphy—ask him to pray. See if he will help raise funds. Call Archbishop Kolini—ask his approval to reinstate the conference. Ask permission to go and meet with the archbishop of Uganda for the same. See if he will host the Great Lakes Conference in Kampala. Set the date sometime in late May, early June.

John was praying for a miracle.

• • •

On the other side of the Atlantic, Chuck Murphy was pleased with the developments of First Promise. In six months, nearly 180 Episcopal clergy had signed on. Fifty of them were registered for the March 2–3 meeting in Atlanta. TJ was fully ensconced in Little Rock and, as he likes to say, "making waves." A large Episcopal church in Houston, Texas, St. John the Divine, was gearing up for a national First Promise event on March 23 for lay leaders interested in joining the movement. George Gallup—famed pollster and noted Episcopalian—had agreed to be the keynote speaker.[3]

And then there was the possibility of an Asian connection.

First Promise was already in dialogue with Africa. But the Kuala Lumpur Statement proved there were leaders in Southeast Asia with the same heart to confront the rebellion in the American church. The question was this: Would the archbishop of Southeast Asia, Moses Tay, be willing to talk with us? Retired Bishop Alex Dickson made the call. To his amazement, Moses Tay was receptive. Alex asked Bishops Fitz Allison and Bill Wantland, plus one clergyman—Jon Shuler—to join him.

"The trip was worthwhile," Alex later reported. "Moses Tay listened to our story. He was a man we could talk to. We told him our experience as bishops in the Episcopal Church. We reviewed the history of the last thirty years that led to the present denial of Christian orthodoxy. And finally, I asked if he would be open to accepting me as a bishop of Southeast Asia and then sending me back to America as a missionary bishop under his oversight to care for clergy and churches unable to stay in the Episcopal Church. The times, we told him, demanded this kind of action.

"The good news," Alex said with a smile, "is that he didn't say no. He said he would talk to his other bishops. But he assured us that nothing would happen before Lambeth."

It was a beginning. Archbishop Moses Tay now knew about us. More than that, he made a wholehearted commitment to pray for First Promise and our effort to right the wrongs in the American church.

As Chuck prepared for the meeting in Atlanta, he could sense momentum building. Everything seemed in its proper place. A few days before going to Atlanta, Chuck and I called John Rucyahana to see if he had news about reinstating the Great Lakes Conference. We couldn't get through. We tried again in Atlanta, on March 2, during the meeting and learned that John had not yet returned from Uganda. He was due back at any time. In the early afternoon of March 3, Alex Dickson, TJ Johnston, and I went to the hotel business office to try John a third time. The two-day First Promise meeting was scheduled to end at four o'clock and already some were peeling off to catch their planes home. We made the call on speakerphone. This time Bishop John answered.

"Bishop John, this is Alex, TJ, and Thad calling."

"Oh, it is good to hear from you! Thank you very much for calling. How are you doing?" he said, with a certain ring of joy in his voice.

After brief introductions, we asked about the Great Lakes Conference.

"I talked with my archbishop," John responded, "and he was very happy about it. He sent me to meet with His Grace, Livingstone Nkoyoyo, archbishop of Uganda. I've just come back. He was also very happy and offered to host the conference in Kampala, the capital city. So, we are ready to move forward."

"When?"

"Sometime in late May or early June."

"What about the cost?"

"I worked on funding while I was in Uganda. To host a four-day conference with lodging, meals, and the cost of transporting nearly fifty bishops and their wives from other countries to Uganda, will be about $44,000 US. It is the exact amount we needed before but could not raise. So the conference cancelled. Now we have to leave it to God to see whether it will again be possible or not."

We told John we'd get back to him and asked him to pray for the response of the First Promise leaders. We hung up the phone and had no more than entered back into the hotel meeting room when Chuck Murphy interrupted the flow of discussion and asked us to report on our conversation with John Rucyahana.

"The bottom line?" one of us said. "They need $44,000 to make it happen."

Chuck had already told the First Promise leaders about the Great Lakes Conference and how John had said, "No strings attached." It had to be African led, not American.

One priest stood up and said, "I pledge two thousand."

Another, "Five hundred."

"One thousand."

And then another, and another. In less than five minutes' time, the money in its entirety was raised to the amazement of everyone in the room. When the last dollar was pledged, we stood up in a spontaneous burst of applause and gave thanks to the Lord for the miracle of His provision. As we joined in a familiar chorus of praise, the joy was tangible and contagious as we greeted each other with handshakes and hugs. Whatever evil forces stood in opposition to these African leaders meeting together before Lambeth to pray and unite their voice, they clearly had not won the day. The Lord had sovereignly moved, and we all knew it. What is more, we were all part of it.

For many of us, it was like a sunlit rainbow amid days of terrible darkness and storm.

The three of us who had called Bishop John left the celebration and went back to the business office. We dialed the number, got him on the phone, and told him the news.

"Praise the Lord!" he exclaimed. "I can't believe it! This is a real miracle!"

We told John that Chuck made it very clear to everyone—*no strings attached.*

"This makes me very happy. The Lord has gone before us. He has answered our prayers. Our people will have a real voice in Lambeth this year. To God be the glory!"

Then he paused and said, "Oh, I must call Archbishop Kolini immediately and tell him the good news."

John could hardly contain himself. The matter was settled. The Great Lakes Conference was on.

•   •   •

I was absolutely shocked to receive a fax from Archbishop Nkoyoyo of Uganda in mid-April.

> I am extending an invitation to you to join us in this conference and to address the bishops and their wives on the topic, "The moral issues facing the Church and Society in general and their effect on the mission of the Church." . . . The duration of the talk . . . will be one hour. . . . We shall be extremely happy to receive you and be graced by your presence and participation.

John Rucyahana's fax came next: "You are requested to give a paper on the effects of liberalism on the Church of Christ. . . . The Bishops need to know how sick the Western Church is. . . . Thad, you have the platform. Please take it with prayer." I called him immediately. He told me on the phone it was necessary to have a clergyman from the Episcopal Church "speak from their lives, from their mind, speak from what they believe, what they have suffered and be able to expose it to the Africans." I never asked him why he chose me for this daunting task. Chuck Murphy thought it was the logical choice, noting my ten-year relationship with John and our work together in Africa and America. He and Rucyahana both encouraged me to begin the research and write the paper. The Great Lakes Conference was set for June 2–5.

Help came from the most unexpected source.

In early May, John Spong, Episcopal bishop of Newark, issued a formal statement of belief titled "Twelve Theses: A Call for a New Reformation." Fancying himself like the reformer of old, Martin Luther, who nailed his Ninety-five Theses to the Wittenberg church door in 1517, John Spong posted his theses on the Internet, believing he would ignite a reformation of the same magnitude. In effect, his theses brought no real surprise. Spong was the author of the Koinonia Statement. He was the recognized episcopal leader of the gay caucus. In the months preceding the "Twelve Theses," he had dominated the Internet with open letters to the archbishop of Canterbury in which he defiantly opposed the bishops who had signed the Kuala Lumpur Statement. He had clearly met his opponents and rightly feared they, at Lambeth, might win the day.

My fears have been enhanced by . . . the much publicized, hostile
and threatening Kuala Lumpur statement, signed by certain bishops
of Southeast Asia. . . . The facts are, I believe, that these religious
voices are significantly out of touch with the knowledge revolution
that marks our generation.[4]

I particularly deplore evangelical zeal which in my experience, is
hardly ever informed by competent scholarship. These people seem
to me to march to the beat of a drummer in another century.[5]

The Christian Church struggles today to articulate a basis for
ethics in a world where the external standards of the past, like the
literal Ten Commandments and the literal Bible, can clearly no
longer be held to be authoritative.[6]

If the evangelical voice triumphs at Lambeth, Spong threatened, "We
will take to the public media to assure the gay and lesbian Christians we
are privileged to serve, that they have not been abandoned by the leadership
of their Church."[7] In my personal view, this material already provided the
African bishops with enough information to convict Spong—and all his
fellow bishops who signed the Koinonia Statement—as a heretic. Moreover,
it reasonably argued the case that the biblical and moral question surrounding homosexuality was simply the presenting issue. Behind it was a matter
of far greater significance: John Spong openly rejected the essential doctrines
of Christian belief, despising both the authority of the Holy Scriptures and
those who faithfully believe and practice them.

The sexuality issue brought him into the secular spotlight, which it
is said he craved. His books published on the open market. He appeared
on national television and radio talk shows. He traveled the country with
speaking engagements defending, as an Episcopal bishop, the rights of the
gay community. As a gifted speaker, he presented his case in the modern
language of scholarship, appealing to new discoveries in science and medi-
cine, remembering the oppression of blacks in our country during the civil
rights movement and insisting that justice demands the full equality of all
oppressed people groups. As a politician, he eloquently defended the gay
cause with flair and compassion. As a bishop, he was forced to argue his case
from a Christian perspective. Since he had no theological precedent in two
thousand years of Christian history, he had to reason from a new, innovative

platform called modernism and scholarship.

And he did. He testified to the world that the Bible was wrong.[8]

This was, in fact, Spong's real message. It revealed an intense hatred for the Bible. It became, rather than the gay agenda itself, the cornerstone for his new reformation. At just the right moment, some ten weeks before the Lambeth Conference opened, Spong brazenly revealed this new theology in his "Twelve Theses," a definitive creed publicly renouncing the basic tenets of the Christian faith. No public Christian leader in all church history had ever gone to this extreme. To give example, John Spong stated publicly:

- Theism, as a way of defining God, is dead.
- Since God can no longer be conceived in theistic terms, it becomes nonsensical to seek to understand Jesus as the incarnation of the theistic deity.
- The view of the cross as the sacrifice for the sins of the world is a barbarian idea based on primitive concepts of God and must be dismissed.
- Resurrection is an action of God. Jesus was raised into the meaning of God. It therefore cannot be a physical resuscitation occurring inside human history.
- The story of the ascension assumed a three-tiered universe and is therefore not capable of being translated into the concepts of a post-Copernican space age.
- There is no external, objective, revealed standard writ in Scripture or on tablets of stone that will govern our ethical behavior for all time.

The Rev. Dr. John Rodgers, systematic theologian and former dean of Trinity Episcopal School for Ministry in Ambridge, Pennsylvania, responded publicly to Bishop Spong in a matter of days. At the end of his statement he said, "One wonders what more needs to happen to have our Leaders take a stand." To "not say No! publicly to 'Bishop' Spong, is failing to say Yes! to Jesus, whom the 'Bishop' is openly denying." Rodgers rightly commented, "Few, if any, in the history of the Christian church have denied so much and still want to claim the name of Christian. . . . We recommend Mr. Spong resign his orders as an ordained minister of the Gospel."

On May 18, John Rucyahana sent me a fax, saying, "You may have heard about the Twelve Theses of John Spong circulating in newspapers in England. My archbishop read them to me on the telephone. . . . They refute violently the Bible and deny traditional canons and disciplines of the Anglican Church. These are heresies that need to be challenged and the Episcopal province USA should be called to Repentance." He told me to include the "Twelve Theses" in my address to the African bishops and said, in no uncertain terms, "You can call the southern provinces to defend the Church of Christ."

I had more than enough to write about. I had all the proper documentation to prove the moral failure resident in the decisions and actions of the leaders of the Episcopal Church. What I didn't have was the ability to communicate the terminal nature of our condition. I was convinced from my experience with John Rucyahana that even if these African bishops took a stand, calling for immediate reform, we in the American church would not hear them. If they, like the prophets of old, demanded the Episcopal Church repent on the threat of excommunication, we would not act. We were an arrogant people, unable to recognize the voice of God in the mouths of poor, black, seemingly uneducated Africans. Our hearts were already hardened. We had already made our choice. We were a people too far gone, and I knew it. I had seen it.

Somehow, with just the right words, I needed to tell them that.

• • •

The Great Lakes Regional Pre-Lambeth Conference officially began on the evening of June 2, 1998. Forty bishops and their wives from five nations, including four archbishops, gathered at a Kampala hotel for dinner and then an opening address by the archbishop of Uganda, Livingstone Mpalanyi-Nkoyoyo. It was the first time in decades that bishops from the Great Lakes region had come together for a regional meeting. From the moment it began, the tone was set. The banners, handouts, and speakers all echoed the chosen theme of the conference: "Be Firm in Faith—Ephesians 4:14." The Africans were there to find their voice, their message, their uncompromised stand. "Lambeth 1998 is soon approaching," Nkoyoyo said that night, "and we need to make ourselves ready."

Archbishop Nkoyoyo stood at the podium—an imposing figure both in size and looks—with an interpreter at his side. After greeting the attendees, he went swiftly to his thesis, stating that at Lambeth the "UK and the US have dominated not only the topics of concern but have influenced most discussions and decisions. . . . We must make certain that our voices are heard and our concerns addressed." The topics for consideration that week in Kampala included the debt burden, justice and reconciliation issues regionally and internationally, local problems of poverty and hunger, and, of course, human sexuality. Even the president of Uganda, Yoweri K. Museveni, was on the roster of speakers.

"The Christian church in Africa," Nkoyoyo uttered emphatically, "knows how to deal with polygamous people. They are not ordained. They are not given full rights and authority in the church. They are preached to repent and turn from their sinful ways. In [the North] homosexuality is a problem which the church wants to compromise on. Some have ordained and sanctioned homosexuals—married them in the church and have authority in churches including leadership. . . . We must make certain that all issues concerning the church as a whole are addressed."

Then, in the stride of a preacher's rhythm, he concluded:

"We must stand united and let our voices be heard.

"We must stand united and let our people be represented at Lambeth and in the world.

"We must stand united and allow the Holy Spirit to work through us as we lead the church in Africa to the new millennium."

At these words, the bishops and their wives stood and broke out in a well-known African song of praise, *Tukutenderezah Jesu* ("We Praise You, Jesus").

It simply didn't matter to Livingstone Nkoyoyo that there was a fundamental incongruity of power. The global North had more money, more votes, and more control of the Lambeth proceedings. They did not have the majority of people. Nor did they understand the Africans' commitment to the uniting power of the gospel. "Evangelism and bringing the good news of Christ to the entire world has to be our first concern," Nkoyoyo stated in his address. "This is the foundation for which we stand as a Christian community." In his mind, and in the minds of the gathered bishops, the common bond could be found only "in the blood of Jesus Christ, which binds us in fellowship with other members of the worldwide Anglican Communion." No amount of money or earthly wisdom or parliamentary claims to nobility and power could convince them otherwise.

A new day was dawning and they said it. They meant it. It was time, Nkoyoyo thundered, for the global North to "look to our leadership for the church approaching the next millennium."

• • •

I gave my address on the second day of the conference, late in the afternoon. I passed out copies in English, armed with an appendix chockful of documented evidence on the moral crisis facing the American church. I told them human interest stories of clergy and church leaders persecuted for calling their bishops to biblical repentance. I told them firsthand, as an Episcopal clergyman, that we were in desperate need of their help. But if they gave that help, I stated factually, we would most certainly reject it—and we would reject them. They needed to know that because it had already happened and, I was convinced, short of a divine intervention, it would happen again.

That afternoon, I told them the American version of the story of Alexander Muge, the late Kenyan bishop of Eldoret. He was one of their own. It was the only way I knew of warning them that we, in the US, had already turned our cold hearts to stone.

• • •

He was forty-four years old, married, with four children ages fourteen to nineteen. In the spring of 1990, he was on a US preaching mission sponsored by African Team Ministries. His schedule took him to St. Luke's Episcopal Church, Walnut Creek, California, on May 17. The Rev. Gary Ost had invited him to speak at an evening worship service, preceded by dinner at a local restaurant.

It was their first meeting. A few others joined them.

The conversation began by asking the bishop about the church of Kenya and its explosive growth, the very opposite of the decline in the US Episcopal Church. For Alexander Muge, this was not a point of speculation. There was reason for the decline and he said so. He pointed out, in his own words, "that the decline of the Church in the USA is due to the secularization of the Gospel and the lack of self-discipline among the clergy in the Church;

those who should set a good example, but fail to."[9] Muge believed the US church could not call the nation to repentance on any moral issue as long as it was "among the institutions perpetuating and promoting immorality."[10] Specifically, he told them at dinner, "homosexuals and lesbians have taken over the Church leadership in the USA, and there is no way God is going to bless this Church with growth."[11]

He said it not knowing his host clergyman, the Rev. Gary Ost, was a practicing homosexual.

What took place next is best said in Bishop Muge's own words:

The Rector changed his face and became very furious at me. . . . I told him the Bible condemns all sorts of immorality: adultery, fornication, and homosexuality, and that confessed homosexuals will not inherit the kingdom of God unless they repent and change their lifestyle—as it says in Ephesians 5:5. The lady parishioner also became furious with me . . . and then confessed that she was also a homosexual and loves Jesus Christ. They told me that my faith was that of the British nineteenth-century evangelicals, for which there is no room today. . . . I pointed out to them that Jesus says that He is the same yesterday, today, and forever; and that they seem to believe that this doesn't apply to them in the USA.

The rector went further to emphasize that homosexuality is not sinful, and that his bishop, the Rt. Rev. William Swing, knows his sexual preference and supports him. He stressed that there is nothing of which to repent and it is now high time that they begin blessing homosexual unions in the church. I told him that it was wrong for a confessed and practicing homosexual to continue as rector of the church.

It was then that Bishop Muge told them he was going to preach that night on this very issue.

I planned to tell them it is evil for people who call themselves Christians to practice homosexuality. I insisted that the Spirit of the Lord was leading me to speak on Sodom and Gomorrah, and there was no way I could restrain the Spirit of God.

Gary Ost told him flatly he would not allow him to preach that night and that he would lose the financial and prayer support of St. Luke's Church. Muge said he was "not prepared to sacrifice Jesus for some dollars." With that, the evening came to an abrupt end. Muge was formally denied the pulpit.

A few days later, the Kenyan bishop called an American press conference. He told the media, "I believe that I am the first bishop in the worldwide Anglican Communion to have been denied the right to preach by a priest." He went on to challenge the church in Kenya to "pray for the church of Christ in the Western world, and particularly in North America," but also cautioned "not all who come to our country or continent with collars for missionary work are true believers of the gospel."[12]

Alexander Muge stepped away from the microphone knowing he had done the right thing. In Africa and throughout church history, the proper role of a bishop was to defend the faith, to exercise godly discipline when leaders who bear the name of Christ publicly err, and to call believers everywhere to pray for the recovery of the church. He had done just that. He expected Gary Ost's bishop to do the same.

But, Muge discovered, it's somehow different for Episcopalians in the US.

Gary Ost's bishop, William Swing, proved the point. He issued a press statement in response to Muge. He said he believed that "poor Bishop Muge" had naïvely allowed himself to be used by dissident elements within the diocese of California who were "orchestrating the event as part of a campaign to discredit church liberals."

In other words, Africans were nothing more than black, ignorant, naïve pawns.

Alexander Muge decided to respond gently to Swing's insults. He said to the news media,

I did not consult anyone on the issue and in case of any blame, I should be the one held responsible. In addition, my press release was not judgmental as such. I attacked the act of homosexuality and not the people involved. I appeal to the people involved to repent and turn to Jesus Christ, who loves them.

It was his last public statement in the United States.

Back home in Kenya three months later, Bishop Muge joined Anglican leaders in denouncing government corruption. This particular time he outraged Peter Okondo, a Kenyan cabinet minister, who turned in retribution and publicly banned Muge from entering the district where he served as bishop. He suggested that Muge would be killed if he defied the order. "They will see fire," Okondo said openly, "and many not leave alive."[13]

Bishop Muge refused to be separated from his people. He told the local Nairobi newspaper, *The Daily Nation*, "Let [Okondo] know that my innocent blood will haunt him forever and he will not be at peace, for God does not approve murder." The next morning, August 14, 1990, he went to Busia Town and spent the day talking and praying with his people. By midafternoon, it seemed as if Okondo's threats were nothing but an African wind tossing up dry dirt into the summer sky. Muge said his good-byes. He got into the car with three of his staff members and, taking the wheel, drove out of town.

He was only a few miles away. It happened so quickly. The truck coming the other way just turned in on him. The papers said "the lorry hit them head on." The truck driver was not injured. Muge's staff members were taken to nearby hospitals. Bishop Muge died instantly.

The government later reported that the threats against Muge's life were "unfortunate." Kenyan president Daniel arap Moi called his family, expressing sorrow.

The Episcopal Church newsmagazine *Episcopal Life* featured the story on the front page of its September 1990 issue. The Anglican bishop was both a hero and a martyr. He had taken a prophetic stand against the corruptions of the Kenyan government in the name of Jesus Christ and it had cost him his life. A tragic but courageous story for our times. Alexander Muge was hardly anyone's "pawn." But, oddly enough, *Episcopal Life* only told the story of the circumstances surrounding his murder in Kenya. They made an editorial decision not to mention the events in Walnut Creek, California, only a few months earlier. Of course, Muge had taken a prophetic stand then, too, in the name of Jesus Christ. But this time he stood against us—their readership—and against the corruption of the gospel in the Episcopal Church. He had called the leaders of our beloved church to repent and reform.

Best not to mention that, the editors decided.

But I did, I had to, at the Great Lakes Conference eight years later.

I could not let his testimony be forgotten. I did not want his voice, which cried out in our American wilderness, to be silenced. What happened to him would most certainly happen again. If the Africans opposed the Americans at Lambeth, they would not be heard. They would be insulted, laughed at, and dismissed out of hand. They would likely suffer the loss of significant funding for their regions. There would be no change. The mighty US Episcopal Church would not repent. In fact, they would look strategically at the African nations as a mission field of opportunity to spread their all-inclusive, highly sophisticated gospel. History, I feared, would most definitely repeat itself.

But still, I reasoned, it was worth the effort. Who knows if the days of Jonah might not return and, by sovereign intervention, the Episcopal Church would hear the African voice and turn from its wickedness? So I closed my address by asking that these African bishops do at Lambeth what their own Bishop Muge had done in Walnut Creek, California.

One more time.

• • •

The bishops listened to six presentations during the conference but spent the majority of their time in group sessions. They were specifically preparing for their effective participation at Lambeth. A committee was chosen from among them to draft a formal statement. Near the end of the conference the draft was presented for open discussion. I remember taking notes during that time and being moved deeply by the force of their convictions and the reality of their fears.

"We need to sit as Africans at Lambeth," one of them said. "Not scattered."

"We must not discuss homosexuality," another argued. "To study it is to continue it. It must be stopped. It is destroying the church." Others stood, agreeing. "It is heresy clothed with power, money, seeming education — still, it remains heresy."

A voice from the back spoke clearly: "Spong is already a heretic." The response was immediate, everyone affirming the verdict. They could not understand why he had not already been removed as a bishop. It should not, must not, be tolerated.

A bishop from East Ankole, Uganda, by the name of Elisha Kyamugambi spoke next. He knew that making a public stand at Lambeth threatened the desperately needed cash flow from the north.

"My brothers," he began slowly, "we have got to become self-sustaining and stop our total dependence on the First World for the ability to serve our needs, and train and take care of our people. We have got to stop being afraid. Fear is preventing our ability to receive from God the riches He would pour out upon us. The sin is *fear*, and we must stop being afraid. We need to stand firm in the faith that God has given us . . . and will give us as He provides the resources as needed, when needed, as we step out and obey God. Our Father is rich. Our Father can provide."

Elisha sat down. The room was suddenly quiet.

I looked around and saw it on their faces—this was a holy moment. There was a real cost to following Jesus Christ. These African leaders knew suffering and poverty intimately. They knew their voice in Lambeth would have repercussions that could hurt their people physically. The temptation to politic by speaking softly, compromising slightly, and allowing fear to govern their witness pressed deeply on their minds, asking, "Isn't there a way to make a stand without paying the cost?" Bishop Elisha confronted the temptation head on. He believed it was necessary to name the fear and, in the name of Jesus, deal with it. But would they? Could they?

I watched them, wondering if I would have the courage in Christ to do the right thing.

As we came to the final service of the conference, the African bishops had made their decision. "The Ugandan martyrs did not compromise their faith—even to death," the preacher said. "They are a living witness to us, for this is our day to be firm in faith and not compromise the gospel. We must go to Lambeth on our knees that we may be firm in our faith. We must pray and fast against Spong and his army." The assembled congregation gave their immediate approval.

They were together in Christ, with one voice, one faith, ready for Lambeth.

A few days later, their resolutions were made public to the press.[14]

• • •

Paul Buckley was at the Lambeth Conference that August, a reporter for the *Dallas Morning News*. His story captured the moment. The sexuality debate was over. A resolution had passed. The Africans had risen to the occasion.

> Canterbury, England—Anglican bishops, struggling with the most volatile issue at their once-a-decade Lambeth Conference, overwhelmingly reaffirmed traditional Christian sexual morality Wednesday and rejected "homosexual practice as incompatible with Scripture."
>
> The battle among bishops from around the world pitted a bloc of conservative Africans and their allies against more liberal bishops from the West, particularly the United States. The vote, which followed more than two hours of passionate debate, was a victory for traditionalists. . . . The tally: 526 bishops (82%) in favor of the resolution on sexuality, 70 against and 45 abstaining.[15]

It was called Resolution I.10—"Human Sexuality." "This Conference," it began, "in view of the teaching of Scripture, upholds faithfulness in marriage between a man and a woman in lifelong union, and believes that abstinence is right for those who are not called to marriage." The resolution, "while rejecting homosexual practice as incompatible with Scripture, calls on all our people to minister pastorally and sensitively to all irrespective of sexual orientation." In addition, it moved against "the legitimizing or blessing of same sex unions nor ordaining those involved in same gender unions."

As journalist David Virtue said, also reporting from Lambeth, "It was a stinging defeat for liberals especially from the U.S., Canada, England and Australia who have long sought to liberalize the church's historic stand on sexual behavior."[16]

But was it a "stinging defeat"? Hidden in Resolution I.10, carefully crafted, were words in direct opposition to the clear edict that homosexual practice was "incompatible with Scripture." The predominantly North American agenda had found its way into the final drafting in one sentence among many: "We commit ourselves to listen to the experience of homosexual persons." This presented a great confusion. If homosexuality was incompatible with Scripture, why leave room for more dialogue? This blatant contradiction in thought made it clear that the debate was far from over.

As the media thundered the word *incompatible* across the headlines, and God-fearing Anglicans gave thanks for the overwhelming preservation of the historic Christian faith, the revisionists knew that this jolting setback was not the end of their story. They had the commitment of the Anglican bishops worldwide "to listen"—not to the authority of Scripture but to the essential authority of their new religion: *experience.*

Their message made its way into the language of the archbishop of Canterbury, George Carey. For him, the sexuality issue was a "difficult and painful debate." He said in a closing statement, favoring the revisionists, "We need to carry on listening to one another." But then, at the same time, he stood with the vast majority of Anglican bishops, saying, "I stand wholeheartedly with traditional Anglican orthodoxy, see no room in holy Scripture or the entire Christian tradition for any sexual activity outside matrimony of husband and wife, and I believe that the amended motion is simply saying what have all held; what Anglican belief and morality stands for."[17]

The double-talk had taken root.

There were other noteworthy decisions made at the Lambeth Conference. For example, the bishops made an indirect response to the "Twelve Theses" of John Spong in two separate resolutions reaffirming the historic primacy of Scripture.[18]

The revisionists were shocked and devastated. They had clearly underestimated the opposition from the global South. Many US bishops sent messages back to their home diocese stating the resolutions—including Resolution I.10—were wrong and they simply would not comply. The Communion was dividing over essentials.

But before the Lambeth Conference ended, another significant resolution passed on geographic boundaries. Bishop Larry Maze of Arkansas got what he wanted. Lambeth reaffirmed its earlier position declaring it "inappropriate for any bishop or priest of the worldwide Anglican Communion 'to exercise episcopal or pastoral ministry within another diocese without first obtaining the permission and invitation of the ecclesiastical authority thereof.'"[19]

This left the crisis in Little Rock at a stalemate. Should Rucyahana go to Little Rock that September? Tension was clearly mounting. Time was running out. By sheer coincidence, Maze had invited Spong to come to Little Rock the very same weekend St. Andrew's and their rector TJ Johnston had invited Rucyahana to come to their church and serve as their bishop.

• • •

It was messy behind the scenes of Lambeth.

John Rucyahana told a journalist shortly after the conference was over that the bishops of the global South, and specifically the Africans, had become "a force to be reckoned with. We know this victory is for the glory of God and the gospel of Jesus Christ," he said, "but we cannot ignore our contribution. . . . We are not ready to be swayed or dictated upon by anybody."[20]

Not everyone believed that.

As expected, allegations emerged. It was believed that a First World right-wing conspiracy "had brokered a deal with Third World bishops in which they would support the plea for debt relief in return for support on the issue of homosexuality."[21] With the allegations came derogatory statements patronizing and insulting African Christians. John Spong led the attack. He first claimed that the Christian faith of Africans was "just a step up from witch-craft. . . . They've moved out of animism into a very superstitious kind of Christianity." Andrew Carey, son of the archbishop of Canterbury and noted journalist, told Spong that "Third World bishops might feel belittled and patronized by such remarks." Spong retorted bluntly, "If they feel patronized that's too bad. I'm not going to cease to be a 20th century person for fear of offending someone in the Third World."[22] In other words, Africans are not twentieth-century people? The same exact reasoning was thrust against Alexander Muge in Walnut Creek, California— *They told me that my faith was that of the British nineteenth-century evangelicals.*

Richard Holloway, archbishop of Scotland, condescendingly repeated Spong's argument: "Africans need to be taught the biblical scholarship of the last 150 years." But Holloway took it a step further—what was he thinking? He publicly accused conservatives from the North of buying Asian and African votes with dinners of "chicken and sausages."[23]

Africans—they said of Muge—*are nothing more than black, ignorant, naïve pawns.*

Emmanuel Kolini, archbishop of Rwanda, heard the accusation from Holloway, his colleague and fellow archbishop. He quietly prayed. He listened to the media playing up the image—*bought with chicken dinners.* He decided this time he could not remain silent. The media picked up his statement.

"We have chicken back home in Africa, you know. Only one thing bought me and still buys me—and that's the cross—and nothing else."[24]

Kolini was hardly anyone's pawn.

Andrew Carey finished his final article on Lambeth 1998. He ended it with one final observation: "After three weeks as a journalist at the Lambeth Conference, it is quite clear to me that there is no right wing conspiracy, merely an honest attempt to enable Third World bishops to have a greater voice in the Lambeth Conference. This initiative has quite frankly worked."[25]

• • •

In the remaining days of August 1998, while Episcopal bishops were returning home, testifying, "Things will not change," a certain fear lingered among the clergy and supporters of First Promise. In all likelihood, the Episcopal bishops were right—there would be no change on American shores. Like the silencing of Muge, who called the church to repent from its sexual immorality, so these Lambeth resolutions—which issued the same resolve—would quickly fade from the headlines, diminished by the mighty force of Episcopal leaders determined to further their cause.

Chuck Murphy wrote a letter to the archbishop of Canterbury inquiring about the inconsistencies and how resolutions would be implemented. He also wrote US Presiding Bishop Frank Griswold, requesting that in light of Lambeth he recant his stance or resign.

But Archbishop Kolini faced his own challenge of how to proceed, since Lambeth had also resolved against crossing boundaries. He determined to give Griswold time—to not let the issue of crossing boundaries attract attention. They would first see what Griswold did. Archbishop Kolini called Rucyahana and told him not to go to Little Rock. Rather, with the help of several Episcopal clergy, they would first observe and document the American church's reaction to Lambeth.[26]

A season of waiting had begun.

For Emmanuel Kolini and John Rucyahana it was hard to shake the sadness in their hearts for what seemed an inevitable end. Americans don't listen to Africans and Asians. Americans didn't hear Alexander Muge. They rejected the Kuala Lumpur Statement.[27] In all likelihood, they would not comply with the Lambeth resolutions—even with more than 80 percent of

Anglican bishops worldwide endorsing them. Kolini and Rucyahana knew this story all too well. The Americans would stay the course. They would continue their public opposition to biblical Christian faith and morality. They would believe in their arrogance that they were right, enlightened by the scholarship of a new day. They would amass their great wealth and go forth as ambassadors to spread their new gospel for a new millennium.

Eventually, they fully believed, though it would take time, the Third World will catch on.

CHAPTER 10

COME AND SEE

These are unprecedented times. What we have is Apostolic Succession without Apostolic Success. It's obvious why. We have no regard for the Apostolic Faith.

— THE RT. REV. C. FITZSIMONS ALLISON[1]

I t was a chance meeting—a moment in time held secret between two men for the next five years.[2] The Lambeth Conference 1998 had just ended. Archbishop Moses Tay of Southeast Asia was headed back to his residence. Bishop John Rucyahana of Rwanda was on his way to a meeting in town. In an open courtyard, under a midsummer afternoon sky in Canterbury, England, their paths crossed.

Moses initiated the conversation. He told John, in no uncertain terms, he was prepared to act. He would give him and Archbishop Emmanuel Kolini his full support to further the work. To this day, John remembers Moses' exact words: "I am ready to help you. Get a plan. Inform me. We do it together."

The two men talked like strategists at wartime.

"I am not happy," Moses said emphatically. "The liberals have forced their way into Resolution I.10. They demand we 'listen to the experience of homosexual persons' while the resolution says clearly we reject 'homosexual practice as incompatible with Scripture.' This is wrong. Leaven leavens the whole lump of dough. It is not a win for the orthodox. The minority view has been accommodated. Satan has a foothold in the resolution. Evil has not been corrected."

"It is true," Rucyahana replied. "It is a complete contradiction. It's like rejecting John Spong as a heretic and then saying we commit to listen to him. What are we doing? Who are we listening to?"

"So, since no correction," Moses reasoned, seeing the days to come, "cancer will surely metastasize. When gangrene sets in, you must amputate. If no action, it spreads to the whole body. This is my concern." He knew it medically, as a doctor. Ministry was his second career. He knew if a medical diagnosis required immediate intervention, it was the doctor's ethical duty to act on behalf of the patient. Not to do so was neglect and malpractice. It went against every fiber of his being—as a doctor, a Christian, and a leader.

He said it again: "We must act."

"We are convinced in Africa," John stated, "the American strategy for dialogue is the devil's own strategy to buy time. It does two things. One, it prevents us from decisive action and therefore gives time for revisionists to advance their agenda. Two, it makes the archbishop of Canterbury very happy. He wants the Anglican Communion to remain united at all cost, even in the midst of heresy. I tell you, this listening thing, this plea for dialogue, is a slow but sure death."

Moses shook his head in disgust.

"We must get the order straight," John urged. "The gospel comes first—then unity."

"You are right, John. I talked with the archbishop of Canterbury about this already," Moses confided. "I spoke to him after we issued the Kuala Lumpur Statement last year. I said, 'Unity is the invisible dress the king is wearing.' We must face facts. Unity was broken long ago. It can never be first priority. Biblical unity must come by being in Christ, by the living way. Then unity is God's gift. If unity is not in Christ through obedience to the Word of God, by becoming a child of God—saved, redeemed, made new in Jesus—then unity is not possible. It becomes an idol."

"This is very dangerous," John warned.

They were both in agreement. In those few minutes together, Moses and John could see the big picture. They knew, in time, the minority opinion hidden discreetly behind the strong orthodox language of Resolution I.10 would become accepted doctrine in Anglicanism. It would have power to tear the church apart and destroy the faith of many. Something had to be done—soon.

John outlined the first step. He believed the Episcopal Church would rebel against the resolution diocese by diocese. Each statement of rejection needed to be fully documented and then sent to Anglican bishops world-wide. "After that, the second step," he said. "We meet. We set a strategy for action."

Moses agreed.

The two shook hands, promising to keep each other in prayer, and then went their separate ways. It was, in hindsight, a historic meeting. It was the first time leaders from Africa and Southeast Asia agreed to set a specific plan of action that—together, from the global South—would confront and oppose America's new religion. That meeting, their handshake, like a picture frozen in time, set in motion an alliance between two Anglican provinces that would, in the days to come, rally a worldwide Anglican reformation.

These formidable gospel men had made the decision to act.

Back home in the US, we at First Promise already knew Rwanda's uncompromised stand. What we didn't know was the strength of conviction that had come upon Moses after the Lambeth Conference. We would soon learn the reason Moses was named Moses—the biblical picture of God drawing out His people from bondage. A church historian once said of him, "Moses Tay saw a window of opportunity in those days, a brief moment in time that he knew, 'if we don't do it now, we will never get to do it again.' There was an edge to his readiness. It was as if he said, 'Throw me out of this plane, and then throw me a parachute.' Moses was Moses! If the Anglican Communion had a flicker of hope for reformation, it was going to take some-one like this—a leader cut from a very different kind of cloth."[3]

After Lambeth, Archbishop Tay flew home to Singapore. Back in his office, sitting at his desk, he felt the bitter disappointment. He knew the Anglican Communion was in trouble. He knew he could not sit idle. It had been a year, almost to the day, since he had read a letter from an Episcopal priest in the US thanking him for his bold witness of the gospel at Kuala Lumpur. His response then had been the same response he had given every-where to this international crisis of faith and leadership:

Repentance is basic and required by God. "Inclusiveness" of people who refuse to repent is clearly against the Word and purpose of God. Refusal to accept homosexuality as sinful is a diabolical contradiction of the Word of God, and is a blatant attempt to destroy the Gospel of Salvation through Jesus Christ. This is an issue of eternal life and eternal death. It is not a matter of opinion or a subject for study by an appointed commission. . . . We need to heed the words of 2 Cor. 6:14–18. . . . May we unite our hearts to pray for an unprecedented *revival* in our churches.[4]

That was a year ago. Every word echoed his firm commitment to do something. It was a call to act—not to listen, but to discipline ungodly leaders; not accommodate them, but to repent from sin, not bless it or tolerate it. It was, as he said, a matter of "eternal life and eternal death." He had waited patiently for Lambeth '98. He had hoped for correction but found an insidious compromise. Now that it was over, he knew the time had come. What remained unanswered was how he would act, and when, and with whom.

• • •

As Tay had foreseen, the American Episcopal Church's rebellion against Lambeth quickly began to take shape. While same-sex blessings continued at great stride, the diocese of Massachusetts passed a resolution at their convention in brazen defiance to Lambeth. By year's end, eighteen dioceses publicly rejected Resolution I.10 with four dioceses passing resolutions contrary to it.[5]

The vehement opposition to Lambeth was found at the highest levels of the Episcopal Church. But no one undermined Resolution I.10 more skillfully than Frank Griswold. As a seasoned politician, he systematically turned the negative rhetoric against the traditional orthodox into a positive strategy for the homosexual community. Griswold was a leader. He saw opportunity and seized it.

The language planted into Resolution I.10 was taking root, and it was beginning to thrive and spread. *Listen to the experience of homosexual persons.* Griswold was nursing a new orthodoxy—a standard that raised personal experience above all else, and certainly above the antiquated words of the Bible. This was his promise for a more advanced spiritual life—listen to our experiences, not the Word.

It was exactly what Moses Tay had predicted. Resolution I.10 had been greatly compromised.

Before August even ended, less than three weeks after Lambeth, Griswold had snagged his first great trophy: George Carey, archbishop of Canterbury, renowned worldwide as a traditionalist, the champion for orthodox evangelicals. The door of hope had first cracked open for Griswold with Carey's concession to Lambeth, calling upon all to "listen to one another."

In the months to come it would become apparent that Griswold not only had a convert but an advocate and evangelist in the highest office of Anglicanism. Soon Carey would even concede that the position of Lambeth could change in the future—his doctrine of sexual ethics no longer rested on the unchanging nature of Scripture, but on the ever-changing philosophies of the human mind.

Griswold's revisionist plan for takeover was successfully and aggressively advancing. He knew that no one in the Anglican Communion had authority to hold the mutinous Episcopal Church accountable. Nothing could stop him.

In mid-January 1999, the Association of Anglican Congregations on Mission sent a two-hundred-page report, "The Petitions,"[6] to over eight hundred Anglican bishops worldwide, appealing for emergency intervention, protection, and the establishment of an alternative Anglican presence in the province of the Episcopal Church of the United States of America.

Chuck Murphy was watching the developments with fascination. Instinctively, he knew the public release of "The Petitions" was not enough to stop Griswold. There had to be one-to-one conversations with international leaders who could effect change. That, in the Anglican context, meant archbishops. He knew the time had come to meet Moses Tay in Singapore and Emmanuel Kolini in Rwanda. These were men who could make a difference. He made the calls, asked for the appointments, and set the itinerary for traveling overseas in late January 1999. Chuck called the principle "leapfrog." It's the risky act of going over the head of those in authority to those with greater authority in order to produce change.[7]

Chuck flew to Singapore that January with Jon Shuler to meet with Archbishop Moses Tay. He then flew to Africa, where my wife and I met him and joined the meetings with Archbishop Emmanuel Kolini and Bishop John Rucyahana. Both Archbishops Tay and Kolini had read through "The Petitions" and agreed that it was time for strategic action.

In Singapore, Moses Tay made two proposals. First, in light of the request for immediate intervention made by "The Petitions," a number of archbishops needed to write Frank Griswold an "open letter" opposing the blatant rejection of Lambeth Resolution I.10 by the Episcopal Church. Second, he believed it was time for a meeting of specially invited archbishops to discuss appropriate action steps. He offered to host the meeting in Singapore in mid-April. Chuck took both proposals to his meeting with Emmanuel Kolini in Rwanda, who readily approved them.

"If there is no repentance in the Episcopal Church," Kolini said bluntly in response, "then there is no communion."

"What we don't understand," Rucyahana said, "is the current position of the evangelical US bishops and those they lead; especially now, after reading "The Petitions." Tell me, what are they going to do? Will they remain silent even in the face of all these facts? You know, we have told you that in Rwanda to be neutral is to be gentle, and to be gentle is to betray Jesus. We can't be gentle and take no action when Jesus is being publicly mocked. So you need to tell us, where do these evangelical Episcopal bishops stand now? What are they saying? What are they doing?"

Chuck couldn't answer. At the end of February, Chuck was scheduled to meet with these US bishops who had united under the banner of the American Anglican Council. He told John and Emmanuel he would have more information at that time and report back. Until then, they agreed to focus on the Tay strategy: an open letter to Frank Griswold and the mid-April meeting of archbishops in Singapore.

They were small steps, but steps nonetheless. We flew home filled with thankfulness in God's abundant kindness and grace. Both archbishops wanted to act. They wanted to challenge Griswold. They wanted to muster support among their own colleagues. They seemed pleased with Chuck's leadership, First Promise, "The Petitions," and our urgent request for intervention. At least for now, they were more than willing to receive us and work with us, fully aware that we were leapfrogging our bishops back home.

• • •

The revisionists responded immediately and severely, led by Bishop John Spong's continued rhetoric against the hard-line biblical stand in Resolution

I.10. He pronounced it "unchristian, uninformed, prejudiced and evil," and the product of "irrational Pentecostal hysteria."[8]

Chuck Murphy subsequently attended the American Anglican Council meeting in Orlando on February 25. He spoke for an hour, challenging American evangelical bishops to break communion with revisionist and apostate colleagues in the church; but by their silence he could tell they were not going to lead. From that moment on, Chuck had a saying he would repeat in nearly all his public addresses: "There are two crises in the Episcopal Church. There is the crisis of faith that was addressed at Lambeth '98. Then there is the crisis of leadership that is supposed to guard the faith, guard the discipline, and guard the unity of the church at a time of major realignment in the whole of Anglicanism."

Chuck believed that if just one bishop were willing to lead, willing to risk his job for the sake of the gospel, the intervention from overseas would happen with lightning speed.

Not one stood.[9]

However, seven of the thirty-eight archbishops did stand and lead by exercising their Christian duty of holding their colleagues accountable before the Lord. Using Griswold's own language, they wrote him an open letter (posted on the Internet on February 26, 1999) urging him to "listen to the Church" at Lambeth. It was nothing less than a gentle appeal to repent and return to the "Christian faith."[10]

Griswold collected his nine-member Council of Advice and, with them, released an international response on March 10, 1999, that masterfully displayed the seductive power behind his gospel. Concluding his rationale, he appealed: "We invite each of you to visit those parts of our church which cause you concern . . . to listen to the experience of homosexual persons, which is mandated by the Lambeth resolution (I.10) on human sexuality. . . . We invite you, in the words of Jesus, to 'Come and see.'" These words, "Come and see," would play a defining role in the upcoming April meeting of concerned archbishops in Singapore.

Behind the courteous tone drenched in compassion and seeming mutual respect stood men of absolute defiance. Griswold and his Council of Advice had no intention of hearing and obeying the corrective call to biblical repentance that the archbishops had issued. The only hope of reconciling the division was for the other side to "Come and see" and, in seeing, repent of their outdated biblical stand. Otherwise, the division would remain and continue to deepen.

Before Chuck Murphy flew to Singapore for the meeting of archbishops, he was given a ten-minute audience with George Carey, who was speaking at a conference in Charleston, South Carolina, on April 8, 1999. Chuck knew the archbishop had been fully briefed on the upcoming Singapore meeting. He had reason to believe that Carey was privately supportive. He was hoping to get his endorsement.

The disappointment began in the archbishop's public address titled "The Precious Gift of Unity." Carey passionately defended his belief that unity—that bond that holds the Anglican Communion together—is to be prized over the truth—the very substance of faith. His exact words were these:

> History shows . . . how immensely difficult it is to rebuild unity once unilateral action has been taken. It is far harder . . . to determine to stay together, until truth emerges. Our fierce commitment to truth and our stand upon it must be moderated within the believing fellowship.[11]

Truth must be moderated for the sake of unity?

Chuck couldn't believe his ears. Basic Christian doctrine, from the apostles to the church fathers, asserts that truth—the transforming and redeeming power of the gospel—is the bond that unites Christians in the body of Christ. It is gospel faith that forms the bond of unity just as the essence of love forms the bond of marriage. Without love, there is no marriage. And without the gospel, which Griswold and company had radically distorted for their own agenda, there is no unity. The archbishop knew better. But enormous political pressure bore down on him. The Anglican Communion was unraveling under his administration. He was driven by a singular passion as archbishop of Canterbury to hold it together—unity at all cost, "The Precious Gift of Unity," even if it meant moderating the truth of the gospel in a day when it was being publicly maligned. Surely this was not what Carey believed privately, was it?

The ten-minute meeting came shortly after the archbishop's address.

Murphy quickly outlined the reasons behind the Singapore gathering of archbishops in light of the massive American rebellion to Resolution I.10 and Griswold's unwillingness to publicly recant in his response to their "open letter." He told the archbishop, "Something has got to be done."

George Carey disagreed and told him so. He warned Chuck against taking any precipitous action. He advised him to step back and adamantly opposed his involvement in Singapore.

Murphy made one more attempt in the remaining time. He gave an analogy of a dysfunctional family where Dad is a drunk. Mom comes down the stairs with a black eye every other night. The family goes along to get along as if nothing is wrong. The day comes when the older son steps forward and calls for an intervention from the outside. Dad gets taken away, and guess who becomes the jerk? Is it Dad, who drinks and beats up Mom? Heavens no! It's the older son. In a dysfunctional system, he's the problem because he ratted. Now he's isolated by everyone because he's the one who broke up the family unity. But in a healthy system, Dad's the jerk. The older son did the right thing by calling for an outside intervention.

"Here's the point, Archbishop," Chuck said in conclusion. "We're in a dysfunctional system. We at First Promise are being perceived as the problem and we're not. The Episcopal Church and its rebellion to Lambeth and the gospel of Jesus Christ is the problem. They are the ones breaking up the Anglican family. What we are asking for is an intervention from archbishops overseas. The situation is intolerable and we cannot keep on keeping on. Your support would help. That's what we're asking for."

The time was up. The archbishop remained firm. He gave no endorsement.

Actually, he asked Murphy to stand down.

• • •

On the last day of the Singapore meetings, the archbishops met alone. In the room were Harry Goodhew (Sydney and New South Wales, Australia), Emmanuel Kolini (Rwanda), Jonathan Onyemelukwe (Nigeria), Maurice Sinclair (Southern Cone), Moses Tay (Southeast Asia), and Bishop Evans Kisekka (representing Archbishop Livingstone Nkoyoyo of Uganda). Bishop John Rucyahana of Rwanda was also present. For nearly two days, Chuck Murphy, John Rodgers, and a host of presenters had made their case for an emergency intervention in the Episcopal Church. Now, on April 15, 1999, it was time for the archbishops to close the doors, say their prayers, speak their mind, and render their decision.

By the end of the day, they had a unified strategy in place.

"We greet you joyfully in the name of our risen Lord!" they wrote in a formal letter to the First Promise leaders. "Let us tell you straightaway that we hear your cry, and are committed to action. . . . We assure you of our commitment to pursue this matter to a satisfactory conclusion."

It was exactly what we wanted to hear.

They completed their first action step that day. They wrote letters to George Carey, Frank Griswold, and their fellow archbishops. Their purpose was twofold: First, they wanted to "do all we can to ensure that our fellow [archbishops] are sufficiently informed." Second, they needed to underscore the urgent state of affairs in the Episcopal Church "for compliance with the Lambeth Resolution on Sexuality."

The second step was to plan "a further meeting of concerned archbishops to take place in November to monitor progress." In essence, they agreed on a set time of seven months to study the situation for themselves. They did not want to intervene, for example, until they appropriately accepted Frank Griswold's invitation to "Come and see."[12] In this way, it could never be said they did not listen to the gay community, as Resolution I.10 mandated. In addition, they wanted to give their fellow archbishops time to reflect and respond to the letters they had written that day. They were convinced an intervention had to come only when all other possibilities had been fully exhausted.

"We cannot take shortcuts," they wrote to the First Promise leaders, "but neither will we allow official procedures to postpone indefinitely necessary action." They closed the letter by asking for prayer "as we continue to address these difficult matters. . . . May we have wisdom and grace, and may you be encouraged and given strength to persevere."

For many of us, it seemed nothing short of miraculous. Six Anglican archbishops, all from the global South, were willing to address the mass rebellion in the Episcopal Church and consider, in seven months' time, a possible intervention. In these men, we found hope. There was a real, tangible passion for the uncompromised gospel of the Lord Jesus Christ and the unity that results from true faith in Him. These were the men who would not submit to some weak attempt to hold the Anglican family together at the expense of the gospel while the greatest heresies the world has ever known ravaged the people of God.

In these men, we saw biblical faith. We saw godly leadership.

We had a way forward and rejoiced in it.

• • •

Griswold's "Come and See" tour was scheduled for early fall, September 27–October 6. The summer of 1999 proved to be difficult at best. Griswold, Carey, and the revisionist camp hardened their hearts with even more resolve against the Singapore archbishops. They continued not to hear the gentle but firm correction from Singapore and amend their ways. In fact, Griswold's triumphant day nearly came on June 21. In Rochester, New York, the Rev. Canon Gene Robinson from the diocese of New Hampshire—renowned for leaving his wife and two daughters for the gay lifestyle—was nearly elected bishop. The church had never elected an openly gay bishop. History was in the making. On the third and fourth ballots, he led the field of candidates but did not have a majority. On the fifth, he lost the election by only seven votes. Afterward, Robinson said he expected to try again to become bishop in another diocese.[13]

That summer we knew it was only a matter of time before Griswold's strategy would play out.

In England, George Carey took the offensive against the Singapore archbishops. He didn't like their joint April 15 letter calling him to "deal decisively with the deliberate deviations from the faith." He knew they were "hurt and distressed by the increasing number of Bishops and [Archbishops] who are deliberately going against the Lambeth Resolutions on Biblical Authority and Morality." He also knew they wanted him to take an unwavering stand by effecting immediate disciplinary action.

He was not going to do it.

The archbishop of Canterbury wrote them all back on May 5. He made it quite clear that their request for action was, in itself, the problem. In no uncertain terms, he told them, they were the ones "exacerbating tensions." He strongly urged them to adopt a "moratorium on correspondence."

Moses Tay was incensed. He met with his provincial leaders in Southeast

Asia and issued a response on August 4. It quite simply said that if there was to be a moratorium, it should be "on Bishops and Dioceses going against Lambeth's position on Biblical Authority and Morality." The letter continued:

> We need to face up to the deep divisions within our Communion because of the continuing deviation from the "faith once delivered to the saints." We cannot value unity above truth which is intolerant of error. Any façade of unity is no more than the proverbial invisible clothes worn by the King. . . . Please be assured, George, that we still respect your office. But look at what is happening in [the Episcopal Church] after Lambeth. . . . I am writing on behalf of our Province, to protest to you and the whole world on this sad state of affairs.

Then he signed it, "Yours regretfully, the Most Rev. Dr. Moses Tay."[14] Once again, battle lines were being drawn at the highest levels of the Communion. Deep divisions, like tremors rumbling miles beneath the earth's surface but rising quickly to the top, were suddenly being felt with regularity. It was going to have to play out. Neither side had any intention of yielding their position for a moment. The "listening" was over. The invitation to "Come and see" was nothing but an impoverished attempt to convert global South leaders to their modern Gnostic spin on Jesus Christ.

Sadly, the archbishop of Canterbury, by choosing sides, had lost his ability to moderate.

That summer Archbishop Emmanuel Kolini decided to "Come and see" on his own. He fully intended to participate in Griswold's fall event by sending one of his bishops, John Rucyahana, as his representative. But he had to see for himself, firsthand. In an interview with journalist David Virtue, Kolini stated, "If we want to help, we have to understand exactly what is going on. . . . I am listening and seeking and making sure what we are doing is the right thing."[15]

But what he saw, he said to Virtue, was "a time of tolerance and a time of decadence." He wanted the Episcopal Church to fix its own problems. But everywhere he went he could see Spong's influence "destroying the church and undermining the gospel." Many Episcopalians were blindly following

Spong's famed "Twelve Theses" by openly disbelieving the absolute necessity of the cross, the bodily resurrection, and the uniqueness of the Lord Jesus Christ. From the African perspective, this terrified Kolini: "If we say Jesus is one among equals and he is not the only way to the Father, we are in danger of Muslims winning. The Muslims are keen to evangelize the entire world and they are focusing on Africa."

"Don't Episcopalians fear that?"

He could not understand why revisionists proactively dismissed and marginalized evangelicals committed to biblical faith. "You don't want to lose them," he said that summer. Yet, he discovered, the revisionists were on the offensive, accusing evangelicals for bringing division and upsetting the unity of the Communion. Kolini dismissed their argument out of hand, saying, "We are not going to compromise the gospel for the sake of unity. That's clear. No compromise with Jesus and the gospel . . . where do we get our unity. . . . Unity meets at the bottom of the cross, where all sinners meet and where we repent and we are forgiven. Outside of that we can't have unity. . . . Never. Never."

That summer, Kolini heard the cries of Episcopalians being oppressed by the revisionist leadership ruling the church. It was impossible for him, a Rwandan, after experiencing the untold, unimaginable suffering of his people from poverty, famine, disease, war—especially the genocide of 1994—to hear the cry of the suffering and not swiftly intervene. He found it unfortunate that Christian leaders, especially the clergy and bishops, had been silent for too long. Why is it, he wondered, when people are being unfairly treated that no one comes to their rescue?

"If we take the world as a sinking ship," Kolini taught, "and Jesus is on the rescue in a small boat, the church is called to be on His team. We are rescuing for life. The gospel is life."[16]

But if Kolini provided an intervention for faithful, orthodox Anglicans in the US, a certain danger awaited him. The archbishop and his province would, in all likelihood, be financially cut off from the flow of money coming from the US Episcopal Church. David Virtue asked him about this possibility. But it simply did not concern the archbishop. Actually, a smile came across his face at the thought of such a power play. "They can't make us any poorer," he said from fifty-four years of experience living in the Third World. "So even if there is hostility I wouldn't mind. It is all part of the suffering of the cross."

That was Kolini. More than anyone can imagine, he knew the cost of suffering.

November was coming, the end of the seven-month investigation by the Singapore archbishops. As Emmanuel Kolini flew back home with his wife, Freda, he prayed for the God of miracles to stretch out His hand over Frank Griswold and the Episcopal Church and cause them to repent. If they did not, if they continued to shipwreck the faith of those holding fast to the truth of the Bible, then something would have to be done. He would not stand back in silence. Never. Never.

It is called "rescuing for life."

• • •

Frank Griswold and his staff hosted the ten-day "Come and See" event in late September. Five leaders from the global South participated, including two archbishops (South America and Australia) and three bishops (representing their archbishops of Kenya, Tanzania, and Rwanda). They traveled to New York, Philadelphia, northern Virginia, Richmond, Orlando, and Boston, meeting both clergy and lay leaders representing all facets and ideologies in the Episcopal Church.

Bishop John Rucyahana kept a journal of those ten days. "I saw a terrible sickness," he wrote. "The authority of Scripture, the fundamentals of the faith, and the basic discipline of the church are being challenged. Why is no one saying it's wrong to 'say what you want to say, do what you like to do'? It was too bad. The Episcopal Church is in trouble. I no longer believe it is reformable from within."

John wrote down four succinct points in his report to Archbishop Kolini:

- Many Episcopal clergy have adopted an attitude of superiority when it comes to the authority of the Bible. They embrace an ongoing revelation from God through culture and science that informs biblical truth, rather than allowing the truth of God's Word to inform and transform the culture.
- There remains a great majority who reject and resent the unify-

ing appeal of Lambeth '98. They believe the resolutions on biblical authority and morality are not binding on them.

- Our request to cease ordaining practicing homosexuals and blessing same-sex unions was not accepted. The bishops and priests who continue these practices will not be disciplined.
- Episcopal leaders are unwilling to discipline John Spong for his "Twelve Theses." This underscores the real problem as a loss of biblical authority and faith, and not the symptomatic issues of sexuality.

Nothing sealed John's conclusions more than the closing meeting with Frank Griswold on Wednesday evening October 6. John reported, "He was very hospitable and welcoming. Most diplomatic. God blessed us with the opportunity to share honestly. The five of us told him we were deeply distressed by the blatant disregard of the Episcopal Church to the Lambeth resolutions. We requested he take immediate action to stop this divisive rebellion in his province. In particular, I had the freedom to ask him personally what he would do if one of his bishops ordained a practicing homosexual. His response surprised me.

"He said he would do nothing. He would not discipline them.

"I asked, 'Why?'

"He gave two reasons. First, he said he holds an honorary office. He presides over autonomous bishops and dioceses who have the right to do what they want to do. Therefore, he reasoned, it would be very difficult to enforce discipline. Even bishops, he said, cannot hold their fellow bishops accountable. The five of us debated him on this point. We argued that minimally an archbishop holds a position of authority and respect. He wields influence. He must speak and be heard. He must do everything possible to deter sinful acts. But the presiding bishop had nothing to say to us in response but 'My hands are tied.'"

My hands are tied?

"He then gave his second reason. He expressed sympathy with those violating the Lambeth resolutions, because he believes that many of them are merely responding to pressure from within their own communities. He himself confessed that he ordained practicing homosexuals while bishop in Chicago as a result of the same pressure. He then reasoned as a seasoned politician that although these actions would most definitely continue in the Episcopal Church, it should in no way endanger our common desire to maintain the unity of the Anglican Communion. The plea for unity in disregard for biblical truth made Frank Griswold no different than any other revisionist we met on our journey."

In light of this conversation and the ten days of "Come and See," Bishop John Rucyahana made his final recommendation to Archbishop Kolini:

> I, therefore, appeal to you and the archbishops meeting in November to offer a clear and direct course of action, which means first breaking of communion with the Episcopal Church until such time that it repents and offers Godly discipline within its structures. Then, second, form a missionary district that will provide oversight and the framework for the proclamation of the Gospel of Jesus Christ in the United States of America.[17]

Archbishop Harry Goodhew was also on the "Come and See" tour. His diagnosis of the Episcopal Church was one and the same with Rucyahana's. In his report, he stated that "we were surprised to find the marked impact that 'liberal' views of the Bible have on the minds of many bishops and clergy. As a consequence there is a weakened capacity to maintain and defend the faith once delivered to the saints." Concerning the issue of "listening" to the gay community, he wrote, "we hold that the dialogue has been abused by the unauthorized introduction of changes that presuppose a particular outcome to that dialogue. This impaired process has in fact jeopardized Anglican continuity."[18]

The five all agreed. The Episcopal Church was in critical condition.

But Harry Goodhew concluded his report with a very different resolve than Rucyahana. There was no recommendation of breaking communion and establishing a new Anglican work in the US. Rather, Goodhew appealed to Frank Griswold to provide "flying bishops" (alternative episcopal oversight) to those clergy and congregations oppressed by the revisionist rebellion to the gospel. This strategy, while providing for the needs of the persecuted, in no way called Griswold and the Episcopal Church to repent from their rejection of Holy Scripture and the blessing of sexual immorality. In fact, it left Griswold in charge, administering pastoral care for the very people who opposed him and his untoward defiance of the gospel.

The Goodhew strategy accommodated Griswold. The Rucyahana

strategy rebuked him. Both men strongly opposed the new religion in the Episcopal Church. But they disagreed on what to do about it. Both men agreed that an intervention was necessary. But they disagreed on how it was to be done. As a result, there was a definable tension in the air. November was coming. The seven months were nearly over. The Singapore archbishops had decided to reconvene in Kampala, Uganda, November 15–19, to discuss their findings and set a strategic action plan. But would this be possible? What happens when two doctors agree on the severity of the diagnosis but strongly disagree on the method of treatment? Two sides, both deeply concerned for the patient, one ready for immediate surgical intervention, the other appealing for noninvasive measures. Both unwilling to compromise. Both trying to honor the other.

Such were the days leading up to Kampala.

Archbishop Moses Tay sent Chuck Murphy an e-mail as early as September 7. He was already aware of the tension that existed between the Singapore archbishops. Somehow he was convinced that the majority would not want to stage an intervention of any kind. They were reluctant to act. Moses believed a new strategy was in the offing that waited for the upcoming meeting of the thirty-eight archbishops set for March 2000 in Portugal. They believed it could be just the right moment for the Singapore archbishops to persuade their colleagues to act unilaterally in disciplining the Episcopal Church.

But Moses shuddered at the thought. He knew such a proposal would be dismissed out of hand.

First, the archbishops have no legal authority in which to enforce discipline. In fact, it is a matter of great controversy as to whether the legislative arm of the Anglican Communion has any legal authority to enforce its own resolutions within any given province. "It has canon law," someone once said, "but no canon jail." Second, Moses knew that the archbishop of Canterbury would immediately thwart such an effort. He had already publicly sided with Griswold. He had lashed out against the Singapore archbishops in his letter of May 5. Save a sovereign act of God, George Carey would bring to bear the powers of his office to extinguish any strategy demanding a disciplinary intervention against the Episcopal Church.

At that point, it would be over.

The Singapore archbishops would be completely powerless. Any decision to act after that time would be in utter defiance to the archbishop of

Canterbury, his office, and the remaining archbishops. Strategically, they would have missed the moment. Up till now, this particular battle for the gospel was being waged outside the means of "permission giving." Griswold and his colleagues led by decisive action. So, for example, it was only after they fully embraced the homosexual community that they opened the channel for discussion. Even then, they never asked permission from the worldwide Anglican Communion.

So why, knowing the strategic nature of this particular battle, were some of the Singapore archbishops needing permission from the archbishop of Canterbury and their colleagues? Did they not know that once permission was denied, it was over? They would give Griswold and the American bishops the right to march on, propagating their gospel with no one holding them accountable and no one providing rescue for those in the United States refusing to compromise their ancient Christian faith.

Moses could see that this was, at best, a failed strategy. "I am afraid," Moses wrote Chuck, "[some Singapore archbishops] are of the view that nothing should be done before the Archbishops' Meeting in March next year."

For Moses, this was nothing less than a tragic development. He would have retired by then. His term as archbishop formally ended before the March meeting. How could he, in good conscience before God, step down having done nothing? What kind of bishop does not rise to defend the faith of Jesus Christ before the heretics of his day? Who refuses to protect the church of God from "savage wolves" who "distort the truth" and do not "spare the flock" (Acts 20:28–30)? How could he stand by and wait for a political, institutional remedy when he knew the institution had no authority in which to act?

Something had to be done. But what could he do?

If only he could sit down with his fellow Singapore archbishops in Kampala and speak his heart. As a matter of history, reformations are rarely born within the hierarchical structures of the church. More often than not they emerge from the grassroots where unknown leaders, in accordance with God's Word, and in obedience to the Holy Spirit, stand up in their generation to defend and proclaim the historic gospel of Jesus Christ. Were these days any different? Something had to be done. It would require an extra measure of grace because this was the wealthy and powerful Episcopal Church leading the rebellion. It was not some poor, remote Third World province. If that were the case, moral discipline would be rendered quickly, effectively.

But this was the mighty United States. The stakes were high, the potential cost to opposing provinces great. The probability of division shattering the visible unity of Anglicanism altogether real. Who would see the urgency of the moment and be willing to do something about it?

Time was running out.

Moses needed to speak his heart in Kampala. The Singapore archbishops needed to act together before George Carey was given public opportunity in March to deny permission for a US intervention.

• • •

On Thursday, October 21, 1999, Bishop John Rucyahana made a private call to Archbishop Moses Tay in Singapore. John was in Pawleys Island, South Carolina, that week. He had finished the "Come and See" tour with Frank Griswold. He had visited several US churches. He was about to fly out to St. Andrew's in Little Rock, Arkansas, to perform his first official duties as their bishop on Sunday, October 24 with the blessing of his archbishop. A new day was dawning, the first rays of morning light pushing back the covering of darkness, and John could feel it. The "Come and see" visit had made it self-evident that nothing—no amount of dialogue, no years of committee debates and resolutions—was going to detract the US church from their defiance of the gospel. John was ready to take up the mantle, fly to Little Rock, and formally welcome this American church under the care of an African bishop.

"Tell me, are you coming to Kampala next month?" John asked Moses Tay on the phone.

"Yes, I will be there!"

"Revisionism and rebellion in the US is contagious and must be stopped!"

"Yes, you are right," Moses replied.

"The situation in the US is worsening. The revisionist bishops say they will not change their actions and admit openly to what they are doing. Also, I met with the presiding bishop. He says he cannot discipline any of his bishops. He says, 'My hands are tied!' He also admitted to me that he has ordained practicing homosexuals. So the 'Come and see' visit was good after all. The revisionists are flagrant in their contempt for Scripture, and their 'in your face' attitude worked against them."

"What about the evangelical bishops? Are they willing to break communion with these heretics?"

"Some of them are coming to Kampala. We need to ask them point blank. If they will not, they are in danger of becoming accomplices with Frank Griswold."

"We must listen to them carefully and encourage them to this end," Moses replied.

"I have a request to make of you, Archbishop," John stated. "Before you retire, can we consecrate missionary bishops and send them back to the US to begin a new province? What do you say?"

"Yes! Can we do it in Kampala?"

"No, Archbishop Nkoyoyo of Uganda is not ready to do this himself. But we must do it soon. The longer we wait, the more we leave the American church in frustration with many being persecuted."

"I agree with you!" Moses said, and that was it. The rest of the phone conversation remained in confidence. The two of them talked for another ten minutes. When John put the phone down, he took the piece of paper he was writing on and slid it into his briefcase. We would later learn that he and Moses had fully discussed the particular details of a US intervention before March. It had to be done. Both men knew they had to go to Kampala with a specific strategy in hand for the Singapore archbishops to consider. Both men felt optimistic. Both men believed that unity was possible in Kampala. They sensed they were on the leading edge of a sovereign move of the Lord God Almighty who, as in times past, acted on behalf of His church. Both men felt a deep conviction in the Lord that the days of a great reformation of the gospel were coming both in the Anglican Communion and worldwide.

But they first had a Christian duty to perform as leaders before God and His people. It is the most solemn of all tasks required of God's ministers in those times when the church refuses to repent of her gross sins and immoralities. It is the act of standing apart, leading the people, and lifting their voice in bold and united proclamation: "Let all who love the Lord, and hate evil, come out of this more and more apostatizing church, lest they be partakers of the plague which will come upon her in the day of her visitation."[19]

For Moses and John, there could be no greater outcome from Kampala than the Singapore archbishops, in full agreement, taking on this Christian duty together. This was their hope. This was their heart.

CHAPTER 11

THE KAMPALA CONTINGENCY

When Dr. Packer spoke on "Unity in Truth: The Anglican Agony" at Latimer House in 1997, he lamented that tolerance of the intolerable had become the Anglican way, yet "felt that there was no alternative but to take G. K. Chesterton's advice and 'Go on gaily in the dark!'" These words, said the reporter, were given with tears in his eyes.[1]

Few understood that for Chuck Murphy, simply boarding the plane for Kampala, Uganda, had been a matter of obedience to God. Already that year, far beyond his comfort zone, he had flown to Singapore twice, Rwanda twice, and Nigeria once. In the privacy of his family and friends he had confided, "God knows my reluctance. He knows I want to please Him, to do the right thing. But it comes with a certain disquiet." Still he kept putting one foot in front of the other.

Now, here he was in Kampala, discussing with Archbishop Kolini just hours before the conference what God had laid on his heart during that flight over.[2] Could Kampala be the moment? If the orthodox Episcopal bishops would stand in biblical and apostolic authority and defend the Christian faith and rescue the church from this apostasy, then First Promise wouldn't be needed. "I believe it is time for me and First Promise to step back from primary leadership in this movement."

Kolini agreed, the best-case scenario was for the US bishops to lead the intervention, not Murphy. Not First Promise. "We must stand firm," the archbishop told Chuck. "We must wait and see what they will do. I am convinced they will reveal their true heart. If they come to Kampala in complete repentance and join us, then, yes, we will work with them. But if they will not join us from the heart, we must begin the new work in America without them. It is their decision. Where are they? What will they be asking of us?"

Kolini spoke with unwavering resolve, like the young David of Scripture. There could be only one outcome: to stop the US Goliaths in their mocking of God's Word and their treachery upon God's people with a gospel that cannot save. Yes, no doubt about it, Kolini wanted the four US bishops to step boldly into their God-given office of leadership. He believed it was their calling. But first they must pass the test. In Kolini's mind, there could be no hesitation, no more waiting yet another forty days and forty nights. The hour had come for action. Were these US bishops ready for that? Were they together?

• • •

The conference room was small, able to hold about a hundred. In the center of the room, long folding tables draped in white linen and arranged in a U shape provided enough seating for the conference participants. Behind them, around three sides, were two rows of chairs designated for invited guests and intercessors. At the front of the room, on a diagonal slant just off to the left, was the head table seating five, and to the right stood a lone chestnut-brown podium rigged for sound.

Eight archbishops attended—from Uganda, Rwanda, Congo, Burundi, Southeast Asia, Tanzania, South America, and Australia, plus two bishops representing Kenya and Sudan. Also present were the four US bishops, as well as other bishops from Africa and leaders from the US and Britain.

The archbishop of Uganda, Livingstone Nkoyoyo, rose from his chair at the head table and went to the podium. As host of the Kampala conference, he welcomed us to his native country, "the pearl of Africa," home of more Anglicans than any other country except Nigeria. He then proceeded to give the opening presentation. His theme dramatically set forth the great tragedy of our times: How is it that those who once brought the gospel to Africa have now abandoned it? The blatant rejection of the gospel in the US, Canada, and England was now spiritually impacting the daughter church of Uganda. Something had to be done, in prayer, by the sovereign hand of God.

"I believe," he concluded, "that God has chosen to gather us here to speak to us in a special way and to show us a way out of darkness and confusion for the purpose of restoring His church and to give Him His right place in our lives and the church. It is my humble prayer and call, therefore, that we allow God His time to speak, counsel, and teach us what type of church He wants us to lead."[3]

With that, he sat down. The irony struck hard: *It was time for the daughter to rescue her mother.*

Archbishop Moses Tay followed.

He gave historical background. He reviewed the events that led to the recent Singapore meeting in April and all that happened since. He made a clear statement: If the US would issue a moratorium on its practices, "we will all shut up. But until then, no more compromise. It is the worst word in the English language."

Then winsomely, passionately, Tay moved into the arena of greatest concern and possible division among the archbishops: a strategy for immediate action. "It is not a mistake that we are in Uganda, a land of martyrs who were willing to pay the price." The revisionists know how to act, he argued, time and time again, against the gospel, in defiance of Lambeth, and without care for Christians worldwide. But we don't act. We talk, postponing action. "Unless you turn off the tap and fix the leak," he reasoned, "don't bother to wipe up the floor!" With masterful precision, Tay concluded his address by urging his fellow bishops to stand up for what they believe: "Someone needs to lead, stand up and be counted."[4]

The four US bishops presented next. Moses Tay could not have set the stage any better.

Robert Duncan, bishop of Pittsburgh, was ready for the moment. He stood at his chair, not the podium, and spoke from his heart, deeply, compassionately, the words we had all hoped an American bishop would make. He did not come in arrogance, but humility, openly confessing "a broken heart at what has happened to my church, the Episcopal Church in the USA." His was an open, disarming confession. He did what sinners do at the time of conversion. He did what alcoholics do at the time of complete surrender. It was the exact message the archbishops needed to hear. He detailed a three-point appeal to them:

- "We in the Episcopal Church USA are in a deplorable state theologically."
- "There is no accountability among us." With that, Bishop Duncan declared the situation irreparable and the church incapable of self-correction.
- "The orthodox ECUSA bishops welcome intervention of foreign [archbishops] to protect the orthodox in the USA and to restore accountability in the communion."[5]

"We need your advice on how to proceed," he pleaded, addressing the archbishops. He confessed that there was nothing more that could be done by him or by any US bishop, and they needed an intervention by the archbishops overseas.

Then Duncan confidently concluded his formal appeal by declaring this was the "agreed position" of US bishops who belonged to the American Anglican Council (AAC). In other words, Bishop Duncan was not alone. His confession was not just personal. It was corporate. He was representing the united voice of evangelical colleagues both in the room and back in the United States. This fact alone was startling, miraculous. We had heard our AAC bishops unite under a common confession of biblical faith. But we had not heard them unite behind a common strategy to confront the American church. Without that strategy, they could not provide leadership. But with it, with this "agreed position," a new day was possible in the US.

These four men, it seemed, had come to Kampala as one man.

Bob Duncan sat down. Now all that remained was the affirmation of the other American bishops. It was a key moment.

One after the other, the three US bishops rose to tell their stories. Each one had great passion for gospel mission in their own dioceses . . . but not for gospel intervention from overseas.

The first one was Bishop Andy Fairfield. He confessed weakly that his own diocesan leaders were not in favor of his coming to Kampala. The second, Bishop Steve Jecko, made it absolutely clear that he would remain in the Episcopal Church until the very end. The third, Bishop Jim Stanton, lead bishop for the AAC, said he favored an intervention from overseas but only if the terms were suitable, negotiable. And then, after many words, it was over. The US bishops were done presenting. It didn't seem possible.

What about the "agreed position"?

Confusion thundered through the room. Fact: These men were not together. But more, these three bishops had quickly deserted Bob Duncan, implicitly denying any notion of an "agreed position" and humiliating him in front of everyone.

Nothing could be clearer, nothing more tragic: The US bishops were still divided. And if they were divided, the US coalition would remain divided. And if the US coalition could not stand with one heart and one voice, how could anyone expect the archbishops to respond favorably and in one accord to our plea for a US intervention?

For many in the room, that was it. The presentation to follow by Murphy and First Promise didn't matter. The Kampala meeting had already unraveled.

• • •

Nevertheless, First Promise was next to be heard. First Promise had come into existence precisely for this reason: The US bisops had refused to lead. Nothing more could be done unless the archbishops provided the leadership our bishops could not. It was our request now. But in Kampala, at this exact moment, we were beggars.

John Rodgers took the floor. No US clergyman had more respect and honor. He was the former dean and president of Trinity Episcopal School for Ministry, a gifted and pastoral systematic theologian, and a renowned champion for evangelical reformation in US Anglicanism. This elder statesman began his remarks by saying, "We come thankfully, humbly, with joy and sadness. You already know how bad things are in the Episcopal Church."[6] He outlined in detail the US rejection "to all of the historic doctrinal and moral norms of Anglicanism." He gently underscored the failure of the US bishops to offer "no plans that effectively redress this situation." Then he made his appeal to the archbishops, saying, "Action is needed. Timely action is urgent. Not to act would send a message that the Episcopal Church's errors do not really matter."

Dr. Rodgers increased the intensity of his message. He was asking for intervention now. It had to be now, governed not by political correctness but by the urgent need to defend this saving gospel.

Chuck Murphy did the same. He said, "We are an alliance of evangelical leaders across the US trying to provide leadership in a leadership vacuum. We are driven by a gospel vision for rebuilding the Anglican Church in North America in the twenty-first century."

Point by point, and in great detail, he exposed the arguments of those who opposed a US intervention: "They say, 'Unity first, truth follows,' but the Bible says truth produces unity! They say, 'An intervention will cause schism and God hates schism,' but the Bible says schism is a wrongful separation over secondary issues. We are not dealing with secondary issues, but the public denial of primary doctrines. They say, 'Wait, stay in, let it work out,' but we must resist the language of compromise and accommodation and insist on the biblical language of repentance."

He recounted David opposing Goliath, Elijah rebuking the prophets of Baal on Mount Carmel, and Nehemiah standing before King Artaxerxes requesting letters of authority that he might go and rebuild Jerusalem burned by fire. "Like Nehemiah," Chuck reasoned, "we are just cupbearers—clergy and lay leaders not bishops—asking for letters of authority from you, the archbishops, that we might rebuild the ruins of the US church."

With that, he proposed a specific action plan in which the archbishops would establish a missionary province in the US under their own authority.[7] This kind of intervention "would restore discipline and accountability in the US. It would grant Anglicans freedom from the tyranny of Episcopal structures that forcefully demand compliance to their heretical teachings. It would give us hope and a future in reaching our nation with the gospel."

Like John Rodgers, he asked for it urgently. "It's time now. Such action will take boldness and courage on your parts. No doubt your colleagues will criticize and scoff. It comes with the territory. It's what happens to leaders when they step out, obey God, and do the right thing. We need you to do the right thing. We need your leadership. We need it now."

And that was it. The cry for help was issued. As reformers, it presented a biblical call to action. As Anglicans, it presented a massive headache, because no one at First Promise held the office of an active US bishop. This fact alone had power to derail an intervention. If the archbishops acted now, in favor of First Promise, the AAC bishops would never support them and might work to oppose them. Back home in the States, the majority of prominent evangelical leaders would remain loyal to the AAC bishops. Like them, they would never endorse an intervention, even by archbishops, unless their bishops blessed it and led it.

This was the dilemma facing the archbishops in Kampala. To act now would further divide the faithful in the US. But not to act would allow the American crisis to spread its infection to the world.

"I am hard-pressed to believe they will act together. Not now," said Murphy privately to a number of us at the end of the first day. "The good news is that Archbishop Kolini is chairing this meeting. The bad news is that some archbishops will not act without support from US bishops. They will argue in favor of action, but not now, not until after all the archbishops meet in Portugal next March. That's what I think."

He was right.

• • •

On the morning of the second day, Archbishop Maurice Sinclair rose to address the conference. At first, he championed the principles that united us: He defended the gospel; he rejected the heresies; he was offended by Episcopal Church leaders who mocked the correction of Lambeth; he was moved with compassion for Anglicans in the US oppressed by the church; he believed a strategic intervention was the only solution. He was confident the Kampala archbishops would engage that intervention—just not now.

The room split in two.

He wanted no talk of intervention until after all thirty-eight archbishops met in March 2000. He called for a reasonable approach, moderated by patience and careful consideration. He urged that nothing be done without the proper consent of the archbishop of Canterbury. This meant it was essential for the Kampala archbishops to meet with him prior to March, share their concerns, get his endorsement, and make certain their decision for action was top priority at the March meeting in Portugal. In addition, he knew there were other archbishops, not in Kampala, who would fully support their position. They needed to be contacted. There was much work to be done before March. It required a tempered, systematic approach.

He then turned to the Scriptures. He knew the division in the room. He needed to challenge the logic of those demanding action without going through proper lines of Anglican authority. He turned to the parable of the wheat and tares in which the Lord Jesus stated a general principle that acting hastily uproots both the good and the bad. Then he applied the text to the moment: Do not act, not now. God will act in His time. We must wait, but not wait passively. There are things to do, steps to be taken. If we do it right, the archbishop of Canterbury will be on our side. He will stand with us. Eventually, we will win the day.

Many agreed. Many disagreed.

Other formal presentations followed. Midafternoon, the archbishops opened the floor for general discussion. The proponents for action rose first. Their first concern was that the parable of the wheat and tares had been misused. It did not apply to matters of church order and discipline, but end times, and the relationship between the church (the sons of the kingdom) and the world (the sons of the evil one.)[8] The Asian coalition strongly opposed the use of this parable as a means to delay a US intervention. Such an interpretation placed it at odds with clear apostolic teaching that requires instant correction and discipline for those inside the church who distort the truth of the gospel.

"Paul took action," argued one Asian clergyman. "He preached the gospel. He denounced and exposed heresy. He did not give in to false teachers for one minute. He gave this charge: 'Do not be yoked together with unbelievers. For what do righteousness and wickedness have in common? Or what fellowship can light have with darkness?' Therefore, the Scriptures teach, 'come out from them and be separate, says the Lord.' This is not a time for delay. It is time to act. We confront revisionists and demand repentance. We declare ourselves in broken communion. We beg archbishops to take bold action. Have moral courage in Jesus. Revisionists have another faith, not a Christian faith. God is on our side—let's do it!"[9]

The next to stand was a bishop from northern Uganda. In broken English, slowly but clearly, he told the story of the death of his wife, killed walking home from the market. She had stepped on a land mine. "We have enemies," he told us. "They come across our borders. They kill our people. They steal our young. They train them to kill. They misuse their bodies and their minds. Do you think we should sit back and wait to do something? No, we cannot. We must protect our children and our families every day."

He paused long enough for common sense to sink deep into our hearts. Then he continued. "We have an enemy destroying the church. It is the devil.

He is at work. Our people, our children, are at risk. Never sit back—always protect them. We have a saying in the African church: *Don't bring sheep into the sheep pen if there's a wolf inside*. No, this is wrong. First we must get rid of the wolf. Then bring the sheep."

He hung the image like a mural on the wall and then quietly sat down.

Bishop John Rucyahana spoke next. He had already given a formal address, but there was more to say. "I believe my dear friend and bishop from Uganda is right. We must deal with the wolf. The Episcopal Church has a different religion. They have abandoned the Christian faith. They have denied the authority of the Bible. They have no structures for accountability. How long can we hug Bishop Spong as a brother in Jesus when he denies the biblical testimony of Jesus? He is a heretic, yet he remains a bishop to this day. We are therefore in danger of making Anglican unity our priority. We cannot do that. We cannot wait upon the archbishop of Canterbury to give his permission to rescue these Christians from heretics. Please, I beg you, we cannot wait anymore. We must act. No more delays. For the sake of the people, we must do it. Therefore, I kindly request the archbishops to come up with a plan of action before we leave Kampala."

The other side was just as adamant.

They reiterated their strategy. More time was needed for a proper intervention. More archbishops were needed. It would strengthen the possibility for the archbishop of Canterbury to back the intervention in front of all the other archbishops. We needed to be patient. Trust the system. If we act before March, the archbishop of Canterbury might turn against us. We can't risk it. Plan for the US intervention after March.

Do it, but do it right.

Late in the day, the meeting adjourned. The archbishops went into private session to discuss the issues, pray together, render a decision, and write their final report. Before they left the room, one last voice trumpeted. It didn't seem possible that anyone could dictate upon the archbishops. But it happened.

US Bishop Jim Stanton set forth an ultimatum, hoping it would have the power to persuade. "If you do act," he said, marking the boundaries of his turf, "act together. We will not follow you if you divide."

Even the words themselves seemed to drop hard on the floor. How could the US bishops demand unity from the archbishops when they themselves were utterly divided and completely unable to lead the US coalition? It reeked of presumption. But this man knew what he was doing. There loomed an unspoken possibility that some archbishops, with or without their colleagues, would lead the US intervention before March. That wasn't negotiable. It needed to be nipped in the bud, now. So he said it once, loud and clear, for the archbishops to hear. For all of us to hear. If it happened, the US bishops would never support it.

•　•　•

The final report was read the next day.

On first impression, the one-page statement gave no possibility for any kind of intervention. Yet at the same time it did outline a vague strategy for the archbishops' meeting in March: "We share your distress. . . . we declare our solidarity with you. . . . we will inform our colleagues of the intolerable situation. . . . we will carefully document and commend a proposal to this meeting [of archbishops in March]." But what exactly did that mean? Were they going to intervene or not? There was simply too much ambiguity.[10]

Chuck Murphy asked for a brief recess. It was far better for First Promise leaders to vent their disappointment in private rather than public. It was a wise step as we took time to regroup, talk it out, and pray for next steps.

When the archbishops called us back to the meeting, Chuck spoke on our behalf. He asked for clarity on paragraph 2. His specific question: "Does this mean if some of the archbishops choose to act prior to March the rest of you would support them?" Journalist Dick Kim told the story:

> The [archbishops] nodded in the affirmative. . . . [they] specifically stated that they had a *plan*, and that they were fully committed to this work, but that they thought it best not to share the plan with us just yet . . . they did not want to talk about what they might or might not do. We were asked simply to TRUST them, and we affirmed that we would.[11]

So they had kept the Kampala Statement intentionally vague. They didn't trust the media. Yes, they had left room in paragraph 2 for an emergency intervention before March. But their primary focus was this secret plan, this effort to present to George Carey, the archbishop of Canterbury, a detailed but classified document that would go before all thirty-eight archbishops in March. Therefore, in Kampala, these eight archbishops, plus two bishops representing their provinces, wrote Carey a private letter. They requested immediate audience with him. They expressed their "concern over this grave situation."

It is our judgment that our Anglican unity cannot long be maintained without a significant strengthening of discipline and order. These necessary things are being ignored in ways that are unacceptable. Order can only be restored through repentance and by discontinuing teaching and practices which contradict our Scriptures and traditions.[12]

The letter was strong, confronting. But it never mentioned what they would do if their demands were not met. What then? There was little we could do. We told them we trusted them.

The Kampala Statement was released to the press that day. David Virtue, renowned Anglican journalist, took one look at it, found no substance, loaded his gun, and fired directly at First Promise:

Depending on whom you talk to, Kampala was a bust or a step on the road towards eventual schism in the worldwide Anglican Communion. Thoughtful observers see it more as two steps sideways. First there was Singapore, then Kampala. The Rev. Chuck Murphy and his First Promise supporters went to Uganda with hopes of a New Province. They left empty-handed. . . .

The Rev. Chuck Murphy, First Promise's articulate leader, is impatient to move forward, and one can't blame him. But he is white, Western, and a Type-A driven man with an agenda. His theological analysis of [the Episcopal Church] is correct, his prescription for its cure is open to discussion. One thing is for sure: he will not move the [archbishops] any faster than they are willing to move. That's a lesson I'm sure he's learned now that he has stuck his chin out twice—first in Singapore, now in Kampala.[13]

The media spin rendered Kampala a non-event, First Promise a failure, and the March meeting as the next great hope for change. But the media was the least of our problems. The heartache came from one of our own.

Bishop Jim Stanton left the Kampala meeting, flew to England, and gave an interview for the *Church of England Newspaper*. Stanton, bishop of Dallas, chair of the AAC bishops—which represented most evangelical and catholic bishops in the Episcopal Church—did what he should never have done. Of course, he opposed First Promise and the strategy for immediate intervention. He opposed any notion of archbishops acting on their own. He said he believed "whatever actions taken had to be in unison. What Lambeth called for was action by the [archbishops] as a whole."[14] But he did not stop there.

He crossed the line. He gave himself back to Frank Griswold. He said he was not alone. He gave the impression that the AAC bishops were unified in this matter. His exact words announced to the world "that the American bishops were keen to support their Presiding Bishop Frank Griswold." It made no sense, not after Kampala, not after we pledged ourselves to defend the nonnegotiable doctrines of Christian faith. There was a unity in Kampala on the nature of the problem in the Episcopal Church, but unity in support of Griswold? Impossible! How could this happen?

Confusion reigned after Kampala. What disappointment, what betrayal, what utter failure to see the leader of the AAC bishops running home to the US, tossing these words recklessly into the air, and then be found buried in the smiling embrace of Frank Griswold.

• • •

Archbishop Kolini gave the closing statement at the Kampala meeting. He rose from his chair at the head table, put down his glasses, and began. He spoke slowly, his tone solemn and resolved, his words crisp yet unexpected. Some of us imagined he would speak on the need for perseverance in times of trial. But instead, he prepared us for the day of action—the very thing we had asked for and didn't get. We were like soldiers taking off our battle gear. He was like a military commander telling us to put it back on.

> We must be bold, ready for action. We must be ready to accept the name "rebel" for Jesus Christ. You must thank the archbishops who are not afraid. You know, it is no accident that we are here in Uganda, the land of martyrs. We must remain obedient at any cost.

We are grateful for First Promise. You've opened our minds, made us think, and shown us the problem. You have given sacrificially for these meetings in Singapore and Kampala. God will not allow you to spend all that money, then go empty-handed. You have been called to be reformers. The church must be reformed. Thank you for your obedience. This is a problem that is bigger than the US. It is worldwide. The US should be a great country for God.

We must remember that Paul went to Jerusalem not knowing what would come. Would he die there? Would he be beaten and thrown in prison? We must be ready to go with him.[15]

But why "must we be ready to go with him" and why "be bold, ready for action"? Of all people, Archbishop Kolini knew the Kampala decision was to postpone the day of intervention, not prepare for it. We listened with politeness. We believed him. We trusted his leadership. We prayed that the promises made for a US intervention come spring would be kept. But what was he doing? Why was he saying this to us now in the midst of our disappointment? He seemed so confident, so ready.

Most of us didn't get it. A couple of us did.

•   •   •

It happened outside the Kampala hotel, on the last day, in the late afternoon. The restaurant had outdoor seating and just beyond, large decorative tents on the lawn with chairs and tables underneath to shield guests from the African sun. The archbishops had completed their deliberations. We had read and processed the Kampala Statement. A few of the participants had already left for the airport.

We were in a break before Emmanuel Kolini addressed us at the closing service. From the corner of my eye, I saw John Rucyahana come out of the hotel and beeline for Chuck Murphy. The two of them, along with Jim Beard, who administrated First Promise, headed for the tents, away from the crowds. I knew something was up. John saw me and motioned for me to follow.

He picked out a table and the four of us sat down. At once, I took out pen and paper to record the moment. He stopped me, said no, and instructed me to put it away. He had come with a message from Archbishops Tay and Kolini.

They supported the secret plan as presented by the archbishops. They would do everything in their power to assist Archbishop Sinclair in his efforts to convince the archbishop of Canterbury of their plan. They believed in reform from within the political structures. But without compromise to their endorsement, they fought for paragraph 2 and got it.

This meant there were two strategies in the same document. One inside the system seeking permission, collaboration, and unity. The other outside the system, acting without permission because they believed it was the apostolic duty of a bishop to defend the gospel in a time of crisis. God required it for the protection of His people and for the glory of His name.

They had sought counsel from their colleagues both in Singapore and Kampala. They had researched the situation thoroughly. Now it was a matter of conscience before God. There must be a response without further consensus. They made their position clear to the archbishops in closed session and together with their colleagues crafted the final wording of paragraph 2: "among us are those ready to respond to specific and urgent situations which may arise in the months before the [archbishops'] Meeting in Portugal."

This was the leadership of Tay and Kolini. Two strategies, both bound together, one inside, one outside, working not in opposition to each other but in alignment for the common cause of the gospel.

John Rucyahana leaned toward us. We were to tell no one. No reporters. No one at the conference. No one back home save essential personnel. No announcements in our churches. No whispers in secret to people who would shout it from the rooftops. No e-mails that could be copied and sent to the wrong people. John said he knew how hard it was for Americans to keep quiet in a world of instant communication. But he was not giving us an option. If word got out, the mission might fail. The forces brought to bear against a US intervention would be swift and overpowering. Were we up to the task? Could we keep quiet?

We swore to secrecy.

Then he said it: Tay and Kolini were prepared to act. We were to go home and make preparations. They had set the date for the end of January. The place, Singapore. We were to document all "specific and urgent situations" as stated in paragraph 2. They would review them at that time and then make the final decision. If they opted to act, they would need names, at least two, from among our clergy.

They had to be men above reproach and able to stand the test of national and international scrutiny. One flaw and it was over. The press, like sharks to blood, would splash it across the tabloids and compromise the mission.

Bring the men to Singapore, John said. If the archbishops approved them, they would consecrate them missionary bishops from their respective provinces. Then they would send them back to the US as fully Anglican bishops outside the legal jurisdiction of the Episcopal Church and Frank Griswold. These new bishops would then oversee the clergy and churches in "specific and urgent situations," and a new day would begin. From that point on it would be possible to be fully Anglican in America and not Episcopalian, freed from those who deny Christ publicly, and free to preach Him everywhere without shame. That was the plan.

Tay and Kolini believed Archbishop Nkoyoyo would join them, but they were not sure. There was much to do, even in their own provinces. Nothing was guaranteed. We must remain in prayer, John said, and work hard. "The devil will come against us. He does not want us to act. We must be prepared."

We told John we already had names. The First Promise steering committee had gone through a selection process in case the archbishops decided to act in Kampala.

John told us to send a letter to Tay and copy Kolini and Nkoyoyo.

Chuck mentioned names of retired bishops who would want to go to Singapore and support the archbishops in this action.

John hesitated. Once again, he reiterated the absolute essential requirement to keep quiet. We must swear these men to secrecy, John said.

Chuck agreed and asked if Archbishop Sinclair would know about this and support it.

John responded quickly. First, Maurice Sinclair signed the Kampala Statement with paragraph 2, so he knows the possibility of it. All the archbishops do. Second, Kolini remains the chair of the Kampala archbishops, not Sinclair who serves as secretary, and he will lead the effort of engaging the secret plan with the archbishop of Canterbury.

Everything was in order. We understood. We prayed together and left for the closing service.

I knew that very moment I would never forget this meeting under the tent. I knew for certain the Lord had answered our prayers. He had raised up leaders able to confront the rebellion of our time and willing to risk their positions of great authority to do so. They had made the decision to act on our behalf and out of obedience to the Lord Jesus Christ.

It moved me beyond words. This decision could cost Tay and Kolini everything. I could hear it in John's voice. I could see it in his eyes.

Moments later, at the closing service, I heard it again in Emmanuel Kolini as he gave his final remarks. He was preparing us for action because action was coming. He was telling us that it would come with cost because following Jesus Christ always comes with cost. He told us to be ready. But he was doing more than telling us.

He was about to take the step and show us.

There would be no more meetings, no more politics, no more statements, no more endless waiting. The date was set. It was time to act in Christ.

• • •

By mid-December, the news leaked. During the last weeks of December Archbishop Sinclair fired off e-mail exchanges with John Rodgers and Chuck Murphy, warning against any consecrations before the March meeting of archbishops. Both responded that they would not lead such but only follow the direction of the archbishops.[16] And then a strange, almost deafening silence followed. E-mail traffic stopped completely.

By the second week of January, less than three weeks before Singapore, we didn't know if the meeting was still on. Neither Murphy nor Rodgers had heard from Kolini since Kampala or Tay since mid-December. Both were convinced the leak had reached the highest levels of leadership in the Anglican Communion and that Tay and Kolini were under the gun to back down.

Rumor had it that Archbishop Nkoyoyo had already decided not to go to Singapore. Rucyahana pursued it. He went to Uganda, talked with Nkoyoyo, and found that it was true. International pressure was mounting. Nkoyoyo said he might send one of his bishops but wasn't sure.

The moment Rucyahana arrived back at his home in Rwanda we talked by phone. We fully expected him to say it was off, but he didn't. He said he had talked with Tay and Kolini. The meeting was on. We were to go to Singapore.

But we knew something wasn't right. We asked, would Kolini be there?

John said he didn't know. He told us to walk by faith and trust the Lord.

But the plane tickets were nonrefundable, we said, and expensive. Should we wait?

No, he responded adamantly. We must not give in. The devil works hard to block our going to Singapore. We must rebuke him at all cost.

Murphy countered, saying the devil might torment us worse if Archbishops Nkoyoyo and Kolini did not attend. This would make Moses Tay the only consecrating archbishop. He retires in mid-March. That means no archbishop would stand to defend this action against the firestorm of worldwide criticism after March. The new missionary bishops would have no credibility, no archbishop, no province in the global South to call home, and no authority to enter the US and effect a proper intervention. That spelled disaster. So why do it? Murphy argued. It would be far better to call it off, step back, regroup, and rethink our position.

For John Rodgers and Chuck Murphy this was no small matter.

Before Kampala, the First Promise steering committee had completed the selection process. They chose these two men to serve as missionary bish-ops if asked. Both men were reluctant at first. Rodgers was retired. Murphy had always said no in the past. But this time, after praying for guidance, after talking with their wives and family, they agreed. "You cannot ask for intervention and then, if they ask you, say no."[17]

Both men were ready but both were concerned. Without Kolini, they argued, the burden of this mission would rest completely on Moses Tay's successor, and that was not right. There must be another archbishop for this mission to succeed in an Anglican world. Without Nkoyoyo, that left Kolini.

Would Rucyahana talk with Kolini again?

Buy the tickets, Rucyahana urged. He had no reason to believe Kolini had succumbed to outside pressure. He would talk with him. He would call when he knew more. But we must keep on the move, he said. Remain in prayer. For the sake of the gospel, the Lord will not let this mission fail. That was enough for Rodgers and Murphy. That day they bought the plane tick-ets, all of them. Murphy went through the list of names with Rucyahana one more time. They made some adjustments and that was it. A few days later, the tickets arrived. One of them, a roundtrip from Kigali to Singapore, bore the name of Emmanuel Kolini.

But would he use it?

Should he use it? He holds one of the highest offices in the Anglican Communion. He is the face of the province of Rwanda to the world. He is instrumental in bringing foreign money and resources both to the church and to Rwanda post-genocide. He sits on an international commission dealing with HIV-AIDS, the rampant killer of Africa. He is on endless committees nationally with both church and government for reconciliation in Rwanda. How could we expect him to go to Singapore for us? For Kolini to be effective, he must be credible. One step on that plane and he risks that credibility.

Internationally, he could jeopardize his influence with foreign investors, especially American and British investors. If that happens, if monies are cut off, the suffering of the poor multiplies exponentially. What greater pressure could Kolini bear than this? He told us in Kampala he might be rejected by other archbishops, even the archbishop of Canterbury. He expected it. He said it was part of the cost of defending the gospel. He didn't mind.

But this wasn't just about him. It was about his office and the political power behind his office to attract resources from all over the world to aid in the recovery of Rwanda. How could he risk hurting the poor, the orphan and widow, the sick and dying, the ability to get clean water, decent nutrition, medicines, education, and housing for the poorest of the poor? What does he do? What was the Lord saying to him? Should he use the ticket?

By the time we boarded the plane for Singapore in late January, we still didn't know whether Kolini was coming or not. In fact, we believed he wasn't. We had enough information pieced together to conclude he had worked a deal with Nkoyoyo. We believed both men wanted to show their support for Tay and the consecrations. We believed they were going to send one of their bishops to represent them. It would be just enough to get the work done and still lessen the political impact to their respective offices.

It was the best of both worlds.

"It makes sense," Murphy said en route to Singapore. "These men are leaders in the Third World. They have got to stay focused. I understand that. It's what I'd do if I were in their shoes. To be honest, I'm amazed at how much time and effort these archbishops have given us in recent years. It is truly remarkable. Think about the problems they face back home. Think about our problems in the US. It doesn't compare.

"So don't get me wrong, I am grateful for these archbishops and whatever they decide to do to help us. But that said, if we're right about this, if Kolini doesn't come, it changes the end result. In the short run, I think the consecrations will make national and international headlines. The media will jump all over it. But six weeks later, it will be gone, a flash in the pan, forgotten. For me personally, it's not a way forward. Without Kolini to see it through after Tay retires, for me, I think it's a recipe for failure.

"If John Rodgers wants to go through with it, fine. If Moses Tay chooses to consecrate someone else, fine. I am not the one driving the decisions. But I am speaking personally now. I just don't think I can do it, that's all."

• • •

Hours before John Rodgers boarded the plane for Singapore, the phone rang. It was a dear friend, the Rev. Quigg Lawrence, rector of Church of the Holy Spirit, Roanoke, Virginia.

The situation was dire. Back in September, Quigg's bishop, Neff Powell, met with him, his staff, and elected leaders. Following the meeting, the bishop issued a letter requesting an amicable separation on the grounds of irreconcilable differences with Quigg and the church. Powell cited that Quigg was too set in his conservative beliefs. He was convinced Quigg would never support the Episcopal Church's irreversible pro-gay, pro-choice agenda. The letter shocked Quigg. What had he done to provoke such an action?

Church of the Holy Spirit was the second largest church in the diocese in attendance — with seven hundred on a Sunday morning — and in giving. He took the letter to the elected leaders of the church. They decided not to act but to pray. A month later, the bishop's office issued a second letter requesting a financial pledge for the year 2000. But how could the bishop ask for a pledge and an amicable separation at the same time?

It didn't make sense. It was best to put the pledge on hold.

The bishop reacted. He issued a formal letter pronouncing Quigg and Church of the Holy Spirit out of the Episcopal Church without a hearing, without a fair trial. If they wanted to return, they would have to conform to his demands. For starters, all church property belongs to the diocese. But Church of the Holy Spirit had a unique legal agreement that the bishop's lawyers could not override. If the church wanted to stay, the bishop said, they would have to turn over all legal rights to building and property.

That wasn't all. Seven other demands followed.

It was now January 2000. Quigg met with his leadership again. They knew it was over. The bishop had left no room for negotiations. In Quigg's language, they had been thrown from the Episcopal Church train without trial or real charge. They were not about to hand over their property. They were not about to compromise the gospel of Jesus Christ. But it seemed a new day had come in the Episcopal Church. The bishops had a new sense of wielding their power. If clergy and church leaders refused to submit to the new teachings of Frank Griswold, John Spong, and Neff Powell, even though their teaching rebelliously and publicly contradicted the Bible and historic Christianity, then out they go. Just like that.

"I felt desperate," Quigg said. "I didn't know what to do. So I called John Rodgers."

John picked up the phone and listened to Quigg's story. It was perfect timing for Singapore. By ousting Quigg and the church, Neff Powell had triggered the second paragraph of the Kampala Statement, which promised "parishes and clergy under threat because of their loyalty to the Gospel and to Anglican standards must be supported and we [the archbishops] will play our part in such support." John Rodgers had a file folder full of clergy and churches "under threat." Some had already left the Episcopal Church. Others were on the brink. But this was different. This was an act of aggression by the bishop.

"Quigg, I can't tell you what is happening," John said, having been sworn to secrecy. "But I think God is about to answer your prayers. Just hold on another few days. I am about to leave the country and I am pretty sure there is nothing to worry about. God is moving!"[18]

John Rodgers put the phone down. He knew he had given Quigg hope. But was that the right thing to do? Deep inside, did he have hope? John knew the story. Kolini might not be in Singapore. Without him, there would be no consecrations, no US intervention, no help for Quigg, and no help for clergy and parishes under the tyranny of heretical bishops. Without Kolini, Singapore was nothing more than another meeting.

John was tired of meetings. He had been to more than he cared to count. In his mind, it was time for action. No one needed another carefully crafted, politically sensitive statement coming out of Singapore promising another meeting in a few months that might result in action. But this was his fear.

He didn't want to travel halfway around the world and come back empty-handed. He didn't want to come home and hear the phone ring, only to find Quigg, or some other clergy, asking what happened. Then John would have to confess, *I gave you false hope. We have to wait for the March meeting of archbishops in Portugal. Maybe that meeting will be the one that triggers a US intervention. Sit tight, be patient. We have to trust the Lord.*

Quigg didn't want to hear that. John didn't want to say it. Quigg was right; he had just been kicked off the Episcopal train. What he needed now was for John Rodgers to come back from Singapore and say, "Quigg, here comes a gospel train sent from our dear brothers and sisters in Rwanda and Southeast Asia! They love us. They are welcoming us on board in the name of Jesus!"

Anything less and flying to Singapore was a big fat waste of time.

CHAPTER 12

THE "SINGAPORE SIX" IRREGULARS

At the genocide in 1994, the whole world stepped back and no one came to Rwanda's aid. We will never stand back when others are similarly threatened, physically or spiritually.

— EMMANUEL KOLINI, FRIDAY JANUARY 28, 2000[1]

W e went to the Singapore Airport to pick up the Africans. Most of the US team stayed at the hotel, their mood expectant. All of us believed Kolini was on the plane. I found the customs area. Standing outside, I leaned against the glass wall, straining to find a familiar face. Nothing but a sea of people. A few minutes passed. I saw Harriet Rucyahana first, then John. I waved, but they didn't see me. I kept my eyes on John. He looked tired but confident, assured—or was I misreading him? He turned back with half a smile and started to talk to someone behind him. I couldn't see who. I waited until the people shifted. For a brief second, I thought I saw him. I looked again, knowing, deep down, I didn't expect him. Why put the church of Rwanda at risk? Why put himself at risk? The crowd shifted again and I was filled with surprise. There he stood, tall and regal in appearance, casually talking with John. Next to him, his wife, Freda. It was then I realized the Lord had answered our prayers. By a sovereign act of God's mercy, Kolini was in Singapore.

• • •

We met in a conference room at St. Andrew's Cathedral. Tay, Kolini, and Rucyahana sat together with their wives next to them. Across the large wooden table sat John Rodgers, Chuck and Margaret Murphy.[2] Kolini opened in prayer. Tay then welcomed us, saying, "This is a historic occasion. It is the beginning of a reformation, and reformations never begin with consensus." He had two letters in front of him. One from Maurice Sinclair, the other from George Carey. Both archbishops were trying to stop Tay and Kolini from consecrating Rodgers and Murphy as bishops to the US. Carey argued it would be a "serious blow to the Communion" and an "irresponsible act." Sinclair said it would betray the "expressed conviction and advice" of the Kampala Statement. Both men urged, wait for the March meeting of archbishops in Portugal. Consider Moses Tay's retirement and his successor. Suspend the consecrations.

Tay and Kolini disagreed. They were done with church politics. If George Carey was concerned about a "serious blow to the Communion," then he needed to consider why Griswold remained in office, why Spong was never rebuked, and why the US Episcopal Church refused to comply with the Lambeth resolutions. For these reasons, the only "irresponsible act" was not taking responsible action to discipline the US church. It was long overdue. Taking action now, in Singapore, might already be too little, too late. Didn't Carey know that the Communion was severely divided and on the brink of an impending split?

They continued down the list of objections.

Kolini challenged Sinclair's reading of the Kampala Statement. In fact, it did provide for pastoral action before March. Moreover, the Kampala archbishops had appointed him to chair this movement. As chairman, Kolini had every right to call the meeting in Singapore and to act according to his conscience.

Tay then responded to the matter of his retirement and the concern for his successor. This too was a matter of conscience. How could Moses Tay stand before the Lord on the last day having done nothing to hold the church accountable? Was he a "naughty boy" doing something before retirement? Or was he a prophet sent by the Lord in a time of unspeakable apostasy? Tay knew what he had to do with or without the blessing of his colleagues. Still, he did call his successor. He shared his heart. His successor listened, prayed, and gave his consent with one stipulation: What he'd do after Tay left office would be up to him.

There was one more objection. Do they act now, in Singapore, or do they wait for the archbishops' meeting in March? Kolini made a general observation: Remember Griswold and Spong acted without ever consulting Carey, and then got support over time. Evangelicals are afraid to act without Carey's approval. Tay echoed this view, saying if they waited for March they would end up asking Carey for permission, which he would never give. How could he? He clearly believed such an action would be a "serious blow to the Communion." But if they acted now, without consulting him, then the archbishops' meeting in Portugal would be forced to deal with their action and, more critically, the US problem that caused it.

It was time to act. Both men were convinced of it. The objections deepened their resolve.

Moses made the announcement: Rodgers and Murphy would be consecrated as bishops under their authority. He proposed an evening service, six o'clock that night in the cathedral. Kolini agreed. The decision was made. We spent the next hour reviewing all legal matters for the proper consecration of Anglican bishops. We worked out the details for the service. We talked about the reactions that would soon come from every corner of the globe. And then we sat back and dreamed of the future as Anglican missionaries in America, unencumbered by the Episcopal Church, able to fully preach the Lord Jesus Christ without hindrance. The more we talked, the more it sank in. This was no small event. On this night, in just a few hours, two Anglican archbishops would stand before the Lord and change the course of history.

• • •

I was struck by the simplicity of it all. A handful of worshippers sat quietly in the first three rows of the cavernous St. Andrew's Cathedral. The organist played the ancient hymns as if the church were packed with a thousand voices lifted in praise. The communion table was lit with a spray of brilliant lights from above and just behind it, on the back wall, an enormous golden crown was painted, or maybe on tapestry, with the words above it, "Jesus Christ, King of Kings," and below it, "Lord of Lords." As I looked behind me, a sea of empty pews stretched to the far back, bathed in a gentle light. Electric fans hung from the vaulted ceiling, cooling the warm Malaysian air. The entry doors stood wide open. I imagined the media storming in with reporters and film crews ready to pounce on the story, but it didn't happen. They didn't know. And I wondered how many great moments of history were like this, perfectly calm, protected under a cloud cover of privacy and utterly common to the casual observer. But this night was far from common. Sometime tomorrow we would come out of the hurricane's eye. The Anglican world would hear of this event at St. Andrew's Cathedral in Singapore and suddenly be hit by the fierce storm of its own making.

At the opening hymn, we all stood. The two archbishops processed into the cathedral with Bishop John Rucyahana and three retired bishops, Alex Dickson, Fitz Allison, and David Pytches. The media would soon call them the "Singapore Six." John Rodgers and Chuck Murphy sat together in the front left pew during the first part of the service. At the time of the sermon, Kolini ascended the lofty pulpit just right of center. He offered two main points: We are called to preach the gospel, and we are called to be obedient to the Holy Spirit.[3] After giving a general exposition, he remembered the prophet Samuel and his fear of anointing young David as king. Samuel knew he would be killed for this act if King Saul found out. And Saul, said Kolini, "always wanted to please men rather than pleasing God . . . that was his trouble." His sermon closed making the obvious comparison: Was he, like Samuel, afraid to lay his hands on these two men in the face of great Anglican opposition? Was his heart set on pleasing men rather than God?

These were his actual words:

> Brothers and sisters, this New Year, new century, new millennium, are we going to please men or are we going to please God? It is not easy. . . . I must work with you in the gospel. . . . I am not afraid of laying my hands. I don't feel guilty. I walk with you. . . . if I do the opposite I would be hurting myself, my God, and the Spirit of God. It is my prayer that you preach the gospel. The Father has sent Jesus Christ as our Lord and Savior. He is calling you to be His servants to preach the gospel at any cost. . . . We shall be praying for you. May the Lord bless the Church in America.

With that, he descended from the pulpit and called Rodgers and Murphy forward. The two archbishops examined them publicly. A few minutes later, the Singapore Six gathered around the two men and laid their hands on them. Each of the six knew the cost of this moment. They had prayed for God's leading. They knew it was better to obey the Lord and risk it all—their jobs, their reputations—than to remain compromised and accountable on the day of the Lord's appearing. It was with this depth of conviction that they first laid hands on John Rodgers, then Chuck Murphy, and consecrated them Anglican bishops.

In that moment, Rodgers belonged to the province of Southeast Asia; Murphy, the province of Rwanda. Both men were officially out of the US Episcopal Church. Neither of them posed a threat to the Anglican Communion as long as they served as bishops within their respective provinces. But that was not going to happen. As they rose from their knees, Tay and Kolini boldly declared the US an open mission field. The Episcopal Church had failed to defend the gospel by willfully introducing "erroneous and strange doctrines contrary to God's Word." For this reason, they were setting apart Rodgers and Murphy as bishops to the US and missionaries to a country that once, not long ago, sent evangelists proclaiming Jesus to them.

Like it or not, the global South had suddenly invaded the global North.

As a first act of celebration, we received Communion. Then, together, we recessed to the front of the cathedral, singing "Great Is Thy Faithfulness." As we walked outside singing the final verse, a handful of people on the street stopped to look at us, and then walked on. Of course, they had no idea what had just happened inside. Nor did anybody, not yet. The press release would go out sometime the next day. For a little while longer, we held the moment to ourselves like parents holding their newborn before telling the world the good news. It gave us a night, and then Sunday morning church, to thank the Lord for His mercy.

•　　•　　•

FOR IMMEDIATE RELEASE: *New Bishops from Africa and Asia Consecrated and Sent to the United States.* An international group of Anglican Archbishops and Bishops today consecrated the Rev. Charles H. Murphy III and the Very Rev. Dr. John H. Rodgers Jr., as Bishops who will be released to minister in the United States of America. . . .

[They] have agreed to step forward at this moment of crisis in an initiative aimed at reversing a 30-year decline of 30 percent in the membership of the Episcopal Church of the U.S.A. . . . .

The Archbishops and Bishops agree that this is a Gospel issue, not a political issue. It is an action to re-establish the unity that has been violated by the unrebuked ridicule and denial of basic Christian teaching. They are convinced it is time to give the faithful in the US a place to remain Anglican. . . . The sending of these bishops back to the United States is offered as an interim step in an ongoing effort to lead the Episcopal Church back to its biblical foundations.

A few quotes were added, as well as listing the names of the Singapore Six. We sent it before noon, which meant, with the time change, it arrived in the States late Saturday night, long after the deadline for Sunday morning papers. Essentially, most people wouldn't hear the news until Monday.

Tay and Kolini met with us Sunday midafternoon for the first order of business. They wanted us to hear their response to Archbishop George Carey. They assumed the press release was already on his desk and believed their letter should be faxed immediately, hopefully reaching him at nearly the same time.

Dear George:

The consecrations in Singapore are an interim action to provide pastoral assistance and nurture to faithful individuals and congregations. The apostasy of the "12 Theses," the continued rejection of the Lambeth Resolutions by a number of dioceses in the Episcopal Church . . . have gone unrebuked as the boundaries of Christian and Anglican Faith have been notoriously breached. The unity of Anglicanism must be understood as grounded not merely in polity but fundamentally in the historic Faith entrusted to us. Far from being an attack on the Communion, this action is an affirmation of the unity of Anglican doctrine and faith which has been frequently and flagrantly violated in the Episcopal Church.

It is precisely our irresponsible inaction that has allowed this division to continue. It is the violation of the Faith that makes unity impossible. This pastoral step establishes no new entity but simply gives pastoral care until faithful doctrine and [church] discipline have been restored. We believe this action will greatly assist the [archbishops] in March to address these issues.

[We are] sure you would agree that this is a pastoral and Gospel issue and not a political one, and should be treated accordingly. Rather than being a serious blow to the Communion, we see this action as reflecting a serious resolve to uphold the Lambeth Resolutions. . . .

Any strategy that seeks to ground the unity of the Anglican Communion with its foundation in political accommodation rather than in the essentials of the Christian Faith is doomed. Only an unapologetic and firm insistence in the Faith entrusted to us will keep us together.

Yours in Christ,
The Most Revd. Dr. Moses Tay
The Most Revd. Emmanuel Kolini

A copy of the letter was sent to Archbishop Sinclair. Next, Tay and Kolini wanted to talk about strategically deploying Rodgers and Murphy in the US. But this, they decided, should wait for morning.

•   •   •

We came to the meeting wanting to understand the word *interim*. How do we implement the statement the archbishops made to George Carey: "an interim action to provide pastoral assistance and nurture to faithful individuals and congregations . . . until faithful doctrine and [church] discipline have been restored"? Strategically, Tay and Kolini knew three major events were about to happen: first, the March meeting of archbishops in Portugal; second, the US bishops' meeting in California soon after Portugal; and third, the Episcopal Church's summer General Convention in Denver. Tay and Kolini wanted to know how each of these meetings would respond to the Singapore event. Would doctrine and discipline be restored? Ideally, the archbishops' meeting in Portugal would diagnose the severe division in the Anglican Communion and call the Episcopal Church, and those like them, to immediate repentance. If they did repent and comply with the Lambeth resolutions, then the Singapore event would have made its mark.[4]

In the minds of Tay and Kolini, every opportunity for repentance should be given.

For this reason, they said, they established an "interim," where Rodgers and Murphy would not serve liturgically as bishops. This meant no confirming or ordaining, not until the Episcopal Church refused the opportunity to repent. At that point, the interim would be over and the new bishops would be released to do their work in the US. With this principle in place, Tay and Kolini still wanted Rodgers and Murphy fully deployed during the interim to preach the gospel in the US, to receive churches wanting to remain Anglican but not Episcopalian, and to start new churches with a missionary passion for reaching the lost.

For John and Chuck, this was exceedingly good news. Both men had churches and clergy ready to come on board. John thought of Quigg Lawrence in Roanoke, Virginia; William Beasley in Chicago; and a half dozen more from around the country. Chuck thought of King Cole in North Carolina; TJ Johnston in Little Rock, Arkansas; and again, a stack of requests on his desk back home in South Carolina.

It was then that John Rucyahana said, "In Singapore, we have acted. Now we must perform. Go home, set strategies. God is calling us into the mission field. We are not called for politics. Go and win people to Jesus. Plant new churches for Jesus. We are free. Now, how will we use our freedom?" He spelled out the dangers, warning us that distractions would come from all sides. Many would oppose and ridicule. The temptation to respond would be great. But we were not to lose focus. Our job was to go home, preach the Lord Jesus Christ, start churches, and build a missionary movement that would last for years to come.

These were the orders given us from the global South leaders.

From my journal—personal:

What would have happened if Tay and Kolini had not acted? I only know this: Our nine-year-old granddaughter Samantha was diagnosed with cancer late last August. For five months, she went through a brutal regimen of chemotherapy. We almost lost her after the fifth treatment. This method of attacking cancer is invasive, violent. But that's the thing about cancer. You can't stand back and let it attack the body. Something has to be done quickly and aggressively. Love absolutely demands it. Today, on January 31, the medical tests came back and reported that our Sammy was cancer free. We could not contain our tears, our joy. The Lord spared her life. Neither of us could imagine her story if no action was taken. How can anyone allow cancer in the body of their own children, or in the body of Christ, to go unattended?

Who does not rise up and defend their own?

• • •

Archbishop Carey was visiting South Africa. He released a brief press statement on February 1.

> The Archbishop of Canterbury has expressed his regret that this action has been taken ahead of the meeting of the [archbishops] of the Anglican Communion in March. . . . It has come as a grave disappointment to the Archbishop, as it is his view that such consecrations are irresponsible and irregular and only harm the unity of the Communion.[5]

US Presiding Bishop Frank Griswold went on the offensive.

He wrote to all Episcopal bishops, copying his letter on e-mail list serves that reached the world: "Their press release says that they have 'agreed to step forward at this moment of crisis. . . . ' I am appalled by this irregular action and even more so by the purported 'crisis' that has been largely fomented by them and others, and which bears very little resemblance to the church we actually know, which is alive and well and faithful. . . ."[6] His message was simple and strategic: *We are healthy!* To the Associated Press he said, "These two men have been ordained outside all formal structures of the Anglican world." The *Washington Post* quoted him, saying, "The church in this country is far from being in chaos and conflict. The Episcopal Church is alive, well, rising and very much focused on its mission of taking Christ to a needy world."[7]

Over the Episcopal News Service he beamed with hope. Reflecting on the archbishops' meeting in March, he said he would give them "a more balanced impression of the Episcopal Church, a church far from being in chaos." He added, "I go to the meeting with an open mind, ready for revelations of the Spirit, ready for the wisdom of the [archbishops]. And I will listen with great care to their stories of mission."[8]

Frank Griswold got out in front, formidably using the media to his own advantage. He spun the word *crisis* until people finally heard the good news that the Episcopal Church was "alive and well." Only quietly and only once did he publish his severe indictment against the action of Tay and Kolini as "dangerous fundamentalism . . . which threatens to turn our God of compassion into [an] idol of wrath."[9]

Carey and Griswold were among the first to react to the Singapore consecrations. Gustav Niebuhr of the *New York Times* called it "an event that sent shock waves among the world's Anglican churches."[10] As expected, those shock waves suddenly produced press statements from across the globe:

We are disappointed that our friends acted against our clear advice and we cannot approve such a step as they have taken at this time.
Archbishops Sinclair of the Southern Cone,
Mtetemela of Tanzania and Goodhew of Sydney[11]

Neither of the two bishops consecrated in this irregular service have authority to minister in the congregations of this diocese.
Bishop Lipscomb of Southwest Florida[12]

From the inception of our church there has always been one binding authority; one that is seldom challenged where it is specific: the Constitutions and Canons.
Bishop Theuner of New Hampshire[13]

Bishops are not intercontinental ballistic missiles, manufactured on one continent and fired into another as an act of aggression. The recent irregular ordination in Singapore is, in my opinion, an open and premeditated assault on Anglican tradition, catholic order and Christian charity. . . . They created bishops in a way that is designed to split the church.
Archbishop Peers of Canada[14]

Some real smart [archbishops] have come up with a novel idea. Let's start an Anglican Airlines and fly in peculiar bishops for special occasions. . . . A bishop who matches your bias will arrive from the sky . . . and you can rack up frequent schism miles. . . . When I look at the modernists in Singapore and their new age Episcopal supporters in the USA, I am keenly aware of being an old traditionalist. A fossil. Someone who has respect for historic episcopacy.

Bishop Swing of California[15]

These new bishops . . . Their ordination was a power grab by an antiquated minority. . . . Anyone who elevates their prejudices to the position where they are defended as the will of God is evil. Anybody who justifies their denigration of another person's being based upon a quotation from an ancient sacred text called the Word of God is simply out of touch with contemporary scholarship.

Bishop Spong of Newark[16]

This is a brief sampling, but it captures the deep emotion of the times. Tay and Kolini had made a direct and violent assault on church order. For some, this was the very heart of Anglicanism. The force of criticism from all parts of the Communion made us wonder if Tay and Kolini would be instantly tried and removed from office. But as sharp as the criticism was, it actually worked in their favor. The Anglican world was now compelled to know why they did it. Eventually, over time, Tay and Kolini believed their voice would be heard over the sound of their accusers. People would know the truth: The church is not built on canons and constitutions. It's built on the "faith that was once for all entrusted to the saints." It's founded on the *sovereign authority and inspiration of Holy Scripture.* This is the heart of Anglicanism!

The archbishop of Canterbury had yet to issue his formal response. With all respect, no matter what he said, no matter what he did, the truth would remain: Church order had no meaning as long as the classic doctrines of Scripture were being formally denied and publicly ridiculed by Anglican bishops and archbishops. For this reason, something had to be done. Tay and Kolini were simply the ones who did it.

• • •

His letter, issued on February 17, went to all bishops in the Anglican Communion.[17] Before rendering judgment, Carey presented three arguments. Concerning the "interim" nature of the act, he wrote, "I fear that this pragmatic view of the episcopacy does not accord with the tradition of the Church." Second, he raised the matter of territorial integrity, saying that it "is a most important element of due episcopal order and collegiality." He stated that this principle "reaches back at least to the Council of Nicea" in 325.[18] In both points, he was defending matters of historic church order.

His third argument brought accusation against the legality of the consecrations, saying that "neither the constitution of the Province of Southeast Asia nor that of the Episcopal Church Rwanda . . . have been followed." This was an unfortunate declaration, since both provinces complied fully with the letter of their respective constitutions. With that, the archbishop addressed the Singapore consecrations:

> Therefore, whilst recognizing John Rodgers and Charles Murphy as
> faithful and committed ministers of the Gospel, I have to conclude
> that I cannot recognize their episcopal ministry until such time as
> a full rapprochement and reconciliation has taken place between
> them and the appropriate authorities within the Episcopal Church
> of the United States.[19]

The statement was clear: The archbishop of Canterbury "cannot recognize" Rodgers and Murphy until the territorial issues are reconciled. But this, for Tay and Kolini, was an enormous gift from heaven.

Moses Tay responded forcefully two days later: "[Carey's] conclusion . . . implies that the consecration is valid but the two consecrated are out of communion with him. This brings more questions than answers. . . . If the Archbishop . . . insists that an individual bishop of a Province is not 'in communion' with him, will he not have to conclude that that Province is also out of communion with him?"[20]

Emmanuel Kolini waited until his House of Bishops met in Rwanda the third week of March. With clarity and unanimity, the bishops issued this response: "The consecration . . . is valid . . . regular and in conformity with the Constitution of the Province of the Episcopal Church of Rwanda." Without hesitation, they assigned the new bishops "to pastoral service within the United States of America."[21]

In a stunning moment of history, the archbishop of Canterbury had surprisingly affirmed both the validity and irregularity of the Singapore consecrations. Even though he did not recognize them, Rodgers and Murphy were fully protected by their respective provinces and archbishops. There was little more that the archbishop of Canterbury could say or do. Ironically, his use of the term *irregular* had a reverse effect on the American scene. Too many people knew the beginnings of American Anglicanism. In 1784, the first Anglican bishop to serve in the US was a man named Samuel Seabury. When the bishops of England refused to consecrate him after the war, he went to the Scottish Episcopal Church for ordination. For several years, the archbishop of Canterbury refused to recognize his *irregular* consecration. Of course, eventually he did. But by then the term *irregular* had become a badge of honor in the Episcopal Church.

Well, that is, until now.

•   •   •

Rodgers and Murphy were deluged by phone calls when they returned home—calls from family and friends, from clergy and church leaders wanting their episcopal oversight, but far more from the media. The new bishops opted not to give interviews in the first few weeks. Better to tame the story, set the tone, and control the spin. Even then, the media would drive the bottom line, twisting the story into an article titled "Homosexuality and the Church." Rodgers and Murphy would have to work hard to stay on message.

John Rodgers:

We're in a church in which somebody can basically . . . deny every major doctrine of the apostolic faith and be undisciplined. . . . we are left with "each one doing what is right in his own eyes."[22] Strong action is already long overdue. . . . The stakes are too high for us to do nothing. This is an issue of the authority and proper interpretation of Scripture and of the heart and soul of the Christian Faith.[23]

Chuck Murphy:

It's unfortunate that many people choose peace with pay, don't rock the boat, don't make waves, don't get in trouble, don't pay the cost. . . . I can't find a way to take the sting out of the cross. And I can't find a way to take the cross out of the gospel.[24] The archbishops who decided to act felt like that action was necessary, and that sometimes leadership needs to get out front, and cannot wait for consensus. . . . A decision was made completely on the highest levels of the Communion and it was their choice, their call, their decision.[25]

During the third week of February, Chuck Murphy called together church leaders from across the country to help strategize their first steps forward. He also brought in a personal contact by the name of Leith Anderson, senior pastor of Wooddale Church, Eden Prairie, Minnesota, since 1977 and a best-selling Christian author. After the conference, Leith, Chuck, John, and a handful of us went to a local restaurant.

"Reforming movements tend to gain momentum quickly at the start," Leith said. "People tend to get on board, invest, and bring others. There's excitement, like an adrenalin rush. A short time later, the movement peaks and then begins a downward trend. They're generally gone within one generation."

"What are the reasons for that?" Chuck asked.

"It's quite simple. When you're born in the negative, you tend to die in the negative. You become known for what you stand against, not what you stand for. Remember the Reformation. Martin Luther nailed the Ninety-five Theses to the door of the Wittenberg Church in his opposition to the Catholic Church. Then came the printing press and the mass publication of the Bible in the commoner's language. The Reformation became known for preaching the gospel of justification by faith alone. The Reformation lasted not because people opposed the Catholic Church but because the gospel changed their lives."

"You're dead-on," Chuck commented. "So if we're not positioned to go forward, this won't last."

"That's right. The media knows you for your opposition to the Episcopal

Church. If this does not change, you're a flash in the pan. Sell papers today, gone tomorrow. You've got to ask hard questions: What do you stand for, not against? In two years, fifteen years, a hundred years, how will you be known?"

"For me, I am done with the Episcopal Church," Chuck quipped. "I think we're about the mission, reaching the lost, impacting our culture with the gospel of Jesus Christ. I think we have something to offer in the Anglican context. I'm telling you, I want to talk about mission and not sex in the Episcopal Church."

"Then stay away from distractions," Leith advised. "Stay with the archbishops who have put their job on the line so you can remain Anglican. Be their missionaries to America. Stop talking to the media. If you have to engage in battle, remember the slogan: Shoot elephants—not squirrels. If you don't, you will live in the negative and die in the negative. Stay positive. Ask, who are you? Well, you represent the best of Anglicanism. You stand with the majority of Christians around the world. You are fully orthodox, fully Anglican on American shores. Now go be missionaries. Glorify God by making disciples of Jesus Christ through the orthodox Anglican tradition. Go preach a positive, vibrant message. Keep your focus."

"Now, that's the hard part," Chuck said, sitting back in his chair, looking thoughtful. "This is very helpful."

We would always remember the lunch with Leith Anderson. It was a pivotal, defining moment for us. It helped frame the language Chuck and John would use to the pioneer leaders of the movement. It would set us on a course from which we would never turn back.[26] We left that lunch making a clear choice: We were not going to be a refugee camp for disgruntled Episcopalians. We were called by the Lord to be missionaries to America, passionately preaching the gospel of salvation in Jesus Christ to the lost.

As often as we tell our story, we always remember and repeat the phrases that Leith gave us that lunchtime: for not against; born in the negative, die in the negative; elephants not squirrels; Anglicans in mission to America—simple phrases that have kept our eyes on Jesus and His call for a true reformation.

•   •   •

Rodgers and Murphy began their work. They traveled the country, preaching the gospel, making news wherever they went. But they both experienced a certain hesitation. The archbishops' meeting was only a few weeks away. They knew that meeting would render some form of judgment on the Singapore consecrations and Emmanuel Kolini. Moses Tay would not be there. His successor, Archbishop Yong Ping Chung, was unknown to us. After the meeting, on or about March 29, the archbishops would issue a formal statement. At that time, it could all come crashing down. Rodgers and Murphy could be marginalized along with Kolini, rendering the consecrations and the US mission ineffective. For this reason, they hesitated. They knew they could not begin the mission in earnest until after the archbishops met.

In the meantime, John Rodgers decided to write an e-mail to his new archbishop from Southeast Asia. A few days later, on March 8, he received an e-mail response, our first recorded words from Yong Ping Chung. He could not have been more gracious.

> Greetings in the name of our Lord Jesus Christ. . . . May I assure you of our warm welcome into our family. As your Archbishop, I will do everything to protect you in all things right, honest and Godly. I hope we will meet in the not very distant future. . . .
>
> Our whole Province will be in Prayer, some will be fasting from 23–29 March 2000 during the [archbishops'] meeting. You may want to mobilize the people under your care to join this prayer wave. We want to pray for faith and unity in truth. We want to pray to cast out all impediments of unorthodoxy, ungodly immorality, doubts and denial of the authority of the Bible from the Anglican Communion. You and all the people under your charge are very much in our prayers. . . . God bless. Yours in Christ.
>
> *The Most Rev. Datuk Yong Ping Chung*

These words brought great comfort and hope. We didn't want Kolini to stand alone in Portugal. We feared that Yong might be a politician, unwilling to align himself with the Singapore consecrations. In addition, we knew Yong was meeting with Archbishop Carey prior to Portugal. We feared Carey would put pressure on Yong to separate from Kolini. But the e-mail of March 8 allayed these fears. We suddenly realized that Yong Ping Chung was as passionate for the gospel as Moses Tay. He had the same strength of conviction "to cast out all impediments of unorthodoxy" as Moses Tay. We found ourselves rejoicing in the Lord's provision of Yong. Here was a man unwilling to go to Portugal without mobilizing a "prayer wave" in Southeast Asia. He wanted the same in the US. This gave us confidence. We had every reason to believe he would stand with Kolini, defend the Singapore consecrations, and do his best to make sure the Anglican Communion remained under the authority of the Bible. What a surprise! What a gift from the Lord.

CHAPTER 13

PORTO DIRECTIVE

It was Kolini who invited us to Porto. He did not want the new bishops there. They would attract the media and it would appear politically motivated. But he did want people around him. In forming the US team, we decided to bring our expert in church law, Ken North.[1] We also brought a few clergy and lay leaders who had suffered at the hands of revisionist bishops. I was there as a witness to the Singapore event and to take notes for Rodgers and Murphy back home. We all knew the gravity of this meeting and the importance of being there to pray. Kolini restated it on our first day with him: "You are here to pray for us."

We booked into a local downtown hotel and waited for Kolini to call. Usually it happened late at night. He would either come to the hotel or we would pick him up and take him to a local diner. Most times he came alone. On two occasions, he came with the archbishops of Congo and Burundi. We did not see Yong. He had been assigned to a committee that convened after meeting hours. But what we did see amazed us. In these late-night meetings, Archbishop Kolini gave us front row seats to see the spiritual battle arrayed against him and Yong. He did it graciously, talking with us in generalities. Most times, he didn't mention names so as to honor his colleagues and not break confidences. But he gave us enough to feel the strength of the opposition so that we might know, and in knowing earnestly contend with him in prayer.

• • •

Early on, he met with Yong. Both men knew a covert plan was in place, first to divide them from the orthodox archbishops who met with them in Kampala, and then to marginalize them. They made an agreement between each other. They chose not to lobby their position. Kolini said, "We will not play politics. It brought genocide to Rwanda. It does the same in the church. The Lord will present people to us." Yong agreed. He added one strategic comment: "When Singapore comes up, we do not talk about the *action*, but the *reasons for the action*. Let them answer: Are these reasons genuine or not?"

From a purely political perspective, Kolini and Yong were in no position to challenge their northern colleagues. One African archbishop said to Kolini in private, "We have said amen for too long. We have been followers for too long. We salute you for what you have done." Another said to him, "Who are you to stand against a superpower like the Episcopal Church USA?" And still another, "It took courage to act in Singapore. I think many bishops in their heart agree with the act. But they are timid. They are [financially] dependent on the US." For Third World Christians, it is hard enough to wrestle with the sufferings of persecutions, famine, war, disease, AIDS, poverty, and the list goes on and on. "We have poverty," one of Kolini's African colleagues rightly argued. "Let the US handle their own problems."

But this kind of detachment was totally unacceptable to Emmanuel Kolini.

"There are two kinds of poverty," Kolini replied, "physical poverty and spiritual poverty. We know the first. Our brothers in the US know the second. We must respond to our brothers in need. That's what 'Communion' is all about." For Kolini, this was a kingdom principle. The gospel demands we act on behalf of those in need, always, even when it costs us. But for those who do nothing, unwilling to "risk their job to do their job,"[2] they are ultimately saying, "Let them handle their own problems."

This pained Kolini. He found the same attitude in the US. He met clergy serving under godly bishops, working hard in their church, but doing nothing to help their fellow clergy suffering nearby at the hands of a revisionist bishop. "How can you be happy," he'd ask them, "while your fellow orthodox clergy are suffering in a diocese right next door?" No one gave him a satisfactory answer to this question.

Letting people suffer was simply not an option for Kolini. At Porto, he wanted his African colleagues to understand that. This was the lesson from the Rwandan genocide: Don't pass by in silence! Don't hear the screams and do nothing! If his colleagues could hear and embrace this kingdom principle, they would understand the reason Singapore had to happen and join Kolini and Yong in their mission.

• • •

We met in the hotel after their first day of meetings. Kolini seemed relaxed but pensive. He told us he was deeply impressed by one African archbishop who had made a strong, impassioned plea during the meeting. This archbishop told everyone he was carrying a message from his bishops back home:

> Tell the Archbishops in Porto our people are dying at the hands of Muslim fundamentalists for professing Jesus Christ. They are paying the price for standing for Jesus. Now they hear you are abandoning the gospel they are dying for. By doing this, you put them in danger. Now they are suffering even more because of your confusion of faith. Anything contrary to the Christian faith received from the apostles is costly to our people.

Kolini smiled. "You know he closed his comments to the archbishops by saying, 'The Bible will set you free!'" He put his head down and laughed. "Why don't Christian leaders know that?" He couldn't imagine saying it to clergy in Rwanda. "It's very sad. The Bible is being rejected." It was then that Kolini told us what profoundly upset him. At some point in the meeting, the archbishops supporting the revisionist agenda presented their opening argument. At first, he thought he misunderstood what they were saying. But they kept saying it. Their new views on human sexuality, they said, were based solely on the fact that they were following the Holy Spirit. He was leading them. The Spirit is speaking a new word to the church if we had ears to hear. Kolini shook his head in disbelief. He summarized their argument: "One, according to these archbishops, we are to follow the Holy Spirit even if He contradicts Scripture. Two, the Holy Spirit is now leaping over the traditional understanding of Christianity to embrace a new sexual morality. By saying this, their apostasy is known to everyone."

• • •

The first confrontation came from a friend on the second day. They met privately and, at first, cordially. This archbishop had been to Kampala, strongly orthodox and deeply loyal to George Carey. He believed the Kampala meeting had endorsed a plan to take several orthodox archbishops to meet with Carey just prior to Porto. Together, with Carey, they would finalize a proposal to be passed at Porto that would discipline the US Episcopal Church and establish an orthodox Anglican witness in the US.

"He told me I ruined his plans," Kolini reported. "He was very angry. He said that our relationship had been damaged by what I did in Singapore. But I asked him, 'Do you understand why? You forced your plan on us at the Kampala meeting, which was not even paid for by you. How could you do that?'

"This made him even angrier. But I said, 'Why are you angry with me? In Kampala, you put a fence around me with your plans and told me to stay quiet. That's colonialism! In Singapore, I knocked down your fence. I will not be manipulated by you—or by anyone. I acted out of conscience. It was dangerous for me to take this stand for my own life, for my family, even for my country. Some look at me as stupid. But I have a responsibility before God to speak the truth of the Bible.'"

We wondered what happened next. "He left upset with me," Kolini responded. "I said to him, 'If we cannot reason together, correct, rebuke—then what?' But he did not respond. The door shut behind him and that was it." He paused, clearly impacted by the event. "I'm sorry the orthodox are not together. It is very troubling. But I shall never regret laying my hands on Chuck and John even in the face of misunderstanding and prejudice. The cost has been high. But first, you must check your conscience. If I am isolated, I don't care what form martyrdom takes. Tay and I knew George Carey would never endorse their plan. We both knew in the Lord that action was required for this meeting in Porto, not a proposal."

• • •

Eventually Kolini and Griswold met privately.

"He wanted to know one thing," Kolini told us. "He asked me, 'What are your plans?' I said to him, 'It depends on you. How will you and George Carey handle this matter? Will you talk with John and Chuck?' But he did not answer. You know, I told him in the African culture, when a child runs away, relatives keep the child until the time of reconciliation. That's what we did in Singapore. I said, 'We are keeping your children. It is not my intention that these Americans become Rwandese. But I keep them where your hand can reach them. John and Chuck are good men. Reconciliation depends on you. I have kept them in the Anglican family. Now go talk to them. Yong and I will accompany you.'"

Griswold had already heard this counsel. Carey, in his public letter regarding Singapore, had made the same recommendation, saying he would not recognize Rodgers and Murphy as bishops "until such time as a full rapprochement and reconciliation has taken place between them and the appropriate authorities within the Episcopal Church of the United States." Griswold was that authority and he knew it.

But would he do it? He told Kolini, "My bishops are very angry."

Kolini said he spoke straight with Griswold. "You are contaminating our Christians. It is past time for these bishops to be accountable for what they have done. If they are angry, they should be angry with themselves first." Kolini then reiterated the way forward: "Reconciliation depends on you."

We are keeping your children.

We asked Kolini if he thought reconciliation was possible. "Yes," he responded, "but it will require repentance, not just dialogue. I told Griswold we will be watching. After Porto, he meets with his bishops. This summer, the Episcopal Church has a convention in Denver. Will he listen to what is being said in Porto? Will he meet with Yong and me, John and Chuck? What will he do? We will be watching."

With sincerity, Emmanuel Kolini extended the possibility of reconciliation to Frank Griswold. He did it in good faith, believing and praying Griswold would accept the offer and comply with the statement made by Carey for "a full rapprochement and reconciliation." Did he actually believe it would happen?

He looked at us with a half smile and then quoted a saying from African Christians: Big men don't repent. Only small ones.

•　•　•

Kolini called the night before the archbishops' report came out. His voice sounded tired. "They are putting pressure on Yong and me." He said it so simply: "The spiritual battle is real." He couldn't meet with us. They were about to go back into session. He requested we get together and earnestly pray for them.

Later he told us there were forces campaigning to condemn the Singapore consecrations entirely. Harsh statements made an early draft of the report. Kolini believed Yong made the difference: "He spoke with great courage and boldness. Sitting next to Griswold, he told everybody, 'The Communion is sick with leprosy. What was done in Singapore was trying to heal the sickness. It was done out of sincerity, a pastoral act attempting to deal with the problem.'" Yong effectively turned the spotlight off the Singapore event and onto Griswold and the repudiation by many US dioceses of the 1998 Lambeth Resolution I.10. Kolini was impressed by Yong's strength in the Lord: "The harsh language never made the final report."

But the night got heated. Kolini and Yong were blamed for Singapore. Some tried to force them to say they were sorry and recant. They would not. They stood together. Others opposed their decision to act without consulting the archbishop of Canterbury, thereby inciting division, rebellion, and irresponsibility. Kolini knew this moment was coming. He had played the scenario out in his mind a thousand times. He had gone to Porto prepared to be marginalized for the sake of the gospel. In his heart, he knew he was ready.

"I did it knowing the cost," he said. "I could not negotiate the cost. Sometimes you have to say yes and obey not knowing how much it will cost. It was the same for Jesus on the cross. He obeyed. He did not negotiate. If all my brothers said to me, 'You are trouble,' I don't mind. I don't regret Singapore. I knew revisionists were undermining orthodoxy. Something had to be done.

"There would have been great danger coming to Porto with no action. The discussion in Porto would never have happened otherwise. Now the archbishops are informed. They know what the Episcopal Church is doing. The whole world knows.

"I am glad to have carried this burden for my brothers and sisters. I went to the US and saw their suffering and tears. No one was listening to them before. Now, from Porto on, they will listen."

●　●　●

Kolini was extremely pleased with the final report: "It's very strong!" The expected condemnation of Singapore never happened. The sovereign authority of the Bible was upheld, and still more surprising, Frank Griswold and the bishops of the US Episcopal Church were put on notice. For Kolini and Yong, the Porto Communiqué was a win. The Lord defended them and their witness. More importantly, He defended the gospel. "It's a wonderful message," Kolini told reporters, "to all Christians."[3]

Concerning Singapore, Kolini and Yong figuratively got their hand slapped. The archbishops expressed "deep concern" that the Singapore event happened "without appropriate consultation." That fact alone, they stated in the communiqué, "poses serious questions for the life of the Communion." Rowan Williams, archbishop of Wales, stated it this way: Singapore "was an unprecedented breach in the received order of the Communion, since no attention was paid either to the views of the official Anglican leadership in the United States or to the counsel of the Archbishop of Canterbury." But Williams, who would later become the archbishop of Canterbury, understood why. For some, he wrote, the "main driving force behind the Singapore consecrations" is found in the "uncritical adoption by Episcopalians of a liberal, multi-cultural, relativist agenda." Williams knew no one portrayed that agenda better than John Spong:

> The theological fireworks of Bishop John Spong, formerly of Newark, New Jersey, who has been cutting long swathes through pretty well every received doctrine and ethical conviction of classical Christianity, have done a lot to sharpen up this discontent. Has North American Anglicanism no means at all, people ask, of reining in pluralism? And if it hasn't, are its structures at all trustworthy? These tensions precipitated the Singapore crisis.[4]

Rowan Williams rightly shifted the spotlight to North American Anglicanism. This is what Kolini and Yong had prayed for to the Lord. "When the family is asleep," an African once told me, "it is wrong to throw a rock through the bedroom window. But when it is thrown to warn the family that their house is on fire and their lives are in danger, they remember the rock with great thanksgiving in their heart."

The analogy seemed to fit. Singapore was the rock. It wrongfully disturbed the "received order of the Communion" and deeply concerned the archbishops. But in Porto, they woke up to see the raging fire consuming their beloved Anglican Communion. At once, their focus turned from Singapore to North America and the rebellion that caused an "unprecedented breach" in the "received doctrine and ethical conviction of classical Christianity." To stop the fire, the archbishops reaffirmed in the communiqué their full commitment to "Scripture's decisive authority in the life of our Communion."

> We believe that the unity of the Communion as a whole still rests on the Lambeth Quadrilateral: the Holy Scriptures as the rule and standard of faith; the creeds of the undivided Church; the two Sacraments ordained by Christ Himself and the historic episcopate.[5]

They were not done. They also reaffirmed their commitment to Lambeth Resolution I.10, which was "overwhelmingly adopted by bishops at Lambeth '98" and yet now "has been rejected in some dioceses of our Church." (This resolution recognized "homosexual practice as incompatible with Scripture" and opposed "the legitimizing or blessing of same sex unions" and "ordaining those involved in same gender unions.") The archbishops took their stand: "Such clear and public repudiation of those sections of the Resolution related to the public blessing of same-sex unions and the ordination of declared non-celibate homosexuals, and the declared intention of some dioceses to proceed with such actions, have come to threaten the unity of the communion in a profound way."

Still, they were not done. To stop the fire, something more than a reaffirmation was needed. The behavior had to stop. And so, with one voice, the archbishops then issued the following declaration: "We urge all bishops to recognize that further public actions of the kind mentioned above strain the reality of mutual accountability in a global Communion."[6]

It is a stunning reality that Frank Griswold both agreed to the wording of the Porto Communiqué and signed it. Had he repented and come to a change of heart? Would he now in fact demand his US bishops comply with this declaration and stop all "further public actions"? Or was this a matter of politics—signing with his colleagues as a show of unity but, on the way home, uncrossing his fingers and doing as he pleased? Had he come to appreciate the gospel witness of Kolini, Tay, and Yong? Or was it possible he underestimated the power of the rock that crashed through the window of the Anglican Communion?

Kolini was jubilant. "The apostolic teaching of the Bible is clearly laid out. The Lambeth Resolution stands as it is! No one can bear to play around with it." If they do, Yong later wrote, it would be "considered as serious ground for breaking fellowship and communion with us."[7]

"Light has to challenge the darkness all the time; that's my belief," Kolini told reporters. "We want to limit the damage and prevent the church from going astray." Therefore, he went on to argue, if the Episcopal Church wants "to belong to the Communion, they have to reform. But it is their choice. . . . God is still waiting for the last person to repent, because He doesn't want to send anybody to hell. Grace may change people."[8]

It was altogether miraculous. "Who are you," said one archbishop to Kolini, "to stand against a superpower?" But then another told him, "Stand firm! Even our Lord Jesus Christ took refuge in Africa!"

The victory was even sweeter.

The archbishops took no further action against the Singapore consecrations. They affirmed the letter written by the archbishop of Canterbury on February 17 (see above). In technical terms, George Carey would not recognize Rodgers and Murphy until there was reconciliation between Griswold, Kolini, and Yong. This meant the Singapore consecrations were valid though irregular, fully Anglican, and under the authority of their respective provinces. It also meant that Kolini and Yong would only negotiate reconciliation with Griswold if, and only if, he truly stood by his public affirmation of the communiqué.

Yong wrote, "It is my hope and the hope of many that the Presiding Bishop of the Episcopal Church will be able to warn some of his Bishops to halt the willful pursuit of the Revisionist agenda."[9]

"We will be watching the US," Kolini said again. "How will Griswold behave now, after signing the communiqué? What will he say to his bishops when they meet next week in California? What happens when the Episcopal Church leaders meet at their convention this summer in Denver? Will they comply with the Lambeth Resolution and the Porto Communiqué? If they do, then we move toward reconciliation."

If they don't, the fire rages on. Kolini and Yong would have no other choice but to fully deploy Rodgers and Murphy. The US mission born in

Singapore would begin without hindrance. Then, at the time, the African saying would come true: "When I see my neighbor's house on fire, I tell him it is on fire. If my neighbor tells me he likes fire, I say, 'Okay, then I will save the children'" (Archbishop Bernard Melango, Central Africa).

• • •

On March 30, two days after the Porto Communiqué was released, Frank Griswold met with his House of Bishops in the San Bernardino Mountains of California. After five days, he called for a press conference. Instead of declaring solidarity with his fellow archbishops by uncompromised allegiance to the communiqué he himself had signed, Griswold turned. Jerry Hames, editor of *Episcopal Life*, reported the presiding bishop's opening words: "We've arrived at a new, deeper place." Hames continued:

> He [Griswold] said it was unrealistic to expect or assume any change in diocesan practice. "Theology is lived out in specific contexts," he said. "Diversity will continue to express itself. I cannot imagine any diocese altering its perspective [on ordaining homosexuals in committed relationships or blessing same-sex unions] as a result of either the bishops' meeting or the [archbishops'] meeting."[10]

The word *unrealistic* caught the media spin.

The *Church of England Newspaper* titled their article "The American Church refuses to bow to [Archbishops'] view."[11] Again they reported the Episcopal Church "is not abiding by the majority vote at all, quite the reverse, it is pressing ahead all the more vigorously with its radical cultural revisionism." And in classic British humor, "The Episcopal Church goes with the flow of its own Californian hormones."[12]

Griswold then announced, "We seek to honor those with a different view as we move to some new place that God has yet to reveal."[13] It was not clear what he meant by "honor" or moving "to some new place." But it was clear he had blatantly rejected the disciplinary correction from Porto. By signing it one week and calling it "unrealistic" the next, he publicly turned against his fellow archbishops and dishonored them. He betrayed them, and he betrayed himself. What kind of man was this?

• • •

The victory of Porto was suddenly diminished.

There is only one kind of victory in the kingdom of God. It happens when a sinner repents and turns to the Lord Jesus for the forgiveness of sins and amendment of life. It is the only reason Kolini, Tay, and Yong opposed Griswold and the US church. They called for repentance in Jesus' name, discipline for Spong and all who teach contrary to the unchanging doctrines of the Christian faith, and commitment to lead US Anglicans back to the saving message of the Bible. For this reason, Griswold's announcement in California deeply grieved them. He had refused to listen to the Lord through his colleagues at Lambeth '98, the event of Singapore, and now, again, at Porto. Unless there was a dramatic turnaround, Griswold would inevitably lead the US General Convention in July to "some new place" of deeper rebellion to the Lord.

Archbishop Yong Ping Chung went before the Lord in prayer. What could he do to stop Frank Griswold at this late date? On May 22, he made the decision to go into his office, close the door, and write.

Dear Frank . . . Greetings to you in the name of our Lord Jesus Christ. . . . I believe none of us want to see the breakup of the Anglican Communion. We do need one another. However, we cannot compromise the authority of the Scriptures nor the uniqueness of Jesus Christ. The center of focus and the reason for our communion must be Jesus. I feel if we have lost our focus we have lost our unity. . . . The whole problem lies in the fact that the church has . . . followed the ways of the world. . . . Many churches in many parts of the world . . . have turned their deaf ears to what Jesus Himself said in John 14:6: "I am the way and the truth and the life. No one comes to the Father except through me."

. . . Many years ago in my late teens, a missionary introduced to me Jesus. He told me about the love of Jesus and the power of the Gospel to change lives. He quoted for me John 3:16. . . . The love of God convicted me and I received His love and His forgiveness and came out of the Kingdom of Darkness into the Kingdom of Light. I was the first convert in my family. Now, praise God, the rest of the family are all believers of Jesus. It saddens me deeply that this wonderful divine love of God through Jesus has been cheapened and has been allowed to be sidetracked by the dictates of human hearts and desires. We have compromised the power of the Cross.

. . . There are some who feel that we in the "2/3 world" are a bit naïve and that we are fundamentalists. Without apology, we stand firm on the authority of the Bible and salvation in Jesus alone. We believe in the creed. . . . To us our God is our life. We acknowledge that we are sinners and we fall short of the glory of God. However, we know that the Holy Spirit is given to us to help us to claim the victory that Jesus, and Jesus alone, has won for us on the cross. We want to say with Paul, "For to me, to live is Christ and to die is gain." Whether we are from the "2/3 world" or the "1/3 world," God is the same. He is still the sovereign God. His standards have not changed. . . . If we can agree that murder, adultery, idolatry . . . are sins then we must also see that homosexuality is also a sin. We believe in the authority of the Bible. We take it seriously, not blindly. We cannot simply choose to believe in one part of the Bible and not the other.

. . . We are ever so grateful to our Almighty God for sending missionaries, some were from your country, so many years ago to our part of the world so we too can know Jesus and the love of God. We know what it was like to live in darkness. But now because of Jesus we live in His marvelous light. It pains us ever so deeply to see those . . . who brought us the faith so long ago are the ones who are telling us that all that was for nothing. With their pluralism, liberalism, and downright rebellion against the sovereignty of God, they introduced to us "another Gospel." . . . They want to enslave their Church. . . . Lord have mercy upon us! . . . we cannot compromise the Gospel.

. . . In your position you can influence and steer the church in the USA back to God. We pray that you will not compromise the uniqueness of Christ Jesus under the pressure of [a] pluralistic society in the USA. We pray that you will stand firm on the authority and the true orthodox teaching of the Bible. As your General Convention approaches we pray that you will have the strength, courage and wisdom to rebuke the erring practices in your church, especially those opposing Resolutions . . . Lambeth 1998, and the Oporto Communiqué. We pray that you will give encouragement to those who truly stand firm in the orthodoxy of their faith. Please be assured that I will request our Province to pray that God will use you to fulfill His purpose.

Yours in Christ Jesus,
Ping Chung[14]

This is what Christians do. It didn't matter that he was an archbishop. He was first a Christian, and his duty as a Christian was to give his testimony of Jesus in the hope that Frank would have ears to hear.

Kolini and Yong decided to meet with Rodgers and Murphy in late July in Amsterdam. They were already scheduled to attend a special conference hosted by the Billy Graham Evangelistic Association. It was "the largest-ever gathering of its kind, about 10,000 evangelists from 190 countries."[15] By then, the US General Convention would be over. Griswold would have made his decision.

It would then be time for Kolini and Yong also to decide. If Griswold repented, calling his bishops to comply with the discipline of the Porto Communiqué, then Kolini and Yong would need to meet and discuss their plan to reconcile with him. But if Griswold refused, then they would have no choice but to begin the US mission. Their position would be the same as the great apostles Paul and Barnabas, who said, "We had to speak the word of God to you first. Since you reject it and do not consider yourselves worthy of eternal life, we now turn to the Gentiles" (Acts 13:46).

On that day, John Rodgers and Chuck Murphy would be fully released in the US. There would be no more talk of the Episcopal Church and its rebellion before God and the church universal. They would be missionaries, sent out from Rwanda and Southeast Asia, to do the one and only thing necessary as Christians and as Anglicans—*to go and preach Jesus.*

CHAPTER 14

THE BATTLE JOINED

If we be schismatics because we have left them, by what name shall they be called who have forsaken . . . the primitive church, forsaken Christ himself, and the apostles, even as children should forsake their parents?

— BISHOP JOHN JEWEL[1]

To leave a church which has become apostate is not schism. This is one's Christian duty and nothing else.

— MARTYN LLOYD-JONES[2]

I n the summer of 2000, the unthinkable happened.

The 73rd General Convention of the Episcopal Church passed Resolution D039, which formally accepted sexual intimacy outside the covenant of marriage. It read, in part,

> There are currently couples in the Body of Christ and in this Church who are living in marriage and couples in the Body of Christ and in this Church who are living in other life-long committed relationships. . . .
> This Church . . . will provide for them the prayerful support, encouragement and pastoral care necessary to live faithfully by them.[3]

It passed by overwhelming majority.[4]

This same resolution carried with it the possibility of ceremonies blessing same-sex marriages. Conservatives fought hard against this piece of the resolution, and won. But for Bishop John Rodgers, this was no victory at all. His once beloved church still adopted what the Bible calls fornication as an acceptable manner of Christian morality and conduct. In disgust, he wrote that the passing of D039 "is clearly in contradiction to the biblical and official teaching of the Church. . . . The Episcopal Church has called evil good. . . . [It] no longer cares what Scripture teaches."[5]

As if that were not enough, tragically, a prominent evangelical bishop broke from conservatives, giving full support to the resolution. The man tried to defend himself to Bishop John Rucyahana of Rwanda, to which John simply replied, "In our country, we do not engage in dialogue with sin. It must be rebuked."

• • •

The archbishops were stunned by D039. Meeting in Amsterdam, while attending the Billy Graham conference on evangelism, Kolini and Yong knew they had to go back on the offensive. Clearly the Singapore consecrations were not enough to signal the depth of their resolve to bring correction to the US. More had to be done. With Rodgers, Murphy, Rucyahana, and other invited guests at their side, Kolini and Yong announced they were moving full speed ahead. They formally released Rodgers and Murphy to expand their work to any US Episcopal diocese. "You are not to begin a new church," they warned. "You are a missionary outreach of the Province of Rwanda . . . to serve in the US mission field . . . to save souls."

With that, on July 28, the movement was named "Anglican Mission in America."

The next morning a press release went out. Without mentioning D039, Chuck Murphy sent this comment to the media: "We believe that what the people of the US need and long for is the uncompromised and undiluted Gospel of our Lord Jesus Christ. We — of Anglican Mission — are resolved to provide an Anglican witness in America that faithfully guards the heart and soul of the Christian message." In any other forum, these words, and this act, would be a formal declaration of war. The birth of Anglican Mission signaled the official decision of Rwanda to cross into the geographic territory of the Episcopal Church. Six months earlier, the archbishops announced the

Singapore consecrations as "an interim action." But now, said the Amsterdam press release, "the interim nature of the mission is over." The orders were given by Kolini and Yong for Anglican Mission to take the US by storm. John Rucyahana captured the moment when he sent out this message to the founding clergy and lay leaders of Anglican Mission:

> I want you to know you have started big. In Singapore, two arch-bishops gave their blessing for this work. . . . Now, you need to go. . . . Go and do the work: Preach the gospel, evangelize, start new churches, bring existing churches into the work and send them into mission. Start with humility. You asked for authority. . . . You got it, . . . now go do it. You have all the tools you need for this Anglican witness in Jesus Christ to grow. . . . now go and preach the Gospel everywhere. Grow the church. We are a part of you. We love you. Keep focused on Jesus.[6]

● ● ●

In the summer of 2000, Anglican Mission in America (AMIA) already had several churches from across the country in places such as North Carolina, Chicago, Denver, Roanoke, Little Rock, and Atlanta. New churches were being started in places such as Raleigh, Charlotte, Chicago, and Austin, Texas. With the passing of D039 and the formal launch of AMIA, another wave of churches came into the mission.

One Episcopal priest, Ken Ross from Littleton, Colorado, reported, "Resolution D039 was the final straw. Recognizing sex outside of marriage . . . did it for us. No church in the history of Christendom has ever done that. . . . Many in the church are simply trying to ignore the problem. . . . But we can no longer, in good conscience, ignore this crisis." With an average attendance of 170 on a Sunday morning, the congregation came to a vote. All but one decided to leave the Episcopal Church. They voted knowing the cost: They would be forced to walk away from their new church building, completed only six months before. "Ironically," Ken said, "it was the biggest givers who said we should leave. There was no hesitation. We couldn't stay."[7] As expected, the local bishop seized the property and evicted the church.

• • •

In Destin, Florida, senior clergyman Mike Hesse described the night of the congregational vote as "unforgettable." They too knew their vote meant the loss of their church building. Still, when Mike called the question in favor of leaving, with 415 in attendance, the people responded "with a thunderous affirmation." When he asked to hear from those staying, he couldn't believe it. "There was total silence." In the days that followed, the number from Destin who transferred into AMIA rose to over eight hundred.

The local bishop fought back. He allowed the congregation to remain in their church building for two weeks after the vote. Mike reported: "We had no place to meet. . . . One of the greatest blessings . . . is the response of every other congregation in Destin. . . . Many . . . offered the use of their facility. . . . The only church facility we were not allowed to utilize, under any circumstance, is the one we built and left." The bishop then moved against Mike, inhibiting him from performing his duties as a clergyman. Mike's pension was frozen. Six months later, the bishop deposed Mike, legally terminating him as an Episcopal priest. But by then it didn't matter. Mike had joined AMIA. He was now a clergyman from the Anglican province of Rwanda and a missionary sent out by Rwanda to serve in the US mission field of Destin, Florida.

"To God be the glory!" Mike said. "We are a people who have been delivered from a very real bondage. . . . We are discovering more of the Lord's heart for those who do not know Him and who need to hear from us the Good News of Jesus in a fresh and life-changing way."[8]

At Christ Episcopal Church, Mobile, Alabama's oldest Protestant church, the congregational vote took place on October 1, 2000. The majority ruled: 251 decided to leave the Episcopal Church with 29 remaining. Senior clergyman Tim Smith wrote that the local bishop "immediately filed a lawsuit freezing all assets and claiming ownership of the buildings. . . . the clergy were deposed and denied the right to make further contributions to their pension funds." The legal negotiations for the building delayed the departure of the congregation from their historic site by one year. On October 7, 2001, with an average attendance of 370 on a Sunday morning, the church began worshipping at the Mobile Convention Center.[9]

•   •   •

Others from across the country made the same decision. They too would pay a high cost for separating from the church's rebellion. Others, seeing the cost, decided not to separate in fear of provoking their bishop to wrath, subjecting their clergy to inhibition, losing their properties, and severely dividing their people and their finances with a congregational vote. In such cases, many clergy and senior leaders opted not to inform their congregations of D039. This too was a great sin. How could anyone keep silent when the church had radically endorsed sexual immorality? Who could stand back when bishops were punishing those taking a stand for the gospel? But many were afraid to take the risk. It was easier not to tell the people, bury their heads in the sand, and pretend the world around them had not changed.

But it had.

And once again, Kolini and Yong rose to the occasion.

They quickly sent a message to Episcopal bishops who had defrocked AMIA clergy: "Such actions are without credible foundation. . . . Each of these individuals remains in good standing as a member of the clergy of the Province of Rwanda." Then they issued a piercing statement: "These punitive actions demonstrate yet another dimension of the pastoral emergency that led to the formation of the AMIA."[10]

But these Episcopal bishops did not flinch. In the fall of 2000, they continued their attacks. If Kolini and Yong wanted to talk about a "pastoral emergency," it was not D039. It was them, and AMIA. These were the ones instigating rebellion, forcing their way into US dioceses, and defying traditional Anglican order out of hand. Surprisingly, US *conservative bishops* who had voted against D039 joined in the protest. Some spoke openly against AMIA. Others threatened punitive action against clergy and churches considering AMIA. Still others mounted legal opposition.[11] It didn't make sense. Why fight AMIA, Kolini, and Yong? Why not unite against the corruption of their colleagues propagating D039?

We would soon learn the answer to these questions. Standing right behind these conservative bishops, in full support, was none other than George Carey, archbishop of Canterbury.

•   •   •

Carey wrote to AMIA leadership in mid-October, with a copy to Frank Griswold. He rendered his strongest judgment to date. He said the "trends set in motion by" the Singapore consecrations were both "regrettable and against the spirit of Christ." For this reason, he found Kolini and Yong guilty for the act of initiating division in the US and in the Anglican Communion. They were men, Carey said,

> who have flouted so sharply the well understood disciplines of our Communion and have opened a deep division between provinces. It is surely clear to all that it is an ecclesiological nonsense for someone to be made Bishop of the Province of Rwanda and whose entire existence is to be a missionary bishop in a sister province. It is a shocking error that weakens our fellowship and imperils our mission.[12]

Carey made no mention of D039 or that it was, in fact, the "shocking error" not just in our day but for two thousand years of Christian history or that it violated Scripture and by definition of Scripture was "against the spirit of Christ." Who cared about "ecclesiological nonsense" in the face of theological corruption?

Kolini and Yong could not stand idly back. Carey had drawn battle lines, siding with Griswold. He had made crossing boundaries a greater sin than D039. He had made unity the "very precious gift which must be protected with might and main"[13] and not the truth of the Bible. Nothing outraged Kolini and Yong more. As a first response, Kolini wrote Griswold on October 17. He wanted him to know AMIA would continue strong in the US as a public rebuke: "The Province you lead, which has come to bear the likeness of John Spong . . . has denied and denigrated our Lord and Savior Jesus Christ."[14] On the same day, he wrote George Carey. He felt constrained in his spirit to argue the proper doctrine of biblical unity:

> I believe, however, that where the cross is denied, belittled, or degraded without challenge or discipline our unity is to me superficial. Just as unity is fundamental, so is the foundation of that unity and there is none other foundation than the cross of Christ.[15]

Kolini and Yong decided to meet. They opted for early December in South Carolina with Rodgers and Murphy alongside. As they prayed and talked together, a number of action steps became clear. First, they decided to issue a formal statement informing Carey, Griswold, and the Anglican Communion that they would never back down. AMIA would remain until the Episcopal Church leaders repented from their gross rebellion and complied with the discipline issued as early as Lambeth 1998. The statement read as follows:

> We will continue on our course until there is some official, public rebuke of those provinces which resist conformity to the mind of Christ as expressed in the Lambeth Quadrilateral, the resolutions of Lambeth 1998 and the Oporto Communiqué. In addition, we must see the fruit of repentance in the American Episcopal Church. Continued oversight of this mission is necessary as a matter of obedience to our consciences and consecration vows.[16]

Their next decision was to advance AMIA by consecrating new bishops sometime in 2001. The first mention of this came in a joint letter to George Carey on December 6. They told him bluntly that the "shocking error . . . continues to be the unrebuked behavior of the Episcopal Church. . . . This being the case," they stated openly, "we are considering additional bishops to meet the growing needs of this work."[17]

Carey fired a letter back on December 21: "I must ask you to consider carefully the implications of going ahead with further consecrations. Such a step would deepen the emerging splits and harden attitudes throughout the Communion. . . . I appeal to you to take the longer view."[18] He then raised the level of his public attack. Speaking to all bishops in the Episcopal Church on Saturday, March 10, 2001, Carey seized the moment. He wanted every US bishop to know with certainty that he was "totally opposed" to AMIA, calling it "deeply schismatic." He made it quite clear, reported US evangelical bishop Bob Duncan, "that he would not support any group that has decided to work outside the system." For Carey, "it was imperative for the orthodox to remain in the Episcopal Church and to work for transformation from within." Duncan went on to say, "I am deeply grateful that Archbishop Carey chose . . . to voice support for . . . our decision to remain in the Episcopal Church."[19]

Kolini and Yong kept pursuing. They set June 24 as the date of the consecrations. They also decided to do it in the US. This infuriated Griswold. With the mind of a winsome attorney, he appealed to his fellow archbishops. In his letter, Griswold re-imaged the Episcopal Church as "flourishing with a renewed sense of mission." He positioned it as wholly orthodox: "Scripture, the historic faith of the Church set forth in the Creeds, and submission to the Holy Spirit . . . supply the ground upon which we all stand." Then he unleashed his venom against Kolini and Yong, charging them with the ecclesiastically illegal act of crossing boundaries:

> Not only are the proposed ordinations a further invitation to schism, but they also involve two [archbishops] who, without informing me and certainly without my permission, are planning to enter this province with the express purpose of acting contrary to a basic principle of the Communion that no bishop is to perform episcopal acts in the diocese of another bishop without obtaining the bishop's permission. . . . the proposed action by our two brothers is a profound violation.[20]

Neither Kolini nor Yong responded. In their view, Griswold's ability to convince Anglicans that he was an orthodox man leading an orthodox church was fast waning. More to the point, they believed Anglican leaders worldwide were seeing through Griswold; that is, if there was a "profound violation" it had little to do with crossing boundaries and more to do with his rebellion against the historic Christian faith.

It was more important for Kolini and Yong to write George Carey and tell him that AMIA "is simply unwilling to follow the corrupt path that is being charted by the present leadership of the Episcopal Church USA. . . . We must now act. We will therefore consecrate more bishops for the Anglican Mission in America in order to provide adequate apostolic and episcopal leadership for this growing ministry."[21]

Carey was more than provoked. He wrote back immediately. This time, without apology, he released a personal letter to Kolini and Yong publicly over the Internet before they ever received it.

> This news burdens and dismays me. . . . I simply cannot believe this is in conformity with the way Christ would want us to

behave. . . . Let me make no bones about it. . . . I cannot recognize John Rodgers and Chuck Murphy as bishops in the Communion with me unless they are fully reconciled to the Presiding Bishop of the Episcopal Church. . . .

How am I to regard those who act without lawful authority? What you propose to do is in blatant disregard of our Anglican ecclesiology. . . . Consider what confusion it would bring and what a scandal to our Communion! . . . I cannot support you if you persist in taking this action. . . . I urge you both to think again. . . . it is not too late for you to draw back from a step which can only do lasting damage.[22]

Even now Carey stood fast by his friend Griswold, defending the US borders.

Kolini and Yong opted not to write back. Not yet. Instead, they asked Chuck Murphy to speak on their behalf at a press conference held on June 23, the day before the consecrations.

Standing in front of the microphone, Murphy said, "While we in the Anglican Mission have made our stand for biblical truth over institutional unity, it is regrettable the present Archbishop of Canterbury has chosen to take the opposite position. . . . We have now come to a moment in which the entire Anglican Communion is facing a realignment along the fault line of biblical truth." Few championed this view of the coming realignment in Anglicanism more than Chuck Murphy. He then reinforced his argument: "When challenges to turf and territory produce a stronger outcry than the relentless challenges in recent years to the basic tenets of our Apostolic Faith and witness, this crisis is only exacerbated."[23]

His words dug deep. Kolini and Yong had invaded Griswold's turf and territory. But more, they had chosen Denver in particular, the same city that had witnessed the passing of D039 one year before. This was the place where the Christian faith was maligned and disgraced, and this was the time for these men to respond. That response was first the consecration of new AMIA bishops. Second, it was their willingness to pay the price for their action. Both men knew it would come. Especially Archbishop Yong. He was already experiencing considerable pressure from leaders in Southeast Asia not to consecrate in Denver. He was already being told—in no uncertain terms—that if he did consecrate, the cost would likely be his job.

•   •   •

Yong had called Murphy back in mid-May. He had met with the bishops of Southeast Asia. He told Chuck simply, "I did not get their support for more consecrations." He later wrote,

> I have discussed this with the Diocesan Bishops of our Province. However, I did not get a consensus from them. . . . They felt they could not support such an action because this would violate our Constitution and the Canon Laws.[24]

Archbishop Yong spoke of his love and deep respect for these bishops. They were men sold out for Jesus and for the mission of evangelizing Southeast Asia in His name. But they did not agree that further consecrations were needed. Southeast Asia, they believed, had done enough. They urged Yong to find an alternative solution, which he promised to do. But if this proved unsuccessful, and if Yong made the decision to consecrate on June 24 in Denver, "I assured them that I would bear the consequences myself."

He knew what that meant. He would face legal charges for breaking their constitution. He would lose his office as bishop and archbishop. The legal process itself would bring heartache and division among leaders in his province. It would turn their focus away from their primary work of evangelism. "It is not something that I want to do," he wrote privately. "I have nothing to gain but everything to lose."

He was being torn in two. As archbishop, he had responsibility before God to defend the gospel on the international stage. In good conscience, he could not ignore what was happening in the US. "When house on fire," he said once in staccato English, "no committees to discuss. Grab bucket! Get water!" In the same way, he could not ignore AMIA. "As you all know," he wrote friends, "we inherited this situation. . . . We have all these people who are already committed to stand with AMIA. We cannot abandon them." It seemed no matter what he decided, Yong wrote, "It will be a very lonely and costly road ahead."

In keeping his promise to his fellow bishops, Yong set up meetings in the US to explore all other possibilities. He also traveled to meetings in Nassau and Canada. "Consecrating more bishops for AMIA is a gigantic step with great repercussions," he wrote to US orthodox bishops. "I cannot and will not take it lightly. Therefore, it is my desire to meet with you and to seek your counsel. Please be assured that I am not asking you to come to persuade you in anything. I want to meet you with an open heart."[25]

In every encounter Yong pursued one line of questioning that most troubled him: "What is being done for faithful US Episcopalians who, for reasons of conscience, can no longer stay in the church? Already there are nearly eight thousand Christians in AMIA. What is the strategy to protect them? Do you have a workable solution?" Everywhere he went, everyone he asked, the answers always came back the same.

Except for AMIA, there was no strategy. And most didn't like AMIA.

US bishop Bob Duncan confirmed for Archbishop Yong that US bishops had no alternative solutions for those leaving the church. More to the point, Duncan said, "Many of our [orthodox] Bishops are hurt or angry or both about AMIA. That is just the way it is, and it is what we are trying to work to change."[26]

Yong left these meetings saddened. He could not understand why the burden of these days still fell to Rwanda and Southeast Asia. He had come in humility to find answers, but there were none to be found. On the morning of June 12, he told Chuck Murphy, "It is with a very heavy heart that I feel I have no other choice but to go ahead and do the consecrations. . . . I must do this for the defense of the gospel, for the sake of my conscience, and for the care of the precious souls in AMIA." He prayed his people back home would understand. He wanted them to know the passion of his conviction and why he felt he had no other choice.

> I pray that our Diocese and our Province will be able to rise up to the occasion and be the small voice in the wilderness speaking out for the Faith that was entrusted to us by our Lord and Savior Jesus Christ. . . . It is our duty to speak and to act when "other gospels" slip in to destroy the faith and the unity that we have in Jesus, and Jesus alone. . . . We must lift high the cross of Jesus. We must stand up against those who want to compromise the Faith that Christ has

given us. We must be firm especially at this time of history. I believe we have been chosen for a time as this. It is time for South East Asia to arise. . . . I could not, by conscience, do otherwise.[27]

Julia, his wife, fully supported the decision. She knew her husband's courage and tears. "If we are deposed for the gospel," she told the leaders of AMIA, "I'd like to be known in history for that."

The opposition came quickly.

On Sunday morning, June 24, Yong Ping Chung was scheduled to preach in Calgary, Alberta. The local bishop, Barry Hollowell, caught wind of Yong's decision to consecrate in Denver and denied him access to the pulpit. He sent the archbishop a fax to his hotel "forbidding me to attend the church." He opposed Yong's "kind of theology" and told him so. Yong's only comment? "He was very liberal."[28]

Yong Ping Chung flew to Denver. That night, with a packed crowd from all across the country to witness the consecrations, he stepped into the pulpit. He was welcomed with honor, respect, and applause. This crowd wanted to hear him preach. In a simple gesture, he lifted up the Bible and declared,

The Bible has life, the Bible is life, and the Bible gives life. . . . But the enemy, the devil . . . reduces the Bible into a common document, void of God and breath. Thus there is no more authority in the Bible. However, the Bible is crucial to life, especially in our ever-changing, confusing and bewildered world. . . . Brothers and sisters, the Bible is the only truth. It held the truth yesterday. It holds the truth today. It will continue to hold the truth tomorrow and forever.

The congregation again erupted in applause. Yong was on a mission. He wanted everyone to know why he was in Denver, why he was consecrating new AMIA bishops, why the Anglican Communion was fracturing in two, and why the people in the US had a right to hear the gospel. He thundered:

Do you accept the Holy Scriptures as revealing all things necessary for eternal salvation through faith in Jesus Christ? . . . When the church loses sight of this and allows the world to dictate the rule of life, it has lost its mission. . . . When the authority of the Scripture is not honored, we face division in the body of Christ. . . . The gospel has power to change lives. If we don't tell our people, we are cheating them.[29]

This was not a new message. Yong was simply stating what the overwhelming majority of Anglican bishops had affirmed at the 1998 Lambeth Conference: the absolute and sovereign authority of Holy Scripture. But there was something new that night. Yong and Kolini, in a united effort, were holding the US Episcopal Church accountable to this nonnegotiable truth. Not with words only, but with action. And by this action, they courageously confronted the fatal weakness in modern Anglicanism. Where is the accountability? Who brings correction and discipline to those who disgrace the gospel and deny the Lord?

And so that night, in the city of Denver, four men were consecrated Anglican bishops. Yong and Kolini released them, along with all clergy and Christians in AMIA, to evangelize the US; to uphold, defend, and preach the Bible without compromise; and to ensure a faithful Anglican witness in the US for as long as the rebellion continued. They did it because they knew, in the Lord Jesus, it had to be done.

It's called discipline, they said repeatedly. It's what Christian leaders do. Anything else is just politics.

•   •   •

The testimony given by Yong and Kolini in Denver yielded two immediate reactions. First, it strengthened clergy and Christians to take risks in standing for the Lord and His saving gospel.

For example, at St. John's just outside Philadelphia more than 350 members—representing 95 percent of active congregants—decided to leave the Episcopal Church and affiliate with AMIA. The Rev. Phil Lyman commented on the vote: "Although this was an agonizing decision . . . they simply could no longer stay . . . and be true to their own consciences. . . . To many of us, the Episcopal Church in the US today is unrecognizable, and we believe it is they, not we, who have departed from the Anglican tradition of faith."[30]

The congregation offered their Episcopal bishop the fair market value for the church they had built and worshipped in for eighty-two years. The bishop was not amused. He ordered them to vacate immediately. He gave Phil Lyman, his wife, and their five children, thirty days to get out of the rectory—their home for thirteen years. The bishop then inhibited the clergy from serving as priests, saying they had "abandoned the Communion."

"We understood the implications of our recent actions," Lyman told a reporter, "and that there would be a price to be paid for our refusal to compromise faith and conscience." But, he went on, "The ministry has thrived not because of our buildings but because of our Lord. . . . Yes, this is a sad day for us. . . . while this may be our last day in these buildings, it is far from our last in mission and ministry. . . . We look forward to new blessings, new opportunities, and to a new place within the Anglican Church."[31]

Phil Lyman said it so well: "We have lost nothing and gained everything."

• • •

The Rev. Terrell and Teresa Glenn had already moved to Raleigh to plant a new AMIA church. At the beginning of 2001, they had one family. In January 2003, they averaged just under three hundred at Sunday worship. The sacrificial love and courageous faith of Yong and Kolini had deeply impacted Terrell.

> Thank you for making a way for me to be an Anglican clergyman. Thank you for providing a place for us. I pray that we will never take any of it for granted and will demonstrate that gratitude by reaching out to the many that have not yet come to know the new life that is found only in Jesus. [32]

• • •

The second reaction came against Rwanda.

Pat Ashworth of the *Church Times* released the story: "In the wake of the Denver consecrations, Trinity Church, Wall Street, in New York, has turned down a request from the Church of Rwanda for a grant of $146,000. It says the province is 'actively working to promote schism within the Episcopal Church of the USA.'" The article quoted Judith Gillespie from Trinity Church, saying,

> We have always felt that we do not have to totally agree with our partners in order to work with them around mission concerns. With the Anglican Church of Rwanda, however, we have now gone past a point of disagreeing on the theology. We have reached the difficult decision that Trinity Church cannot provide support to a Church that undertakes such divisive activity within our own Church.[33]

Once again Rwanda was portrayed as instigating the "divisive activity" rather than responding to it. Bishop John Rucyahana responded quickly by fax, which AMIA published over the Internet.

> We have heard about Trinity Church's decision to punish our Province. . . . It is clear to all the people that Trinity expects us to swallow their position as we receive their money. God forbid, we cannot. . . . They don't think Africans and Asians can oppose anybody who is in the wrong. . . . We are not ready to accept apostasy . . . in exchange of money to meet the needs of our poor communities. . . . May the Almighty Father judge between us.[34]

In a private note, the African bishop took it a step further: "It's more than colonialism. It's an applied method to dehumanize the needy." Archbishop Yong agreed. In a quote to the *Washington Times*, he said,

> I am very outraged that money . . . is being controlled, manipulated and applied as a pressure point to poorer churches to comply with the will and agenda of the givers. I suspect that more pressure will be applied and more money will be used as the battle for the truth of the Gospel intensifies. The whole intention is to silence any voice that dares to speak up against the mighty donors.[35]

• • •

The Bible says "the Lord disciplines those he loves" and that "God disciplines us for our good, that we may share in his holiness" (Heb. 12:6, 10). With discipline comes choice. We either receive it and amend our ways or we continue headstrong in our rebellion. Although few may have considered the Denver consecrations an act of discipline from the Lord, one thing was certain: The leadership modeled by Yong and Kolini to act in faith, with conviction and at great personal risk, served to embolden both sides. Without question, in the latter half of 2001 and beyond, choices were made and the chasm grew wider.

Sadly, George Carey's position hardened. He continued to blame Yong and Kolini for initiating the crisis — "Your action in support of AMIA has brought us to a troubling point in the life of our Communion." He continued to defend Griswold — "In my view, the Episcopal Church of the United States remains orthodox in faith and doctrine." What else could he do with Yong and Kolini but exercise the powers of his office against them? For the first time, he took his sword out of its sheath and asked, "Must there not come a point at which I must declare that I am no longer in communion with you?"[36]

Yong and Kolini both wrote back, but the time for words was fast waning.[37] In January 2002, they sat down and met with George Carey at Lambeth Palace. It had no lasting value. Carey continued to condemn "the schism created by the AMIA" and would leave office in late 2002 holding the same view.[38] As a matter of record, in his last days as archbishop of Canterbury, Carey denied money to a Rwandan bishop and told him plainly it was because of "the activities that your [archbishop] is engaged in."[39]

Nothing could be clearer: Grace and mercy to Griswold, punishment to Yong and Kolini.

Ironically, Carey's hardness helped Yong, for the bishops of Southeast Asia had opportunity to experience it firsthand. For example, when the bishops wrote Carey a private letter, they soon discovered Carey released it publicly to the media.[40] This hurtful act helped set the stage for early March 2002, when the province met for their annual meeting. When it was over, Yong wrote to the leadership of AMIA saying there would be no constitutional action against him. He would remain in office. But, Yong said, "it was a very hard and long battle." He knew he had a very important task facing him. He needed to come to his fellow bishops and provincial leaders in humility, not to rescue his position, but to be right with them in the Lord.

"I would like to apologize again to you all for the distress, unease and pain that I have caused you in regard to . . . the consecration of the four mission Bishops for AMIA."[41]

Although he believed he did the right thing, to "discharge my duty as the Archbishop," he knew he had hurt them. Before each one he asked for their forgiveness in truth, not politics; in Christ Jesus, whether in office or not, for the sake of their relationship and for the uninterrupted mission of their province. The other bishops in turn worked hard with Yong to resolve their differences and helped establish principles that strengthened their relationship for the future. In the end, their love for the Lord and each other, for the truth of the gospel and the passion for winning Southeast Asia for Jesus Christ, won the day.

"God won!" Yong wrote with joy in his letter to AMIA. The reconciliation begun was clearly the Lord's doing, and it lasted. In November 2003, they reelected Yong to serve another term as archbishop.

CHAPTER 15

OPEN REBELLION

Post-Denver, post-9/11, the battle intensified.

Yong knew why, and so did Kolini. The Anglican Communion had no formal mechanism to discipline the leaders of the rebellion. With no correction, chaos reigns. Lawlessness prevails. Ask any parent; they live this principle every day, 24-7. Without practical authority to stop the behavior, the behavior continues. Without intentional resistance, the invasion marches on; the fire spreads; the poisonous infection spreads; the leaven seizes the lump; the terrorists gain absolute control. And that is exactly what happened.

Kolini, Yong, and Moses Tay knew from the beginning that as long as that renowned heretic John Spong remained unrebuked there would be no end to the devastation. For this reason, they did more than sit back, watch, and complain. They took action. And with that action, they persistently called upon the archbishop of Canterbury to use the authority of his office and stop the rebellion before it was too late, before the Anglican Communion suffered irreparable damage. But discipline and correction never came.

These were days when the rebellion raged beyond control.

- Former Archbishop Richard Holloway of Edinburgh made the announcement in a publication by the Lesbian and Gay Christian Movement that "he no longer believed Jesus was the Son of God" but rather "an extraordinary man." He was never disciplined or formally charged with heresy.[1]
- Bishop William Smalley of the diocese of Kansas announced he was "authorizing the blessing of persons living in committed relationships other than Holy Matrimony." The clergy and lay leaders

supported their bishop by resolution at their next diocesan convention.[2] The infamous national resolution D039 supporting sexual intimacy outside of marriage did not allow ceremonies blessing same-sex marriages. Smalley therefore stood in lawless defiance to the laws of his own Episcopal Church, let alone historic Christianity. He was never disciplined or formally charged with heresy.

- The confirmation and consecration of John Chane as bishop of Washington, DC, came with the full knowledge of his public denial of the Christian faith. In his Easter sermon of 2002, the bishop-elect preached openly, defiantly: "And yet, the Easter story of the resurrection, which defines the core of our Christian theology, is, at best, conjectural. . . . the concept of Jesus' physical, bodily resurrection, was not even part of the early Christian experience. . . . At their very best, the stories of the resurrection of Jesus as contained in the Gospels and Acts of the Apostles are contradictory and confusing." Instead of charging him with heresy, the church consecrated him bishop.[3]

- On June 14, 2002, Canadian Anglicans in the diocese of New Westminster "voted to approve a rite for blessing same-gender relationships." Immediately following the vote, a priest rose up, "declared a state of 'pastoral emergency' and led the walkout of nine conservative parishes . . . along with members of at least six other parishes."[4] Among those who walked out was the renowned Anglican theologian and professor at Regent College, Vancouver, J. I. Packer.

Packer responded to the Canadian decision in an article for *Christianity Today*:

Why did I walk out with the others? Because this decision, taken in its context, falsifies the gospel of Christ, abandons the authority of Scripture, jeopardizes the salvation of fellow human beings, and betrays the church in its God-appointed role as the bastion and bulwark of divine truth. . . . To bless same-sex unions liturgically is to ask God to bless them . . . something that Scripture, canonically interpreted, clearly and unambiguously rejects as sin. This has never been done before, and ought not to be done now. . . . It is a watershed decision for world Anglicanism, for it changes the nature of Anglicanism itself. It has to be reversed.[5]

But it wasn't. There was no mechanism in Canadian or international Anglicanism to discipline the bishop or the diocese. The only means of protest was to walk out of the church. For Packer, this could not have been easy. A dear friend had urged him to walk out years before. In a public address given in October 1966, the great preacher Dr. Martyn Lloyd-Jones believed the primary doctrines being challenged then by English Anglicanism already warranted the act of separation: "We spend most of our time . . . united with people who deny and are opposed to these essential matters of salvation. . . . Now, I say, that is sinful." Lloyd-Jones was rebuffed out of hand by evangelical Anglican leaders. And yet his words live on:

God, I believe, has given us a solemn charge of guarding and protecting and defending the faith in this present evil age in which we find ourselves. . . . we are the modern representatives and successors of the glorious men who fought this same fight, the good fight of faith in centuries past. Surely, as evangelicals, we ought to feel this appeal. We are standing in the position of the Protestant Reformers. . . . let us rise to the occasion. . . . May God speed the day.[6]

For Packer, the great reformer, that day finally came.

The archbishops issued their protest in late May 2003 as they met together under the direction of the new archbishop of Canterbury, Rowan Williams.[7] In the context of their pastoral statement, they rendered their decision concerning the act of blessing same-sex unions as raised by the US and Canadian church: "we as a body cannot support the authorization of such rites."[8] Griswold signed it. So did the archbishop of Canada. But it didn't matter. Both men proved by their actions that they didn't mean it.

And the defiance escalated.

On May 28, three days after the archbishops' statement was released and in full awareness of their formal rebuke, the Canadians conducted their first official same-sex blessing service. Yong spoke out sharply: They "timed their outrageous act . . . so as to challenge, defy and mock all the [archbishops] of the Anglican Communion."[9] The archbishop of Canada did nothing to stop it. The bishop in Canada would remain in office for years to come, never disciplined, and never formally charged with heresy.

With no correction, chaos reigns. Lawlessness prevails.

Ten days after that, the defiance escalated again in shameless rebellion.

This time it was New Hampshire. From the *Washington Times*: "On June 7, the Rev. Gene Robinson became the world's first openly homosexual bishop-elect in the Anglican Communion."[10] His election was confirmed on August 5 by the leadership of the Episcopal Church at their General Convention. From *USA Today*: "His ratification makes the Episcopal Church the first major denomination to say that people in committed gay relationships are not barred from ordination or leadership."[11] Frank Griswold did nothing to stop it. He could have used the authority of his office to oppose Robinson and the diocese. But he did the exact opposite. In fact, he voted for Robinson, and worse, he did everything possible to encourage delegates at convention to support Robinson's election and "respect the action of the Diocese of New Hampshire."[12] And it worked. Griswold got what he wanted. And he got more.

During convention, the bishops voted to reject Resolution B-001, which reaffirmed "Holy Scripture as the foundation of authority in our Church." The bishops could not, with any integrity, back Robinson for bishop and, at the same time, affirm the sovereign authority of Holy Scripture. This reasoning was in keeping with the logic of the 1998 Lambeth Resolution I.10, which identified "homosexual practice as incompatible with Scripture." To keep one, the other had to go.

So they kept Robinson, and they let the Bible go. Griswold had already made this choice. Before taking office he said, "the Episcopal Church is in conflict with Scripture" and the Holy Spirit was presently leading the Church to "contradict the words of the Gospel."[13] Gene Robinson agreed. In his own words: "Just simply to say that it goes against Tradition and the teaching of the church and scripture, does not necessarily make it wrong. . . . We worship a living God [who] leads us into truth."[14]

Without blushing, Robinson defied the teaching and authority of Scripture.

He stepped into the spotlight, front and center on the world stage for all to see and marvel. He was, after all, the first openly gay bishop in two thousand years of Christian history. But he was more than that. Much more. He was a man, by his own confession, who stood in open contradiction to the gospel. This made him, according to Christian doctrine classically defined, both biblically and historically, a heretic.

It was therefore the solemn duty of every US Episcopal bishop, called by God to guard and defend the Christian faith, to bring Robinson under discipline and call him to biblical repentance.

But what did they do? They joined him. They applauded him. They put him into the pulpit instead of taking him out. They stood him in front of the media as their mascot, the face of the Episcopal Church. They called themselves innovators and prophets, preachers on the cutting edge of social justice, defenders of the rights and dignity of every human being. But they were not. They were heretics, all of them, for they rejected the absolute authority of Holy Scripture. They cast their vote in favor of Robinson. By so doing, they committed treason. They betrayed their office. They despised the gospel they had vowed to uphold. In this act of mutiny, they mocked and ridiculed Christians unwilling to turn their backs on biblical faith in Jesus Christ. They abandoned Anglicans in other parts of the world who were suffering persecution and martyrdom for their faith in a gospel these bishops vetoed by resolution. Who could believe it? How was it possible?

These were days like no other; days when rebellion seized control of the Episcopal Church; days when no one was left inside the church with any authority to stop the inevitable consecration of Robinson in early November. If there was any hope for discipline, any possibility for intervention, it had to come from the Anglican archbishops overseas. But what could they do now? What authority did they have?

Was anyone able to rebuke these rebels and swiftly bring them to trial?

• • •

Within days after the Robinson vote, Rowan Williams decided "to convene an extraordinary meeting" of all archbishops. He set the date prior to Robinson's consecration, in London, October 15–16.

On the first Sunday morning after the vote, the Rev. Steve Randall stood in his pulpit at St. Timothy's Episcopal Church in Catonsville, Maryland, and announced, "I can no longer submit to our bishops." The two-hundred-member congregation gave an immediate standing ovation. "People will say I am just bailing out," he went on, "but I am following God's call as best I can.

I don't have a golden parachute. I will lose my pension, insurance, paycheck, and all my benefits." And he did. It also cost the church their building. But, he told reporters, how can anyone stay in a church "doomed to destruction and despair"? A few weeks later, Randall and a majority of both leadership and congregants left to start a new church.[15]

So why weren't hundreds of Episcopal clergy doing the same thing?

Bob Duncan issued a statement immediately after the convention approved Robinson: "I have not left, and will not leave, the Episcopal Church or my apostolic role as Episcopal Bishop of Pittsburgh."[16] Evangelical leaders circulated a document with the same message, saying emphatically, "Do *not* say you are leaving the Episcopal Church." They called a meeting for all evangelical Episcopalians in Plano, Texas, October 7–9 and urged no one to consider leaving the Episcopal Church for at least six months.[17] In January 2004, twenty-six hundred Episcopalians met in northern Virginia and again heard the message repeated: "Hold on; be patient; work from within." Duncan told the crowd succinctly, "We're not going anywhere."[18]

From Africa, a number of archbishops responded quickly after the Robinson vote. From Kenya: "The decision . . . is wrong. It is against Biblical teaching, it is sin and it damages the Body of Christ." From Uganda: "We condemn this decision. . . . they are abandoning the faith." From Nigeria: "They have enthroned the will of men over the authority and revealed will of God in Scripture." From Central Africa: "We will not be part of it." From Rwanda: "These actions do now create a real breach in communion."[19]

John Rucyahana said it this way: "The Episcopal Church has denied the teaching of the Lord Jesus and nullified the transforming power of His cross. They stand in contradiction to Scripture. We cannot go with them. Jesus saved me. He rescued me from my sin. I cannot betray Him — no, never."[20]

●　　●　　●

The archbishops met in London that October. In a public statement following the meeting, they acknowledged the Robinson consecration "will tear the fabric of our Communion at its deepest level":

> If his consecration proceeds, we recognize that we have reached a
> crucial and critical point in the life of the Anglican Communion and

we have had to conclude that the future of the Communion itself will be put in jeopardy. In this case, the ministry of this one bishop will not be recognized by most of the Anglican world, and many provinces are likely to consider themselves to be out of communion with the Episcopal Church (USA). This will tear the fabric of our Communion at its deepest level, and may lead to further division on this and further issues as provinces have to decide in consequence whether they can remain in communion with provinces that choose not to break communion with the Episcopal Church (USA).

There was more. The Lambeth Conference 1998 had requested the archbishop of Canterbury to "establish a commission to consider his own role in maintaining communion within and between provinces when grave difficulties arise." The archbishops in London therefore decided to form the commission at once and requested its members deal with the "issues raised at this meeting, within twelve months."[21]

In other words, they formed a committee. There would be no discipline, not now. No rebuke of Robinson or the diocese of New Hampshire or the bishops of the Episcopal Church or Griswold himself. No stopping the November consecration. Nothing for a year's time, not until it comes out of committee. Even then, Chuck Murphy quipped, "Only maybe. . . . Griswold must be happy."

John Rucyahana was stunned there was no call to repentance. He wrote every archbishop at once: "Putting up with their actions for a whole year is a dangerous move. It gives the devil the upper hand. It demoralizes the churches in our Provinces. It exposes the Church to ridicule. It causes the members of the Church to lose confidence in their leaders . . . because there were no disciplinary actions taken."[22]

None whatsoever.

• • •

"The consecration is not negotiable," said Kolini sternly.

"The breaking of communion is their fault," Yong replied. "It is not ours."

Both men sat in a conference room in a nearby London hotel. The archbishops' meeting was over. They had brought with them Benjamin Nzimbi, archbishop of Kenya. They had invited Chuck Murphy and John Rodgers to be with them as they processed this historic meeting. None of them were happy with the public statement, knowing it had been politically softened. But it did not diminish the strength of their resolve, as Yong stated: "Many archbishops have given notice we will break communion if Griswold goes ahead with the consecration of Gene Robinson." These men were not waiting a year to respond.

"This was real spiritual warfare," Kolini said, recalling the meeting. "I could feel pressure on my heart. My breathing became hard. All I could do was close my eyes and pray. When you are at the end of your own strength, you turn to the Lord to fight the battle." He remembered one moment in particular. It was Griswold. He said publicly what should never have been said, ever, by anyone — the unimaginable.

The unforgivable.

Kolini's eyes became wet with tears, his face contorting in painful distress. Nzimbi and Yong listened as men who had been there and were there again, reliving the scene, the horror, the shock. A palpable presence of grief filled the room, both solemn and terrifying. These men believed the Bible. They believed what the Lord Jesus had said about the unforgivable sin. But to be there when it happened, to hear it said with conviction, without fear and trembling, without conscience, made them physically retch.

"Griswold told us," Kolini said quietly, factually, "the New Hampshire decision was done prayerfully and canonically. And then he said it was done by the Holy Spirit."

Kolini shook his head in disbelief and disgust. It was one thing to defy Scripture and tradition. But this was altogether different. This was an act of speaking against the Holy Spirit and he knew it. He felt it. He heard it with his own ears. Not just once. "Griswold said it three times. It broke my heart. I can't be in communion with that kind of person. This is a different spirit. We are in different religions."[23]

• • •

Gene Robinson was consecrated bishop on All Saints Day, November 2, 2003.[24]

The tear was immediate. Twelve of thirty-eight international Anglican provinces either broke communion or cut ties or declared "profound impairment of communion" with the US Episcopal Church: Nigeria, Rwanda, West Africa, Southeast Asia, Tanzania, Kenya, Uganda, the West Indies, Central Africa, South America, Congo, and Zambia. Archbishop Nkoyoyo spoke for the Church of Uganda: "We deplore, abhor and condemn [this act] in the strongest possible terms. . . . The Church of the Province of Uganda cuts her relationship and Communion with the Episcopal Church of the United States of America."[25]

Archbishop Nzimbi of Kenya told reporters: "The devil has clearly entered the church. God cannot be mocked." Sydney's Archbishop Jensen stated emphatically, "he is not a bishop."[26] Archbishop Akinola of Nigeria spoke on behalf of his church leaders: "We condemn in totality this consecration . . . this divisive and unscriptural act."[27] Archbishop Venables from South America wrote Griswold: "You have done what you had no right to do . . . absolutely scandalous. . . . It is my fervent hope that you will repent."[28] Archbishop Melango of Central Africa also wrote Griswold, saying, "In charity and heartbreak, I call you to repent. Until that time, you have broken our fellowship. To sit with you and meet with you would be a lie. We are not one. We do not share the same faith or Gospel. You should resign."[29]

By February 2004 four more provinces had broken from the Episcopal Church: Sudan, South India, Pakistan, and the Philippines. Their archbishops, joined with nine others, sent a letter to faithful Anglicans all over the world encouraging them "to engage in loyal witness to the risen Christ and to resist and confront the false teaching undergirding these actions and which is leading people away from the redeeming love of Jesus into error and danger. . . . we invite you to stand with us."[30]

But at what cost?

Archbishop Dirokpa from Congo said his bishops were profoundly aware of the cost. "We have already been warned. . . . there is little hope that we will be able to secure financial support from the United States for our dioceses. . . . Congo is already very poor and will consequently suffer even more. But, we have made our decision. . . . No one can force us to sell or to exchange our faith in Jesus Christ. . . . We will hold firm to the side of Jesus in spite of our poverty. . . . This is the cost of following Jesus."[31]

It was a stunning, miraculous moment in Anglican history. Suddenly there was leadership coming from the archbishops in the Anglican Communion. But not from the North. Not from Lambeth Palace. Not from a meeting or by democratic vote or by a statement made from a year-long committee. It came from deep within the hearts of archbishops from the southern hemisphere. These leaders rose up one by one in a time of crisis, linked arms, and knew they were appointed by God to lead the Anglican Communion into the future. Without pomp and ceremony yet filled with grace and dignity, the torch of God's anointing and leadership passed from North to South, from ancient Canterbury to Third World archbishops who refused to compromise their faith in the Lord Jesus Christ. The Anglican Communion would never be the same.

There were new leaders at the helm, marked by their passion to follow Jesus. Standing among them were two men, the forerunners, Kolini and Yong. Men who prayed this day would finally come.

● ● ●

The tear meant nothing to Griswold. He continued to campaign with renewed vigor. "God's truth is still unfolding," he said, defending why his actions contradicted the closed canon of Scripture. This truth, he kept insisting, did not come from his own mind but by divine inspiration: "The Holy Spirit is still leading us on."[32] And his bishops believed it. Peter Lee of Virginia, a supporter of Robinson, said smugly, "I like to think that down the road I'll be remembered as a bishop who did the right thing."[33]

Instead of being severely disciplined, these men received a gentle hand slap on October 18, 2004, when the year-long committee published their extensive work titled the "Windsor Report."

> We recommend that the Episcopal Church (USA) be invited to express its regret that the proper constraints of the bonds of affection were breached in the events surrounding the election and consecration of a bishop for the See of New Hampshire, and for the consequences which followed, and that such an expression of regret would represent the desire of the Episcopal Church (USA) to remain within the Communion.

This act of expressing regret for breaching bonds of affection was accompanied by an invitation "to effect a moratorium" on the election of another gay bishop "until some new consensus in the Anglican Communion emerges." The moratorium made no mention of disciplining or removing Gene Robinson from office and therefore, by implication, sanctioned his continued role as bishop in New Hampshire.[34]

In the same breath, and with equal weight of concern, the Windsor Report hand-slapped Kolini, Yong, and those who had initiated cross-boundary interventions for the sake of the gospel.

> We call upon those bishops who believe it is their conscientious duty to intervene in provinces, dioceses and parishes other than their own: to express regret for the consequences of their actions, to affirm their desire to remain in the Communion, and to effect a moratorium on any further interventions.[35]

The archbishops from the global South were outraged.

Peter Akinola, archbishop of Nigeria's nearly eighteen million Anglicans, issued an immediate statement: "Instead of a clear call for repentance we have been offered warm words of sentimentality for those who have shown no godly sorrow for their actions. . . . Where is the language of rebuke for those who are promoting sexual sins as holy and acceptable behavior?"[36]

Henry Orombi, the new archbishop of Uganda, agreed: "For us, the Windsor Report's call for expressions of 'regret' is not a sufficient response to the crisis the Episcopal Church's actions have created in the Anglican Communion. What is needed is clear repentance in both word and deed."[37]

Peter Akinola was equally upset that "We have been asked to express regret for our actions [of crossing boundaries]. . . . How patronizing! We will not be intimidated." From Lagos, Nigeria, archbishops meeting from all over Africa expressed their opposition: "To call on us to 'express regret' and reassert our commitment to the Communion is offensive."[38] They were not going to stop crossing boundaries. None of them were. Not until the Episcopal Church repented of their sin. And that wasn't about to happen.

In January 2005, the US Episcopal bishops made their first response to the Windsor Report by saying, "we as the House of Bishops express our sincere regret for the pain, the hurt, and the damage caused to our Anglican bonds of affection by certain actions of our church."[39]

This apology, or regret for causing pain, was a far cry from repentance. The global South leaders rejected the US apology outright, saying, "An apology . . . does not go far enough." Archbishop Melango of Central Africa told reporters, "They have . . . not repented." At his side was Archbishop Nzimbi of Kenya, who said, "Apology does not make sense to us. The biblical word is repentance."[40]

Archbishop Venables of South America was insulted by US arrogance:

[They will] have to repent and conform their teaching and practice to historic and biblical faith, in order to have the broken relationship restored. . . . Any thought that the passage of time will soften the resolve of the majority (of global South archbishops) is unfounded. To do so would be a rejection of our core values. It would be a rejection of the gospel itself, and a denial of the price that Jesus paid on our behalf.[41]

Again, Griswold simply didn't care. He was not going to repent. He made it clear in February 2005 on a nationally televised news broadcast with Jim Lehrer, saying "he regretted the pain he caused" by consecrating Robinson. "But that does not mean that we necessarily regret the action itself. Certainly, I, having participated in the ordination of the bishop of New Hampshire, do not regret having done so."[42]

Griswold had stepped over the line of no return.

From that moment on, it didn't matter what anyone said or didn't say. The US Episcopal Church and the Anglican Church of Canada were unable to hear the cry for repentance coming from all corners of the globe. On they marched: "We believe that God has been opening our eyes to acts of God that we had not known how to see before," wrote key Episcopal leaders as they affirmed their "support for gay clergy, and appealed for the contentious issue not to split the 77 million-strong Anglican Communion."[43]

But it was going to. They knew it. And they didn't care. Truth be told, they wanted it. In June 2006, as the 75th General Convention of the Episcopal Church met in Columbus, Ohio, they demanded it.

•　•　•

At General Convention 2006, Episcopal Church leaders made a mockery of the Windsor Report.

With Resolution A161, they rejected any hint of a "moratorium" on ordaining more gay bishops or blessing gay marriages. Instead, they passed Resolution B033, which promised "to exercise restraint" for anyone "whose manner of life presents a challenge to the wider church." The resolution meant nothing. Within weeks, the diocese of Newark, New Jersey, put forward a gay candidate for bishop.

Resolution D058 stated the simple message of Christian faith: Salvation through Christ alone, "the only name by which any person may be saved." It never made it out of committee, being vetoed by 70 percent majority. It would have gone unnoticed except Jeff Chu from *Time* magazine picked up on it. In an interview with Bishop Katherine Jefferts Schori, he asked her directly, "Is belief in Jesus the only way to get to heaven?" Her answer was of paramount importance. This woman, by vote of General Convention, had just become the next presiding bishop of the Episcopal Church, replacing Frank Griswold. Was she a Christian? Did she believe in the uniqueness of Jesus Christ—His deity, His saving death and resurrection?

This was her moment, in the national spotlight of *Time* magazine: "But for us to assume that God could not act in other ways is, I think, to put God in an awfully small box."[44]

What religion was this? Of course, the news of Schori's election stunned the world. She was the first female archbishop in Anglicanism. But to Anglican leaders in the global South this news paled in comparison to the confession of her beliefs. They had hoped for a leader who would honor the Christian faith and heal the divisions. Instead they got an activist, a supporter of Robinson, a campaigner for same-sex blessings. "Homosexuals were created by God," she told the world press. But they asked, how could she blatantly contradict Scripture? She replied: "The Bible was written in a very different historical context by people asking different questions."[45] The Bible no longer mattered. Not now. Not for her.

For this reason, Schori had no problem leaping beyond Christian recognition, using language unknown to Scripture or two thousand years of Christian witness. In her first sermon as presiding bishop-elect, she spoke of Jesus as no one had ever done before: "Our mother Jesus gives new birth to a new creation and we are his children." This woman, by her own confession, stood in open contradiction to the gospel. This made her, according to Christian doctrine classically defined, both biblically and historically, a heretic.

Instead of bringing her to justice, the Episcopal Church elected her as their leader. With great applause, Griswold rose in celebration, made his final bow, and declared without shame, "I believe the election of Katherine Jefferts Schori, Bishop of Nevada, to be the 26th Presiding Bishop was the work of the Holy Spirit."[46] With that, the fabric of the Anglican Communion ripped in two.

• • •

Archbishop Melango of Central Africa knew it was over. He also knew his people would suffer without money from the Episcopal Church. But physical suffering, and suffering for faith in Jesus, was common for African Christians, and expected. Melango welcomed it, saying, "their treasure chest has lost its luster. We would rather have Jesus and poverty. In that combination we find ourselves rich."[47]

Anglicans in Kenya received $70,000 from the Episcopal Church. They needed it. But what would they do? How could they call the US church to repent and at the same time, in good conscience, take their money? What kind of witness would that be? So they did what Christians do, even poor Christians. They sent it back, saying, "We are sorry to have lost a long-time relationship with the Episcopal Church, but we will not compromise the gospel of Jesus Christ."[48] They made the choice to suffer in Jesus.

Can we make the same choice? As Christians living in the US, this kind of suffering in Jesus is not common, expected, or welcomed. When it comes our way, it scares us. We are too much like our affluent culture. We opt for comfort. We medicate our pain. We choose not to choose suffering.

I have seen it countless times in my work with Anglican Mission. An Episcopal priest calls me. I sit across from him at a diner and listen. His conscience is tormented. He is living a lie and he knows it. He is a Christian man who has come to a living, saving faith in the Lord Jesus. His church has betrayed him. The bishops have denied his Savior and no one seems to care. No one brings the bishops to account.

He looks at me like a deer staring into the headlights. He is tired of pretending it will all go away. He is tired of meetings that promise change, and there is no change. As time passes everything gets worse.

Deep inside, he knows what to do. The Lord is pricking his heart. He must take a stand but he can't. It will cost him too much. He is afraid of losing his salary and benefits. He thinks about his wife and children. How will he provide for them? How will he make ends meet? He fears rejection from friends and colleagues. He agonizes over the people at church. He doesn't understand why they have to suffer. And they will. If he takes a stand, they will lose the church property. Some will go with him. Some will stay. They will divide. He doesn't want that to happen. He wants to protect them. But how can he protect them by staying under the authority of Episcopal bishops who have publicly blasphemed the name of Jesus?

He says it over and over again: He wants it all to go away. But it doesn't.

I tell him I will help him. We will walk through the suffering together. I remind him that Jesus promised to meet us in suffering. He is doing it with Christians in persecuted lands. He will do it with us. The priest makes no commitment. He tells me he will pray about it and call me. But he doesn't. So I call him a few weeks later. He tells me he can't do it, not now. The stakes are too high; maybe later.

He chooses not to choose suffering.

I immediately think of the Anglican leaders in Africa and Asia. They have already taken their stand against the US. Their poor are already suffering without US money. Why won't we suffer with them?

I don't understand it. I put the phone down. If I am certain of anything, it is this: We need the help of these Christians in Africa and Asia. We are weak in faith. They are strong in Christ. We are hesitating, compromising, and rationalizing. But they, by their actions, are choosing to follow Jesus regardless of personal comforts. We need their help. We need to be taught how to choose suffering for the sake of the gospel. Only then will we be strong and courageous to follow Jesus no matter the cost. Only then will we be able to join them in singing this triumphant song of praise and glory to God: "We would rather have Jesus and poverty. In that combination we find ourselves rich."

PART 3

RAISING THE CROSS

CHAPTER 16

GRANT US SUFFERING

For to you it has been granted for Christ's sake, not only to believe in Him, but also to suffer for His sake, experiencing the same conflict which you saw in me, and now hear to be in me.

— PHILIPPIANS 1:29–30 (NASB)

John Rucyahana and I met for one last interview before completing this book. We sat in a hotel lobby in Pittsburgh on a rainy Sunday afternoon in April. We talked for hours, as old friends do. Even now, after all these years, I am struck by the difference between us.

I remind him of the night he stepped into the pulpit at Beeson Divinity School in Alabama. In a chapel replete with images from the past, the great heroes down through Christian history, I saw John turn and look behind him. He focused on the carved bust of a man named Luwum and pointed to it. Before his sermon ever began, before the congregation ever sat, John lifted up his voice and said, "Do you see that man? That man was my father in the faith." And that is where the difference between us begins.

Janani Luwum held the office of Anglican archbishop of Uganda during the days of Idi Amin's presidency. The last time John saw him was in February 1977. They were together, in the western part of Uganda, preaching side by side at an evangelistic crusade. John told the crowd at Beeson,

We were working in the mission field, preaching Jesus. Many people were coming to faith in Christ. In the middle of the crusade, Idi

Amin's soldiers came for him. They arrested him. They took him back to the capital city of Kampala where Amin put a gun to his head and killed him.

I look at John with amazement. He was mentored in Christ by men like Janani Luwum, who gave his life for the sake of the Lord Jesus. His earliest years as a Christian, an evangelist, and a clergyman were under Muslim domination. He grew up in faith experiencing a biblical principle that makes no sense to the human mind: *The church comes alive in suffering and martyrdom.* I think of Acts 8. Persecution came against the church after Stephen's death. Instead of frightening Christians into silence, the exact opposite happened: they "went about preaching the word . . . and proclaiming Christ." How is it possible? I think of Tertullian, a church father from the third century, describing it in these terms: "The blood of the martyrs is the seed of the church." What is this divine grace resting on the church in times of persecution?

But this is typical of me. I say this to John because I've read it in the Bible and church history. He knows that grace. He has experienced it in times of persecution. He has lived it and been discipled by it.

I make my confession. I tell John my fathers in the faith were American preachers and academic scholars. We have not known suffering and martyrdom in the US. We have not experienced that grace that comes in times of persecution. We pray for the persecuted church in faraway lands. But personally, I don't know it. I've not lived it. I'm not shaped by it and I am strangely unaware of what I am missing without it.

John looks at me and says quietly, "It is already here in the US."

He tells me again the story of an Episcopal priest from Alabama who was fired from his church. The bishop and lay leaders politically forced him out and, when he left, nearly two hundred went with him. The issue was simple: This man preached Jesus according to the Bible. He was maligned, slandered, and mistreated for being an evangelical. Shortly after he left, the two hundred began meeting in a school gym for Sunday morning services. They wanted their priest to come and lead them, but he wouldn't do it.

I met with that priest, John tells me. I said, "Go, lead this people. Jesus said, 'If they persecuted Me, they will also persecute you.' You have been persecuted. It's an honor to be persecuted for Jesus. Now go, these people need you." But the priest said no. He said he was too wounded from the pain of it all. He needed counseling and rest. So he took the severance money and left for three months. By the time he got back, the people had chosen another priest to lead them. You see, persecution is already here and you don't know how to handle it. And if you can't handle this, what are you going to do when it gets worse?

He doesn't have to convince me. I remind him of the day a reporter came to him at a conference and asked, "What can African bishops do to help Americans keep their church properties?" John was horrified. He was in America for one reason: to fight for the gospel against Episcopal heretics. Church property meant nothing in comparison. Nor was it reasonable to ask Third World bishops living in poverty to help Americans rescue their properties. John did not mince words. He spoke to the reporter and challenged him: "What are you doing? We Africans have come to rescue you from a burning house. We are helping to save your souls. Why are you asking us to run back in and save your furniture? Are you ready to follow Jesus or not?"[1]

Even now, this African bishop has no patience with me on this subject.

Here's the problem, I tell him. Some of our most respected evangelical preachers in the Episcopal Church are waging a different war: They're fighting Episcopal heretics for their buildings. Some of them are famous, long-time leaders of large, successful churches. Their properties are worth millions, paid for by the people. For this reason, many have gone to their bishop to work out a financial settlement. Others have hired lawyers and taken their bishop to court. Still others are waiting out the storm, believing the Episcopal Church will one day extend mercy and allow them to leave with their church buildings.

John shakes his head in disgust.

He says sharply, "You cannot serve two masters. These clergymen have a duty before God to stand for Jesus, call their bishops to repent, and suffer the pain of being evicted from their buildings for the sake of the gospel. You do not negotiate money with heretics. Never! If they evict you, you accept suffering. Then go, stand outside your buildings, and let the world know you are clinging to Jesus Christ, not your buildings. My brother, it's time you Americans take up your cross and follow Jesus. What are you waiting for?"

Why are you afraid to suffer?

I have no answer for him. I only know this: Some of these great preachers discipled me in Christ. They are faithful ministers, profoundly gifted in ministry. To this day, I believe they were appointed by God to lead the recovery of Anglicanism in North America. And they would have, if it hadn't come at the high cost of losing their church properties. I believe John is right. We fear suffering. We believe the Bible is true but deceptively hold a First World view of the Bible: *The Lord never allows Christians to suffer.*

But how can I tell that to this African who knows *true* suffering in Christ?

He reminds me his American professor, Stephen Noll, wrote an article called "It's the Property, Stupid!" Noll said the main problem among evangelicals of our generation is tragically not theological but financial; it's not the outrage of heresy but the loss of property.[2] You see, John argued, Americans can't always hear the voice of poor Africans. So let them hear Stephen Noll. He's a respected theologian and yet he condemns you. He knows you have more passion for church property than for Jesus. Now, why is that?

His question hits hard, deep. It hurts. I say it quickly, honestly, almost under my breath: *because we think we can have both.*

• • •

Of course, this doesn't apply to everyone.

I tell John about Rick Terry. He served eleven years as rector of St. Paul's Episcopal Church in Chillicothe, Ohio. He may not be famous, but what he did was remarkable. Together with his leaders, he challenged the bishop of southern Ohio to uphold sound doctrine. When the bishop refused to comply,[3] Rick made a choice. He resigned as rector and left the church building behind.[4]

> I have sought to remain obedient to the Lord Jesus, endeavoring to be a faithful minister of God's Word and Sacraments. . . . I have decided to leave quietly. This is not about me. This is about fidelity to the Gospel of Jesus Christ.[5]

With church leaders and parishioners at his side, he rented space at a coffee house in the middle of town and began meeting for Sunday morning worship. Rick and his wife, Dody, lost their home at the church rectory.

With a cut in salary and two boys in college, Rick had no choice but to paint houses as he pastored the new church: "I'd much rather do that than compromise what the Lord Jesus Christ did for me."

I tell John that Rick isn't alone. Recently, I met Kenyan clergy in the Boston area who work eight-hour night shifts, five days a week, while pastoring their church full time. It is their testimony in the Lord Jesus Christ that they will not serve Tom Shaw, bishop of Massachusetts; they will not share in his sin of promoting immorality; and they will not worship in his buildings.[6] I've met clergy wives who are raising their children and, at the same time, working long hours to help finance their husband's cut in salary. And I've met Christians from all over the US and Canada who sacrificially give time and resources to help their churches — meeting in rented spaces — be a strong witness for Christ in their communities. These people have welcomed suffering and hardship, and they have done it joyfully.

People like Margaret Hughes. I will never forget the day I met her.

I was preaching at an Anglican Mission church outside Philadelphia. I still remember Margaret, in her late eighties, sitting by herself after church at coffee hour. As I sat next to her, she asked me — in her most elegant British accent — if I knew her late husband. Little did I know I was talking to the widow of the great twentieth-century theologian Philip Edgcumbe Hughes. I asked her gently, "What are you doing with these Christians? They are nomads. The bishop forced them out of their building. Why have you gone with them?"

"Because I wouldn't have it any other way," she said with a smile.

"Yes, but isn't your husband buried at the old church?"

"My dear," she said to me, her hand resting on mine, "I never promised to follow my husband's bones. I promised to follow his faith. And he would have done the very same thing."[7]

• • •

John opened his Bible.

As he was looking for a particular verse, he said, "Archbishop Moses Tay told us to remember Lot's wife. In Southeast Asia, Muslims are persecuting and killing Christians. People have no choice. They are forced to answer the question, are you a Christian or not?[8] So what do they do? Do they speak up or do they remain quiet? If they speak up, they know they will suffer persecution, and they don't want to suffer. So the devil tempts them to remain quiet. But the Bible is clear: If we are Christians, we must speak up and confess Jesus. If we don't, we are ashamed of Him. We deny Him.[9] We become like Lot's wife, turning back to the comforts of Sodom. This we cannot do and escape the fire of judgment."

With that, he read a passage from the gospel of John: "Yet at the same time many even among the leaders believed in him. But because of the Pharisees they would not confess their faith for fear they would be put out of the synagogue; for they loved praise from men more than praise from God" (John 12:42–43).

"Look carefully at these verses with me," John said. "These men were politicians. They believed in Jesus privately but they would not confess Him publicly. If they did, the cost would be too great. They'd be thrown out of the synagogue. This means real personal suffering. They would lose their position of power as leaders, their respect in the community, their financial income, and any hope for success in the future. As men confessing Jesus, they'd be rejected as Jesus was rejected and treated as outcasts and lepers. He was despised. He was nailed to a cross. If you confess Him, you get thrown out of the synagogue with Him only to bear the weight of His cross. Do you think they wanted that? The Bible says no. They feared suffering. They loved praise from men more than from God. This was their time of testing. They made their choice."

"You mean the choice to keep quiet," I responded.

"Out of self-protection," John thundered.

"Yes, because they didn't want to suffer. Like many of us, they wanted the best of both worlds."

"No," John shot back. "You can't have both. My brother, listen to me. We have come from Africa and Asia to help you. You cannot stay under the authority of religious leaders and bishops who deny Jesus as God's unique and eternal Son, the only Savior of the world; who reject the Bible as the Word of God; and who promote immorality as the church has never known. You cannot stay at the communion table with these people. You cannot stay and worship the Lord in their buildings. You must speak up as Christians. Testify against them. Call them to repent of their sin. They will throw you out on the street. They will call you names. You will suffer for Jesus. But this is what it means to love praise from God more than praise from men. My brother, the time of testing is here, right now. You must choose: Are you Christians or not?

Are you nothing more than politicians?

I was struck by the force of his words. I had not seen the chasm of John 12:42–43, separating private belief and public confession. I was deeply convicted. There have been many times I have kept quiet about my faith in Christ. I've made that political choice because I feared personal rejection. In these days of heresy in the Episcopal Church, many of us have kept quiet. We have made the argument: "Why speak out? We're orthodox Christians, right believers in Christ. We're safe. That's all that matters." But is that true? If we do not speak out, are we denying Him by our silence? Have we become like these men in John 12?

"I don't know, John. This is confusing to me."

"But why is it confusing?"

"Many of us," I said, "who know and love the Lord are guilty of this sin. We have kept quiet in the face of persecution and heresy. I think about evangelicals who are still in the Episcopal Church. They may speak out a little, but they will never speak loudly enough to risk personal suffering. They will never take that one step, cross the line, and risk it all for Christ. What are you saying about them? Are they not Christians?"

"Listen to me," he responded. "I am saying they are under a test. It's not enough to say, 'We are orthodox! We are evangelicals!' The Lord Jesus Christ requires obedience. We must obey Him. He asked Peter, 'Do you love Me more than these?' If so, 'Follow Me!'[10] If these people are truly converted by the Holy Spirit, they will not stay with heretics who distort the Bible to their own destruction and speak against the name of Jesus who saved them for eternal glory. Eventually, they will leave the Episcopal Church and not be far behind you."[11]

"But, John, many won't. It's a fact. They have made the decision to stay in and keep quiet."

"Keep quiet?" With that, a certain pain washed over John's face. He sat back in his chair, his eyes fixed on mine, his finger pointed directly at me. From deep within his African heart came three words I have heard him say time and time again. These words have long shaped his identity in Christ. He learned them as a young boy under his father's care, as a teenager in Rwandan refugee camps, as a Christian under Muslim persecution, and as an Anglican bishop of Rwanda in the aftermath of genocide. These three words, he believed, could have saved a million Rwandan lives in April 1994 if the US and the United Nations had had the moral courage to act on them. But they didn't and, for John, there can be no greater sin. There can be no excuse, no compromise. We must always act on them, no matter the times. No matter the situation.

Never keep quiet.

He said it again and again, until my American ears could hear and understand.

Never keep quiet.

● ● ●

He first pressed these words into my heart on the day he took me to Rwanda and showed me the corpses of his fallen people. He spoke simple truth: "We cried out for mercy. You in America heard our cry.

"You did nothing."

Never keep quiet.

"Remember," he said that day, "those who see the crime and keep quiet are as guilty as those who commit the crime. It was true during the days of genocide. It is equally true in the days of persecution and heresy: If you say you are orthodox, and keep quiet, you are as guilty as the heretics."

Never keep quiet.

"We may suffer for it. It may come at a high cost. But it doesn't matter. This is the gospel we preach. The Father heard our cry when we were lost in sin. He could have turned away but He didn't. He acted. He sent His beloved Son. Thanks be to God, the Lord Jesus came down from heaven. He went to the cross. He suffered for us. With His blood, He forgave us. He reconciled us to the Father."

Jesus did not remain quiet. As Christians, we cannot remain quiet —ever.

● ● ●

People ask me, "What are these Anglican bishops and archbishops from Africa and Asia doing here in America?" I answer, "They have come to teach us." Then I am asked, "But what have they come to teach us?"

Three words, I tell them, which are simple to say, hard to hear, and much harder to act on.

And then I say, "If only you could meet these men."

When John Rucyahana came to the US in 1997, he saw the rebellion in the Episcopal Church. He met clergy and Christians oppressed by heretical bishops. They needed protection. He made appointments with as many evangelical Episcopal bishops as possible. He urged them to take immediate action: *Go to them. Cross diocesan boundaries. Rebuke the heresy. Defend the faith. Risk your job.* But they were not willing. They gave him no choice. He could not walk away in silence. So he did what these US bishops refused to do. He took action. He crossed provincial and diocesan lines. He started in Little Rock, Arkansas, and the news went everywhere: *An African bishop oversees an Episcopal church in America.* This African did more than tell us. He was the first to show us. He did what most of us were afraid to do.

Never keep quiet.

John did not ask permission; not even from his archbishop, Emmanuel Kolini. He knew he could lose his office as bishop. He could bring international disgrace to the Anglican Church of Rwanda. But what choice did he have? He is a survivor of the Rwandan genocide. He is a Christian, a bishop, and a defender of the faith. In his mind, these biblical principles are not to be compromised or negotiated.

Never walk away from the cry of the persecuted.

Never play politics with heretics.

Never keep quiet.

John's archbishop, Emmanuel Kolini, is no different. He fully agreed with John's decision to take the church in Little Rock. So did all the Anglican bishops of Rwanda. From that time on, they spoke out with one voice, publicly denouncing the rebellion of the Episcopal Church. And they suffered for it.

Emmanuel Kolini once said at a national gathering for Anglican Mission,

> Money has been used as a threat to my people and Province because we supported Anglican Mission. Even brothers and sisters turned against us. It was the same in times past and is the same in the church

today. We are viewed as traitors crossing the ocean looking to help. But liberation has come to you. Do we love Jesus more than ourselves? Do we love Jesus more than our properties? Do we love Him more than anything else? Then let us go forth and do His mission.[12]

And that's Emmanuel Kolini. He went to Singapore in January 2000 to consecrate two American priests as bishops and send them to the US to begin the rescue work. He could not sit back in silence and allow the *spiritual genocide* in the Episcopal Church and Canada to continue. He had no choice. He had to act. He is a Christian, a survivor of the Rwandan genocide, a bishop, and a defender of the faith. If this act in Singapore meant being removed as archbishop of Rwanda, then so be it. Obedience to Jesus Christ comes first.

My soul is crying. I will *never keep quiet* as the world did to my people. You in Anglican Mission asked us to come help, and we came. We had not asked your missionaries of times past to come to Africa—but, thank God, you came. Now we come to you.[13]

The Rwandans did not come to America alone. Archbishop Moses Tay of Southeast Asia hosted the Singapore consecrations. Yong Ping Chung, his successor, refused to let the Rwandans fight the battle in isolation. These Asians stood strong in their faith in Christ, not willing to shrink back in silence at the Anglican rebellion in North America. Instead, they acted. Alongside Kolini and Rucyahana, they stormed the US as missionaries of a gospel that demands they *never keep quiet* in the face of heresy and opposition.

Yong said it this way:

Our God is a loving and merciful God. But He will not tolerate compromises to the essentials of our faith. . . . He will intervene. . . . He will raise up leaders after His own heart. He will begin new work and ministry that is obedient to His call and command.[14]

These men were the first. They opened the door for bishops and archbishops to come from Kenya, Uganda, Nigeria, Congo, Bolivia, and many other Anglican provinces. These missionaries have come to defend the Anglican Church from the tyranny of unthinkable heresy and to help us. They want us to be strong in our faith in Christ Jesus; unwavering in our devotion to the inspiration and authority of the Bible; uncompromised in our resolve to speak up and *never keep quiet* in days of immorality and injustice; and then, in humility, to accept the suffering that comes as a result. And suffering does come.

They know it back home, and they know it on our behalf.

Who could have guessed that US monies would have been cut off from them and their poor? Who could imagine Episcopal revisionists mocking these great men as ignorant, simple-minded fundamentalists? But they expect slander. They want us to expect it too. They want us to know that obedience to Jesus Christ comes first; and with it comes suffering; and with suffering comes "grace upon grace" to endure it.

These are the missionaries who have come to America.

The Lord has sent them for a purpose; not just to Anglicans, but for all in North America who bear the name of Christ. For they see our culture lost in arrogance, pride, and lust. They feel the demonic grip upon the hearts and minds of powerful church leaders. They know that spiritual forces of darkness have already begun to descend hard upon our land. They are convinced persecution is coming with greater force against believing Christians. They want us to be prepared — not just for these present days, but the days yet to come.

And not just for us, but for those who come after us.

●　　●　　●

I opened my Bible to Romans 5:1–5 and read it to John.

> Therefore, since we have been justified through faith, we have peace with God through our Lord Jesus Christ, through whom we have gained access by faith into this grace in which we now stand. And we rejoice in the hope of the glory of God. . . . And hope does not disappoint us, because God has poured out his love into our hearts by the Holy Spirit, whom he has given us.

I skipped verses 3 and 4.

It's these two verses, I tell John, that separate you and me, your church and my church. You see, with verses 1, 2, and 5, I still get to preach the great doctrines of the Bible: justification through faith, peace with God, standing in grace, rejoicing in hope, His love poured into our hearts, and His power given us in the Holy Spirit. These are exalted themes. They lead people to Jesus Christ and the work of His cross. They declare that God's promises in Christ are available to us right now for the asking. Our Christians want that. They need that. The last thing they want to hear is preaching on verses 3 and 4, and I'll tell you why.

Most Americans live pressured lives, full of anxiety and stress. When they come to church, they want relief. They want an experience that's positive and upbeat. American preachers know that. If we want them back, if we want our churches to grow, we need to provide services and programs that are engaging, relevant, not too demanding, not too serious, but focused on making sure their needs are met. If we don't, they will find churches that will. That's life in our consumer culture. So we preach 1, 2, and 5, not 3 and 4.

He laughed at me. "You can't do that!" And then he read the missing verses: "Not only so, but we also rejoice in our sufferings, because we know that suffering produces perseverance; perseverance, character; and character, hope."

He said quietly, "You are cheating your people."

"It's true," I responded. "We're not telling them that they will suffer if they bear His name, if they live godly lives in Christ Jesus, if they give strong, uncompromised testimony of Him at opportune times. Our culture will beat them down. We're already seeing it. More Christians than ever are facing immoral practices at work. They know if they speak up, they risk their jobs. College students are calling home and testifying of the daily pressure to give in to the lifestyle of their peers. Some are giving in and their parents don't know what to do about it. Do they speak up? Do they risk pushing their children away from them?

"Fourteen-year-old Jennafyr Giuffrida goes to public school in Massachusetts. She wears a cross around her neck because she is a Christian. Her classmates know it. Every day someone ridicules her for her faith in Jesus, often to the point of tears. But every morning she makes the same decision to wear the cross. She is living verses 3 and 4. She is a missionary to her generation and suffering for it in Jesus' name."

"It's true," John said. "You have to make choices like this young girl. Do you come to church as a consumer to get your needs met or do you come for Jesus? If you come for Jesus, He will send you out to be a witness in His name and a missionary to your people. If you do that, He promises you will suffer."

He looked down at his Bible and went through the text of verses 3 and 4 point by point.

- Because of the great salvation given us in Christ Jesus, as stated in verses 1–2, believing Christians are promised suffering in this world.[15]
- We are to expect it.[16] But much more, we are to rejoice in it.
- Then, in the midst of Christian suffering, the Lord works in us these divine graces of perseverance, tested character, and hope.
- As He does that, we experience His love poured out into our hearts by the Holy Spirit, who helps us face suffering and persecution, even if it means we die.

"You can't avoid this," he stated.

"But we can," I reply. "We make another choice. We leave church and stay quiet about Jesus. If we stay quiet, we don't suffer for Him. It's that simple. Our faith is then shared only between Christians."

He looked away and didn't respond.

"John, you decided a long time ago to live boldly for Jesus. You were persecuted for it. But in the midst of your suffering, you found these verses to be true. The more it happened, the stronger you became as a witness for Christ. I saw that strength in you. I didn't see it in me. When you took me to Africa, I saw these same biblical principles at work in the church. These Christians knew persecution for their faith in Jesus. They knew physical suffering from daily life in Third World poverty. I expected to see them beaten down. But instead, I saw the joy of the Lord on their faces. I heard it in their testimonies, their songs of praise, and their unbridled passion to evangelize their people for Jesus Christ. I couldn't believe it. I still can't. I'm amazed the church comes alive in times of suffering. Seeing it, experiencing it, was beyond me.

"I knew then that something had to change in the US. You showed me these verses from Paul's letter to the Philippians: 'For it has been granted to you on behalf of Christ not only to believe on him, but also to suffer for him, since you are going through the same struggle you saw I had, and now hear that I still have' (Phil. 1:29–30).

"I came home praying for it: 'Lord, grant us suffering in the US on behalf of Christ.' And I began preaching it across the country. I must tell you, it annoyed people. They came up to me and told me they didn't like it. But it didn't stop me. I'm convinced we need it. If we're going to be filled by the Holy Spirit to be missionaries to our country, then we have to make the same choice: Are we going to live boldly for Jesus or not? If so, we need to expect suffering and believe the Lord will meet us in that suffering. Then, and only then, will we know verses 3 and 4 by experience. We will begin to feel the kind of strength in Christ you and your church know so well. We will taste joy from the Lord like we've never known before. And we will find a new passion welling up inside us to evangelize our people for Jesus Christ. It's what happened in the book of Acts. It's happening in your church in Africa. It needs to happen here in America."

He nodded, looking straight at me.

"Then we need your help, John. We need the testimony of your Christians in the pulpits of our country. I know you've come to rescue us from the heresy of our denomination. But we need more from you. Call us to repent of our self-indulgence. Teach us to be missionaries in a country hostile to the gospel. Grab our hands and walk us into verses 3 and 4 that we might win our generation, and the next, for Christ."

Help us choose Jesus.

CHAPTER 17

THE HILLSIDE

A few minutes passed before John said, "You know this isn't easy."

As we talked, my thoughts went to Bishop Chuck Murphy. For ten years I worked at his side as he chaired Anglican Mission in America. Every day I saw him plagued by all kinds of distractions. Every day he made the same choice to stay on message: "We're a missionary movement. That's it." Chuck refused to direct time and energy to the heretics screaming for attention in the Episcopal Church. He was done with them and said so on more than one occasion: "I am convinced that our call is to remain focused on our mission, make the decision to 'leave alone' the various 'blind guides' that would otherwise distract and deflect us . . . and boldly press on."[1]

He also had little interest in the political restructuring of orthodox Anglicanism in the US. There were too many meetings, too many people vying for position and power. This, too, he believed, was a great distraction. So he asked Archbishop Kolini to grant one request: Let Anglican Mission be protected under the province of Rwanda. In this way, Chuck could do what he does best: cast the vision for a missionary movement in America. Keep the leaders focused and on task and not distracted by changes taking place in Anglicanism worldwide. Recruit a new generation of leaders who live and breathe evangelism and mission,[2] and provide every resource possible to help Anglican Mission churches succeed to the glory of God.

Year after year, Chuck's message simply did not change:

As a missionary outreach of Rwanda, we have a secure Anglican home in that Province. As a missionary outreach to the United States, we have a clear focus on the 130 million unchurched people in this country. As I have said before, that is our charge. That is our calling. That is our mission.[3]

It always surprised me when evangelical leaders spoke harshly against Chuck, and even more when it didn't seem to deter him. Every day he made the same choice. Every day he kept pursuing one thing and one thing only: It's about mission. It's about the 130 million in our country who don't know Jesus. It's about faithfulness to Christ, being true to the gospel, and then doing something about it. It's saying no to distractions and politics, every day. And every day, saying yes to the mission given us in Christ Jesus.

•   •   •

"Again I tell you," John said, "this isn't easy." He stood up, went to the counter, and poured a cup of coffee. He turned and said, "There are three principles I want you to know."

"One, heresy has a purpose. You see, it is the devil himself tormenting the church. He distorts the Bible. He confuses Christians. He stirs up division among us so we become ineffective in our mission to preach the gospel to the lost. Therefore, we must oppose heretics immediately. The apostle Paul said he did 'not yield in subjection to them for even an hour.'[4] We must never waste time. We stop them, recover the church, preach the Bible, and get back into mission. If we don't do this, we become politicians.

"Two, we must never play politics. We cannot allow the devil to scare us from speaking the truth. I've told you before that Bob Duncan, bishop of Pittsburgh, once said to me, 'John, you are not politically seasoned.' He is right! I thank God for that. I told him I am not called for politics, and neither is he. We are called to speak the truth in Jesus' name so the church can remain healthy and be a light to the world."

John was emphatic: "We must be persistent. We can never let up."

Then he said, "I remember when the archbishops met in Tanzania in February 2007. They called the Episcopal Church to repent of their sin of practicing sexual immorality.[5] But this confused me. Why did they do that? The Episcopal Church has denied the Bible. They have denied Jesus as the only way of salvation. I tell you, this sin is greater. They should have been called to repent of that first. Then, if they do that, they will know why they must repent of the other. You see, we must be careful to speak the whole truth. When we hold back, when we water it down, we become politicians. This is very dangerous. The Lord will hold us accountable on the day of judgment for that. You must teach this in your churches."

As he sat back down, I noticed John was restless. I asked him to continue, but somehow we started talking about other things. Eventually I circled back and asked again about the third principle.

He sipped his coffee and became quiet. I watched him stare deep into his cup as if he had already escaped to another place, another time. Without raising his eyes, he said gently, "I told you, it isn't easy."

•   •   •

As John often does, he painted pictures with his words. In telling the story, he took me to Rwanda, to a field on a hill overlooking one of the prisons. The countryside is once again spectacular, the lush green hills of Rwanda all around, all neatly cultivated and terraced, with workers tilling the land for as far as the eye can see. To me, the sky has always seemed a deeper blue, the clouds a richer white than back home. The sun is hot on my skin and strong. The brightness hits down on the lakes and makes them come alive with beauty. The volcanic mountains in the distance rise to meet the clouds in the air and then stretch high to touch the heavens.

It all seems perfect until my eye again catches sight of the prison below and the soldiers standing at the entrance, dressed in military uniform, their rifles strapped over their shoulders and hanging down at their side. I know about these prisons from John. They are packed with the killers of the genocide. I wonder why he has brought me here.

"I have one more thing to say. I want you to know the sin that has been in my heart."

I look at him in surprise. I don't understand.

"You know," he states, "God has called us to preach the gospel to sinners. But He tells us to speak truth in love. Do we do that? When we speak to church leaders bound in the lies of the devil, do we love them? Do we want them to know Jesus? Are we begging the Lord to have mercy on them? Or are we angry for what they have done to us and to our people? Are we guilty of pride because we stand in the truth and they do not? Do we look down on them, judging them in our hearts? Are we like Jonah preaching to the people of Nineveh? He didn't want them to repent. He didn't want the Lord to extend mercy to them.

"My brother, have we become that?"

I watch as tears fill his eyes.

He points down at the prison. He tells me that more than 110,000 fill the jails of Rwanda since the genocide. He has been inside. He has listened to story after story. He tells me again, like he has done so many times before, "They still hear the screaming voices of those they killed. The scenes replay in their mind. They can't stop them. It torments them in the day. It wakes them at night. The guilt is fresh, like an open wound still bleeding. They feel the presence of evil haunting them. The smell of death still burns deep in their nostrils. The pain presses down hard on them. It's too much for anybody to bear."

John knows their only hope is the Lord Jesus Christ. When he was asked to serve as chairman of Prison Fellowship in Rwanda, he agreed.[6] But he had no idea what it would cost him personally. Not until the day he came here, to this prison. He came by invitation. They asked him to preach the gospel in front of a large gathering. As he stood in front of the prisoners, he knew exactly what to say.

"They have to repent," John tells me. "They have perpetrated the genocide. They are guilty of a great sin before the Lord. They will never be able to pay for what they did. If they do not repent, they will perish in the flames of hell. Only Jesus can save them. They need to know that. They need to know what He did for them at the cross. I told them plainly, they must run to Jesus, repent of their sin, and beg for His mercy.

"But the moment I said that, I saw tears rolling from their eyes. Many started crying out loud. Others were calling on the Lord in repentance. I knew what was happening. I am part of the East African revival. I know what it means to see the Holy Spirit bringing people under conviction of sin and into saving faith in Jesus Christ. When I saw that, I reacted. I stopped preaching. They didn't want me to stop. They wanted to hear more from the Bible about Jesus. But I couldn't do it.

"I ran out of the meeting room and out of the prison, until I came to this hill. Tears were streaming down my face. Pain was gripping my heart. I couldn't believe the depth of anger I felt against them. It shocked me. It overwhelmed me."

I watch him, there on the hillside—his voice rises, his fists clench.

"They killed my people. They killed my family.

"They killed my niece, Madu.

"They stripped her naked, using machetes to peel the skin off her arms from shoulder to wrist, and they gang-raped her. They cut off her head.

"They raped her mother, and then they killed her and her brother also.

"What was I doing preaching to their killers?"[7]

He looks away, his face wet from tears.

"I tell you the pain was too great for me. I fell on my knees and wept. I thought I wanted those men to know Jesus, but it's not true. I wanted them to pay. I opposed them, and I opposed the Lord. Why was He reaching out to save those men? How could He forgive them for what they did to me and my family?

"I could not stop the crying. I didn't understand it. But I knew this truth: The confusion and pain was coming from within me. Bitterness had taken root. The desire for revenge was choking me. If anybody needed to run to Jesus and repent, it was me. I needed Jesus. I needed Him to forgive me. I was no different than the prisoners. I was locked behind bars of resentment and unforgiveness and I knew it.

"I kept praying: *Lord Jesus Christ, help me. I have sinned against You. Take this pain from me.* But He didn't do it. I continued to pray until the Holy Spirit made it clear to me—*I must forgive the killers of my family.* I told Him no, I couldn't do that. The pain was too great. The hurt was too deep.

"But He said it was past time. He wanted me to remember the Lord Jesus Christ and what He did when He was nailed to the cross. He did not turn away from His killers. He faced them. He looked them straight in the eyes and cried out from the midst of His pain, 'Father, forgive them; for they do not know what they are doing.'

"It was hard for me to hear that. I knew the Lord was challenging me: *Did Jesus wait until He got off the cross to forgive His killers, or did He do it while He was still in pain?* I said to the Lord, *He did it while He was still in pain.* I said it many times until it sank deep into my mind: *He forgave us while He was still in pain.*

Just then, John stretches out his arms from side to side as far as they can go. I have seen him do this a thousand times when he speaks about the cross. I see the pain still etched on his face as he says, "When the Lord Jesus Christ was hanging on the tree, stripped, beaten, mocked, despised, nails tearing through His flesh, nails in His feet, and a crown of thorns on His head, from within the pain He cried, 'Forgive! Forgive!'"

He keeps his arms extended, and he tells me, "I immediately got up from my knees. I wiped the tears from my eyes. I went down the hill and did what He was telling me to do. I went back into the prison. It was time for me to go and forgive those men in the name of Jesus. It didn't matter that pain was still gripping my heart. Anger was still inside. The Lord had not taken it from me. But He showed me: We can't wait until the pain is gone; we must forgive while we are in pain. This is what Christians do, and He gives us the power to do it."

"You went back?" I ask, startled.

"Yes. There is no time to waste. It is now, as tears flow down from our cheeks that we must learn to forgive. We must tell them about Jesus who loves them. He holds no grudge. He hates their sin. But He calls them to repent. It is high time they know that and surrender their lives to Jesus Christ. They have nowhere else to go. He will heal them. He will forgive them by His blood shed on Calvary. He will save them by His own power for eternal life. He will bring them together in love and reconciliation so that Hutus and Tutsis are united together for His glory. It is the only way for my nation to be put back together."[8]

John sits back in his chair and put his arms down.

I can feel my insides churning. I am not like him. I could not go back into that prison. Not now. Not for a long time. I watch him as he pulls out a clean handkerchief and wipes his face.

He tells me, "To this day I go to the prisons in tears. I can still feel the pangs of bitterness. It is not easy for me." But then, in the same breath, John tells me story after story of testimonies in Rwandan prisons. His face lights up when he says, "You can't believe it! The Lord is performing miracles in the prisons. We are seeing men and women cry out to the Lord like never before. They are coming to saving faith in Jesus Christ and then they're becoming evangelists! They are winning fellow prisoners to Jesus. We are seeing repentance catch fire from prison to prison. It is true. It is miraculous. It is the glory of God. The Lord Jesus Christ is healing Rwanda from inside the prisons of the killers! Who would ever imagine that!"

And then he smiles from ear to ear, giving thanks and praise to the Lord.

• • •

I listen, I smile. I join him in giving the Lord praise. But I am distant. I am still strangely stuck on that hillside in Rwanda. His story has pierced to something deep inside me, and I need to work through it. I need to talk it over with him. But the moment I begin, I realize it's not going to happen.

From behind me, I hear people coming toward us. Their voices are familiar. John is scheduled to preach at a local church, and these people have come to pick him up. I look at my watch and realize our time is up. I react immediately. I don't want them here, not now. I don't want this moment interrupted. I need more time with John.

But that's not going to happen. It's over. John is the first to get up and greet them. I stand next, and we enter that horrible zone of small talk.

"We're sorry we're a few minutes late," one of them says. John reaches down for his briefcase. Someone else grabs his luggage. We all shake hands and linger for a moment in conversation.

As we conclude, I turn to hug John good-bye and thank him.

"Remember," he says to me, "the Lord Jesus Christ forgave us while He was still in pain. Trust Him to meet you there. He will help you by His Holy Spirit to do the same."

He takes a step back and points his finger at me. I know that look. I know the unspoken words. He has said them to me so many times: *Now go, put a torch into the darkness, and tell people everywhere about Jesus.*

Then he turns and walks away.

• • •

I watch him as he leaves the hotel lobby and gets into the car with the others. He stops and does what he has always done with me. He lifts both hands in the air and waves them in an African greeting. I wave back and watch him disappear into the car. As it pulls away, I see myself still standing on the hillside. As the car passes from view, I think of John walking down the hill, past the guards, through the front gate of the prison with his Bible in hand. He has gone where I still cannot go.

Why can't I deal with the pain in my own heart?

I know his story applies to me. It applies to so many of my friends and colleagues in the States. We are in pain and we're not dealing with it. Obviously we've not been through the slaughter and savagery of genocide. But we have been through a great spiritual darkness. The devil has waged war against us in his fury. The church has been rent asunder; heretics have risen to power; the name of Jesus has been openly blasphemed; people have been led astray into lies and immorality; Christians who have refused to compromise the gospel have suffered persecution.

And yet, we have also sinned. Many of us have turned against each other in anger, slander, and hatred. We confess Christ but we are divided. I know it. I'm guilty of it. I have felt the pain of resentment and bitterness in my own heart, and I've done nothing about it. I have not helped my colleagues deal with it. I have not come running to this hillside to weep and repent. I have not gone to those I've locked up in the prison of my unforgiveness. It is still in me. I know I must deal with it—but I really don't want to. Not now . . . not ever. I'd rather keep it pressed down and hidden deep inside.

Why am I still wrestling with these same old issues?

I am strangely aware that this is where my story began. I met John in the fall of 1988. I had just finished reading a book by an African Anglican bishop named Festo Kivengere. He knew the stench of anger and bitterness in his own soul. For him, it was the brutality and killings of his Ugandan president, Idi Amin. But the Holy Spirit convicted Festo and called him to forgive and pray for Amin in Jesus' name. Festo obeyed. He began to see Amin through the lens of the cross, as one for whom the Lord Jesus Christ shed His blood. I read the book twice. I didn't understand it. *How could anyone forgive a man like that?*

And there stood John, arms outstretched.

He walked it through with me then. He is still doing it now. His words come back to me: "My brother, we must face our sin. We feel its weight. We bear its pain. Then we run . . . to the hillside, in tears—to the cross of our Lord Jesus Christ. And we repent."

I take out a note pad and pen. I write John and Harriet's names, Emmanuel and Freda Kolini, Moses and Cynthia Tay, Yong Ping Chung and Julia; a dozen more Asian, African, and other global South missionaries who have come storming through the gates of our American churches. I write simply,

They have come, but it's hard to see them. They have come to help us, but we are proud. Like the Laodiceans of old, we are wretched, miserable, poor, blind, and naked—clueless. The Savior is standing outside our church, knocking. They have come to strengthen us in faith. They want us to declare our loyalty to the Lord Jesus Christ and to the Bible as sovereignly inspired. They want to teach us how to live godly lives in Christ and then how to suffer in the face of opposition. I know that. But now I know more. I know where suffering begins. It's right here, on this hillside. It begins in humility, under the convicting power of the Holy Spirit, in the open confession of my sin, and in true repentance before the Lord. It begins on my knees in tears.

"If we tell people about Jesus without these tears," John has always told me, "we are nothing more than a noisy gong, a clanging cymbal." The suffering begins here. The mission begins here.

When am I going to let the tears come?

I turn to look down the hillside at the prison. It is hard enough to face the pain of my own sin, but to face the people who have bound my heart in anger and bitterness? To go to them while the pain is still fresh, the wound deep and exposed, and forgive them as the Lord Jesus Christ has forgiven me? But this is what the global South missionaries are demanding from us. They've come to mentor us in Christ; to shake us from our sins of arrogance and prosperity that have lulled us to sleep and rendered us passionless.

They want us on this hillside. They want us to do the hard work of repentance. They want us to know the kind of pain and suffering that comes as a gift from the Lord. And then they want us to go down the hill, down into the prison. They want us in the mission field with those who are lost without Jesus.

They want us to hear the cries of the suffering and, in hearing, they want us to act immediately. Always act. This has been their greatest testimony. We cannot hear their screams and do nothing. We must go to them. We go to them when the risk is high. We go to them when we are suffering and in pain. We go every time, all the time, and we act. We stand with them. We love them. We tell them about the Lord Jesus Christ, who is reaching out His hands in power to save. This is the gospel message passed down from every generation. Now it is our turn. No amount of anger and bitterness, no amount of personal suffering can ever shut our mouths. We go to the prisons. We go to the mission field. We go to the lost and suffering and we tell them about Jesus. This is what the Lord has commanded us to do, and we must do it.

No matter the circumstance. No matter what it costs.

Never silent.

APPENDIXES CONTENTS

1

TRUTH'S MISSION FIELD

From Chapter 7, p. 91

In the late 1980s, Allan Bloom, professor at the University of Chicago, warned us about the shifting winds of change among his students and wrote, "The recent education of openness . . . is open to all kinds of men, all kinds of life-styles, all ideologies. There is no enemy other than the man who is not open to everything."[1] Bloom rightly called this new philosophy *The Closing of the American Mind*. His students—their generation and their manner of thinking—now lead our country.

Without absolute truth, without boundaries to discern right from wrong, good from evil, holy from unholy, all that remains is subjective truth—which means that people can decide truth for themselves. Our judicial system, for example, has not upheld the biblical, unchanging laws of God for the well-being of America but has, instead, placed a higher value on the ever-changing constitutional rights of each American citizen. With no sense of fundamental moral accountability, we have become like that generation of old, spoken of in the Bible, where "every man did that which was right in his own eyes."[2]

The Barna Research Group reports that at the beginning of 2000, 38 percent of Americans believed in eternal, unchanging moral truths. Soon after the terrorist attack of September 11, 2001, that figure dropped to 22 percent. George Barna, president and founder, suggested "that it's just too much work to claim very specific and detailed beliefs and then to try to follow them in daily life. . . . It's too limiting on their behavior. . . . most Americans want to keep their options open."[3] Ironically, polls indicate that interest in spirituality is on the rise in our country. "But this new interest in spirituality," said Frank Newport, editor of the Gallup Poll, "is showing up in what people are feeling, not what they are doing."[4] In other words,

America has moved beyond Christianity. We are religious, but we will make sure our religion enhances our rights to live the lifestyle we choose best. It cannot, and will not, impose moral and doctrinal regulations that challenge our freedom or restrict our behavior.

In this setting, the American church has had a choice: Would it move with the culture or against it? Would it encourage this vague, feeling-based spirituality, or would it hold firm to the standard of an ancient gospel message? According to research, for most American Christians attending church, the Bible is no longer seen as the source and revelation of absolute truth, nor is it honored as God's Word. Even among born-again Christians, says Barna, "Only 32% . . . still believe in the existence of absolute moral truth."[5] This shocking statistic states that at best, by two-thirds majority, the American church has already made up its mind. We do not want the straightforward preaching of the Bible. We want our pastors, preachers, seminary professors, and leaders of our denominations to encourage our freedom to be who we are, live as we please—like all other Americans—and, at the same time, assure us that we have the approval and blessing of almighty God: Father, Son, and Holy Spirit.

We have embraced the philosophies of our time—and I am not just talking about the Episcopal Church.

In recent days, scholars of church history, world mission, and sociology have discovered that Christianity in the global North is shrinking while, at the same time, it is exploding in the global South. University of Chicago sociologist, Martin Marty, has described this massive shift statistically:

> In the part of the world that stretches west from Poland across western Europe, crosses the northern United States and Canada, and includes Japan, "there are 3,000 fewer Christians now than twenty-four hours ago, whereas in sub-Saharan Africa, there are 16,000 more Christians than twenty-four hours ago."[6]

We are living "in the middle of a large-scale transformation in the nature of Christianity."[7] For example, in 1900, "80 percent of Christians were either Europeans or North Americans. Today, 60 percent are citizens of the 'Two-Thirds World'—Africa, Asia and Latin America."[8] In raw numbers, church growth in Africa alone has escalated "from 10 million in 1900 to 360 million by 2000."[9] There is a new move of God in our day. "Christianity is spreading faster than at any time or place in the last 2,000 years."[10] But it is not happening in Europe or in the United States of America. The facts clearly indicate that the "center of Christianity has shifted southward."[11]

In this emerging global South church, there is no confusion about absolute truth. It is conservative, traditional, and firm in its conviction that the Bible is God's Word, the revelation of that truth. Nor is there confusion in dealing with the immediate culture around them and choosing, in the light of New Testament exhortation, not to "conform . . . to the pattern of this world, but be transformed by the renewing of your mind."[12] When it comes to conversing with the church of the global North, there is a certain unrelenting rigor among its leaders in setting forth biblical and traditional moral values, faithfully passed down from generation to generation. In fact, it goes beyond that. Ironically, Africans, Asians, and Latin Americans now view the northern church and culture as a mission field in need of repentance toward God and true faith in the Lord Jesus.

We have become their mission field?

And they are coming. Scholars call it a "reverse evangelization."[13] Fifty years ago, the United States sent out "two-thirds of the 43,000 Protestant missionaries active around the world."[14] Today, missionaries from the global South are "travelling northward."[15] In a feature article in *Newsweek*, April 2001, Kenneth L. Woodward confirmed the deteriorating condition of the North: "Countries that were once considered Christian homelands have become the mission territories of the new millennium."[16]

These missionaries are not simply coming to reach the unchurched in the United States—though researchers now tell us that the US "is the largest mission field in the English speaking world."[17] They are specifically coming to the American church and calling us to biblical repentance. They are keenly aware of the secularization of our mainline denominations. They know our church policymakers have turned from the clear teaching of Scripture to publicly condone the morality of our time. They know our temptation to build large and "successful" churches that boast in numbers, programs, money, and facilities and have more interest in attracting the consumer than converting the sinner. They know we are wealthy, educated, and powerful—yet completely ignorant that our American church is shrinking, their church is growing, and that "the churches that are doing best in the world as a whole are the ones that stand farthest from Western liberal orthodoxies."[18] But the greatest obstacle is that they also know how quickly we dismiss them as inferior. They step into our pulpits with their accents, different color skin, their love for the Lord Jesus, and a divine authority from the Word of God and the Spirit of God to speak directly to our situation. They know all too well how hard it is for us to hear them.

The dynamic at work is not new.

> But God chose the foolish things of the world to shame the wise; God chose the weak things of the world to shame the strong. He chose the lowly things of this world and the despised things — and the things that are not — to nullify the things that are, so that no one may boast before him.[19]

The missionaries from the South have come to help us make the right choice. The time has come for the reformation of the American church. We are in need of a new wave of Christian leaders who refuse to compromise the preaching of the Bible as the authoritative Word of God and who will challenge us to live godly and holy lives in distinct contrast to the world around us. We are in need of the mighty and sovereign move of God — the kind that is taking place in the global South — to happen here on American soil. Nothing else has the power to awaken the sleeping church in the United States into a reviving missionary force that can change the course of our country and the lives of generations to come.

We need these missionaries to come help us.

2

KUALA LUMPUR STATEMENT (SELECTIONS)

From Chapter 7, p. 94

The Kuala Lumpur Statement, recorded here in part, was like a trumpet blasting from ancient Mount Zion, declaring the church's unwavering commitment to the authority of the Bible, the need for repentance with compassion, and a genuine plea for mutual accountability within the Communion.

- "It is, therefore, with an awareness of our own vulnerability to sexual sin that we express our profound concern about recent developments relating to Church discipline and moral teaching in some provinces in the North—specifically, the ordination of practicing homosexuals and the blessing of same-sex unions."
- "The Scripture bears witness to God's will regarding human sexuality, which is to be expressed only within the lifelong union of a man and a woman in [holy] matrimony."
- "The Holy Scriptures are clear in teaching that all sexual promiscuity is sin. We are convinced that this includes homosexual practices, between men or women, as well as heterosexual relationships outside marriage."
- "We believe that the clear and unambiguous teaching of the Holy Scriptures about human sexuality is of great help to Christians as it provides clear boundaries."
- "We find no conflict between clear biblical teaching and sensitive pastoral care. . . . We encourage the Church to care for all those who are trapped in their sexual brokenness and to become the channel of

Christ's compassion and love towards them."
- "We are deeply concerned that the setting aside of biblical teaching in such actions as the ordination of practicing homosexuals and the blessing of same-sex unions calls into question the authority of the Holy Scriptures. This is totally unacceptable to us."
- "We live in a global village and must be more aware that the way we act in one part of the world can radically affect the mission and witness of the Church in another."[1]

Four days later, leaders from the province of Southeast Asia, under the direction of Archbishop Moses Tay, met and immediately, unanimously, endorsed the Kuala Lumpur Statement. But as strong as it was, they were not satisfied. Something more was needed—something that demanded a response. They were convinced that the substance of these issues critically threatened the core teaching of the Bible and the very fiber of unity that held the Communion together. Between February 19 and 20, these Christian leaders drafted a resolution that, with one added point, decidedly drew a deeper line in the sand:

> That this Province supports and be in communion with that part of the Anglican Communion which accepts and endorses the principles aforesaid and not otherwise.

The phrase "and not otherwise" signaled that a breach in the Anglican Communion was possible. If the US Episcopal Church, for example, did not repent from its ungodly actions and embrace the clear admonishment of Scripture, as outlined in the Kuala Lumpur Statement, then the province of Southeast Asia and the province of the Episcopal Church in the United States would no longer "be in communion."

3

THE FIRST PROMISE STATEMENT

From Chapter 7, p. 98

TJ Johnston

Chuck Murphy has a theory that the best decisions are made with the best information. So we spent most of the first morning making sure everyone knew the latest developments. We simply got on the same page. Then, before we processed this information and determined what, if anything, we should do, Chuck called us to a time of extended prayer. We made our way to the old church—which is where All Saints holds the eight o'clock Sunday morning service. Really, it's where All Saints has worshipped since the mid-1700s, and possibly under the same live oak trees that are there today.

I believe that prayer time was a turning point for a lot of us. I had a sense first, that we were being set apart and called out to do a new work; and second, that there would be dramatic changes for some of us both in our ministry and in our personal lives. I can't speak for everyone, but a number of us left the old church with a deeper awareness of God's peace, direction, and energy for taking a bold step forward.

After lunch, we mainly worked in small groups, giving everyone a chance to process the massive changes happening in the Episcopal Church and how we should appropriately respond. Then Chuck did what he does best. He called us together, stood at this easel and newsprint, asked the small group leaders for feedback, and pulled the bits and pieces of all our conversations into a coherent and emerging voice. Up to that point, I wasn't sure what to expect. We could easily have come back from our groups without any consensus. But that's not what happened. We were basically together. It was clear to me, from the conversations around the room that afternoon, that this group of leaders was ready to act.

We asked Jon Shuler, who is a gifted wordsmith and holds an earned doctorate in church history, to take what was on the newsprint and write a statement as a working draft for our review the next morning. Jon did an incredible job. Two major principles surfaced. First, we based our response on the first promise made at our ordinations; namely, to "be loyal to the doctrine, discipline, and worship of Christ as this Church has received them."[1] This was critical for us. In fact, we called our statement the "First Promise." In Philadelphia, the House of Bishops made decisions contrary to essential biblical doctrine—the very thing they had promised God they would not do. We, therefore, made it clear that our ordination vow bound us "to a most sacred trust" and that "this trust is incapable of compromise or surrender by those who have been ordained."[2] We then took the next step and declared the authority of the Episcopal Church impaired:

> We believe that [this Church has] departed from "the doctrine, discipline, and worship of Christ as this Church has received them," and we declare their authority to be fundamentally impaired, and that they are not upholding the truth of the gospel.

The second principle that emerged was to align ourselves directly to the Kuala Lumpur Statement and those bishops and archbishops of the global South who were boldly correcting the heresy of the global North and modeling loyalty to the "doctrine, discipline, and worship of Christ." It was imperative for us to acknowledge their voice—which was not heard in Philadelphia at the convention—and stand with them in their defense of the gospel. So we wrote,

> We hereby endorse the "Kuala Lumpur Statement" [1997] as a true and accurate statement of the apostles' teaching concerning biblical authority and human sexuality. We affirm it as expressing the faith of Jesus Christ which we have received in this church, and we call upon the bishops of the Anglican Communion to endorse it as such and to discipline those who have departed from it.

But here's the key: Once these principles were in place, we took one more step. These times demanded more than a bold statement opposing the decisions in Philadelphia. We needed to send the signal that we were prepared to act, to move out and, if necessary, sacrifice our careers for the reformation of the church. So we decided, after much intense discussion, to embrace the resolution that came out of the province of Southeast Asia immediately following the signing of the Kuala Lumpur Statement, which said, "We intend to 'be in communion with that part of the Anglican Communion which accepts and endorses the principles aforesaid and not otherwise.'"

The ramifications of this statement were huge. For example, as part of the First Promise Statement, we agreed that we would "not fund, nor recommend funding, any legal institution, organization or person whose actions aid or further teaching . . . contrary to God's Word written." For some of us, that meant going to our bishops and telling them, if they did not repent—which basically meant embracing and implementing the pastoral corrections clearly detailed in the Kuala Lumpur Statement—then we would declare ourselves out of communion with our bishops and no longer financially support them. If, after that, they still did not repent, we pledged to look for another bishop who would be willing to cross into our bishop's territory [diocese] and provide proper and biblical oversight.

It was a strong statement.

Many of the senior clergy gathered in Pawleys Island on September 8–9, 1997, had bishops who voted for the new presiding bishop, stood against the Kuala Lumpur Statement, and were actively promoting the new sexual agenda for the church. To sign the First Promise Statement on the afternoon of September 9 committed each of us to two immediate and well-defined action steps. First, we were promising to go to our vestries [an elected council of elders] in the next few days, stating clearly what we had signed and why. Then, we were promising to make an appointment with our bishops to do the same.

In principle, it was a strategic moment. We knew something had to be done immediately. We knew it required both leadership and decisive action. I was particularly pleased with the way we closed the First Promise Statement. It caught the same sense of urgency we felt in those two days of meetings:

This departure from apostolic truth must be stopped. The call for repentance and a season of biblical reform, which has been sounded by many, must begin today, and by the grace of God we commit ourselves to this task. We desire nothing more nor less than to exemplify in word and deed that Jesus Christ is Lord of this Church, and we pledge to stand with all who make it their desire "to obey all that He had commanded" (Matthew 28:20).

Once the document was finalized, the questions we had to face were these: Were we ready to sign it and lead at a time when leadership was so critically needed? Were we ready to pay the cost — putting our positions, careers, families, and churches at risk? Or would we step back? It was crunch time. But here's the good news: Twenty-seven senior clergy of large evangelical churches from around the country signed the First Promise Statement.

I believed then, and I believe now, that I was witnessing a sovereign move of God.

Now here's the bad news: Some of the guys heading home weren't even off the plane when this story hit the Internet. They never had a chance to set up those meetings with their vestries or bishops. Major media outlets — religion writers from newspapers and magazines, radio talk show hosts, you name it — were picking up the story and calling our offices, homes, and cell phones for interviews. Within forty-eight hours, First Promise, and the names of those who signed it, had become public knowledge. Immediately, a number of our guys caught flack both from their vestries and bishops. Within a couple of days, we were getting phone calls and emails from a handful of them who were telling us, after reflection and prayer, they were backing off. They wanted their names off the First Promise Statement pronto.

It was a costly moment.

But honestly, I think Jon Shuler got stung the quickest and the hardest. He was elected as our spokesman for media coverage. His name was out there — and as a guy who made his living from benefactors in the Episcopal Church who had a vision for church planting, he suddenly found the money-well running dry. That happened in a matter of weeks. But I think all of us, to some degree or another, felt the heat. I don't think any of us realized when we signed First Promise just how significant that moment was in our lives — and in the life of the Episcopal Church.

But here's the home run: We were calling the church to biblical repentance. We were willing "to risk our jobs to do our jobs."[3] It was clear that the church was in trouble and that the evangelical bishops were either unable or unwilling to lead. Now, twenty-plus senior clergy from around the country—with little or no legislative authority in the church—stepped up to the plate and hit the ball. Together, we believed Jesus Christ was calling us to stand for Him, and for the truth of the Bible, and to lead in such a way that would, in His strength—and His strength alone—make a significant impact.

4

THE DALLAS STATEMENT (SELECTIONS)[1]

From Chapter 7, p. 100

In particular, four points must be noted from the Dallas Statement.

- "We fully endorse the statement on human sexuality which came out of this [Kuala Lumpur] conference."
- "We share in the affirmation that the biblical sexual norm is clear, and . . . we agree that the Church has no authority to set aside biblical teaching by ordaining non-celibate homosexuals or authorizing the blessing of same-sex relationships."
- "The Church's teaching on human sexuality has been seriously impaired in recent years by the open endorsement of homosexual practice by some Anglican leaders. It is not acceptable for a pro-gay agenda to be smuggled into the Church's program or foisted upon our people, and we will not permit it."
- "Those who choose beliefs and practices outside the boundaries of the historic biblical faith must understand they are separating themselves from communion, and leading others astray."

More than the statement itself, the international Anglican leaders attending the Dallas conference believed it both necessary and urgent to write a pastoral letter to the US Episcopal bishops. In the main body of the letter, these questions were posed:

Why then have some of you acted in opposition to the teaching and discipline of your own national church? Why in this matter have such bishops failed to consider the judgment of their colleagues in other parts of the Anglican Communion, nor taken into account the repercussions of their actions in different areas of the world? Do those who perform or sanction such ordinations and blessing knowingly set aside the authority of scripture and the doctrine of marriage given by God in creation and affirmed by His Son, Jesus Christ?

The letter closed with a request: "We ask from among you answers to these questions before the end of this calendar year."

5

CORRESPONDENCE

From Chapter 8, p. 110

The Rev. Dr. Jon Shuler made a strategic decision to "assist this group of people [in Little Rock, Arkansas] to build a healthy, growing, disciple-making congregation in the Episcopal tradition, even if, for a season, they find themselves outside the Diocese of Arkansas."[1] He wrote the bishop, shortly after a private visit with him, over the matter:

> Let me summarize my understanding of your position. Several dozen active and committed lay people, baptized and confirmed in this part of the body of Christ, and eager to follow and serve Christ Jesus in this church will not receive your support or your blessing to begin a new congregation in this city of Little Rock. This is so even though they desire to do so in response to what they believe to be God's call, and with the intention of building an Episcopal congregation which will be primarily focused on reaching unchurched and unbelieving persons living and working in the city.[2]

Then Jon took it a step further. In their meeting, Larry Maze had called these people "dissidents." Jon believed this comment revealed the bishop's mind in the matter and said so near the end of his letter.

> They do not see themselves as "dissidents," and I told you neither do I. They do indeed feel excluded by the theological drift of the diocese, particularly on human sexuality. . . . This doctrinal objection to their proposal seems to me to be the core of your disapproval. Am I in error here?

The bishop responded.

Did you not hear me say to you that if *any* group came to me saying that they were unhappy with the "theological drift" of the church, be that group conservative, liberal, high church, low church, whatever, we would not respond by allowing the establishment of a new "party-line" congregation?[3]

Party-line congregation?

Larry Maze had tipped his hand. What he did not say in the April meeting with Judge David Young was now typed in a letter with the bishop's signature. Maze believed the leaders of the new church were politically motivated and, for this reason, withheld his blessing. Nothing convinced him otherwise. He did not want Jon Shuler—an Episcopal priest from South Carolina—to help this new congregation grow; not in his diocese, not under his watch, and he told him so. From that point on, two distinct sides emerged. Eventually, the media picked up the story with the sexuality issue being the banner headline.

Arkansas Democrat-Gazette

U.S. Magistrate Judge H. David Young, a member of the new group, said formation of the new church had nothing to do with the controversy in recent years over the Episcopal Church's position on ordaining noncelibate homosexuals. "That wasn't a driving force in this," Young said. "It isn't in reaction to anything; it's something positive. We want to build, not tear down."[4]

The Living Church

In [David Young's] view, the sexuality questions presently roiling the church had no bearing upon the planting of [this church]. "If that issue did not exist, this church would still have been called into existence." The group, which is not part of the Diocese of Arkansas, and is not an Episcopal church at the moment, is "positive, forward moving—not saying 'We've got to fix this or that.'" The emphasis, he said, is on building the church.[5]

Larry Maze didn't buy it, plain and simple. He, and those with him, spun words like *special interest, political, fundamentalist,* and *renegade.*

Arkansas Democrat-Gazette

Maze said . . . "[I] told them that special-interest groups, which is what I suspect they are, are not generally encouraged to start new churches."[6]

The Living Church

The Rt. Rev. Larry Maze, Bishop of Arkansas, said the "disen-chanted" group was denied permission to form a new Episcopal mission because "another congregation in Little Rock was not needed. We have an active and involved mission strategy. Another [church] based on political reasons was not acceptable."[7]

Integrity/Arkansas—Promoting a Conference Supporting Gays in the Episcopal Church

The Right Reverend Larry E. Maze . . . has been very supportive of Integrity/Arkansas. . . . Since its founding in July 1995, Bishop Maze has made a yearly visitation. In large part because of his support for Integrity/Arkansas, a group of fundamentalist conser-vatives from Trinity Cathedral in Little Rock broke off and formed a renegade church without his blessing.[8]

In October 1997, the Rev. Dr. Peter Moore, a strong, steady voice among evangelical Episcopalians and dean of Trinity Episcopal School for Ministry in Ambridge, Pennsylvania, gladly accepted the invitation to come and lead the service. A few weeks after his visit, Dr. Moore decided to write Bishop Maze with his perceptions of this emerging congregation:

The purpose of my visit was to encourage a group of faithful Christians who desire to be a congregation reaching out to the younger profes-sional community (of which most of them are a part) in a way that commends the gospel and honors their own Anglican heritage.

This was my first visit to Little Rock.

What I found was a group of highly intelligent, gifted and devoted followers of our Lord who had begun to coalesce into a genuine congregation of Christ's flock. Without clergy leadership, yet clearly desiring such leadership, they have begun to meet, worship, share their vision and mutually care for each other in such a way that they are now the very solid nucleus of a future congregation.

Their own disagreements with you on issues of sexuality were clearly on their minds, but by no means did I find them focused on these issues. Their focus was on the gospel, on learning more about their faith, on worship and outreach. Whoever ultimately leads this flock will indeed be . . . fortunate . . . Having laity with their resources and commitment would be the dream of most clergy I know.[9]

Larry Maze would have little time to reflect on this letter. On November 18, 1997, the bishop had a phone message left on his answering machine. The new church had called its first senior pastor.

6

THE KOINONIA STATEMENT

From Chapter 8, p. 113

Some ninety bishops, active and retired, signed the Koinonia Statement. It appeared in August 1994 as the first major declaration of support for the gay movement. Bishop John Spong led the way, presenting it to all the bishops in the US Episcopal Church. It stated, in brief, the following principles:

- We believe that some of us are created heterosexual and some of us are created homosexual.
- We believe that homosexuality and heterosexuality are morally neutral, that both can be lived out with beauty, honor, holiness, and integrity.
- But we also believe that those who know themselves to be gay or lesbian persons, and who do not choose to live alone, but forge relationships with partners of their choice that are faithful, monogamous, committed, life giving, and holy are to be honored. We will continue to relate to these couples with our support, our pastoral care, our prayers, and our recognitions, in whatever form is deemed appropriate, that God is indeed present in their life together.
- We are aware of the presence in the church of gay and lesbian clergy. We bear witness to the fact that they have served and continue to serve this church with effectiveness and integrity. Some of them are single, many more of them are living in committed partnerships. . . . We pledge to these clergy, whom we honor as part of this church, our support and protection, and we will continue to hold them to no standard higher than that we would hold any heterosexual priest whether he or she be single or married.[1]

7

TJ'S FIRST SERVICE

From Chapter 8, p. 115

Linda Caillouret covered TJ's first service for the *Arkansas Democrat-Gazette*:

A group of "renegade" Episcopalians in Little Rock met Wednesday night in a Presbyterian church for the first service with their new priest . . . [who] arrived uninvited by the Rt. Rev. Larry Maze, bishop of the Episcopal Diocese of Arkansas. . . . The new group formed in the spring of 1996 with about six families. Today it has about 100 members. They gathered Wednesday night in the Pulaski Heights Presbyterian Church fellowship hall in Little Rock's Hillcrest section.[1]

Larry Maze wasn't happy with the public coverage in the newspaper. On the next day, January 16, 1998, he put out a public statement, in which he said,

What must be considered is that not a single Canon that governs the establishment of new congregations has been observed. . . . However, the irregular call of an Episcopal priest to this diocese constitutes a canonical offense which must be addressed in some way. . . . What is new, at least in my experience, is the disregard for the authority of Canon, that which has ordered this Church for generations. For years we have disagreed, sometimes vigorously, but we have stayed in communion with one another because Canon law provided boundaries for our conversations.[2]

On February 18, 1998, Bishop Maze wrote TJ:

I needn't tell you that you are in clear violation of both the intent and the letter of Canon 14, Sec. 4(a) (1) and will soon be in violation of Canon 16, Sec. 2. If your only interest is to have a viable ministry unfettered by further confusion and conflict, I would urge you to renounce your Episcopal Orders and let us all be free to continue the Lord's work apart from disagreement. Short of that, we feel compelled to ask your Bishop [in South Carolina] to bring his judgment and discipline to this situation.[3]

On March 4, 1998, TJ sent this letter to Bishop John and Archbishop Kolini:

I would ask you to consider accepting me as a member of the clergy of the Province of Rwanda. In making this request I acknowledge that I am willing to come under your authority and direction in my work in Little Rock. . . . I would ask you to consider accepting me . . . until such time that an orthodox bishop could be found to provide oversight in the United States. . . . The sixty days is now about to expire and it seems that Bishop Maze will soon present me for trial and deposition as an Episcopal Priest. . . . I am very encouraged by your willingness to extend support to the proclamation of the Gospel in Little Rock.[4]

TJ then sent what he calls his "Gamaliel letter" to Bishop Maze:

I have carefully considered your view that St. Andrew's is motivated by a special interest and an agenda regarding the debate on sexuality that is sweeping the Episcopal Church. I have not found that to be the case. . . .

Even if, for argument's sake, your assessment of this group a year and a half ago was correct, that position is clearly not reflected in the present make-up of St. Andrew's Church. . . . Since my arrival I have intentionally avoided raising issues that would define us over against the Diocese. . . . We are not sitting back looking for a fight but rather moving ahead seeking to be faithful witnesses to Jesus Christ. . . . It is our desire and purpose to build a Church with a Great Commission mindset that can strategically impact LR with the gospel of Jesus Christ. . . .

Would it be wise for the two of us to take the counsel of Gamaliel in Acts chapter 5 and allow a season of time to pass to see what the fruit of St. Andrew's Church will be? If St. Andrew's is a group motivated simply by special interest, it will surely fail. On the other hand, if it is, as I believe it is, a Great Commission minded Church, then the fruit of that will also be evident. . . .

I am also aware that sometime around the 14th of this month my sixty days of "grace" will have run [out]. . . . May the Lord grant each of us wisdom and grace in the days to come.[5]

TJ received this response to his letter to Bishop John:

We have accepted you under our ecclesiastical authority and pastoral oversight. We hope that you will remain and be even a greater witness to the saving gracious power of Jesus Christ in the Shyira Diocese community. We stand to believe and teach the Divine Lordship of Jesus Christ as the living Son of God. We hold and believe that the Bible is the Active and Authoritative Word of God. We cherish the Anglican tradition. You are so welcome in the Lord Jesus and assured of our love and fellowship.

Yours in Christ,
The Rt. Rev. John Kabango Rucyahana [6]

A month after the "Gamaliel letter," TJ informed Bishop Maze of his transfer to Rwanda. Maze, in turn, wrote a letter to the members of his diocese, dated April 16, 1998. He was clearly outraged by the "failure to respect diocesan boundaries." Internationally, resolutions that help spiritually govern the Anglican Communion are brought up every ten years at the Lambeth Conference, in which all Anglican bishops and archbishops worldwide meet. For Larry Maze, Resolution 72 from the 1988 Lambeth Conference gave him the legal edge he needed—and he cited it in the letter to his diocese:

Resolution 72 of the 1988 Lambeth Conference reads: "This Conference: 1. Reaffirms its unity in the historical position of respect for diocesan boundaries and the authority of bishops within those boundaries; and in the light of the above—2. Affirms that it is deemed inappropriate behavior for any bishop or priest of this Communion to exercise episcopal or pastoral ministry within another diocese without first obtaining permission and invitation of the ecclesial authority thereof."

He concluded his letter by saying, "What is new to me is the total disregard for those boundaries that give us a container for ongoing discussion. Once a group declares that the Constitutions and Canons of the Episcopal Church and the commonly held practices of the entire Communion are not binding, can there be a community in which the discussion can continue? I think not."[7]

Maze capped the brief letter with a final paragraph:

I am frankly saddened that you have been brought into a disagreement that should have been contained by work within the American Church. However, that situation has changed and I must now respectfully request that you re-deploy Mr. Johnston to a diocese that might request his presence. It is unacceptable, and a violation of canon law, that a priest remain uninvited and without license in this diocese. The leadership in Arkansas stands united in our effort to resolve this situation and respectfully asks your earliest response.[8]

Bishop John responded to Bishop Maze, stating succinctly, "The unity of the Church is centered only in Jesus Christ our Lord and Savior, who died for our sins, rose from the dead and lives (as we have it in the Christian creeds). So the issue of boundaries and collegiality cannot hold when the central unity in Jesus is damaged. We have to revisit some issues. Faith is our priority and the rest [Church law] are supportive measures."[9] As long as Larry Maze refused to accept this basic principle, TJ and St. Andrew's would have refuge in Rwanda.

"I hope," Bishop John closed the letter, " that you and your province will find a solution."

A few weeks later, John decided to write George Carey, the archbishop of Canterbury who, among the thirty-eight archbishops worldwide [overseeing the thirty-eight provinces in the Anglican Communion] is regarded as the "primary among equals." John believed Archbishop Carey would be sympathetic since he was, by reputation, an evangelical. After consultation with Archbishop Kolini, John wrote the following:

> We are faced with an obligation to defend faith in the Communion and to give protection to the faithful. Secondly, we can no longer pretend that there is no need for us to get involved in this case which scandalously exposed itself to the extent that one our fellow Bishops (John Spong) has produced [*The*] *Koinonia* [*Statement*] which is in opposition to biblical teaching and the Anglican discipline. . . . Bishop Maze of Arkansas signed the . . . document.
>
> Jesus, and our faith in Him, with the guidance of the Spirit, through the teaching of the Bible is the central focus and our unity. When we disagree in our faith and concept on the Person of Jesus, and the Authority of the Bible, we cannot pretend we are in union. I therefore call upon the Communion to set priorities to discipline ourselves.
>
> Be it made that those bishops, provinces, who do not believe in the Deity of Jesus Christ, [that] His Cross, Death and Resurrection, was an act of God for our salvation, and do not believe in the authority of the Bible and its orthodox interpretation cannot claim the unity and respect for their territory (we don't have any territorial obligation to the non-Christian religions).

Finally, John wrote, it was time that the bishops and archbishops worldwide "take a decision to declare Bishop John Spong, and those bishops who prescribed to his document, *Koinonia*, out of the fellowship of the Anglican Communion."[10] As far as John was concerned, this was a pivotal moment in church history. The apostles faced controversy with the circumcision party in Acts 15. Martin Luther penned the Ninety-five Theses in opposition to false doctrines that had permeated the Catholic Church of his day. The times were different, but the apostolic call to defend the Christian faith remained the same. For this reason, John took St. Andrew's and TJ under his wing. Now it was up to the archbishop of Canterbury to defend the faith, not church law, not territorial boundaries but *apostolic faith in the Lord Jesus Christ.*

John expected a swift, positive response. He was shocked to find Archbishop George Carey's swift response in the negative. Evangelical or not, the archbishop sided with Larry Maze and the argument from church law:

Dear John,

Thank you for your letter of 11 July, asking for support with respect to your decision to take St. Andrew's under your care. I strongly urge you and Bishop Larry Maze to have a word about this. . . . It is my clear view that what you are doing is completely illegal and I hope you will quickly disentangle yourself from something that is quite unconstitutional. May I therefore, once again, strongly urge you to have this conversation with Bishop Larry.

Yours warmly,

George Cantuar [Archbishop of Canterbury][11]

8

ALEXANDER MUGE'S PRESS CONFERENCE

From Chapter 9, p. 137

Kenyan bishop Alexander Muge held a press conference a few days after having been refused the pulpit at St. Luke's Episcopal Church, Walnut Creek, California, on May 17, 1990.

This was a total surprise and the shock of my entire life. I believe that I am the first Bishop in the worldwide Anglican Communion to have been denied the right to preach by a priest. . . . I was turned away from preaching nothing but the true Gospel of our Lord Jesus Christ.

I have called this press conference to express my sorrow at the state of the Church of Christ in this country, with a hope that my public displeasure might be a means of encouragement to the remnants of the Lord's flock, not only in the USA, but the world over. I wish to appeal to the Episcopal Church in this country and the world-wide Anglican Communion to pray for a revival of the Spirit of Our Lord and the Gospel in order to restore the integrity of the Church which has been, and is still being eroded. Dry theology without the Spirit of God will not lead the Church anywhere. We need to rekindle the Fire of the Lord in our hearts and churches. We have to make it plain and clear that Scripture condemns all sorts of immorality. Ordaining practicing homosexuals and appointing them as Rectors, and blessing homosexual unions are indeed signing the death certificates for our Churches. Our historic and loving God does not appease people when they go wrong. He calls upon them to repent and be put right with God. We need to go to the foot of the Cross for the salvation of Christ. . . .

My sincere appeal to the Christian community of Kenya is that we should pray for the Church of Christ in the Western World, and particularly in North America. There are many Christians in the USA who are faithful to the Lord despite the rampant secularization. They deeply need our prayers so that they may be firm in the true faith.

It is also a warning to the Christian community of Kenya that not all who come to our country or continent with collars for missionary work are true believers of the gospel. We need to do some thorough screening before accepting the collar unequivocally. We are not being judgmental as such, the discipline of the Church of Christ throughout the world must be maintained. Sin should be rebuked by any and all means.[1]

9

UGANDA PRE-LAMBETH CONFERENCE RESOLUTION, JUNE 1998

From Chapter 9, p. 142

The Great Lakes Regional Pre-Lambeth Conference, Uganda, Africa: Resolution

Affirming the clear and unambiguous teaching of the Holy Scriptures in all matters of Christian faith and practice . . . We hereby resolve:

- The Holy Scriptures are clear in teaching all sexual deviations and promiscuity is sin.
- Convinced that this includes homosexual practice as well as heterosexual relationships outside of marriage,
- It is therefore the responsibility of the Church to lead to repentance all those who deviate from the teaching of the Scriptures and live in sin,
- Those who practice such things, as well as those bishops who ordain them or encourage these practices, have automatically cut themselves from the Anglican Communion when they fail to repent,
- However, as the Church we have a pastoral responsibility to them, loving and counseling them to follow the traditional biblical teachings on sexual ethics.

10

LAMBETH, RESOLUTIONS III.1 AND III.5 (EXCERPT AND REACTION)

From Chapter 9, p. 142

This Conference . . . reaffirms the primary authority of the Scriptures, according to their testimony and supported by our own historic formularies [Resolution III.1]. This Conference . . . affirms that these Holy Scriptures contain "all things necessary to salvation" and are for us the "rule and ultimate standard" of faith and practice [Resolution III.5].

The revisionists were shocked and devastated. They had clearly underestimated the opposition from the global South. Many US bishops sent messages back to their home diocese stating the resolutions—including Resolution I.10—were wrong and they simply would not comply. Suffragan Bishop Catherine Roskam of New York issued this statement: "I think this [Conference] is an advisory body. It's not legislative, and it won't be treated that way in the Episcopal Church. We will continue to discern the will of God within our own province."[1] Bishops Grein and Sisk, also of New York, added, "the resolution passed at Lambeth will not change the character of our life together." Bishop William Swing of California, who once opposed Kenyan bishop Muge, reported, "the Diocese of California and its bishops are advised but nothing will change in our practice." Frederick Borsch, bishop of Los Angeles, echoed the defiance: "Things will not change." Bishop Spong simply added, "Be assured that today's minority will inevitably be tomorrow's majority."[2]

On August 5, 1998, Bishop Ronald Haines of Washington, DC, issued a pastoral letter to lesbian and gay Anglicans. In essence, it was a letter of apology to the gay community for the gross mistake of Resolution I.10 on

Human Sexuality by Anglican leaders:

> We apologize for any sense of rejection that has occurred because of this reality. . . . It is our deep concern that you not feel abandoned by your Church. . . . We pledge that we will continue to reflect, pray, and work for your full inclusion in the life of the Church. . . . We must not stop where this Conference has left off. You, our brothers and sisters, deserve a more thorough hearing than you received [at Lambeth]. . . . We will work to make that so.[3]

By August 8, 146 Anglican bishops worldwide had signed it. The overwhelming majority came from the United States, England, Canada, and Australia.

The Communion was dividing over essentials.

11

STALEMATE IN LITTLE ROCK

From Chapter 9, p. 144

On the one hand, Bishop Maze had international support by formal resolution of Lambeth, stating that Bishop Rucyahana was not welcome in Little Rock without Maze's consent. On the other hand, the Africans had international support by formal resolution of Lambeth, stating that it was biblically and morally wrong for Maze to continue his ardent support of Spong's political and theological agenda.

Lambeth did not resolve the conflict. Rather, it defended both positions.

Larry Maze remained defiant. He was simply not going to change his ways. He had already invited Spong to Little Rock that September, saying, "I welcome Bishop Spong as a bishop and a teacher." In the same breath, however, Maze was "pleading with Rucyahana not to [come] to Little Rock, because that's when the illegality will become apparent to the whole world."[1] Somehow, in Maze's mind, it all worked. He could rebel against Lambeth when it suited him and embrace Lambeth when it defended him. For the Africans, the choice was not that easy. It was one thing to break a man-made resolution dealing with turf issues. It was altogether different, in their mind, to break with the commands of Holy Scripture.

On August 20, 1998, Chuck Murphy sent a letter to the archbishop of Canterbury, signed by a host of First Promise clergy and lay leaders. In it, Chuck wrote, "we wish to respectfully inquire about several matters which were not clarified by this momentous Lambeth Conference." The time had come to ask how these resolutions would be enforced. For example, what would be done to John Spong in light of his Twelve Theses?

Why was there no formal disassociation from Bishop John Spong or his teaching? He has departed from the faith of the apostles as delivered to the church, and has made a mockery of the person and work of Jesus Christ. This was reported widely, and is beyond dispute, and yet no specific actions were taken against him, of any kind.

There were more questions to ask: In defending the sanctity of Holy Matrimony, would the Episcopal Church be called "to renounce and rescind its recent decision to develop same-sex blessing rites"? Would bishops be rebuked for knowingly ordaining practicing homosexuals? Would the bishops who signed the Koinonia Statement, including the presiding bishop, be called to publicly recant?

In the aftermath of Lambeth, the defining issue was *implementation*. What was the plan for putting the Lambeth resolutions into daily practice in the Episcopal Church hell-bent on defying them?

On the same day, Chuck Murphy also sent a letter to US Presiding Bishop Frank Griswold, also signed by First Promise supporters. The request was simple: "that you bring yourself, your staff, and the stewardship of your office into line with the Scriptures as expressed in decisions at Lambeth." In other words, it was his duty, as the elected leader of the Episcopal Church, to bring the church into conformity with the resolutions. First, this required personal accountability—he had signed Koinonia. He openly advocated the gay agenda.[2] Would he openly recant? Then, it required the same accountability from all his bishops in the Episcopal Church. If he refused to act on these two levels, then the letter called for "the resignation of your office, for the sake of unity in the Gospel of Jesus Christ as received in the Anglican Communion."

One fact was abundantly clear: Without repentance or resignation, Frank Griswold—in his gentle and pastoral manner—would continue to lead the Episcopal Church in direct opposition to the Anglican Communion worldwide and in open defiance to the gospel of Jesus Christ as recorded in Holy Scripture.

Rwandan archbishop Emmanuel Kolini received a copy of these two letters. He wondered how the archbishop of Canterbury and the presiding bishop of the US Episcopal Church would respond. He knew they would respond one day, if not directly then indirectly. Eventually, their words and actions would tell whether they were complying with biblical truth as stated by the African and Asian voice at Lambeth.

It would most likely take time. He knew that.

But this meant he was faced with a strategic decision. Should he send Bishop Rucyahana to Little Rock in mid-September? To do so would cause a sensational media blitz. The Americans would seize the moment and accuse Rwanda of rebellion to the recent Lambeth resolution on boundary crossing. In turn, it could justify their decision to continue their rebellion to Lambeth resolutions on human sexuality and the authority of Scripture. No, he thought. He shouldn't make the first step. Let them choose first. If they repent, Bishop John will not go. But if they refuse to listen and obey, then yes, Bishop John will go.

Faith first—then we talk about boundaries. After all, he reasoned, what are boundaries when the name of Jesus Christ is being publicly blasphemed?

Frank Griswold wrote Emmanuel Kolini. Griswold didn't want John Rucyahana coming to the US. He made his appeal to Kolini based on "the long established Anglican principle respecting the territorial integrity of dioceses and appropriate episcopal ministry." George Carey said the same: "And I have been urging the bishops in Rwanda to decline the invitation to Little Rock."[3]

Kolini read the statements carefully. He knew he was making the right decision. Griswold was making his appeal based on "Anglican principle" concerning boundaries. Therefore, Kolini argued to himself, Griswold would be challenged to uphold the Anglican principles on human sexuality and the authority of Scripture in the same manner—if he were to remain consistent in his leadership.

But would he? Kolini wondered.

The strategy was coming together: Give Griswold time. Don't let the issue of crossing boundaries attract attention, not yet. First, see what Griswold does.

Archbishop Kolini called Rucyahana and told him not to go. Rucyahana called TJ in Little Rock and issued a joint statement in the US that Rucyahana, bishop of St. Andrew's, would not be coming to Little Rock at this time:

We are in a new season, post-Lambeth, where we are urging and praying that the leadership of the Episcopal Church will return to, and embrace, the biblical and theological foundation of the Anglican

Communion as it has been reaffirmed during Lambeth. . . . The counsel of Archbishop Kolini is to allow the leaders of the Episcopal Church to reflect on what happened at Lambeth Conference and to allow them a grace-filled opportunity to respond.[4]

For Kolini and Rucyahana, a few vital questions remained: How would they know the American response? Who would inform them of decisions made by diocesan bishops across the Episcopal Church? How would their fellow African bishops, let alone bishops and archbishops worldwide, find out?

There had to be a proper strategy.

Rucyahana knew exactly what to do. Clergy from across the US had asked to meet him in Pittsburgh on August 29. They wanted John to give them immediate episcopal oversight, just as he had done in Little Rock. He had agreed to the meeting but made no promises.

"This could be the forum," he told his archbishop. "I will tell them I can't take them now, not yet. But there is something they can do. They can help us know the mind of the Episcopal Church after Lambeth. I will ask them to tell us. One, write the facts. Two, make copies for all Anglican bishops and archbishops worldwide. Three, if the Episcopal Church refuses to listen to the biblical counsel of Lambeth and turn from their sinful ways, petition us to intervene."

"Yes," said Kolini. "For the Bible teaches that we must go to our brother who sins against us and show him his fault. If he listens, we have won our brother.[5] That's what we have done. We have gone to the Episcopal Church. We have spoken clearly. We have done this at great risk. We did it in the name of Jesus. Now what will they say? What will they do? Have they listened to us?"

Everyone needed to know their response.

John Rucyahana made the proposal to the clergy gathered in Pittsburgh, and it was accepted. There was a general agreement to document and make public the response of the Episcopal Church to Lambeth — and Resolution I.10 in particular.

A season of waiting had begun.

12

THE AMERICAN REBELLION

From Chapter 10, p. 150

B ruce Bower, an attorney from Chicago, accepted the task of document-
ing the American rebellion to Lambeth. He had a group of men around
him for research, counsel, editing, and encouragement that included the Rev.
Dr. John Rodgers, former dean of Trinity Episcopal School for Ministry
in Ambridge, Pennsylvania; the Rev. William Beasley, rector of Church
of the Redeemer in Chicago; and John Jones, a successful and brilliant
Christian businessman. By December 1998, four months after Lambeth, a
two-hundred-page report with documented evidence was ready for distribu-
tion. The title itself petitioned "The Primates of the Anglican Communion
for Emergency Intervention in the Province of the Episcopal Church of the
United States of America." The introduction cited the grounds for requesting
immediate intervention:

> A case of exceptional emergency within [the Episcopal Church]
> has been caused by the widespread rejection of the authority of
> Scripture and other tenets of the orthodox Anglican faith and the
> approval of sexual relations outside of marriage by [the Episcopal
> Church's] revisionist bishops and other leaders.[1]

The rebellion was staggering.

In October 1998, Bower reported, the Episcopal Church's own newspaper issued this statement: "In the metropolitan areas of New York, Baltimore,
Detroit, Chicago, and Los Angeles, bishops wrote messages of reassurance that
their diocesan life would not change."[2] Hays H. Rockwell, Bishop of Missouri,
said the same: "The resolutions of Lambeth, useful perhaps for that discourse,

are not going to change practice in the congregations of our diocese."[3] Same-sex blessings continued at great stride. The diocese of Massachusetts passed a resolution at their convention in brazen defiance to Lambeth. It affirmed "that God calls some homosexual people to live together in committed relationships and that the Church can and does appropriately bless such unions, and that God calls some homosexual people in such relationships to ordained ministry and that the Church can and does appropriately ordain them." It passed by an overwhelming majority.[4] By year's end, eighteen dioceses publicly rejected Resolution I.10 with four dioceses passing resolutions contrary to it.[5] Other dioceses refused to acknowledge it. Ken Ross, an Episcopal priest outside of Denver, wrote a report on the Colorado Diocesan Convention where Resolution I.10 "didn't even pass a vote for consideration." He went on to say, "the resolution calling the diocese to 'disassociate ourselves from the Rt. Rev. John Shelby Spong as a bishop of the Church with regard to his 12 Theses'—failed. . . . It was, in all, a terribly sad and appalling day."[6]

The vehement opposition to Lambeth was found at the highest levels of the Episcopal Church. On October 10, the House of Deputies Committee on the State of the Church reported that "No resolution of bishops of the Anglican Communion can negate the official acts of the Episcopal Church."[7] Frank Griswold, presiding bishop of the Episcopal Church, couldn't have agreed more.

No one undermined Resolution I.10 more skillfully than Frank Griswold. As a seasoned politician, he systematically turned the negative rhetoric against the traditional orthodox into a positive strategy for the homosexual community. Within days after Lambeth, he sent letters to the *New York Times* and the *Wall Street Journal*. He needed the world to recognize him as a worthy opponent and not a victim of a stunning defeat. While acknowledging the strong convictions from the global South, Frank Griswold did what he did best. He began to sing his song from the very words he had planted deep into the famed Resolution I.10:

The truth is that Anglicanism is far more resilient than any one action would suggest, and Lambeth Conferences, which are advisory not legislative, have with the passage of time changed their minds on a number of sensitive and controversial subjects. I rather doubt, therefore, that we have heard the last word on the subject of homosexuality, inasmuch as the pertinent resolution states "while rejecting homosexual practice as incompatible with Scripture," at the same time "we commit ourselves to listen to the experience of homosexual persons." That process of listening, which is well under way in some places of the Anglican Communion, has yet to begin in others, particularly those in which homosexuality is viewed as a Western phenomenon.[8]

Griswold's initiative to the press made it clear that the revisionists' response to Lambeth had been well planned and on the offensive. Like a campaign stump speech, it had impeccable clarity, precise simplicity, and just the right mix of emotion that appealed gently to common-sense compassion: It's *not* about Scripture. It's about the "process of listening."

It's exactly what Moses Tay had predicted. Resolution I.10 had been greatly compromised.

Frank Griswold was on the attack. His strategy demanded that what was "incompatible with Scripture" today would be compatible with the Anglican Communion tomorrow. The method of accomplishing this ambitious task was to move the authority of God's Word away from Holy Scripture and onto the ever-changing drama of human experience. That is to say, God was speaking not so much through the archaic words of the Bible but in the immediate context of our present, more advanced lives. As early as 1994, Griswold advocated this doctrinal switch:

> Some see the Word most active in terms of Scripture and Tradition, and others see the Word most active in terms of human experience and what's actually being lived by men and women in our dioceses and congregations. My sense is that there is no way to reconcile these different perspectives. . . . And then the question is, as I said earlier: Do we do that in peace? Do we do that with respectfulness toward one another recognizing that there is integrity in a number of positions? No one has the corner on the truth in this area.[9]

By the fall of 1998, it seemed as if Griswold did have the "corner on the truth." For years, he and his many colleagues had effectively deployed their doctrine of experience to maneuver a takeover of the Episcopal Church. It had required skilled and exacting leadership to effect such massive, systematic change—resolution by resolution, election after election. But in the end, it had worked. They had decisively won the day. The US bishops who held to the ancient doctrine of the sovereign authority of Holy Scripture were now in the vast minority and greatly weakened by a crippling inability to bring correction.

Griswold was a winner and he knew it.

He came out of Lambeth ready for the biggest challenge of his life. He was not defeated by Resolution I.10. He was not scrambling in front of the media trying to put a positive spin on a humiliating loss. Nor was he some second-string politician stuttering religious nonsense in front of the cameras. In his mind, the game had just started. His playbook worked before and it would work again. He had Resolution I.10 on his side. Yes, it advocated biblical orthodoxy. But in it, he had everything he needed to build his platform, preach his gospel, and prepare the church for a new way to worship God.

Frank Griswold was poised to engineer his next great takeover—the Anglican Communion.

The moment was his. As the spotlight hit his face, the media in August 1998 actually saw him as a loser and Lambeth as a setback for his radical revisionist agenda. It was now public knowledge that he had abstained from voting on Resolution I.10. Was this, they wondered, an act signifying a change of mind? Reporters challenged him: Would he stop ordaining practicing homosexuals in light of Resolution I.10? He candidly "refused . . . to say he would stop doing so."[10] Some thought they had him on the ropes. But Griswold knew exactly what he was doing. He was not a loser. He had not changed his mind. He was the Anglican archbishop of the most powerful and wealthiest province in the Anglican Communion. All he had to do was stand in front of the cameras, open his mouth, turn on his soft, pastoral charm, and then preach his winning message of compassion and inclusion for all.

Griswold was a leader. He saw opportunity and seized it. Before August even ended, less than three weeks after Lambeth, he had snagged his first great trophy. He had gone to the top. Who better to endorse his new gospel than George Carey, archbishop of Canterbury, renowned worldwide as a traditionalist, the champion for orthodox evangelicals? But how was such a feat possible?

George Carey had been resolute after Lambeth. He said he stood "wholeheartedly with the traditional Anglican orthodoxy." He added, "I see no room in Holy Scripture or the entire Christian tradition for any sexual activity outside marriage."[11] Somehow the "no room" position shifted a few weeks later. He was preaching at Christ Church, Greenwich, Connecticut, on August 30 with Frank Griswold in attendance and a small congregation of fifty gay supporters. Without hesitancy, George Carey restated his belief in the biblical sexual ethic. But then, with stunning surprise, with the news media in full attendance, he publicly endorsed Griswold's new gospel. The great reversal came when he said,

> Let me assure you that the resolution from Lambeth calls upon all to listen to one another and I am committed to that, for my experience tells me that in giving hospitality to the "stranger" we may be entertaining angels unknowingly.

The door of hope cracked open and Griswold lunged at it, saying, "he was heartened to hear Carey say that Lambeth's resolution was the beginning, not the end, of a dialogue." Griswold went on assuring the congregation that "The Lambeth Conference . . . invites us to engage in a process of listening and learning so that [your] experience can become the occasion for greater inclusion in the life of the church."[12] The media sound bite rang out "inclusion" not "incompatibility with Scripture," a dramatic distortion of the intent of Resolution I.10. The news eventually went worldwide. The Griswold gospel, under the deceitful cloak of "listening," now had the full backing of the archbishop of Canterbury.

Amazingly, George Carey was not finished.

In a letter to Archbishop Michael Peers of Canada, as staunch a revisionist as Griswold, Carey wrote, "First, let us remind ourselves, that, in reality, the discussion at Canterbury was the very first time that the bishops as a body had discussed this at any length. A resolution was passed that indicates where bishops stand now on the issue. It does not indicate that we shall ever rest there. That may be the case, but who knows?"[13] The archbishop of Canterbury was now allowing for the possibility of future change. His doctrine on sexual ethics no longer rested on the unchanging nature of Holy Scripture (isn't that what he said clearly after Lambeth?) but like the American revisionists, on the ever-changing philosophies of the human mind. Who could have imagined such a Damascas road conversion to the new Griswold religion?

The timing was perfect.

Carey said it again on September 10, 1998, in a letter to Louie Crew, founder of the gay Episcopal caucus in the US called Integrity: "I do want you to know I am committed to dialogue with gay people, and I have already had a discussion with the Presiding Bishop of the Episcopal Church about how we can ensure that the Lambeth Conference resolution is pursued in this respect. . . . I hope that you will recognize that what I said in my sermon at Christ Church [Greenwich] is what I believe."[14]

There could be no question about it. What incredible fortune! What unrestrained blessing! Griswold not only had a convert but an advocate and evangelist in the highest office of Anglicanism.

Strategically the unholy alliance between Griswold and Carey fanned into flame the widespread rejection of Resolution I.10 in the US Episcopal Church. The rebellion would be so complete that, in one year's time, the Rev. Michael Hopkins, president of Integrity, confirmed that gay ordinations continued at a strong pace. He was quoted as saying, "The Lambeth Conference has had no effect on the American Church. Gay people are still being ordained, and there is no sign that people are changing their minds or that the practice is slowing down."[15] For Griswold and his colleagues, the words "no effect" rang like church bells announcing the day of their sweet unprecedented victory. They had winsomely overcome the hateful biblical doctrines on Scripture and sexuality in Resolution I.10. The word *incompatibility* had magically turned into the word *inclusion* in the compassionate name of "listening." No one seemed to notice that Griswold's high doctrine of listening had effectively drowned out any ability to listen to the word of God as written in Holy Scripture let alone the voice of the global South Christians who had risen to defend the ancient faith and call Griswold and the Episcopal Church to repent of their sin.

He who has an ear, let him hear what the Spirit says to the churches.

Plain and simple, Griswold was not interested in listening. His revisionist plan for takeover was successfully and aggressively advancing. He knew that no one in the Anglican Communion had authority to hold the mutinous Episcopal Church accountable. Nothing could stop him. His gospel had the freedom to march on at will like an uncontained cancer coursing through the body, unchecked and untreated.

13

"LEAPFROGGING"

From Chapter 10, p. 151

What Chuck Murphy calls the principle of leapfrogging is the risky act of going over the head of those in authority to those with greater authority in order to produce change. For Chuck and the clergy of First Promise, this meant going over the heads of their bishops and the presiding bishop of the Episcopal Church to Anglican archbishops overseas. "It's the Ralph Nader story," Chuck taught.

> In 1965, he wrote the book *Unsafe At Any Speed* because he didn't agree with the Detroit auto-makers who said the high rate of traffic fatalities was due to the idiot behind the wheel. So Nader went over their heads to Congress and demanded Detroit take responsibility for auto safety by requiring seatbelts and the like. That's what leadership does sometimes. It means risking your job. Your boss might not take kindly to being leapfrogged. But there are certain moments, certain occasions, when you take risks because it's the only way to get results. I knew it was time for us. We had spent years trying to reform the Episcopal Church from within. It led nowhere. It was a failed strategy. The only solution, as I saw it, was to leapfrog the House of Bishops in the Episcopal Church USA and make our appeal to the archbishops overseas. And that's exactly what we did.

His conviction only deepened on November 20, 1998, when Chuck went to Charleston to hear Frank Griswold address the diocese of South Carolina. The following Sunday, Chuck reported to the congregation at All Saints Church, Pawleys Island, that Griswold had publicly confessed his belief in ongoing revelations from God that often supersede the Bible. "The same kind of doctrine" Chuck taught that Sunday, "was embraced in the 19th century by Joseph Smith who claimed to receive a revelation called *The Book of Mormon*. The same is true with Islam's *Koran*, and more recently, David Koresh and Jim Jones. The Bible is pushed aside for new truth. When asked about this, Griswold simply stated again, "We have to live with ambiguity. What we need to do is discover truth."

It was that Sunday Chuck told the congregation about leapfrogging:

We are, at present, in conversations with archbishops overseas. They are taking a strong stand by saying, "The Episcopal Church is out of line. If it does not repent, we will have broken communion." I believe our time to stand is now. The choice is clear: Are we to go along with the "new gospel" in the Episcopal Church or are we to remain firm in the faith "once for all delivered to the saints"?[1]

Only a small handful objected that Sunday. The rest of the congregation (we were about six hundred in attendance at the time) rose to their feet with applause.

14

A CRISIS OF LEADERSHIP

From Chapter 10, p. 153

Bruce Bower, John Jones, and their colleagues at the Association of Anglican Congregations on Mission sent "The Petitions" in mid-January 1999 to more than eight hundred Anglican bishops worldwide. Julia Duin at the *Washington Times* picked up the story. She reported that "Conservative Episcopal leaders have sent out an international SOS in hopes of countering the influence of liberal US church leaders."[1] The appeal for international archbishops intervening, protecting, and establishing an alternative Anglican presence in the United States was repugnant to the revisionists. Bishop Ronald Haines of Washington said, "This is unheard of. It's more like ecclesiastical terrorism." Bishop Mark Dyer, professor at Virginia Theological Seminary, prophesied, "Are they aware they would not ever be recognized by the Archbishop of Canterbury? There isn't the slightest chance. Whatever differences the archbishop has with some practices in the Episcopal Church, he would never recognize this group." Bishop Edward Lee of the Diocese of Western Michigan rejected the effort, stating boastfully, "That is the genius of Anglican ethos. . . . It does not lock itself into hardened positions which it considers definitive for the ages."[2] Bishop Jack Spong, addressing the annual convention of the diocese of Newark, simply continued his rhetoric against the hard-line biblical stand in Resolution I.10 as "unchristian, uninformed, prejudiced and evil," and the product of "irrational Pentecostal hysteria."[3]

But Julia Duin wisely noted the effects on the local church. The conservative priests in the diocese of Pennsylvania, for example, were under extreme pressure from their bishop, Charles Bennison, who brashly supported the gay agenda. This was the same diocese that voted against a resolution affirming the divine inspiration of the Bible and the saving work of Jesus Christ as the only way to the Father.

The Rev. Phil Lyman, rector of St. John's Episcopal Church, Huntingdon Valley, Pennsylvania, knew in his heart he had to make a stand. In unison with the vestry and fellow clergy, Phil first decided to withhold monies from the bishop, saying, "If our diocese can't affirm that Jesus is the Christ, then we shouldn't be giving to it." Second, he joined with two other local rectors to refuse their bishop permission to preach in their pulpits until he recanted. Bennison immediately threatened to depose the three clergymen.

Julia Duin published Phil Lyman's response:

I've been told if I persist, I'll be liable for trial. This is uncharted territory for a lot of us. What we're doing is not compromising. We wonder: Will we be able to stay on this property? We don't know if we will have to move. We have five kids. I say to my wife that I am sorry your husband has gotten you into this mess. She says, "No, it's a blessing. What a blessing for our children to see their father take a stand for the truth of God and have to pay a price for it."[4]

Unfortunately, Duin had no quotes from evangelical bishops ready to do the same.

Stephen Noll knew "The Petitions" demanded a public response by the US evangelical bishops. Most were members of the American Anglican Council (AAC), a conservative voice working for reform within the Episcopal Church. Noll, professor at Trinity Episcopal School for Ministry and board member of the AAC, decided to write a series of articles in preparation for their February 25, 1999 meeting in Orlando, Florida. He wanted the AAC to boldly endorse "The Petitions" and take the necessary action steps to break communion with what he called "Episcopaganism." Knowing that God doesn't honor "those who choose politics over principle," Noll argued his position dramatically:

If the Episcopal Church were to approve a Baal liturgy for trial use, would this immediately lead to "impaired communion" and a "reception period"? God forbid! Similarly, if fornication is abominable in God's eyes, then it is equally inappropriate to respond to

the authorization of fornication (a.k.a. same-sex blessings) by negotiations or even a declaration of "impaired communion." In the
latter case, broken communion is the appropriate response.

Noll concluded one of his articles with a serious, indeed prophetic,
warning:

> How will it turn out? I do not know, God knows. I am convinced
> that the sword of God's judgment has been dangling over the
> Episcopal Church for many years now. Will He turn His face in
> response to a faithful remnant who turn to Him? Or is it too late
> to avert the complete disintegration of Anglicanism in the United
> States?[5]

Chuck Murphy attended the AAC meeting in Orlando on February 25.
He spoke for an hour, echoing Stephen Noll's plea for the fourteen bishops
present to break communion with their revisionist colleagues. He argued,
"We can either get involved in shaping what's going to shake down, or we
can watch and say, Now what do you want to do?" Chuck told them that
their fellow bishops in the global South were asking, "Why is there such
silence in the American church?" They want to know, he said, because they
believe there is a tear in the fabric of Anglicanism. They believe the American
evangelical bishops should be leading the reformation. They believe it's time
to break the silence and break communion. "By your action," he said, "you
could say there isn't silence."

Chuck felt the resistance in the room. They were not going to break
communion. They were not going to lead.

"Is this a strategy or a showdown?" one of the bishops challenged.

"It's a strategy with an implicit showdown," Chuck responded and added,
"You'll never provide leadership without risk."[6]

Form that moment on, Chuck had a saying he would repeat in nearly all
his public addresses like a scratched CD skipping again and again: "There
are two crises in the Episcopal Church. There is the crisis of faith that was
addressed at Lambeth '98. Then there is the crisis of leadership, which is
supposed to guard the faith, guard the discipline, and guard the unity of the
church at a time of major realignment in the whole of Anglicanism." This

latter crisis irked Chuck. If there was just one bishop with the same kind of courage, faith, and fire in his bones as Phil Lyman in Pennsylvania, ready to risk his job for the sake of the gospel, the intervention from overseas would happen with lightning speed and with great effect. He was sure of it.

15

ARCHBISHOPS' OPEN LETTER TO FRANK GRISWOLD

From Chapter 10, p. 153

The "Open Letter from Primates of the Anglican Communion to the Most Reverend Frank Griswold, Presiding Bishop of the Episcopal Church United States of America" was posted on the Internet on February 26, 1999. Seven of the thirty-eight archbishops were involved plus one retired.[1] The two-page letter was nothing less than a corrective. After cordial greetings and general introductory statements, the archbishops wrote, "None of us can rightly ignore the fellowship of the Spirit which the Lambeth conference represents. Each Province is accountable to the whole Communion. True Christian freedom lies within the compass of truth and love and not in the satisfaction of mere autonomous desire."

Then came the punch:

It is therefore with sorrow and disappointment that we have heard from different parts of our Communion statements at variance with what was resolved at Lambeth. . . . We know too that there are leaders within your own Province who do not wish to follow, and in the past have even broken, the teachings reaffirmed at Lambeth. . . . The Church must listen to all her members, but they must listen to the Church as well.

Fidelity to Christian truth cannot be reduced to aspiration; it entails definite and present obligations. Our particular responsibilities oblige us to say that the continuance of action at variance with the Lambeth resolutions, within your own or any other province, would be a grievous wrong and a matter over which we could not be indifferent. We therefore ask you, dear brother, to examine the directions apparently proposed by some in your Province and take whatever steps may be necessary to uphold the moral teaching and Christian faith the Anglican Communion has received. In doing this you will have the prayers and support of us all and you will bring healing and renewal to your church.

The archbishops were simply exercising their Christian duty in holding their colleague accountable before the Lord. Using Griswold's own language, they urged him to "listen to the Church" at Lambeth. They appealed for a proactive course correction without which they "could not be indifferent." It was nothing less than a gentle appeal to repent and return to the "Christian faith."

Griswold dismissed the letter out of hand. If anyone needed to be corrected, and in time would be corrected, it was the biblical traditionalists from the southern hemisphere. But this would be proven in the years to come. For now, Griswold collected his nine-member Council of Advice and, together, released an international response on March 10, 1999, which masterfully displayed the seductive power behind Griswold and his gospel.

The letter opened with thanks for the "fraternal concern" of his colleagues. He then reasoned that the issue between them was not a biblical matter but simply a sociological one: "we are aware that what happens in one part of the Communion can affect other provinces because of the very different historical and cultural contexts in which we seek to live our lives in response to the gospel." Second, he moved the argument of homosexuality into the realm of multiple opinions: "We write to emphasize to you that within the Episcopal Church, USA, as in other provinces of our Communion, there exist divergent opinions on the question of homosexuality." After reviewing four such opinions, Griswold tried to assert that "We therefore find ourselves in a process of discernment and 'testing the spirits.'" It was his weakest argument, implying that the sexuality issue had not been resolved by the majority of elected leaders in the Episcopal Church.

But then came his knockout punch. He masterfully and discreetly dropped the name and gave a quote from his prominent new gospel ally, George Carey, archbishop of Canterbury. Griswold wrote,

We . . . are instructed by the observation and wise words of His Grace, the Archbishop of Canterbury in a letter addressed to one of our primates, and which I have his permission to quote. 'First, let us remind ourselves that in reality the discussion at Canterbury was the very first time the bishops as a body had discussed it [homosexuality] at any length. A Resolution was passed that indicates where bishops stand NOW on the issue; it does not indicate that we shall ever rest there. That MAY be the case—but who knows?'

With the authority of his own office and the archbishop of Canterbury's, and in the name of Christian hospitality, Griswold then threw Resolution I.10 right back in their faces:

Therefore, in answer to your concerns . . . we invite each of you to visit those parts of our church which cause you concern. . . . Such visits will afford you the opportunity not only to query some of our bishops and representatives of their dioceses but also to listen to the experience of homosexual persons, which is mandated by the Lambeth resolution (I.10) on human sexuality.

Griswold closed the letter by repeating the invitation: "With the love of God in our hearts and the upbuilding of the body of Christ as our hope, we invite you, in the words of Jesus to, 'Come and see.'" These words, "Come and see," would play a defining role in the upcoming April meeting of concerned archbishops in Singapore. But so would the rest of Griswold's letter. Behind the courteous tone drenched in compassion and seeming mutual respect stood men of absolute defiance. Griswold and his Council of Advice had no intention of hearing and obeying the corrective call to biblical repentance that the Singapore archbishops had issued. Their letter made it clear that a line had been drawn in the sand. There were two distinct sides. The only hope of reconciling the division was for the other side to "Come and see" and, in seeing, repent. Otherwise, the division would remain and continue to deepen.

16

JOURNEY TO KAMPALA

From Chapter 11, pp. 167-169

Few understood that, for Chuck Murphy, boarding the plane for Kampala, Uganda, was a matter of obedience to God. Already that year, far beyond his comfort zone, he had flown to Singapore twice, Rwanda twice, and Nigeria once. In the company of his family and friends he confided, "God knows my reluctance. He knows I want to please Him, to do the right thing. But it comes with a certain disquiet." Still he kept putting one foot in front of the other—"take a step, take a step" as he loved to say—not knowing what would be required of him next. It was especially true now as he made his way to Kampala in November of 1999.

Nagging at the forefront of his mind were big-picture strategic questions: What happens if the archbishops in Kampala decided for immediate intervention in the US? How would they do it, and when, and with whom? Would the US evangelical bishops be part of it and support it? Would the archbishops still take the risk if their colleagues, even the archbishop of Canterbury, moved against them? But they must, he thought. Without intervention, the US rebellion spreads worldwide. Yes, but would they? Would these men be like the reformers of old who courageously defied the religious authorities of their day and suffered for it, even died for it? Or would the political pressures in Kampala be too much to bear? Would they buckle? Would they divide? Would they wait for some other time? Or, in God's mercy would they act? And if they did act, he asked for the hundredth time, how do they act? And with whom?

The last question surfaced with a deep, unutterable groan. He didn't want it to be him.

"Lord," he prayed, "what will be required of me then?"

For Chuck Murphy, the sixteen-hour plane ride from the States to Africa,

331

the layovers and time changes, always took a toll on him. Others may like it. He did not. He would rather be home. He dreamed of going back to his church full time. It was what he loved best. He never asked for all this, not once.

On this particular flight, as he settled in over the Atlantic, he pulled out his teaching notes of the past year. One more time through, he thought, just to make sure his Kampala presentation, perhaps the most important of his life, hadn't missed anything. As he scanned the pages, one biblical text kept surfacing over and over again. It was, he believed, the perfect picture of the present time. It was taken from 1 Samuel 17, when young David reached the camp of Israel and heard the shout of a war cry. For the first time David saw Goliath, the mammoth military hero of the Philistines. He heard him publicly curse the people of God. The Israelites had endured the blasphemous reproach for forty days and forty nights in paralyzing fear. They had no plan of action. But when David heard Goliath for the first time, he instantly reacted: "Who is this uncircumcised Philistine that he should defy the armies of the living God?" (verse 26). He immediately stepped forward. He wanted to fight Goliath himself, believing that the "LORD who delivered me from the paw of the lion and the paw of the bear will deliver me from the hand of this Philistine" (verse 37).

Chuck's teaching notes recorded the obvious parallels:

- We are living in perilous times when God's people who believe God's Word are being publicly cursed and ridiculed.
- We are behaving like the Israelites, listening to our Goliath without decisive, prayerful action.
- We are needing Davids—leaders with courageous faith who are willing to act without fear or hesitation and oppose the forces of evil.

As the plane pierced through the night, he wrote in the margins of his notes, "God is calling for a few people who will stand firm, stand strong." Just maybe, he thought, those gathered in Kampala would unite as one man, rise to the occasion, and be the David of our times. The stage was clearly set. Just as David was the youngest in his family and still a youth, so from the heart of Africa, Rwanda was the smallest, if not the poorest and most war beaten, of all Anglican provinces. Southeast Asia was the newest, the youngest. The global South as a whole was considered the most impoverished and least educated.

Was not this the perfect place for God to call forth a David once again? Were not these the leaders to take up the sling and five stones of God's Word and confront the political power and religious pride of the US church?

Yes, but would they?

Chuck's mind wandered back to the four US Episcopal bishops coming. They were men of strong biblical faith, yes, but they had not stopped the mass rebellion among their own House of Bishops, nor did they have a strategic plan to do so. To be honest, they tolerated Chuck, keeping him at arm's length, giving little or no support to the work of First Promise. And yet, in the providence of God, they were coming to this event sponsored by First Promise. At the very least, it gave an appearance of solidarity, as if the threat against the gospel and the urgency of its proclamation in the US superseded any political differences. At the most, it meant that solidarity was actually something God was bringing about. If that were the case, would Chuck be open to it? Would he embrace it? What if these bishops changed their minds in Kampala and stretched out their right hand of fellowship with him and First Promise? What if this was their moment to shine? What if they, under the authority of the global South archbishops, suddenly became the young David of our present times and led the US intervention against their own House of Bishops? What then?

He began to reason it out.

Actually, it would be the best possible scenario. First, it fully engages the historic and biblical office of the bishop, essential to true Anglicanism. Second, it instantly unites US Episcopalians faithful to the Bible behind these bishops. Third and most importantly, it gives incentive to the Kampala archbishops to fully endorse an immediate US intervention led by US bishops. No question about it, it was the best, most effective way forward. It made good, reasonable sense. But, Chuck realized, if this was God's perfect and sovereign plan, then it dramatically impacts First Promise and his leadership. It means First Promise completes its mission in Kampala. It means the leaders of First Promise must graciously step back and let the four US bishops step forward and be bishops indeed, biblical and apostolic, defending the Christian faith, and rescuing the church from one of the greatest evils it has ever known. What could be more desired than this? If it happens, Kampala could become the beginning of a historic reformation. Imagine it: global South archbishops and US bishops, together in Jesus Christ and together in a common mission to reclaim the power and uncompromised authority of the gospel on American soil.

Chuck needed to get behind it. He needed to encourage it.

Before the plane ever touched down in Africa, Chuck resolved in his heart to talk with Archbishop Kolini. He needed to say it clearly, before the conference began, and he did. In a private meeting between the two of them, Chuck made his case: "I believe it is time for me and First Promise to step back from primary leadership in this movement and here's why." The logic was irrefutable, and Kolini agreed, the best-case scenario was for the US bishops to lead the intervention, not Murphy. Not First Promise.

Murphy agreed. "I'm not driving this thing," he told us on the eve of the Kampala meetings. "We're passengers in the back of the bus. If the archbishops choose to go with us, we step forward. If they go with the US bishops, which is actually more preferable, then we support their decision and let the US bishops take the lead. At the end of the day, the archbishops make the call. For me personally, I am more interested in results. We need an intervention. We need the archbishops to back the intervention. That's all. No matter how it's done, something's gotta change back home."

●   ●   ●

Eight archbishops were in attendance from Uganda, Rwanda, Congo, Burundi, Southeast Asia, Tanzania, South America, and Australia, plus two bishops representing Kenya and the Sudan. The four US bishops came, as did local African bishops and dignitaries, a handful of clergy from First Promise, plus specially invited Anglican leaders from the US and England, most of whom knew each other. The formal meetings began on Tuesday morning, November 16. The night before was a social occasion, a "Welcoming Tea," which had all the joy and delight of Christian fellowship. Political agendas were simply undetectable. Cultural differences between North and South, East and West, dissolved in the sweet communion of those who gather in the name of the Lord Jesus Christ. These were people who loved Him and who had traveled great distances because it mattered deeply that their Savior was being publicly maligned and the historic gospel openly rejected. For this reason alone, expectation filled the room. God was in our midst and there was a sense that He Himself was about to act. He had given us front row seats to witness a great reforming moment of history, not for us but for His church; not just for His church, but for the glory of His name.

Such was the joy that spilled over into the morning worship as we heard the gospel preached, said our prayers, confessed our sins, and received the Lord's Supper. It was the perfect start for the meeting.

The tone rightfully shifted after worship to the business at hand. The Archbishop of Uganda, Livingstone Nkoyoyo, rose from his chair at the head table and went to the podium.

> At the beginning of this century Western missionaries zealous and full of the Spirit of God came to Africa and went to other mission fields. They were committed. They did their best as they communicated the Gospel. Most of them had exemplary life styles. Many Africans and other people in most parts of the world received, believed, owned, lived, and died for the Christian faith. Their blood became a seed for Christianity. We praise God for the fruits of the Gospel.
>
> As we come to the end of the century . . . there are divisions over the fundamentals as attested at and after the Lambeth Conference, 1998. The unity of the Body of Christ . . . is threatened by internal disagreements on Christian values, morals, and ethics.
>
> We are committed to stand by the Holy Scriptures. We are ever prepared to uphold the Lambeth resolutions. We want the Anglican Communion to remain one Church.

Nkoyoyo made his case: the blatant rejection of the gospel in the US, Canada and England was now spiritually impacting the daughter Church of Uganda. Something had to be done, in prayer, by the sovereign hand of God. "I believe," he concluded, "that God has chosen to gather us here to speak to us in a special way and to show us a way out of darkness and confusion for the purpose of restoring His Church, and to give Him His right place in our lives and the Church. It is my humble prayer and call, therefore, that we allow God His time to speak, counsel, and teach us what type of Church He wants us to lead."*

With that, he sat down. His words had stuck hard. What irony! What a sad twist of affairs. *It was time for the daughter to rescue her mother.*

---

* Livingstone Nkoyoyo, *Welcome and Opening Remarks by the Most Rev. Dr. Livingstone Mpalanyi Nkoyoyo at the Great Lakes Regional Primates' and Bishops' Fellowship*, 16 November 1999.

17

THE KAMPALA REPORT (SELECTIONS)

From Chapter 11, p. 176

The Kampala Report vaguely affirmed, "We will inform our colleagues of the intolerable situation that you and others like you are facing. We will carefully document and commend a proposal to this meeting which, we believe, will address the problems in our Communion." It went on to say, "We will be seeking agreement on and the progressive implementation of effective measures to ensure a return to historic standard for ordination, moral and marriage disciplines where in our communion these have been notoriously breached."

A careful reading of paragraph 2 suggests that the archbishops had left room for an intervention before March.

We assure you, too, that among us are those ready to respond to specific and urgent situations which may arise in the months before the [archbishops'] Meeting in Portugal from 23rd to 28th March. Parishes and clergy under threat because of their loyalty to the Gospel and to Anglican standards must be supported and we will play our part in such support.

18

WARNINGS AGAINST
EARLY CONSECRATIONS

From Chapter 11, p. 182

Archbishop Sinclair fired off an e-mail to John Rodgers, saying, "We will do all we can to build consensus behind the orthodox proposal and persuade Archbishop George [Carey] to come in behind it." But, he wrote, as if paragraph 2 never existed, "should consecrations take place before the March [meeting of archbishops], the orthodox position will be seriously weakened."[1]

Rodgers wrote back the next day: "As you know, we at Kampala committed ourselves to follow the leadership of the archbishops. We will do as the archbishops request. . . . rest assured that we will not take the initiative. It is imperative from our point of view that you archbishops take the lead. . . . we are the followers at this point."[2]

Sinclair was not satisfied. He wrote to Murphy the day after Christmas: "The renewed witness you are working so hard to establish in the States needs the full backing of Archbishop George [Carey] and the majority of archbishops. We are working with you for this, but do not want premature consecrations of bishops which would jeopardize this progress."[3]

Murphy wrote back: "Please know that nothing could be clearer to me (and to First Promise) than that we are not leading, directing—much less driving—any of the specific Archbishops involved with us in this struggle. . . . I fully understand that the Archbishops are directing this work. . . . What I would say, however, is that I am certain that you will find satisfactory answers to your questions and concerns when you get a chance to catch up with Moses Tay and/or Emmanuel Kolini."[4] Again, it did not satisfy.

Sinclair went back to Rodgers. He knew Tay "favored early consecrations" and was fully convinced that Kolini had "shifted his position substantially" after Kampala. He put pressure on Rodgers to use his "influence for the suspension or at least postponement of plans to consecrate new bishops in January." He then increased the pressure, jumping to an unfortunate conclusion: "So basically First Promise is taking advantage of a minority position in the group of archbishops which appears to accord with their own agenda."[5] This statement did not bless John Rodgers. He wrote back quickly:

> We are aware that not all of the archbishops consider early consecrations of missionary bishops the best approach. We assume that paragraph two of the letter you wrote to us reflected a willingness of both views to live together in solidarity if some took earlier action. That does seem to be the meaning of that paragraph. . . . Once again please know that we are submitted to your corporate leadership and that we are putting no pressure on anyone. Your thought that First Promise is taking advantage of anything other than what we presented to all of you at Kampala is simply incorrect. It disturbs me personally that you think that could be true.[6]

And that was it. A strange, almost deafening silence followed. E-mail traffic stopped completely.

NOTES

Dedication

1. Richard Baxter, *Five Disputations* (1659), p. 165, quoted in Eifion Evans, *Daniel Rowland and the Great Evangelical Awakening in Wales* (Carlisle, PA: The Banner of Truth Trust, Edinburgh, Scotland, p 58, 1985).

Introduction

1. This introductory anecdote was recounted to the author by a friend who witnessed the exchange, and confirmed by Bishop John Rucyahana.

2. For more information about John and his account and experience of the 1994 genocide, see his book (written with James Riordan) *The Bishop of Rwanda* (Nashville: Nelson, 2007).

3. Electing and consecrating an openly gay man as bishop "makes the Episcopal Church the first major Christian denomination to say that people in committed gay relationships are not barred from ordination or leadership" (Cathy Lynn Grossman, "Episcopal Church Approves Gay Bishop," *USA Today*, August 6, 2003). Concerning the blessing of same-sex unions, J. I. Packer wrote in "Why I Walked" (*Christianity Today*, January 2003), "A major change in Anglicanism is involved: Writing into a diocesan constitution something that Scripture, canonically interpreted, clearly and unambiguously rejects as sin. This has never been done before, and ought not to be done now."

4. The 75th General Convention of the Episcopal Church held in 2006 voted down Resolution D058 "Salvation through Christ Alone" (70.5 percent to 29.5 percent), which declared "its unchanging commitment to Jesus Christ as the Son of God, the only name by which any person may be saved."

5. Michael Massing, "Bishop Lee's Choice," *New York Times*, January 4, 2004. In the article, Lee's wife, Kristina, is quoted as having asked her husband, "Peter, do you want to be on the side of the future or of the past?"

6. Concerned Women for America, "Washington's New Episcopal Bishop Promises Liberal Activism in Debut Sermon," June 5, 2002. The article reads, "With reference to the celebration of Easter, he [Chane] said, "*The Easter Story* . . . the event of the resurrection, which defines the core of our Christian theology, *is, at best, conjectural,* based upon what we are able to read from the Gospel accounts and the Book of Acts."

7. Julia Duin, "Heresy Better Idea than Schism Says Virginia Bishop," *Washington Times*, January 31, 2004.

8. *The Book of Common Prayer*, 1549. The bishop asks the one being ordained presbyter, "Will you be ready, with all faithful diligence, to banish and drive away from

the Church all erroneous and strange doctrines contrary to God's Word?" The text, removed from the Episcopal Church 1979 *Book of Common Prayer*, remains in use in most Anglican ordinations around the world.

9. Chuck Colson, "As Long As We All Get Along," *BreakPoint*, February 5, 2004. It should be noted that John Rucyahana serves as the chairman of Prison Fellowship, Rwanda.

Chapter 1

1. Bishop Festo Kivengere, *I Love Idi Amin* (Old Tappan, NJ: Revell, 1977), 62–63. Festo once said, "No matter what grace has done for me in the past, I still need to experience daily the power of the cleansing blood of Jesus. . . . And that is not easy" (quoted in Anne Coomes, *The Authorised Biography of Festo Kivengere* [Eastbourne, UK: Monarch, 1990], 258).

2. Ibid., 10.

3. Ibid., 11.

4. Ibid., 55. Bishop Festo was actually standing next to the archbishop when he was called to stand before the president. He whispered to Festo, "They are going to kill me. I am not afraid." His last recorded words came as he was being taken away. He turned and smiled at his bishops, saying, "I can see the hand of the Lord in this." Armed soldiers then took him away (Coomes, *The Authorised Biography*, 361–362).

Chapter 2

1. Allan Bloom, *The Closing of the American Mind* (New York: Simon and Schuster, 1987), 26.

2. See, for example, Romans 10:17; 1 Corinthians 1:21–24; 15:1–4.

3. Trinity Episcopal School for Ministry in Ambridge, Pennsylvania.

4. The Mustard Seed Babies Home in Hoima, Uganda, provides a Christian home for children either abandoned or orphaned by parents who died of AIDS. For more information about the Babies Home, go to www.mustardseedproject.org.

5. The president of Rwanda, His Excellency Paul Kagame, officially dedicated The Sonrise School on February 22, 2002. John Rucyahana said on that occasion, "Planted in the hearts of these precious children is the powerful love of Jesus Christ. This has the power to change Rwanda's future." For more information, contact Mustard Seed Project at www.mustardseedproject.org.

6. John Rucyahana wrote, "In the East African revival, believers emphasized their need to be in light with each other, sharing their joys and pains, learning to put matters right with the Lord every day as they studied the Scriptures (1 John 1:7–9)" (from his master's thesis, "The Impact of Christianity on Bunyoro Uganda, East Africa," May 1990, 69; available at Trinity Episcopal School for Ministry, Ambridge, PA).

Chapter 3

1. *The Book of Common Prayer* (New York: Oxford University Press, 1979), 876–878.

Chapter 4

1. Gerald Prunier, *The Rwanda Crisis: History of a Genocide* (New York: Columbia University Press, 1995), 5.

2. Ibid., 13.

3. Ibid., 63.

4. Ibid., 51.

5. Ibid., 56.

6. Ibid., 222.

7. Ibid., 133.

8. Ibid., 170.

9. Philip Gourevitch, *We wish to inform you that tomorrow we will be killed with our families: Stories from Rwanda* (New York: Farrar, Straus and Giroux, 1998), 3.

10. Prunier, *The Rwanda Crisis*, 249.

11. John Rucyahana, in a personal interview in October 2002, stated, "We must give credit to many Hutu husbands who hid their Tutsi wives, children, and friends during the genocide to protect them. They miraculously live today as witnesses in our country. At great personal cost, they laid down their lives for their families. If they had been discovered, even as Hutu men, they would have been immediately killed."

12. Prunier, *The Rwanda Crisis*, 247.

13. Ibid., 260.

14. Ibid., 246.

15. Ibid., 284.

16. Ibid., 261. Samantha Powers wrote, "The Rwandan Genocide would prove to be the fastest, most efficient killing spree of the twentieth century. In 100 days, some 800,000 Tutsi and politically moderate Hutu were murdered" (*A Problem from Hell: America and the Age of Genocide* [New York: Basic Books, 2002], 334). She also reported that by 1992, "Hutu militia had purchased, stock-piled, and begun distributing an estimated eighty-five tones of munitions, as well as 581,000 machetes—one machete for every third adult Hutu male" (337).

17. Nancy Gibbs, "Why? The Killing Fields of Rwanda," *Time*, May 16, 1994.

18. Prunier, *The Rwanda Crisis*, 73.

19. Ibid., 327.

20. Powers, *A Problem from Hell*, 343. Powers went on to say, "In Washington Dallaire's alarm was discounted" even though by "February 23 Dallaire reported that he was drowning in information about death squad target lists" (345).

21. Ibid., 338.

22. Ibid., 349, 356.

23. Prunier, *The Rwanda Crisis*, 274–275.

24. Powers, *A Problem from Hell*, 369. The UN Security Council Resolution 912 slashed Dallaire's peacekeeping troops to 270. In fact 503 remained. General Dallaire's constant plea for more reinforcements throughout the 100 days of genocide fell on deaf ears. Powers noted, he "commanded the same 503 soldiers as he had since late April. Not a single additional UN soldier had been deployed" (381). Dallaire would later say, "It seems . . . inconceivable that one can watch . . . thousands of people being . . . massacred . . . every day in the media . . . and remain passive" (386).

25. Ibid., 386.

26. Samantha Powers, "Bystanders to Genocide: Why the United States Let the Rwandan Tragedy Happen," *Atlantic Monthly*, September 2001. In her book *A Problem from Hell*, she wrote, "It is shocking to note that during the entire three months of the genocide, Clinton never assembled his top policy advisers to discuss the killings" (366).

27. Prunier, *The Rwanda Crisis*, 275–276.

28. Prunier tells the story of Felicite Niyitegeka of Gisenyi, Rwanda, who was a Hutu

Catholic lay worker. She helped Tutsis across the border to safety. Her army colonel brother found out and demanded she stop. She refused. They found her with thirty refugees, all of whom were killed "one by one before her eyes. . . . The militia leader then told her she would die and asked her to pray for his soul before shooting her" (*The Rwanda Crisis*, 260).

29. Ibid., 125.
30. Ibid., 252.
31. Ibid., 254.
32. Ibid., 132; see footnote 10 on that page, and page 34.
33. John Rucyahana noted that there were three active Rwandan bishops who were either outside the country at the time of the war, or who fled. These men eventually returned and gave themselves wholeheartedly to the rebuilding of the church and the country.
34. Powers, *A Problem from Hell*, 334.

Chapter 5

1. For more discussion on the 72nd General Convention of the Episcopal Church, held in Philadelphia in late July 1997, see chapter 7.
2. Catherine Claire, "Charting a Route to Restoration, *Jubilee Extra*, Prison Fellowship Ministries, April 2006.
3. The Anglican bishops of Rwanda met on September 15, 1997, to elect a leader from among them to serve a five-year term as archbishop. Before the war, this was a prestigious political position, determined with no small help from the government. This time, it was different. John reported with great excitement that the bishops met together in humility, prayer, and Bible study, without anyone campaigning for the office. By the end of the meeting, they spoke with one voice, choosing Emmanuel Kolini to serve as archbishop and their representative to the Anglican Communion worldwide. John reported, "It is a miracle—and everyone in Rwanda will know. Our bishops are not politicians! We are united together in the Lord. We have sought Him in prayer and He has answered."

Chapter 6

1. Luke 23:34.
2. Ken Ringle, "'The Haunting: He Couldn't Stop the Slaughter in Rwanda. Now He Can't Stop the Memory,' an interview with General Romeo Dallaire" (Commander of the United Nations peacekeeping force during the days of the Rwandan genocide) *Washington Post*, June 15, 2002. General Dallaire said, "In 100 days, 800,000 people were killed, 300,000 of them children. That's not counting 500,000 that got hacked a few times, maybe had a leg chopped off, but survived."
3. Ephesians 6:12.
4. Samantha Powers, *A Problem from Hell: America and the Age of Genocide* (New York: Basic Books, 2002), 335.
5. Ibid., 352.
6. Ibid., 367, 366.
7. Ibid., 370.
8. Samantha Powers, "Bystanders to Genocide: Why the United States let the Rwandan Tragedy Happen," *Atlantic Monthly*, September 2001.
9. Gerald Prunier, *The Rwanda Crisis: History of a Genocide* (New York: Columbia University Press, 1995), 277.

10. Ibid., 276.
11. Ringle, "The Haunting."
12. Powers, *A Problem from Hell*, 388–389.
13. Powers concluded in her book that "Clinton, one of the most eloquent presidents of the twentieth century, could have made the case that something approximating genocide was under way, that an inviolable American value was imperiled by its occurrence, and that U.S. contingents at relatively low risk could stop the extermination of a people. . . . In short, the United States could have led the world" (383).
14. Ibid., 377.
15. Harry Griffith, during his days as executive director of Anglican Mission in America, had a sign on his bookshelf that read, "The hottest places in hell are reserved for those who remain neutral in the times of moral crisis. —Dante."

Chapter 7

1. Philip Jenkins, *The Next Christendom: The Coming of Global Christianity* (New York: Oxford University Press, 2002), 95. Philip Jenkins is "Distinguished Professor of History and Religious Studies at Penn State University."
2. See appendix article "Truth's Mission Field."
3. Jenkins actually cited our story in his book *The Next Christendom* as an illustration to his thesis that American conservatives are turning to the global South for help (193, 202–204). In this context, he pictured the new era as "White soldiers following Black and Brown generals."
4. Stephen F. Noll, *The Handwriting on the Wall: A Plea to the Anglican Communion* (Solon, OH: Latimer Press, 1998), 3. Noll cites two strategic facts. First, in 1920, Anglican bishops worldwide (Lambeth Conference) passed Resolution 66 upholding both holy matrimony and chastity outside of marriage as the "unchangeable Christian standard" (2). Second, Presiding Bishop Edmond Browning, elected leader of the Episcopal Church in 1984, had publicly declared in 1979 that he would "not obey or enforce the Church's official traditional teaching on sexuality." His declared rebellion became the driving force behind the church's new morality.
5. Noll, *Handwriting on the Wall*, 20. This second bishop was brought to trial in 1996—and won his case. The favorable verdict for homosexual ordinations both further isolated Episcopal evangelicals and, as Noll rightly stated, "permitted homosexual activists to advance their agenda to a new level: the advocacy of same-sex marriage" (4).
6. Noll, *Handwriting on the Wall*.
7. See appendix article "Kuala Lumpur Statement (selections)."
8. Jude 3.
9. Noll, *Handwriting on the Wall*, 5. The convention took the polite method of rejecting the Kuala Lumpur Statement by sending it to a committee for further study.
10. Noll, *Handwriting on the Wall*, 20. Noll reported that Frank Griswold gave an interview for *Christianity Today* (January 10, 1994) in which he admitted he had ordained homosexual priests and stated, "The question with respect to sexuality is, How is this person's sexuality part of their living of the gospel." Noll went on to quote that Griswold did not base his argument on Scripture but, in Griswold's own words, "on my own experience of grace in the lives of persons whose sexuality has been expressed outside these classical and normative categories."
11. Ibid., 20.
12. This convention made it clear by action, not legislation, that a policy of "local

option" was in place. As Noll pointed out, "Openly practicing homosexual layperson and clergy spoke without reproach at the Convention. A number of bishops made clear that they now permit blessing of same-sex unions in their dioceses" (4). In addition, the issue of women's ordination—a major issue of debate for over two decades—was now mandatory. Legislation was passed "to remove from power all who oppose the ordination of women" (5).

13. *The Book of Common Prayer* (which "conforms to the Standard Book of 1928") (New York: Seabury Press, 1952), 555.

14. For a detailed account of the conference, see appendix article "The First Promise Statement."

15. *The Book of Common Prayer* (New York: Oxford University Press, 1979), 526, 538.

16. The "First Promise" statement was signed on September 9, 1997, by twenty-seven of the original thirty senior leaders who attended the meeting. This document in full can be found on the Anglican Mission in America website: www.theamia.org.

17. Robert E. Quinn, *Deep Change: Discovering the Leader Within* (San Francisco: Jossey-Bass, 1996), 156. The actual phrase by Quinn is, "If you are not risking your job, you are not doing your job." This book was an extremely helpful tool to First Promise leaders early on in our development. It outlined both leaders who "sacrifice their principles for pressure" and leaders who "accept the necessary risk because it is the right thing to do" (158).

18. The Dallas Conference had forty-five bishops and four archbishops from sixteen nations including Australia, Africa, India, New Zealand, Pakistan, and South America.

19. See appendix article "The Dallas Statement (selections)."

20. The Right Reverend John Spong's letter to Archbishop George Carey, November 12, 1997.

21. Bishop Spong's other letters to Archbishop Carey, November 26, 1997, and February 19, 1998.

22. Presiding Bishop Frank Griswold's interview with the *Philadelphia Enquirer Magazine*, December 28, 1997.

Chapter 8

1. David Young, "A History of St. Andrew's Church: The Early Years: 1996–1997," a document sent to Archbishop Emmanuel Kolini and Bishop John Rucyahana on July 3, 1998 in preparation for the Lambeth Conference, August 1998.

2. Ibid.

3. Larry Maze, "A Statement to the Episcopal Church in Arkansas from the Rt. Rev. Larry E. Maze, XII Bishop of the Diocese of Arkansas," April 16, 1998.

4. Larry Maze, letter to the Rev. Dr. Jon C. Shuler, December 2, 1996. In this same letter, Bishop Maze wrote, "It is beyond my comprehension that with seven local congregations from which to choose, the group . . . simply cannot find a home."

5. Laurie Pierce, "State Wins Support in Authority Battle," *Arkansas Democrat-Gazette*, August 8, 1998.

6. Larry Maze, letter to the Rev. Dr. Jon C. Shuler, December 2, 1996.

7. Young, "A History of St. Andrew's Church."

8. Jon Shuler, letter to the Rt. Rev. Larry E. Maze, November 12, 1996.

9. See appendix article "Correspondence" for selected details of the correspondence.

10. See appendix article "The Koinonia Statement."

11. John Kabango Rucyahana, letter to Thaddeus and Erilynne Barnum, December 26, 1997.

12. See appendix article "TJ's First Service."

13. Thomas Johnston, letter to the Rt. Rev. Larry E. Maze, February 10, 1998. TJ later wrote, "I was not . . . prepared to take that step because I believe that I have been called to serve as priest in this community of faith that desires to witness to Jesus Christ and to faithfully live within the Anglican Tradition." Note: Arrangements had been made for TJ to meet with Bishop Maze, but that meeting never took place.

14. See appendix article "TJ's First Service," Bishop Maze's February18, 1998, response.

15. John Kabango Rucyahana, letter to Thaddeus and Erilynne Barnum, February 13, 1998. Bishop John is on record as taking oversight of the Little Rock church prior to going to his archbishop. He needed to stand with the marginalized before asking permission.

16. See appendix article "TJ's First Service," TJ's March 4, 1998, response.

17. See appendix article "TJ's First Service," TJ's "Gamaliel letter" to Bishop Maze.

18. John Kabango Rucyahana, letter to Thaddeus Barnum, March 12, 1998.

19. Thomas Johnston, letter to the Rt. Rev. Edward Salmon, March 22, 1998.

20. Edward L. Salmon, letter to the Most Rev. Frank T. Griswold, July 29, 1998.

21. April 16, 1998.

22. Laurie Pierce, "Little Rock dispute sets precedent for national Episcopal Church," *Arkansas Democrat-Gazette*, April 25, 1998.

23. See appendix article "TJ's First Service," Bishop Maze's April 1998 responses.

24. See appendix article "TJ's First Service," Bishop John's correspondences to Maze and to the archbishop of Canterbury.

25. Laurie Pierce, "State Wins Support in Authority Battle," *Arkansas Democrat-Gazette*, August 8, 1998.

26. "American priest links with Rwanda Diocese: Canon Lawyers tackle new conundrum before Lambeth Conference," *Church of England Newspaper*, May 8, 1998.

27. Ronald Haines, letter to our Pawleys Island office addressed: To Whom It May Concern, July 8, 1998.

28. Pierce, "State Wins Support."

29. "Rwandan Link with Arkansas Parish, Priest, Befuddles, Frustrates ECUSA," *Christian Challenge*, Summer 1998.

30. Thomas Johnston, "A History of St. Andrew's Church: November 1997 to the Present," a document sent to Archbishop Emmanuel Kolini and Bishop John Rucyahana on July 3, 1998 in preparation for the Lambeth Conference, August 1998.

31. Stephen Neill, *Anglicanism* (Harmondsworth, UK: Penguin, 1958), 31. Nothing could have been more offensive to Larry Maze. Speaking before the gay and lesbian caucus in the Episcopal Church, Maze said, "In the church there are those who have mistaken certainty for faith—who believe that to walk faithfully is to walk with certainty that they have determined the mind and the heart of God. . . . Those of us who live in the mystery of God's unfolding plan for our lives and for the universe and accept the ambiguities of such mystery, simply do not measure up to the test of faith that demands certainty. . . . And now, gay and lesbian people are demanding that they join the search for truth—that opinions that have for generations been layered in sanctified language—are, nonetheless, opinions."

From a sermon titled "May God Grant Us the Grace to Not Deify Our Own Opinions" delivered on September 19, 1998, at the closing Eucharist of the South Central Regional Conference of Integrity, Inc., Little Rock, AR.

32. "God's Little Rock: A Church the Local Episcopal Bishop Never Wanted is Helping Reshape Anglicanism," *Foundations*, October 1998.

Chapter 9

1. Stephen F. Noll, *The Handwriting on the Wall: A Plea to the Anglican Communion* (Solon, OH: Latimer Press, 1998), v–vi.

2. Rwandan House of Bishops, "Statement on Homosexuality by the Anglican Province of Rwanda," a unanimous decision by all nine bishops, signed on January 31, 1998.

3. Five hundred fifty attended the March 23 Houston lay leaders conference. George Gallup stated that American Christians in general practice a "do-it yourself religion" designed for "comfort not challenge." Larry Hall, senior clergy at St. John the Divine's in Houston advised it was time "to be awake, to be alert, to be fearless, to face forces that are intent to destroy the one, holy, catholic, apostolic faith that has been given to us; to say to the forces— 'We will go no further'" (reported by *Foundations*, the newsmagazine of the Episcopal Synod of America, April 1998).

4. John Spong, letter to the Primates of the Anglican Communion, November 12, 1997.

5. John Spong, letter to the Most Rev. and Rt. Hon. George L. Carey, January 26, 1998.

6. John Spong, letter to the Most Rev. and Rt. Hon. George L. Carey, February 19, 1998.

7. John Spong, letter to the Most Rev. and Rt. Hon. George L. Carey, November 12, 1997.

8. John Spong, letter to the Most Rev. and Rt. Hon. George L. Carey, November 26, 1998. Charles E. Bennison, bishop of the diocese of Pennsylvania and colleague of John Spong, states his view of the doctrine of Holy Scripture in this manner: "The Church existed before the Bible. The Church wrote the Bible and the Church can rewrite the Bible" (spoken publicly at the Church of the Good Samaritan, Paoli, PA, December 1997).

9. "A Tale of Two Cultures," *St. Andrew's Messenger*, published by St. Andrew's Episcopal Church, Fort Worth, TX, Summer 1990. The bishop's name is pronounced *moo-gay*.

10. Doug King, "Muzzled African Bishop Speaks Against Immorality," *Foundations*, the newsmagazine of the Episcopal Synod of America, June 1990.

11. "A Tale of Two Cultures," *St. Andrew's Messenger*, and, King, "Muzzled African Bishop Speaks Against Immorality," *Foundations*. The following dialogue is taken from these two articles, which recorded Bishop Muge's reflections of that night at a press conference days later.

12. See appendix article "Alexander Muge's Press Conference."

13. Nan Cobbey and Jerry Hames, "Kenyan bishop killed in road crash—Received death threat," *Episcopal Life*, September 1990. The facts concerning the tragic death of Bishop Muge are found in this article.

14. See appendix article "Uganda Pre-Lambeth Conference Resolution."

15. Paul Buckley, *Dallas Morning News*, August 6, 1998.

16. David Virtue, "Bishops Vote Overwhelmingly for Biblical Standards on Sexuality," http://www.virtueonline.org, August 5, 1998.
17. Ibid.
18. See appendix article "Lambeth, Resolution III.5 (excerpt and reaction)."
19. Laurie Pierce, "State Wins Support in Authority Battle," *Arkansas Democrat-Gazette*, August 8, 1998.
20. Buckley.
21. Andrew Carey, *Church of England Newspaper*, August 14, 1998.
22. Andrew Carey, "African Christians? They're Just a Step Up From Witchcraft: What Bishop Spong had to say about his fellow Christians," *Church of England Newspaper*, July 10, 1998. The Rev. George Conger in his work, "Anglican Mission in America, An Apologetic Vindicating its Creation, Organization, and Purposes," quoted John Spong after Lambeth, saying, "This action flows directly out of the strange, almost pathological, action taken at the Lambeth Conference 1998. . . . The winning resolution revealed an attitude toward Holy Scripture that reflected total ignorance of the last 100 years of critical biblical scholarship. It also revealed an absolute void in knowledge of contemporary medical and scientific data in regard to the origins and nature of homosexual orientation. . . . Let me say this carefully, but clearly. Anyone who elevates their prejudices to the position where they are defended as the will of God is evil."
23. Ibid.
24. Ibid. Carey also reported that the archbishop of Nigeria, Joseph Adetiloye, "noted that Africans are dying for their faith, paying a far greater price than any alleged dinner, bribery or inducement."
25. Ibid.
26. See appendix article "Stalemate in Little Rock" for a more detailed account of this strategic time.
27. The Association of Anglican Congregations on Mission reported in their document "Petition to the Primates' Meeting and the Primates of the Anglican Communion" that Resolution B032 presented at the 1997 General Convention of the Episcopal Church endorsing the Kuala Lumpur Statement was soundly defeated by the House of Bishops with forty-two bishops in favor, ninety-four against, and two abstaining. It should be noted that the next two subsequent conventions—2000 and 2003—never disciplined John Spong or other bishops who hold his views. Spong, up till his retirement, was allowed to continue to head the theological committee of the House of Bishops.

Chapter 10
1. The Rt. Rev. C. FitzSimons Allison at a First Promise advisory committee meeting, June 28, 1999.
2. Bishops Tay and Rucyahana met again in Raleigh, North Carolina, on October 24–25, 2003, at a regional gathering for Anglican Mission in America and there spoke openly of this providential meeting in Canterbury at the Lambeth Conference 1998.
3. Documented in an interview with the Rev. Dr. Jon C. Shuler, June 10, 2002.
4. The Most Rev. Dr. Moses Tay, letter to the Rev. Dr. Timothy R. Smith, rector of Christ Episcopal Church, Mobile, Alabama, August 21, 1997.
5. See appendix article "The American Rebellion" for a more detailed account.

6. Bruce Bower documented the American rebellion (see appendix), and he was supported by a team that included the Rev. Dr. John Rodgers, the Rev. William Beasley, and John Jones.

7. See appendix article "Leapfrogging" for a more thorough explanation and rationale.

8. Bruce Bower, Association of Anglican Congregations on Mission, as reported in the "First Supplement" of "The Petitions," released on April 7, 1999, p. 12. The Newark Convention took place on January 29, 1999.

9. See appendix article "A Crisis of Leadership" for a more detailed account of events surrounding "The Petitions'" circulation and subsequent AAC meeting.

10. See appendix article "Archbishops' Open Letter to Frank Griswold" for a more detailed accounting of the open letter and response.

11. The Most Rev. Dr. George Carey, "The Precious Gift of Unity," given at the S.E.A.D. Conference.

12. The Most Rev. Emmanuel Kolini told our First Promise leaders that in Africa there is a saying that parents who hear the cry of their children must also investigate to see if what they are saying is true. Kolini believed it was essential for him personally to take two months traveling the US in the summer of 1999 so that he might witness for himself the rebellion portrayed in "The Petitions."

13. Bruce Bower, Association of Anglican Congregations on Mission, as reported in the "Second Supplement" of "The Petitions," released on November 5, 1999, p. 17. Bower also cites a quote from the Rev. Dr. Stephen Noll concerning the near election of Robinson: "I predict five years max before we get our first out-of-the-closet gay bishop. Maybe not before the General Convention of 2000, but surely Gene Robinson, or a Gene Robinson, will wear an Episcopal mitre before long. This election will then, like the ordination of women, in 1974 and 1976, set a new precedent. 'The Church has made up its mind,' they will say, and will already have the canons in place to enforce the new precedent on the basis of 'justice'" (39). Noll's prediction came true on November 2, 2003, when Gene Robinson was consecrated bishop of New Hampshire with the blessing and presence of Frank Griswold.

14. The Most Rev. Dr. Moses Tay, letter to the Most Rev. and Rt. Hon. George Carey, on behalf of the province of the Anglican Church in Southeast Asia, August 4, 1999.

15. David Virtue, "We Will Never Compromise Truth for Unity," in an interview with Archbishop Emmanuel Kolini at Ridgecrest, North Carolina, June 6, 1999.

16. Ibid. Many thanks to David Virtue for his in-depth interview with Emmanuel Kolini that important summer of 1999. It was during this time that Kolini became convinced in his prayers that an intervention from overseas was inevitable.

17. The Rt. Rev. John Kabango Rucyahana, "Come and See Report to His Grace, the Right Rev. Emmanuel Kolini," October 25, 1999.

18. The Most Rev. Harry Goodhew, "Come and See Report," published on the Internet on December 22, 1999.

19. Iain H. Murray, *The Forgotten Spurgeon* (Carlisle, PA: The Banner of Truth Trust, 1966), 133. C. H. Spurgeon also said, "It now becomes a serious question how far those who abide by the faith once delivered to the saints should fraternize with those who have turned aside to another gospel. Christian love has its claims, and divisions are to be shunned as grievous evils; but how far are we justified in being in confederacy with those who are departing from the truth?" (143).

Chapter 11

1. Iain H. Murray, *Evangelicalism Divided: A Record of Crucial Change in the Years 1950 to 2000* (Edinburgh: The Banner of Truth Trust, 1982), 143.

2. For a detailed account of how God led Chuck to this new direction, read the appendix article "Journey to Kampala."

3. Livingstone Nkoyoyo, "Welcome and Opening Remarks by the Most Rev. Dr. Livingstone Mpalanyi Nkoyoyo at the Great Lakes Regional Primates' and Bishops' Fellowship, 16 November 1999."

4. Moses Tay. Note: His address was not published. Many thanks to the extensive notes taken by Mr. Jim Beard during the Kampala meetings.

5. Robert Duncan, "Remarks of the Rt. Rev. Robert Duncan, Bishop of Pittsburgh, USA to the Primates meeting, Kampala, Uganda, 16 November 1999." It was later reported that US Presiding Bishop Frank Griswold received word of Bishop Duncan's three-point confession and used it publicly, quoting it verbatim, to ridicule Bob Duncan in front of his colleagues during an address to the House of Bishops' meeting in the spring of 2000.

6. John Rodgers, "An Outline of a talk at Kampala by the Rev. Dr. John H. Rodgers, Jr."

7. Geoffrey W. Chapman, Rector of St. Stephen's Episcopal Church, Sewickley, Pennsylvania, said it this way in his presentation before the archbishops: "We ask for a new jurisdiction on American soil, under the temporary oversight of an overseas province." He argued that such a jurisdiction "would establish the framework for a renewed American Anglicanism committed to biblical Christianity and Great Commission ministry." In a moving final appeal, he remarked, "we beg you, our leaders in the faith, to not be silent."

8. Matthew 13:24–30, 36–43.

9. The Asians used the following Scriptures to argue for immediate church discipline in the face of grievous apostasy: 2 Corinthians 6:14–18; Galatians 1:6–9; 2:4–5; 2 John 7–11; and Acts 20:28–31.

10. See the appendix article "The Kampala Report (selections)."

11. Dick Kim, "A Letter from the Kampala Primates' Meeting, published on the internet by frkim@aol.com, November 1999.

12. The Kampala archbishops, in a private unpublished letter to George Carey, archbishop of Canterbury, dated November 18, 1999.

13. David Virtue, "Singapore, Kampala and Portugal: Commentary," http://www.virtueonline.org, November 25, 1999.

14. James Stanton, quoted in the *Church of England Newspaper*, November 26, 1999.

15. Emmanuel Kolini, "Closing Comments," as recorded by the Rev. Chuck Murphy at the time of the address.

16. For a more detailed account of this e-mail exchange, see appendix article "Warning Against Early Consecrations."

17. An interview with John Rodgers and Chuck Murphy, London, October 2003. John Rodgers admitted, "Frankly, I had gone through my purple passion. I was no longer looking to become a bishop. But in this case, they asked us to stick our necks out, oh I had to do it. I didn't have to think about it that much."

18. An interview with Quigg Lawrence in the spring of 2004.

Chapter 12

1. Robert Duncan, bishop of Pittsburgh, letter to all clergy and lay leaders of the diocese, on January 30, 2000, in response to the Singapore consecrations of John Rodgers and Chuck Murphy by Archbishops Moses Tay and Emmanuel Kolini.

2. Also in attendance: Bishop Fitz and Martha Allison, Bishop Alex and Jane Dickson, Bishop David Pytches, the provincial secretary, the dean of the cathedral, William Beasley, Jennifer Suvada, my wife, Erilynne, and me. Jennifer and I were given the task of taking notes for the meeting.

3. Kolini was careful to start his message with the preeminent call of gospel proclamation, citing Galatians 2:20 as his text, before moving to his second point of obedience to the Holy Spirit. Modern liberalism has dangerously embraced the doctrine of guidance by the Holy Spirit. They use it to justify their rejection of the inspiration of the Bible and the call to preach the full, unchanging gospel message. In the mind of modern revisionists, the Holy Spirit has led them to new truth that contradicts Holy Scripture.

4. Julia Duin, in an article in the *Washington Times* (February 1, 2000) titled "American Episcopal Priests' Consecration May Expand Rift," quoted Bishop John Rodgers: "If the [Episcopal] Church repents and turns around at General Convention . . . we'll quietly turn around and have other things to do."

5. Press statement from the archbishop of Canterbury, received from the communications department of the Anglican Communion Office, London, February 1, 2000.

6. Frank Griswold, letter "For All Bishops of the Episcopal Church," January 31, 2000.

7. Richard N. Ostling, AP Religion Writer, *Religion Today*, February 3, 2000. The article was carried by the *Washington Post* and included the quote to the Associated Press.

8. Kathryn McCormick and James Solheim, "Singapore Consecration Provokes Strong Response Throughout the Church," Episcopal News Service, February 3, 2000.

9. Frank Griswold, letter "For the Primates of the Anglican Communion," January 31, 2000. For Bishop John Rucyahana of Rwanda, the charge of "dangerous fundamentalism" was a "clear expression of anger and possibly embarrassment by Bishop Griswold, hurling insults on Africans and Asians because they are exposing his evil and failures as the leader of the Episcopal Church, USA."

10. Gustav Niebuhr, "Consecration of Two Splits Anglicans," *New York Times*, Sunday, March 5, 2000.

11. Maurice Sinclair, Donald Mtetemela, and Harry Goodhew, "Statement of the Consecration of Bishops Charles Murphy and John Rodgers in Singapore on January 29," February 5, 2000.

12. John Lipscomb, "To the Clergy and People of the Diocese of Southwest Florida," February 7, 2000.

13. Douglas Theuner, "The Episcopal Church's One Binding Authority," e-mail to Louie Crew, February 14, 2000. It is incredible to see this statement in writing. What better describes the unprecedented demise and hypocrisy of the Episcopal Church than a statement by a bishop who esteems the "Canons and Constitutions" over the sovereign binding authority of Holy Scripture?

14. Michael G. Peers, "Statement by the Archbishop of Canada," February 7, 2000. The bishops of South Africa issued a similar statement on March 4, 2000, saying,

"The action taken is thoroughly anarchic and undermines proper order in the Church of God."

15. William Swing, published over public Internet list serves, February 11, 2000. Swing was the same bishop who opposed the late Kenyan bishop of Eldoret, Alexander Muge (see chapter 9).

16. John Spong, "Anglican Battle over Homosexuality Takes a 'Bizarre' Turn," March 18, 2000.

17. Carey's letter began, "Because the principle of communion by which the Anglican Communion stands promotes the See of Canterbury as the focal point of our relationship one with another, there are many people who are expecting me, as the current occupant of the See, to make my views known."

18. In 2005, N. T. Wright weighed in on this issue, telling *Christianity Today*, "The important thing to say is that border crossings are disruptive. Not only are they against the spirit and the letter of Anglican formularies, they are against one of the decrees of the Council of Nicea. . . . it's important to say this was a question that the early fathers faced." (Ted Olson, "Still Fighting Over Nicea," *Christianity Today*, February 2005.) George Conger has written extensively on the historic precedent of border crossing in Anglicanism, especially when there are "false doctrines not only tolerated, but promulgated by many . . . bishops" (George Conger, "Anglican Mission in America: An Apologetic Vindicating its Creation, Organization and Purposes," published in-house by Anglican Mission in America, 2002.)

19. It should be noted that before he closed his letter, George Carey dramatically lowered the expectations on the Portugal meeting of archbishops: "It is assumed that at the end of a week-long consultation, we shall produce an authoritative answer to the searching questions of faith and morals which are currently challenging the Communion. That is unrealistic." This statement more than justified Tay and Kolini's belief that Portugal was not going to produce action and that something had to be done prior.

20. Moses Tay, a personal e-mail to John Rodgers and Chuck Murphy, February 19, 2000. This e-mail would be his last correspondence as archbishop before his formal retirement. Tay's successor, Yong Ping Chung, would meet with the House of Bishops February 27–28. Together, they issued a statement affirming their belief that "the unity of the Anglican church must be grounded fundamentally in Scripture and in the historic Faith entrusted to us." They also affirmed that the new archbishop would inherit and protect John Rodgers (in the same way Kolini was protecting Chuck Murphy).

21. "The Statement of the House of Bishops: The Province of the Episcopal Church of Rwanda" was formally sealed on March 21. It should be noted that Kenneth North, an American lawyer specializing in Anglican canonical law, made careful inquiry and declared these consecrations valid.

22. The Living Church, "Bishop John Rodgers talks about the reasons for his consecration in Singapore," February 27, 2000.

23. David W. Virtue, "Virtue Interviews John Rodgers," http://www.virtueonline.org, February 24, 2000.

24. Dave Munday, "Murphy ready to launch new network of churches," *The Post and Courier*, Charleston, SC, March 12, 2000.

25. The Living Church, "Pivotal Moment," March 26, 2000.

26. Two years later, Leith Anderson was the keynote speaker at our second winter

conference, held in Little Rock, AR, January 2002. Leith addressed clergy and lay leaders from across the country, some 750 in attendance. He told Chuck Murphy that he was pleased the conference focused entirely on equipping Christians for the US mission without focus on the apostasy of the Episcopal Church. This, he said, was a testimony of the Lord's grace and gave hope for the future of the movement.

Chapter 13

1. Ken North was simply an extraordinary man. He was husband and father, lawyer, professor, and director of the Canon Law Institute. Harry Griffith once commented, Ken's "expertise and counsel in the study of Church law is unmatched. . . . [He was] an invaluable resource to our work and a dear Christian brother." Ken's defense of the canonical legitimacy of the Singapore consecrations remains uncontested to this day. On April 10, 2000, Ken died in his sleep at the age of fifty-four.

2. Robert E. Quinn, *Deep Change: Discovering the Leader Within* (San Frandisco: Jossey-Bass, 1996), 156. This book greatly impacted our leaders just prior to Singapore. Quinn argues that most leaders choose "a dangerous tactic: keeping our heads down, our mouths shut, and simply taking our paychecks to the bank—a no-passion, no-risk, no-commitment work ethic" (front jacket-flap). True leaders "initiate action . . . because it is the right thing to do. They care enough to risk dying for the organization, which would kill them for caring" (158).

3. David W. Virtue and Auburn V. F. Traycik, "Rwandan Archbishop Says ECUSA Must Conform to Lambeth Resolutions or Face the Consequences," e-mail from Portugal on March 29, 2000.

4. Rowan Williams, "Our Differences Need Not Destroy Us," April 8, 2000. Williams served on the commission that produced the Porto Communiqué. His closing remark in this article is noteworthy: "The next few years will undoubtedly be increasingly painful and difficult for many."

5. "A Communiqué from the Primates of the Anglican Communion," March 28, 2000, went on to say, "Only a formal and public repudiation of this [Quadrilateral] would place a diocese or Province outside the Anglican Communion." By Williams's assessment of Spong quoted above, and the state of North American Anglicanism, it would seem the "formal and public repudiation" had already taken place.

6. Ibid.

7. Yong Ping Chung, letter to Bishop John Rodgers, April 13, 2000. He went on to say that the communiqué rightly "upheld the authority of the Bible, Priority of Evangelism, Orthodoxy of Human Sexuality based on Scriptures. . . . I also believe that the prayers and fasting of our people around the globe for this [archbishops'] meeting had given us the result."

8. Virtue and Traycik, "Rwandan Archbishop Says ECUSA."

9. Yong Ping Chung, letter to Bishop John Rodgers.

10. Jerry Hames, "Episcopal Bishops Drawn to a 'New, Deeper Place,' at California Meeting," Internet, April 7, 2000.

11. "American Church refuses to bow to Primates' view," *Church of England Newspaper*, April 13, 2000.

12. "The hole revealed at Oporto," *Church of England Newspaper*, April 3, 2000.

13. Hames, "Episcopal Bishops Drawn."

14. Yong Ping Chung, personal letter to Frank Griswold, May 22, 2000. This letter came after the House of Bishops in Southeast Asia met on April 25 "greatly perplexed and deeply saddened" by Griswold's comments after meeting with his bishops in California. It was for them "a clear denial of the basic authority of the scriptures and repudiation of the 1998 Lambeth Resolution . . . on The Authority of the Bible and Biblical Morality." They restated that such a position was grounds for broken communion.

15. Ted Olsen, "Billy Graham a No-Show at Amsterdam 2000," *Christianity Today*, July 31, 2000.

Chapter 14

1. John Jewel (1522–1571), *The Works of John Jewel*, vol. III (Cambridge: Cambridge University Press, 1848), 69.

2. Martyn Lloyd-Jones, *Knowing the Times* (Carlisle, PA: The Banner of Truth Trust, 1989), 253.

3. Resolution D039: "Human Sexuality: Issues Related to Sexuality and Relationship," passed at the 73rd General Convention, Denver, Colorado, July 2000.

4. The House of Bishops passed this resolution 119 for, 19 against, and 4 abstaining.

5. Harry Griffith, "Missionary Bishop John Rodgers Reflects On ECUSA's General Convention 2000, published in-house by Anglican Mission in America, 2000." Noteworthy: Dr. Louie Crew, founder of the gay-lesbian movement in the Episcopal Church, was elected by this convention to the executive council, the church's highest policy-making group, with the highest vote total of the candidates. The unity behind this new gospel was staggering. In a surprise move, Gene Robinson announced his withdrawal from candidacy for bishop in Vermont. Even then conservative bishops called him "the most dangerous man in the American Church" (George Conger, "Conservatives Relieved as Gay Cleric Says He Won't Be Bishop," www.churchnewspaper.com, July 20, 2000).

6. Thanks to Harry Griffith, who took copious notes of the July 27–29, 2000, meeting in Amsterdam and to Tim Smith for his work in compiling historical data on these early meetings.

7. David Virtue, "Fifth Episcopal Parish Flees Diocese of Colorado and ECUSA for Anglican Mission in America," http://www.virtueonline.org, December 4, 2000. Virtue reported that the local bishop, Jerry Winterrowd, chose not to depose Ross but described his actions, and not the resolution, as "immature and irresponsible."

8. "Faith Steps: Walking the Path to Mission: The Journeys of Nine Anglican Mission in America Congregations," AMIA, 2003.

9. Ibid. In the fall of 2006, by the grace of God, this congregation (Christ Anglican Church) completed their new church building under the leadership of the Rev. Conlee Bodishbaugh. In AMIA, each congregation has sole ownership of their land and property.

10. Douglas LeBlanc, "American Bishops Support Two Primates," December 5, 2000. Three active and five retired bishops signed a "Statement of Support" for the stand made by Archbishops Kolini and Yong. In Anglican polity, a clergyman can be transferred from one Anglican province to another. It is usually done with the blessing of both the sending and receiving bishops. In these cases, the sending bishops were not consulted and therefore were angered. Helpless to stop the transfers to Rwanda, they decided to defrock the departing clergy. This action was

senseless and not recognized by Archbishop Kolini.

11. For example, in the late summer of 2000, an evangelical Episcopal bishop put a lien on the property of a large conservative church in his diocese. Knowing the church might transfer to AMIA, the bishop took steps to ensure the property and the buildings, worth millions, would be retained by the diocese. Eventually the church went to AMIA. The legal settlement for the property was in the courts for years.

12. George Carey, letter to Bishop Chuck Murphy, October 18, 2000. Griswold used Carey's support to his advantage. In a letter to all US Episcopal bishops on December 21, 2000, Griswold wrote, "George Carey and I are in very frequent contact. . . . he strongly disapproves of the Singapore consecrations. If there is to be any 'regularization' of the same, it can only come from the Episcopal Church."

13. George Carey, letter to Bishop John Rodgers, December 21, 2000. Carey continued his discourse on unity, saying, "To rebuild unity, John, is much more difficult than destroying it." Carey also wrote Yong on the same day, saying, "Unity is a theological and spiritual issue and we need to bear in mind that it takes far longer to rebuild unity and heal the wounds than it does to break our unity in the first place."

14. Emmanuel Kolini, letter to Frank Griswold, October 17, 2000. Kolini added, "In our Constitutions and Canons, the primary obligation of the House of Bishops of the Province of Rwanda is to: 'Defend the faith and Biblical authority as the supreme rule and ultimate standard of faith and practice.'"

15. Emmanuel Kolini, letter to George Carey, October 17, 2000. It is an important historical note that John Rodgers also wrote George Carey on November 30, stating the necessity of "setting theological and moral limits to membership within the Anglican Communion." Without it, he said rightly, "I believe the realignment [of the Anglican Communion] will move along the fault-line of biblical truth."

16. Emmanuel Kolini and Yong Ping Chung, "Joint Statement," press release by Anglican Mission in America, published on the Internet December 6, 2000.

17. Yong Ping Chung and Emmanuel Kolini, letter to George Carey, December 6, 2000.

18. George Carey, letter to Yong Ping Chung and Emmanuel Kolini, December 21 2000.

19. Bruce Mason, "Archbishop Carey Speaks Out on the Anglican Primates Meeting, ECUSA, AMIA, and the AAC," American Anglican Council, March 16, 2001. These were difficult days for evangelicals. Archbishops Maurice Sinclair and Drexel Gomez had published a significant work titled *To Mend the Net*. It was presented at the archbishops' yearly meeting in early March 2001. In it, they urged archbishops worldwide to set proper limits on theological innovations that deny the Christian gospel and to assume the needful authority to hold such innovators accountable to discipline. Tragically, the work was barely given a hearing. The only positive note, reflected Chuck Murphy, was that this book deepened the growing awareness among archbishops of the serious nature of the problem in the Episcopal Church.

20. Frank Griswold, presiding bishop's letter "For the Primates" regarding AMIA consecrations, June 19, 2001.

21. Emmanuel Kolini and Yong Ping Chung, letter to George Carey, June 12, 2001.

22. George Carey, letter to Emmanuel Kolini and Yong Ping Chung, June 19, 2001. Yong later wrote Carey on November 30, 2001, saying, "You publicly showed your wrath and published in the Internet a very hurting letter. That letter was addressed

to Archbishop Kolini and me but the whole world received it before we did!"

23. Dick Kim, message from Bishop Chuck Murphy, June 23, 2001.

24. Yong Ping Chung, letter to all clergy in the diocese of Sabah, July 6, 2001.

25. Yong Ping Chung, letter to all US orthodox Episcopal bishops, May 30, 2001.

26. Robert Duncan, letter to Yong Ping Chung, May 30, 2001.

27. Yong Ping Chung, letter to all clergy in the diocese of Sabah. Upon hearing of Yong Ping Chung's decision, Bishop John Rucyahana wrote, "We all do admire and respect him. . . . God will protect Yong. He stands as a witness in this present time in the history of the Anglican Church."

28. David Virtue, "Asian Primate Denied Pulpit in Calgary Parish By Canadian Bishop," http://www.virtueonline.org, June 25, 2001.

29. Yong Ping Chung, excerpts from his sermon in Denver on June 24, 2001. Consecrated that night were Thaddeus Barnum, Alexander Greene, Thomas "TJ" Johnston, and Douglas Weiss. "When Barnum arose," reported *Time*, "he was a much changed man. For one thing, he was a bishop. But not of the Episcopal Church USA, whose collar he had worn for 14 years. He was now a missionary — to the U.S. — from the Episcopal Church of Rwanda, pledged against the American church's laxity." David Van Biema, "Episcopal Turf War," *Time*, July 9, 2001.

30. David Virtue, "Episcopal Diocese of Pennsylvania Boots Traditionalist Christians From Church Buildings," http://www.virtueonline.org, May 30, 2001.

31. David Virtue, "PA Bishop Rejects Million Dollar Offer for Parish Property," http://www.virtueonline.org, June 4, 2001. "We have been and continue to be blessed," Phil Lyman said, "by the outpouring of support by the churches in our local community." In particular, Huntingdon Valley Methodist Church offered the use of their facilities on Sunday mornings at their own inconvenience — moving service times, providing office space, and so forth. This kindness extended even for a year until St. John's found a permanent space (David Virtue, "Saint John the Evangelist Anglican Church in PA Finds a New Home," http://www.virtueonline.org, June 8, 2001).

32. "Faith Steps."

33. Pat Ashworth, "Communion Threatened, says Dr. Carey," *Church Times*, July 13, 2001. The grant request was not new. In 1998, Trinity Church awarded the province of Rwanda a three-year grant for $132,000. Consideration for renewal happened to come up following the Denver consecrations.

34. John Rucyahana, letter to AMIA in response to Trinity Church, July 9, 2001.

35. Julia Duin, "Episcopalians Withhold Grants to Africa," *Washington Times*, August 22, 2001. Forty AMIA churches responded by raising $159,000 to offset the decision by Trinity Church, Wall Street.

36. George Carey, letter to Emmanuel Kolini, July 5, 2001.

37. Kolini was especially troubled by Carey's branding AMIA as "schismatic." "The sin of schism," he wrote Carey on August 1, 2001, "is unnecessary separation. The classic definition is in Augustine (4th century): 'schism applies to those who have the same doctrines . . . and choose to meet separately.' Of course, such separation is wrong. . . . The division of our day is clearly over primary, fundamental issues of faith. Surely you understand this." Yong also wrote, "While you take every opportunity to strike at the action of Archbishop Kolini and mine, you have never proved how serious you were in dealing with the recalcitrant stand of the Episcopal Church, USA . . . which is divisive" (November 30, 2001).

38. George Carey, archbishop of Canterbury's presidential address, given at the 12th meeting of the Anglican Consultative Council, Hong Kong, September 16, 2002.

39. David Virtue, "Carey Denies Funds to African Bishop, Says Primate Kolini is to Blame," http://www.virtueonline.org, December 20, 2002. The Province of Rwanda had asked for monies to build a home for the bishop of Kibungo.

40. Yong Ping Chung, archbishop's address, given at the provincial synod meeting of Southeast Asia, March 4–9, 2002. In his address, Yong reported on the letter appropriately sent by the other bishops to George Carey privately protesting Yong's involvement in the Denver consecrations. Yong said, "It was only recently I found out that our Diocesan Bishops did not release their letter of protest into the hands of the media. It was unethically released by Canterbury. This placed our own Diocesan Bishops in a very difficult situation."

41. Ibid.

Chapter 15

1. Victoria Combe, "Jesus Was Not the Son of God, Says Former Bishop," *Daily Telegraph*, April 4, 2001.

2. William Smalley, letter to the clergy of the diocese of Kansas, June 13, 2002. Melodie Woerman, "Kansas Blessing Policy Upheld by Narrow Margin," Plenteous Harvest, newspaper of the Episcopal Diocese of Kansas, October 24, 2002. Bernard Melango, archbishop of Central Africa rightly diagnosed the times: "No one envisioned that we would face a situation where the guardians of the faith, the bishops, would be the source of the problem" (address given at the Forward in Faith National Assembly, published September 2002).

3. John Chane, Bishop-elect Chane's Easter sermon: "Easter Beginnings and Endings," March 31, 2002.

4. Jan Nunley, "Canadian Diocese First to Pass Rite for Same-Gender Blessings," Episcopal News Service, Summer 2002.

5. J. I. Packer, "Why I Walked," *Christianity Today*, January 2003.

6. Martyn Lloyd-Jones, *Knowing the Times* (Carlisle, PA: The Banner of Truth Trust, 1989), 254–255. Packer added his endorsement to the work of AMIA, saying, "Emergency situations require emergency responses. The Anglican Mission in America was brought to birth to regain freedom for Anglican authenticity. . . . The Mission has my thankful support."

7. Ruth Gledhill, "Archbishop Fails to Condemn Unmarried Sex," *The Times*, October 1, 2002. Gledhill reported that Rowan Williams "refused to sign up to traditional Christian teaching that sex outside marriage is wrong" and "has knowingly ordained a practicing homosexual." Alister McGrath wrote, "Rowan has written extensively on issues of human sexuality, and is firmly committed to the full inclusion of homosexual persons in the life of the Church" ("The Writings of Rowan Uncovered, Part 1," www.churchnewspaper.com, August 8, 2002).

8. The archbishops met May 19–26 in Gramado, Brazil, and issued a pastoral letter on Pentecost Sunday 2003.

9. Jay Greener, "Response to Same-Sex Blessing," Anglican Mission in America, May 31, 2003.

10. Julia Duin, "Episcopal Bishop Presses for Same-Sex 'Marriage,'" *Washington Times*, June 23, 2003.

11. Cathy Lynn Grossman, "Episcopal Church Approves Gay Bishop," *USA Today*, August 6, 2006.

12. Frank Griswold, "The Presiding Bishop Writes to the Bishops Before General Convention," June 12, 2003. Also, Rachel Zoll ("Episcopal Head Defends Choice of Gay Bishop," The Associated Press, September 30, 2003) reported that Griswold explained his vote for Robinson by saying, "I wasn't settling the question of sexuality, I was affirming the choice of a diocese."

13. "Interview with Frank Griswold," *Philadelphia Enquirer Magazine*, December 28, 1997.

14. Auburn Faber Traycik, "No Turning Back," *The Christian Challenge*, August 2003. Robinson's most significant statement concerning his view on the doctrine of Scripture came in November 2004: "We believe God didn't stop revealing God's self when the canon of Scripture was closed. We worship a living God, not one who checked out 2000 years ago." It is the same position held by Mormons, Jehovah Witnesses, and others. Robinson went on to say, "The Bible has been hijacked by the religious right. That is our Bible. It's time we take it back. . . . I keep on saying to gay and lesbian people: Let's reclaim this book. It is our story. . . . Exodus is the greatest coming-out story in the history of the world" (Julia Duin, "Gay Bishop Dismisses Anglican Report," *Washington Times*, November 10, 2004).

15. Julia Duin, "A Priest Speaks His Mind," *Washington Times*, September 1, 2003. The local Reformed Episcopal Church graciously offered Randall their facility to start the new church. A short time later they joined Anglican Mission and called the church Emmaus Anglican Church, Catonsville, Maryland.

16. Robert Duncan, statement on the confirmation of Canon Gene Robinson, August 5, 2003.

17. American Anglican Council, "AAC Answers the Question: 'What Do I Do Now?'" August 2003 (distributed by AAC at General Convention).

18. Alan Cooperman, "Episcopal Dissenters Plan Their Strategy: Many Traditionalists Prefer Not to Flee," *Washington Post*, January 11, 2004.

19. Benjamin Nzimbi, a statement from the archbishop of Kenya, August 5, 2003. Livingstone Nkoyoyo, a statement from the archbishop of the church of Uganda, September 14, 2003. Auburn Faber Traycik, "No Turning Back," recording the quotes from Peter Akinola of Nigeria and Bernard Melango of Central Africa. Emmanuel Kolini, "Resolution of the House of Bishops of the Episcopal Church of Rwanda," September 6, 2003.

20. Thaddeus Barnum, "Time to Act," AMIA (Internet), November 4, 2003.

21. A statement by the primates of the Anglican Communion meeting in Lambeth Palace, October 15–16, 2003.

22. John Rucyahana, letter to the primates of the Anglican Communion, November 3, 2003. The quote from Murphy and the following quotes of Kolini and Yong were recorded immediately following the London meeting of archbishops. Minutes take by Thaddeus Barnum and AMIA executive director Tim Smith.

23. Frank Griswold, letter for the primates of the Anglican Communion, October 23, 2003. Griswold wrote, "Please know that broadly across the Episcopal Church the New Hampshire election is thought to be the work of the Spirit." From the diocese of New Hampshire, October 17, 2003: "We reaffirm our belief that the Diocese of New Hampshire faithfully and prayerfully considered and followed a Spirit-led process for the election of our new bishop."

24. The Province of Southeast Asia, "Statement of Breaking Communion," November 20, 2003. This document records the names of sixty-three US diocesan bishops

who voted for Robinson's election as bishop and the fifty bishops who participated in his consecration. Frank Griswold and his predecessor, Edmond Browning, were both consecrators, as was (noted with unspeakable sadness) the author's uncle.

25. Statement from the House of Bishops of the church of Uganda, November 20, 2003. Most provinces declaring broken communion with the Episcopal Church also reaffirmed solidarity with those still inside the church who, rejecting the Episcopal heresy, remained true to the historic Christian faith.

26. "Gay Bishop's Consecration Divides Anglicans," MSNBC News Service, November 3, 2003.

27. "Impaired Communion," *Church of England Newspaper*, December 5, 2003.

28. "The Fallout Continues," Forward NOW!, January 2004.

29. Jan Nunley, "Some Anglican Provinces Declare 'Impaired' or 'Broken' Relationship with the Episcopal Church," Episcopal News Service, December 8, 2003.

30. "Thirteen Global Primates State 'The Episcopal Church USA has Separated Itself,'" press statement released February 9, 2004.

31. Dirokpa Balufuga, "The Archbishop of Congo Addresses Anglican Mission in America," January 18, 2004. Dirokpa endorsed Anglican Mission with these words: "We have come here to bring you the support of the House of Bishops and the Christians of Congo . . . for your courage, having stood firm in the traditional faith of the Anglican Church, and in the doctrinal foundation: The Bible. . . . Our great hope is to see Anglican Mission prosper and become a powerful instrument of mission and witness to the Risen Christ in the United States and around the world."

32. Frank Griswold, "A Word to the Episcopal Church," January 22, 2004. The same quote appeared in *USA Today* (Cathy Lynn Grossman, "Anglicans Await Word," October 18, 2004).

33. Michael Massing, "Bishop Lee's Choice," *New York Times*, January 4, 2004.

34. The Lambeth Commission on Communion, "The Windsor Report," The Anglican Communion Office, London, UK, October 2004, (par. 134).

35. Ibid., par. 155.

36. Peter Akinola, statement on the Windsor Report, October 19, 2004.

37. Henry Orombi, "Archbishop of Uganda to Bishop of Los Angeles," November 2004.

38. The joint statement from African archbishops was titled "A Statement from the Primates Gathered At the First African Anglican Bishop's Conference Held in Lagos, Nigeria," October 2004.

39. "Statement from the House of Bishops in Salt Lake City," Episcopal News Service, January 12–13, 2005.

40. Tom Maliti, "Anglican Archbishops from Africa, Asia, and Latin America Say Apology from U.S. Episcopal Church Not Enough," Associated Press, January 28, 2005.

41. Gregory Venables, "Suddenly, An End to Western Arrogance," *Church Times*, March 4, 2005.

42. David Virtue, "ECUSA Has Chosen to Walk Apart," http://www.virtueonline.org, February 14, 2005.

43. Jill Lawless, "U.S. Episcopals Defend Openly Gay Bishop," Associated Press, June 21, 2005.

44. Jeff Chu, "10 Questions For Katherine Jefferts Schori," *Time*, July 10, 2006.

45. David Virtue, "New US Church Leader Says Homosexuality No Sin," Reuters,

June 19, 2006. In August 2006, the archbishop of Canterbury went on record saying he agreed "homosexual practice is incompatible with the Bible . . . and that homosexuals must change their behavior. . . . I do believe conversion means conversion of habits, behaviors, ideas, emotions." Hilary White, "Archbishop of Canterbury Says Homosexual Sex Incompatible with Bible," LifeSiteNews.com, distributed by David Virtue, August 28, 2006.

46. Frank Griswold, "From the Presiding Bishop: A Word to the Church," http://www.virtueonline.org, July 11, 2006.

47. David Virtue, "Central African Primate Blasts ECUSA and Rips Church of England," http://www.virtueonline.org, January 13, 2006.

48. David Virtue, "Anglican Province Pays Heavy Price for Rejection of TEC Money over Sodomy," http://www.virtueonline.org, August 4, 2006.

Chapter 16

1. Dick Kim published this quote on the Internet (frkim@aol.com) on January 26, 2004.

2. Stephen Noll, "It's the Property, Stupid!" (frkim@aol.com) November 2003. His argument has been sadly true: "While there are many high principles of theology and ecclesiology worth discussing at this time of historic crisis, the bread-and-butter political issue facing most conservative leaders in [the Episcopal Church] is how to keep the property. Or, as they see it, how do they get out of Egypt with the booty?"

3. In the days after Gene Robinson's consecration, Rick Terry and his vestry withdrew financial support of the diocese until the bishop issued a clear statement on biblical sexuality. At the same time, they affiliated with an evangelical movement in the Episcopal Church called the Anglican Communion Network (ACN). Bishop Herb Thompson saw this affiliation as a "step towards breaking communion with me." In a letter dated June 3, 2004, the bishop wrote Mr. Terry, saying, "This act constitutes a violation of your ordination vows." He required an immediate withdrawal from the ACN. Knowing that disobedience to the bishop would result in his being deposed as a priest, Mr. Terry responded on July 29, 2004: "I know in my heart I cannot follow your admonition. . . . I have chosen to leave quietly."

4. A business owner in Chillicothe later commented on Rick Terry's decision to leave St. Paul's: "I don't understand how Mr. Terry could have left that church building with its beautiful tiffany window."

5. Rick Terry, letter of resignation to St. Paul's Vestry, July 20, 2004.

6. In October 2006, American clergyman Lance Giuffrida and All Saints, Attleboro, Massachusetts, broke their affiliation with Tom Shaw and the diocese of Massachusetts. They made a formal request to purchase their building at fair value. In late January 2007, this request was denied and the church was given less than ten days to vacate the premises.

7. Margaret Hughes (1914–2006) could have been buried next to her husband at the old Episcopal church but not with her Anglican Mission clergy officiating the funeral service. Her family decided to bury Margaret elsewhere, bringing her husband's casket alongside. Margaret's testimony has been a great encouragement to many elderly Christians who, in the midst of the present Episcopal conflict, have tried to argue, "I'm too old to leave my church."

8. Moses Tay, then-retired archbishop of Southeast Asia, at an informal meeting with Anglican Mission leaders at Church of the Apostles in Raleigh, North Carolina, October 24–25, 2003.

9. Matthew 10:32–33; 2 Timothy 2:11–13.

10. John 21:15, 19.

11. Fr. Larry Carew, a Catholic priest in Connecticut, rightly commented that truly converted clergy and laypeople who have stayed in the Episcopal Church for various reasons, live in torment, as Lot did while in Sodom. (See 2 Peter 2:7–10.)

12. David Virtue, "AMIA Winter Conference Draws Overflow Crowd," http://www.virtueonline.org, January 17, 2003.

13. Harry Griffith, press release of the Denver consecrations, sent out from the Anglican Mission office, July 2001.

14. Yong Ping Chung, AMIA winter conference opening address, January 11, 2006.

15. See John 15:18–20; Mark 8:34–38; 2 Timothy 3:10–12; Acts 14:22.

16. 1 Peter 4:12–14; 1 Thessalonians 3:1–4; and note Philippians 3:10.

Chapter 17

1. Chuck Murphy, "Reflections on the 2006 General Convention of the Episcopal Church," published by Jay Greener, communications officer, Anglican Mission in America, June 2006.

2. In January 2007, nearly 50 percent of Anglican Mission churches had come out of the Episcopal Church. Most lost their properties, church homes, clergy salaries and benefits, and started over in rented facilities. The other 50 percent were new church starts. Clergy such as Jon Shuler, Terrell Glenn, Gerry Schnackenberg, William Beasley, Christian Ruch, Dan Claire, Ken Ross, Jon Holland, Matt Kessler, Carlos Miranda, and many more, took courageous steps to start new churches in communities all across the US. Their mission, now free from the Episcopal Church and its heresy, fully focused on reaching the lost and unchurched for Jesus Christ.

3. Jay Greener, "For Anglican Mission Leadership," Anglican Mission in America, February 18, 2005.

4. Galatians 2:5.

5. "The Communiqué of the Primates' Meeting in Dar es Salaam, 19 February 2007." The statement reads, "At the heart of our tensions is the belief that The Episcopal Church has departed from the standard of teaching on human sexuality accepted by the Communion in the 1998 Lambeth Resolution I.10 by consenting to the episcopal election of a candidate living in a committed same-sex relationships, and by permitting Rites of Blessing for same-sex unions." Compliance was therefore requested by the House of Bishops in the Episcopal Church by September 30, 2007. A few weeks later, the House of Bishops met and resolved not to comply (March 20, 2007).

6. For more on Prison Fellowship, go to www.pfm.org.

7. Catherine Claire, "Charting a Route to Restoration: Prison Fellowship Rwanda Helps to Bind a Nation's Wounds," *Jubilee Extra*, a publication of Prison Fellowship, April 2006. Claire's interview with Rucyahana paralleled my conversation with him.

8. Ibid.

APENDIXES

1: Truth's Mission Field

1. Allan Bloom, *The Closing of the American Mind* (New York: Simon and Schuster, 1987), 27.

2. Judges 17:6; 21:25 (KJV).

3. Terry Mattingly, "Spirituality up, doctrine down," September 11, 2002. The Barna Research Group, Ltd. is an independent marketing research company located in Southern California. Since 1984, it has been studying cultural trends related to values, beliefs, attitudes, and behaviors. For more information, contact www.barna.org.

4. Ibid.

5. Ibid. Barna has stated, "There was just such a radical gap between what we heard Christians professing they believed and the values and the lifestyle that grew out of the values." This quote was taken from an interview of Barna by Tim Stafford, "The Third Coming of George Barna," *Christianity Today*, July 26, 2002. Stafford concludes in the article, "A morally relativistic American culture was shaping Christians more than Christians were shaping the culture."

6. Thomas T. Clegg and Warren Bird, *Lost in America* (Loveland, CO: Group, 2001), 28.

7. Dana L. Robert, "Shifting Southward: Global Christianity Since 1945," International Bulletin of Missionary Research, April 2000. She is "the Truman Collins Professor of World Mission, Boston University of Theology, Boston, Massachusetts."

8. Kenneth Woodward, "The Changing Face of the Church," *Newsweek*, April 16, 2001.

9. Philip Jenkins, *The Next Christendom* (New York: Oxford University Press, 2002), 4. He cites that Uganda, "a land the size of Oregon," may well have by 2050 "more active church members than the four or five largest European nations combined" (90–91, see also 59–60). In Rwanda today, about the size of Vermont, it is estimated that over 1.2 million Anglicans attend Sunday worship. For Episcopalians in the United States, the average attendance is under a million. The same is true for the Church of England (87).

10. Woodward, "The Changing Face."

11. Woodward, quoting Andrew Walls from the University of Edinburgh, Scotland, "expert in the history of Christian missions" who believes the "events that are shaping 21st-century Christianity are taking place in Africa and Asia."

12. Romans 12:2.

13. Philip Jenkins, quoted by Uwe Siemon-Netto, UPI religion correspondent, in "Christian Ferment in Third World," from the Life and Mind Desk, United Press International, July 1, 2002.

14. Jenkins, *The Next Christendom*, 35.

15. Ibid., 108.

16. Woodward, "The Changing Face." Dr. Stephen F. Noll, in his book *The Handwriting on the Wall* (Solon, OH: Latimer, 1998), said it this way: "re-evangelization of the original colonizing nations is called for" (15).

17. Clegg and Bird, in *Lost in America*, state that the unchurched population in the United States is so extensive that "if it were a nation, it would be the fifth most populated nation on the planet after China, the former Soviet Union, India and Brazil" (25).

18. Jenkins, *The Next Christendom*, 14.

19. 1 Corinthians 1:27–29.

2: Kuala Lumpur Statement

1. Stephen F. Noll, The Handwriting on the Wall (Solon, OH: Latimer, 1998), 45–50. Noll documents the Kuala Lumpur Statement on Human Sexuality in its entirety as well as their appeal for Anglican Reconstruction that calls for "ways of strengthening mutual accountability and interdependence."

3: The First Promise Statement

1. *The Book of Common Prayer* (New York: Oxford University Press, 1979), 526, 538.
2. The following quotes come from the First Promise Statement signed on September 9, 1997, by twenty-seven of the original thirty senior leaders who attended the meeting. This document in full can be found on the Anglican Mission in America website: www.theamia.org.
3. Robert E. Quinn, *Deep Change: Discovering the Leader Within* (San Francisco: Jossey-Bass, 1996), 156. The actual phrase by Quinn is, "If you are not risking your job, you are not doing your job." This book was an extremely helpful tool to First Promise leaders early on in our development. It outlined both leaders who "sacrifice their principles for pressure" and leaders who "accept the necessary risk because it is the right thing to do" (158).

4: The Dallas Statement

1. See Stephen F. Noll, *The Handwriting on the Wall* (Solon, OH: Latimer, 1998), 51–61 for the complete text of the Dallas Statement.

5: Correspondence

1. Jon Shuler, letter to the Rt. Rev. Larry E. Maze, November 12, 1996.
2. Ibid.
3. Larry Maze, letter to the Rev. Dr. Jon C. Shuler, December 2, 1996.
4. Linda S. Caillouret, "S. Carolina Priest Pastors Episcopal Congregation that Diocese Won't Recognize," *Arkansas Democrat-Gazette*, January 15, 1998.
5. "For Now, an Independent Church," *The Living Church*, April 19, 1998.
6. Caillouret, "S. Carolina Priest."
7. "For Now, an Independent Church." Note: Bishop Maze argued vehemently that new church work should never be initiated solely because of special interests. TJ writes, "His statements in this regard were received with irony by the founders because of the particular issue [human sexuality] with which he attempted to marginalize this congregation. The irony grows out of the fact that several years ago Bishop Maze sanctioned the initiation of a special mid-week worship service for homosexuals at the Cathedral in Little Rock. His endorsement of this service was at the behest of Integrity, a well-known 'special interest' group in the Episcopal Church supporting the gay agenda."
8. Integrity/Arkansas, a promotional piece for the South Central Regional Conference: "Are You Empowered? Tomorrow Beckons." Integrity, a movement within the Episcopal Church promoting the gay and lesbian agenda, held a conference in Little Rock with Bishops Spong, Maze, and Dr. Louie Crew as the guest speakers September 18–20, 1998.
9. Peter C. Moore, letter to the Rt. Rev. Larry E. Maze, November 14, 1997.

6: The Koinonia Statement

1. John Shelby Spong, "The Koinonia Statement," delivered on August 25, 1994, at the 71st General Convention of the Episcopal Church "to the Members of the House of Bishops and through them to the whole Church."

7: TJ's First Service

1. Linda S. Caillouret, "S. Carolina Priest Pastors Episcopal Congregation that Diocese Won't Recognize," *Arkansas Democrat-Gazette*, January 15, 1998.
2. Larry Maze, letter to "All Clergy, Senior Wardens, and Members of the Standing Committee" as a response to the January 15 article in the *Arkansas Democrat-Gazette*.
3. Larry Maze, letter to the Rev. Thomas Johnston, February 18, 1998.
4. Thomas Johnston, letter to the Most Rev. Emmanuel Kolini and the Rt. Rev. John Kabango Rucyahana followed by "A Proposal from the Rev. Thomas Johnston" wherein he requests formal transfer from the diocese of South Carolina to the diocese of Shyira, March 4, 1998.
5. Thomas Johnston, letter to the Rt. Rev. Larry E. Maze, March 9, 1998.
6. John Kabango Rucyahana, letter to the Rev. Thomas Johnston, April 11, 1998.
7. Larry Maze, letter to rectors, vicars, and wardens of vacant congregations, April 16, 1998.
8. Larry Maze, letter to the Rt. Rev. John Kabango Rucyahana, April 27, 1998. Maze did not copy the letter to TJ Johnston.
9. John Kabango Rucyahana, letter to the Rt. Rev. Larry E. Maze, June 19, 1998.
10. John Kabango Rucyahana, letter to the Most Rev. and Rt. Honorable Dr. George Carey, July 11, 1998.
11. George Carey, letter to the Rt. Rev. John Kabango Rucyahana, July 20, 1998.

8: Alexander Muge's Press Conference

1. Doug King, "Muzzled African Bishop Speaks Against Immorality," *Foundations*, newsmagazine of the Episcopal Synod of America, June 1990, and "A Tale of Two Cultures," the *St. Andrew's Messenger*, St. Andrew's Episcopal Church, Fort Worth, Texas, June 1990.

10: Lambeth, Resolution III.5

1. David Virtue, "Bishops Vote Overwhelmingly For Biblical Standards On Sexuality," http://www.virtueonline.org), August 5, 1998.
2. Association of Anglican Congregations on Mission, Petition to the Primates' Meeting and the Primates of the of the Anglican Communion for Emergency Intervention in the Province of the Episcopal Church of the United States of America, January 1998.
3. Ronald Haines, "Pastoral Letter," circulated openly, picked up by Dick Kim (frkim@aol.com), August 5, 1998.

11: Stalemate in Little Rock

1. Laurie Pierce, "State Wins Support in Authority Battle," *Arkansas Democrat-Gazette*, August 8, 1998.
2. "Griswold believes not all homosexual Christians are called to celibacy. Griswold acknowledged in an interview with *Christianity Today* that he has ordained homosexual priests" (Douglas L. LeBlanc, "Homosexual Ordinations Cause Parishes

to Leave," *Christianity Today*, January 10, 1994). Griswold himself said, "Can the values of the Gospel and the taking up of one's cross and following Jesus be found in sexual expression outside marriage or celibacy? . . . I have to answer 'yes' based upon my own experience of grace in the lives of persons whose sexuality has been expressed outside these classical and normative categories. Are not all such expressions of sexuality sinful? I cannot say that they are" (Bishop Frank Griswold, "Defining a Lifegiving Sexuality Outside the Norms," *Anglican Advance*, July/August 1993).

3. Pierce, "State Wins Support."

4. TJ Johnston, as recorded in a letter to St. Andrew's Church, August 20, 1998, and in an interview with *United Voice* posted on the Internet immediately following a First Promise meeting in Little Rock on September 20, 1998.

5. Matthew 18:15.

12: The American Rebellion

1. Bruce Bower, "Association of Anglican Congregations on Mission, Petition to the Primates' Meeting and the Primates of the Anglican Communion for Emergency Intervention in the Province of the Episcopal Church of the United States of America," published privately, December 1998, 3. At this time, the Episcopal Church had not formally approved sexual relations outside of marriage, although it was common practice, passed by implication in resolutions, and endorsed by the presiding bishop. It should also be noted that the term "primate" is used to signify the office of an archbishop.

2. Ibid., 28, as reported by Jerry Hames, "Post-Lambeth talk focuses on sexuality issue," *Episcopal Life*, October 1998. Bishop Herbert Donovan was quoted in that article: "We believe that there is much room for debate and no unified understanding of sexuality within our sacred texts." It eventually became clear that the cry for debate was merely a refusal to comply with the Lambeth resolutions on sexuality and the authority of Scripture.

3. Ibid., appendix vol. 2, 121–124. Hays H. Rockwell, in "Reflections on Lambeth—November 3, 1998," stated that the sexuality debate at Lambeth was an issue of hospitality and not, as global South leaders argued, a matter of infidelity to historic biblical theology on the doctrine of sin: "At issue was the question of whether, and to what extent, Anglicans are going to be hospitable to people of homosexual orientation. When the issue came to be debated in open session, the main contributors were African and Asian bishops, and they made it plain that they were not prepared to be hospitable at all." Bishop Rockwell then rendered a piercing racial judgment: "Until very recently, many of the bishops of those churches were English. Now nearly every African bishop is an African, and they are understandably eager to assert themselves in the presence of their former 'masters.'" Simply put, the Rwandan bishops in particular were deeply insulted by these prejudicial comments.

4. Ibid., 31. According to Auburn Traycik and David Virtue, writing for *The Christian Challenge*, in an article titled "Post-Lambeth Backlash Continues in Parts of ECUSA," the motion was supported by 95 percent of the delegates.

5. The Most Revs. Maurice Sinclair, Emmanuel Kolini, Moses Tay, Harry Goodhew, Jonathan Onyemelukwe, and the Rt. Rev. Evans Kisekka, representing Uganda, letter from Singapore to the primates of the Anglican Communion, April 15, 1999. The statistics cited in the letter came from the careful study of "The

Petitions" by the archbishops' meeting in Singapore.

6. The Rev. Kenneth Ross, "A Brief Report," filed at the request of the First Promise office.

7. Bruce Bower, "Association of Anglican Congregations on Mission," appendix vol. 2, 112, 120. Reported by Douglas L. LeBlanc, *Anglican Voice*, November 9, 1998.

8. Ibid., 21. Bishop Griswold's letter to the *New York Times* dated August 17, 1998.

9. Ibid., 4, appendix vol. 1, 1. Peter Toon, "Prescience," written for The Prayer Book Society of the Episcopal Church, August 31, 1994.

10. Ibid., appendix vol. 1, 15. Madeleine Bunting, "Hardline on gay sex strengthens ecumenical bond," written for *The Guardian*, August 8, 1998.

11. Ibid., appendix vol. 1, 35. David Skidmore, "Lambeth struggles over homosexuality in emotional plenary session," written for the Anglican Communion News Service, August 7, 1998.

12. Ibid., appendix vol. 2, 108. Jerry Hames, "Post-Lambeth talk focuses on sexuality issue," written for *Episcopal Life*, October 1998.

13. Ibid., 29. Terry Mattingly's syndicated column of October 7, 1998 convincingly argued that revisionism was spreading rapidly through Canada. He reported that Canadian bishop Michael Ingham had openly denounced the essential Christian doctrine that salvation is found only through faith in Jesus Christ. Such a view, said Ingham, "is narrow, rigid and blind. . . . Such a god is not worthy of honor, glory, worship or praise."

14. Ibid., appendix vol. 2, 145.

15. Ibid., "Second Supplement" to "The Petitions," (November 5, 1999), 14. *The Christian Challenge* picked up this story in September 1999.

13: "Leapfrogging"

1. Charles H. Murphy III, "The 'New Gospel' in the Episcopal Church," published by First Promise and widely distributed over the Internet.

14: A Crisis of Leadership

1. Julia Duin, "Conservative Episcopal leaders have sent out an international SOS," *Washington Times*, February 2, 1999.

2. Ibid.

3. Bruce Bower, Association of Anglican Congregations on Mission, as reported in the "First Supplement" of "The Petitions," April 7, 1999, 12. The Newark Convention took place on January 29, 1999.

4. Duin, "Conservative Episcopal Leaders." David Virtue and Auburn Traycik quoted the Rev. Philip Lyman in their article, "State Set For Creation of Separate Orthodox Province in Anglican Communion" (February 11, 1999), saying the central issue was "Biblical fidelity" and that he must "be loyal first to the doctrine, discipline and worship of Christ."

5. Stephen Noll, "Thoughts on the Future of the Episcopal Church," prepared for the board and bishops' council of the American Anglican Council in a series of articles written in February 1999. At the First Promise regional conference held in Atlanta, GA, on March 15, 1999, the Rev. Dr. Larry Hall, rector of St. John's the Divine in Houston, said much the same: "The Holy Spirit can be withdrawn if churches abandon repentance. I think it is entirely possible that the vengeance of God on the Episcopal Church has begun, that the Holy Spirit is being withdrawn."

6. Doug LeBlanc, "AAC bishops seek middle ground," *Anglican Voice*, March 1, 1999.

15: Archbishops' Open Letter to Frank Griswold
1. The "Open Letter" was signed by Archbishops Gitari (Kenya), Goodhew (Sydney), Kolini (Rwanda), Malik (Jerusalem and the Middle East), Mtetemela (Tanzania), Sinclair (Southern Cone), Tay (Southeast Asia), and Bazley (retired from Southern Cone).

18: Warnings Against Early Consecrations
1. Maurice Sinclair, e-mail to John Rodgers, December 17, 1999.
2. John Rodgers, e-mail to Maurice Sinclair, December 18, 1999.
3. Maurice Sinclair, e-mail to Chuck Murphy, December 26, 1999.
4. Chuck Murphy, e-mail to Maurice Sinclair, January 1, 2000.
5. Maurice Sinclair, e-mail to John Rodgers, January 6, 2000.
6. John Rodgers, e-mail to Maurice Sinclair, January 6, 2000.

INDEX